IN THE WORDS OF ELDERS WITHDRAWN

Aboriginal Cultures in Transition

Edited by Peter Kulchyski, Don McCaskill, and David Newhouse

Over years of teaching, it became increasingly apparent to the editors of this book that students in their Native Studies classes were dissatisfied with many of the texts they were assigned, which were usually anthropological in nature. Their response was to propose a new text that would provide an overview of the thought-worlds of Aboriginal cultures from the inside.

Bringing together the voices of sixteen Elders and traditional teachers from across Canada, this collection allows readers to compare the vision and experience of a generation of Aboriginal people. Today, Elders are the historians of the Aboriginal past and the keepers of cultural events and ceremonies. They are teachers, healers, and experts in survival, sharing a world-view based on the knowledge that all things in life are related and are governed by natural laws. Those represented here include men and women from a variety of traditions and geographical locations.

This unique collection sets a new standard for the representation of First Nations cultures in the academic context. Not only does it mark a shift in the production of knowledge, it fulfils a need for a closer and more respectful collaboration between Native and non-Native communities.

PETER KULCHYSKI is Associate Professor in the Department of Native Studies, Trent University.

DON MCCASKILL is Professor in the Department of Native Studies, Trent University.

DAVID NEWHOUSE is Chair and Associate Professor in the Department of Native Studies, Trent University.

IN THE WORDS OF ELDERS

Aboriginal Cultures in Transition

Pauloosie Angmarlik

Ernest Benedict

George Blondin

James Carpenter

Mary Anne Mason

Eva McKay

Liza Mosher

Twylah Hurd Nitsch

Margaret Paul

Elizabeth Penashue

Martha Rabesca

Alex Skead

Vince Stogan

Wilf Tootoosis

Rachael Uyarasuk

Albert Ward

Edited by Peter Kulchyski, Don McCaskill, David Newhouse

UNIVERSITY OF TORONTO PRESS

Toronto Buffalo London

© University of Toronto Press Incorporated 1999
Toronto Buffalo London
Printed in Canada

Reprinted 2003

ISBN 0-8020-4106-X (cloth)
ISBN 0-8020-7953-9 (paper)

Printed on acid-free paper

Canadian Cataloguing in Publication Data

Main entry under title:

In the words of elders : aboriginal cultures in transition

ISBN 0-8020-4106-X (bound)   ISBN 0-8020-7953-9 (pbk.)

1. Native peoples – Canada – History.*   2. Indians of North America –
Canada – History.   3. Indians of North America – Ethnic identity.   4. Indians
of North America – Cultural assimilation – Canada.   5. Indians of North
America – Canada – Social conditions.   I. Kulchyski, Peter Keith, 1959– .
II. McCaskill, Don N.   III. Newhouse, David.

E78.C2I42 1999   971′.00497   C98-933050-8

All authors' royalties for this book will be used to support cultural activities and
traditional teaching in the Native Studies Department at Trent University.

University of Toronto Press acknowledges the support to its publishing
program of the Canada Council for the Arts and the Ontario Arts Council.

To Fred Wheatley and Chief Jacob Thomas

Contents

Acknowledgments

The editors of this text understand that the act of creation is not the act of a single person, especially in this instance where an advisory collective, the editors' collective, and the Elders themselves were all contributors to the final outcome. We would like to thank the Elders who shared their knowledge with us, who gave graciously and kindly of their time and allowed their words to be transported across space and time. Without their consent and assistance this book would not have been possible. We owe special thanks to Emily Faries, who spent a year interviewing Elders and transcribing the interviews. Her work was vital to the success of this project and we remember it with gratitude. Three graduate students assisted at various stages: we would like to thank Sheldon Krasowski, who became consumed by the interviews and their transcription, D'Arcy Rheault, for his technical assistance in working with the computer programs to assemble the text in its final form, and Anup Grewal, who helped with the copy editing. Staff at the Department of Native Studies gave their usual outstanding service and devotion to the project and we are immensely grateful to Louise Garrow, Joyce Miller, Kathy Fife, Barb Rivett, and Chris Welter for their contributions. An Elders' Text Advisory Committee helped to design and guide this project; its members included Sylvia Maracle, Vern Douglas, Tim Thompson, David Newhouse, Shirley Williams, Edna Manitowabi, Paul Bourgeois, Louise Garrow, Don McCaskill, and Peter Kulchyski. Their work and advice were greatly appreciated. We also thank the Ministry of Education and Training in Ontario for the development of its Aboriginal Education initiative, which provided generous financial support. The Trent Aboriginal Education Council co-sponsored the project and oversaw its development; we are very grateful to it as well. In this circle of giving thanks we must also acknowledge and thank the Creator for the beauty of our lives and the world we live in.

THE EDITORS

Introduction

PETER KULCHYSKI, DON McCASKILL, DAVID NEWHOUSE

The text you hold in your hands is remarkable on several counts, not least because as recently as thirty years ago it is unlikely that a work like this could or would have been produced. This text can be seen to mark a shift in the production of knowledge. The shift can be associated with the development in universities and colleges across North America of a relatively new academic discipline – an 'interdisciplinary field of study' variously called Native Studies, Native American Studies, Aboriginal Studies, or First Nations' Studies. In order to describe the nature both of this shift and of this text, it is useful to reflect on the state of the field of study.

Where the study of Aboriginal peoples in Canada takes place in a Native Studies department or program, rather than through a specific disciplinary lens (such as political studies, anthropology, geography), the focus tends to be on Aboriginal peoples described from the cultural 'inside.' This involves a new kind of intellectual project, new forms of teaching strategies, new methods of research and enquiry, and, indeed, new ways of working in a scholarly environment. At the very least, it also involves showing a new respect for the thought of Aboriginal cultural, spiritual, artistic, and political leaders. This new respect has multiple functions, not least of which is providing a greater legitimacy in academic settings for the teachings of those leaders. In traditional Aboriginal culture, the most important teachers are the Elders.

Like every people upon the face of the earth, Aboriginal people have been trying to make sense of their world; they have been thinking about themselves, their place in the cosmos, their relationships to the newcomers to this land, the changes occurring around them and to them. This thinking, however, has not been valued by many non-Aboriginal people and in some respects by many Aboriginal people themselves. And not many Aboriginal people have been asked about this body of thought, either to document it or to analyse it. Many generations of Elders have been lost, and with them, much knowledge and thought. Now many Aboriginal people desire to examine and develop the systems of thought

that Elders represent and to use this knowledge as the basis for the recon-
struction of Aboriginal societal institutions.

Native Studies can be characterized as a partnership between Aboriginal and non-Aboriginal peoples, for the purpose of producing and vali-
dating accurate knowledge about Aboriginal peoples, knowledge that will
be of greater use to Aboriginal peoples. At a teaching level, it involves
helping Aboriginal students achieve their individual goals through the
reflection of Aboriginal thought and experience in a setting that can
maintain or enhance their cultural values. Native Studies can be an
intensely personal experience for students and faculty, as it addresses the
whole person. Non-Aboriginal students in Native Studies learn about and
experience the historical and cultural legacies of Aboriginal people and
their contemporary realities, and receive a grounding in Aboriginal
thought.

The partnership approach means that Native Studies programs do not
rest easily in the 'ivory tower' of academia. Our success depends in large
measure on the relevance of our efforts to Aboriginal communities, both
urban and rural. These are the principles behind the production of this
text. They were not principles held by many in the university setting thirty
years ago. Even when Native Studies programs began to develop, it took
some time to establish this new ethos. Now, in the nineties, as Native
Studies turn to a new generation of scholars, it has become possible to
produce a text of this kind.

In the Words of Elders was produced because of a need for a text that
would provide a description of Aboriginal cultural thought in Canada
from the inside. Since culture is such a critical dimension of life, many
courses in Native Studies deal with the diversity of Aboriginal cultures
in Canada, and a critical dimension of the field is that of the nature
of Aboriginal traditions. While introductory books exist that describe
Aboriginal cultures – for example, Diamond Jenness's *The Indians of
Canada* (U of Toronto P, 1984; originally National Museum of Canada,
1932), John Price's *Indians of Canada: Cultural Dynamics* (Prentice-Hall,
1979), and Alan McMillan's more recent *Native Peoples and Cultures of
Canada* (Douglas and McIntyre, 1988) – these descriptions are from the
'outside,' as it were, imposing the authors' agenda of what is important,
often emphasizing areas like so-called material culture that are of less
interest to Native Studies' students, and not paying a great deal of attention to Aboriginal people's own thoughts and views of their lives, cultures,
and place in the world.

Each of the above books, for example, pays more attention to the theory that early ancestors of Aboriginal peoples came to this continent by crossing the Beringia land mass (now Bering Strait) than to Aboriginal people's rich heritage of stories relating to how and when they were created and placed on Turtle Island (North America). Furthermore, the anthropological view tends to search for cultural 'purity,' to assume that this purity existed only in the past, and therefore tends to treat Aboriginal cultures as 'dead' cultures. It uses the past tense in describing Aboriginal peoples. It also tends to emphasize the material aspects of culture, ignoring the spiritual world-view so central to Aboriginal people.

We wanted to produce something different, something that listened to creation stories in a respectful way, without holding a so-called Bering Strait 'truth' in the back (or fore) ground; that looked at Aboriginal cultures as evolving and adapting, borrowing from old and new neighbours, and therefore being modern cultures; and that used the names the people themselves used, rather than what outsiders have called them. We also wanted the work to reflect the system of thought of Aboriginal peoples and to portray it as a legitimate and valid system that has much to offer.

The idea for the text originated in 1991 with a Trent University faculty member in Native Studies who was frustrated by the annual complaints from students about the anthropological nature of the assigned cultural texts. A new and different text seemed to be required, one that would attempt to provide an overview of the thought world of Aboriginal cultures from the inside.

It was obvious to us that a text of this magnitude could only be produced by a team. At Trent University, an Aboriginal Education Council, with representatives from a variety of Aboriginal communities in Ontario, oversees all initiatives pertaining to Aboriginal education. The council members were enthusiastic about the project when it was first broached, and agreed to attempt to secure funding for it. The department received a grant from the Ontario Ministry of Education and Training's Aboriginal Education and Training Strategy to carry out research for the volume. An Elders' Text Advisory Committee was set up, and it oversaw all aspects of production of the text from an initial meeting in the summer of 1993 through to completion in summer of 1997.

The committee consisted of two representatives from Aboriginal organizations in Ontario, two Aboriginal counsellors at Trent, three Aboriginal and two non-Aboriginal faculty members.[1] The first major decision made was to hire a research coordinator, and after a well-advertised search an excellent candidate, Dr Emily Faries, of Cree descent from northern Ontario, was appointed. The committee met through the

1993–4 academic year to select Elders to be interviewed and to discuss the questions that would be posed. There was a great deal of discussion about both of these issues, which were resolved in workshop-like, day-long meetings at which the committee consistently worked towards consensus.

In the spring and summer of 1994 Dr Faries conducted a first round of interviews with the Elders and traditional teachers selected. She travelled to the Elder's home community, and spent two to four days with each, working through an interpreter when necessary. Elders and traditional teachers were paid an honorarium for their participation. Through the fall of 1994 she transcribed the interviews and made minor editorial changes. The committee continued to meet, discussed the material that was being compiled, suggested follow-up questions, and discussed the editing process. The transcribed interviews were sent back to the Elders to ensure the information was accurate. By summer of 1995, the interviews had been revised based on follow-up questions. Early in the project we decided that authorship of the text would be attributed to each of the Elders and traditional teachers; 'we' would not substitute our own names for theirs, as editors, compilers, or whatever. We would, on the other hand, put our names to this introduction and accept responsibility for those words we did write. Copyright for the volume would remain with the Trent Aboriginal Education Council, which would use any royalty revenues to support Aboriginal students in financial need at Trent University.

The text that emerged from this process, though not without limitations, will, we hope, be of great use to Native Studies students and all those interested in Aboriginal peoples in Canada. The limitations of the text are largely related to the degree of depth one can reach in working with an Elder. The desirable duration might be a period of several years, whereas what was possible was short visits of only a few days. It is unlikely that any of the chapters herein match the richness, for example, of Julie Cruikshank's remarkable *Life Lived Like a Story* (U of British Columbia P, 1993). Furthermore, the text does not contain the traditional sacred teachings of Elders, provide lists of what plants they used as medicines, or discuss anything, in fact, that any particular individual felt uncomfortable talking about.

On the other hand, what the text may lack in depth it makes up for in breadth. Female and male Elders and traditional teachers from across the country, two from each region, were interviewed; this enables the reader to compare the different experiences of a generation of Aboriginal people, to notice the cultural differences and the similarities. Each chapter, each interview, each story, offers its own flash of humour or sudden moment of genuine insight. We think, for example, of James Carpenter's comparison of the Shaking Tent Ceremony to a television.

It is our hope that just as this text had to be produced out of a new kind of ethical relationship – 'written,' that is, in a new manner – so it will also be 'read' in a new manner. Just as it takes years of training to address and understand a Canadian Supreme Court Justice, for example, so it can take many years of apprenticeship to hear the words of Elders and traditional teachers. These teachings do not come in the prepackaged form to which students are accustomed. Traditionally teachings were not written down but rather given as a 'gift' by an Elder within a specific cultural context such as a ceremony, event, or time spent with an individual at a particular stage of his or her development. Frequently individuals receiving the teachings were expected to 'earn' them by performing a task or participating in a ceremony such as Fasting, the Longhouse, the Midewiwin Lodge, or the Potlatch. Elders sometimes determined the state of readiness of individuals to hear certain teachings, particularly spiritual teachings.

Some stories or teachings were told only at certain times of the year. There can often be allegorical levels or layers of meaning behind a story or teaching. In keeping with the important relationship established between the Elder and the student, the teachings are often very personal, involving intuitive understanding in addition to ideas that address the intellect. Humour is usually central to the teaching style of Elders. In their teachings Elders stress listening, observing, and waiting in an attitude of respect. Knowledge can often come in a moment of experiencing a hidden meaning. Learning is thus a matter of personal awareness and responsibility. Elders often request that the learner be 'of a good mind' when listening to the teachings, in order to more fully understand their meaning. The teachings frequently involve moral lessons that pertain to an individual's behaviour, often linking that behaviour to spiritual understandings.

Many teachings pertain to appropriate ways to live with Mother Earth and all Creation. Indeed, at the heart of most Elders' stories and teachings is the idea that it is important for an individual to attempt to live *Bimaadiziwin*, 'the way of good life' or 'everyday good living' in accordance with the teachings of the Creator. Perhaps the best approach is to read these lines with the same respect and attention one would pay when listening to an Elder. Sometimes, as a result, what lodges in memory only unfolds as 'meaningful' days, weeks, months, or even years later.

In traditional Aboriginal societies Elders were and still are evolved beings who possess significant knowledge of the sacred and secular ways of their people, and who act as role models, often assuming leadership positions in their communities. They are highly respected by the people. They are the teachers, healers, and experts in survival, guiding individuals' behaviour towards an understanding of the natural ways of Mother Earth. The Elders teach a world-view based on the knowledge that all things in life are related in a sacred manner and are governed by natural or cosmic laws. Mother Earth is therefore held to be sacred, a gift from the Creator. In their relationship to the land, people should accommodate themselves to it in an attitude of respect and stewardship. Proper conduct is determined by natural laws that obliterate the distinction between sacred and secular. This is why so many of the Elders in the book speak of the central place living on the land had in traditional Aboriginal culture.

Elders emphasize the belief in unseen powers in all natural phenomena and that all things are dependent on one another. It is through an understanding of the reciprocal relationship between ourselves and Mother Earth and living in a balanced way that we are provided with the sustenance, both physical and spiritual, necessary for life. We are all related and therefore we must be constantly aware of how our actions will affect others, whether they are plants, animals, or people. Thus, human law is a reflection of natural law, and all the structures, customs, and ways of life of Aboriginal society grew out of this central understanding.

The term 'Elder' has itself gained a somewhat fashionable currency in recent years. The 'wisdom' of Elders is now much sought after and admired. A major resurgence of interest in traditional Aboriginal culture, thought, and spirituality emerged in western Canada in the early 1970s. In the fall of 1972, on Vancouver Island, an event occurred that raised the consciousness of Aboriginal people to the importance of their culture and spirituality and the crucial role of Elders. It was a twelve-day gathering that brought together, for the first time, Elders and Aboriginal leaders to discuss the future of Aboriginal people in Canada. That gathering provided direction and inspiration to the participants and changed people's lives.

As Joe Couture, a participant in the gathering, put it: 'That moment symbolized a significant raising of consciousness in the Native mind ... the focus of this awareness development bore on the central importance of Native Elders ... Elders, usually under pressure from younger Natives, are resuming their traditional role and prominence, a manifest role variously expressed as teacher, counsellor, interpreter of history, expert on survival.'[2]

Louis Crier, on behalf of the Elders, stated that being an Indian in the future would entail searching for 'the harmonies between the two cultures, between the basic values of the Indian Way and those of Western Civilization – and thereby forge a new and stronger sense of identity. To be fully Indian today, we must become bilingual and bicultural ... in so doing we will survive as Indians, true to our past.'[3]

The renewal of traditional Aboriginal culture began to take root and grow all across Canada. In Alberta, for example, a number of Elders, including Peter O'Chiese, Edward Bellrose, Abraham Burnstick, Albert Lightning, Joseph Smallboy, Joe Cardinal, Rufus Goodstriker, among others, 'brought out' the traditional teachings, performed sacred ceremonies, supervised fasts, counselled individuals, held cultural workshops, and assisted in the formation of culturally based Aboriginal organizations. In Central Canada other similar events occurred through the efforts of such people as Ernie Benedict (Mohawk), who instituted the North American Indian Travelling College, which brought traditional Iroquois culture to numerous communities. Similarly, Anishinabe individuals such as Edward Benton-Banai, Jim Dumont, and Edna Manitowabi contributed to the renewal through the teachings of the Midewiwin Lodge.

Since that time Elders have played an increasingly important role in Aboriginal communities and organizations in defining and supporting Aboriginal culture and identity. Today Elders are the historians of the Aboriginal past, passing on their knowledge through recitals of the Great Law of the Iroquois in the Longhouse, speeches at Potlatches, or storytelling or guest-speaking in classrooms and Elders' gatherings. They are the keepers of cultural events and ceremonies such as Sweat Lodges, songs, Sundances, and Pipe ceremonies. Some Elders have been given the gift to perform spiritual ceremonies such as the Sweat Lodge, Sundance, or Shaking Tent.

Young people often apprentice with an Elder for a period of time to learn the rituals and ceremonies of their First Nation. Approaching an Elder in a culturally appropriate manner, for example, presenting an Elder with Tobacco, Sweetgrass, and a Pipe, is an important first step for many young people interested in learning the ways of their people and strengthening their identity as Aboriginal persons. In many communities Elders are counsellors, assisting individuals in time of need.

Many Aboriginal social service organizations, as part of their effort to develop a culturally based service model, are integrating Elders in their programs through Healing Circles, traditional medicine, one-to-one counselling, and teaching of the traditional ways through such means as the Medicine Wheel. Cultural-survival schools and Native-language immersion schools as well as public schools across the country use Elders to develop cultural curriculum and act as instructors. Elders such as those included in this volume are playing an important role in the continued development of Aboriginal cultures.

The Native Studies Department at Trent University has adopted a philosophy of education that attempts to address the teachings of the Elders. Its involvement with Elders and traditional teachers goes back to the early 1970s, when the department hired an Anishinabe Elder, Fred Wheatley, and a Cayuga Elder and Confederacy Chief, Jacob Thomas, to teach Ojibwe and Mohawk languages and cultures. The university took an important step in recognizing Aboriginal Elders when it awarded academic tenure to Professor Thomas, thus acknowledging the validity of Aboriginal wisdom as equivalent to scholarly knowledge earned through academic degrees.

Since that time the Department of Native Studies has always had Elders and traditional people, both as faculty, teaching language and culture courses, and as support staff, providing counselling and cultural assistance to students and the community. The department also has sponsored numerous cultural events and ceremonies involving Elders. In the 1970s the first Elders' gatherings were held, a series of four-day cultural workshops for students, facilitated by Elders from Alberta, including Peter O'Chiese, Abraham Burnstick, Edward Bellrose, and Michael Thrasher. The workshops were centred around the teachings of the Medicine Wheel. The desire for cultural events soon spread to Aboriginal communities throughout Ontario.

The department began sponsoring Elders and traditional peoples' gatherings that were open to the community; these attract people from across the country. The gatherings are organized by more than three hundred student volunteers and involve more than twenty Elders and traditional people annually. The gatherings include Elders' workshops, Healing Circles, Sunrise Ceremonies, drumming and dancing, feasts and socials, and women's and men's circles, and have proved so popular that they have grown from fifty participants in the early 1980s to more than three thousand in 1995. In 1996, at students' request, the department scaled down the events, to provide more time for Elders' in-depth teaching.

For purposes of this text, we use a loose meaning of the word 'Elder.' Traditionally an Elder is thought of as a very highly respected older person who has the knowledge of the ancient spiritual and cultural ways of her or his people. Among some First Nations, to become an Elder requires elaborate initiation processes involving various degrees of knowledge, as in the Anishinabe Midewiwin Lodge, or the system of Clan Mothers in Iroquoian cultures.

In other cases, Elders may become recognized as such by their people when they reach a certain age. Few Elders call themselves Elders, and there is no institutional process that recognizes or validates them as such. The Aboriginal community to which an individual belongs is likely the only genuine source of recognition of that individual's status as an Elder. For this text, we talked to highly regarded individuals, some of whom would be considered Elders; others, perhaps because they are too young or for other reasons, would be considered traditional teachers.

Our selection was based on a combination of factors. Our own varied personal contacts and knowledge of individuals and First Nations played a key role. A number of Aboriginal leaders, community people, and Trent personnel came together in a workshop to select the Elders to be included in this volume and to determine the questions we would ask the Elders. We wanted to ensure that we talked to men and women from the east-coast fishing peoples, the Longhouse cultures of the eastern woodlands, the Sweat Lodge cultures of the Canadian Shield, the Sundance cultures of the Prairies, the Potlatch culture of the Pacific coast, the hand-drum cultures of the western sub-Arctic, and Inuit of the Arctic.

In selecting the Elders and questions we were guided by the circle or Medicine Wheel, a central expression of Aboriginal culture today. The wheel, as a circle, expresses a unifying force in life. The Medicine Wheel is a representation of traditional theology, philosophy, and psychology. For Aboriginal people it represents the teachings of the Creator about all aspects of life. There are different but related versions of the Medicine Wheel for different Aboriginal groups. In fact many Medicine Wheels are depicted as concentric circles, each one representing different teachings, often dimensions of human psychology or key values.

One common aspect of Medicine Wheels is that they are based on the four directions and four seasons. Each of the seasons is associated with a direction in the circle, and each life moves through the four seasons and directions, beginning in the eastern spring and ending in the northern winter. The power of the world always works in circles. A circle is the symbol of completeness and perfection. Central to the teachings of the

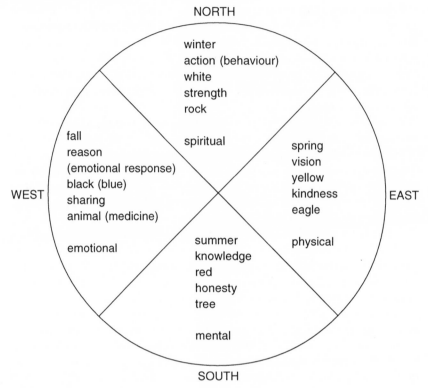

Figure 1: Medicine Wheel

Medicine Wheel is the goal of *Bimaadiziwin*, or 'living in a good way in life,' which entails balancing in oneself the aspects of all four quadrants of the wheel.

In one Medicine Wheel, the four directions represent the four aspects of self: physical, mental, emotional, and spiritual. In addition, four fundamental values in traditional Aboriginal culture are used to guide an individual's behaviour: kindness, honesty, sharing, and strength. There are also four levels to be found in traditional culture represented on the wheel: the individual, the family, the clan, and the nation. Figure 1 illustrates the Medicine Wheel used by the Elders' Text Committee for guidance in the selection of Elders and the knowledge to be obtained from them.

While the Elders and traditional teachers we talked to would likely not claim to 'represent' their whole people or culture, their words offer insight into how their people see the world and life in their communities. It is important to remember that these Elders and traditional teachers grew up as much in a world of Christianity and residential schools as they did in a world of ancient spiritual practices and life on the land. Many of them were born 'in the bush' and, as their life histories attest, have seen a remarkable degree and pace of change. However, these individuals are not relics of some outdated way of life; they are contemporary people, struggling (like many of us) sometimes to resist, sometimes to ride the waves of change.

In putting the text together, we had to remember that there might be many aspects of what an individual said to us that we did not immediately or fully understand. This meant we had to be very respectful of the words of the Elders, trying not to change them so as not to distort or change what the Elder or traditional teacher was attempting to communicate. There are already enough changes involved in taking an Elder's oral teachings, which may be highly situational and related closely to the context of the specific time and place when a teaching is spoken, and translating them into the English language and onto the page as written words.

The reader will not find in these pages a comprehensive or definitive list of the 'traits' of all Aboriginal cultures in Canada or their thought world. This is not by any means a definitive work, nor do we think it possible to produce one in this field. Instead, the reader will find highly personal reflections on sometimes weighty, sometimes more mundane matters. There are life stories. There are some stories of ancient heroes and tricksters. There are descriptions of this or that aspect of life, in old times and in new, but one can always discern the principles of the reflection.

There are some areas where issues of unusual complexity emerge. For example, the theme of Christianity is expressed in almost diametrically opposite ways by different Elders and traditional teachers. Some embrace it and see it as entirely compatible with their cultural and spiritual traditions, while others are antagonistic, seeing it as a very harmful force in the lives of their people and one that has been disruptive and disrespectful of traditional values. Similarly, Elders and traditional teachers sometimes commented about their Aboriginal neighbours in unflattering ways where the neighbours have been enemies or opponents.

To point to a third example, Elders had a diverse range of responses on the question of the place of same-sex couples in their communities: some said they didn't exist, and found the whole idea peculiar; others pointed to cultural traditions that included acceptance and respect for the individual's sexual preference. None of these answers, at least in our view, needs be treated as a gospel truth or as a reflection of how all individuals in a particular First Nation feel about an issue. Reading the collection provides a sense of the variety and depth of different Elders' and traditional teacher's opinions.

We asked all of the people we interviewed the same set of questions. Some had nothing to say about particular topics, while going on at great length about others. Hence, even the comparative nature of the text has its limits. We also gave each Elder and traditional teacher an opportunity to introduce anything else they felt was important that we had not included. So, while some chapters may have a great deal to say about, for example, traditional spiritual values, others may focus on practical matters, such as how to live on the land. However, sometimes an Elder uses a practical lesson or story from her or his life to communicate much more important issues about traditional values. An Elder might tell about how to braid Sweetgrass, not just to instruct in the mechanics of preparing Sweetgrass for smudging ceremonies, but to talk about how it is necessary for people to work together. This allegorical level of traditional teachings can be found most commonly in stories that Elders tell and is one of the sources of this text's richness.

The issues raised by the text, in our view, include the relevance of tradition in the modern world: What is the value of traditional knowledge? Can traditions be maintained? How is traditional knowledge communicated and passed on? The experiences of Aboriginal people in Canada also raise questions: What was the impact of residential schools? What were the key events of the past few decades? How has life changed for Aboriginal peoples?

The substantive cultural values of Aboriginal people could be taken as another set of issues: What similarities does this range of peoples have culturally? What are the differences and what are the sources of those differences? How do Aboriginal people view the modern world they are a part of as well as the non-Aboriginal people they share it with? What are their criticisms? What do they like about life today as opposed to life in the old days? What does it mean to be an Elder or a traditional teacher today? What is an Elder's role in her or his community? Not all the Elders and traditional teachers speak to all of these questions.

The Elders' tales are rich in diversity. Their life histories demonstrate that they came to their understanding of their traditional culture through many different routes. Some were 'tested' on their life path through alcoholism and other personal difficulties. Some came to the teachings late in life. Others were born and raised on the land and have consistently lived a life in the bush. Many emphasize the importance of the land, Mother Earth, as central to Aboriginal culture. Some speak of the different stages of life an individual goes through on the path of life. Throughout, there is a theme of concern for the loss of the traditional values, beliefs, and way of life among the young people of today. How can Aboriginal culture survive against the powerful influences of the dominant society?

At the same time, the volume illustrates that many of the Elders are thoroughly modern people, fully engaged in the contemporary world. Many of the demands made on the Elders involve placing Aboriginal language and cultural teachings at the centre of contemporary Aboriginal life. This is evidenced in the multitude of roles Elders are asked to play in their communities. Elders are involved in prison programs, as teachers in schools, as facilitators of workshops, as speakers at conferences, as counsellors in Aboriginal organizations, in writing books, as spokespersons in the media, and so on. The Elders' stories in this volume attest to the important challenge of integrating Aboriginal values and spirituality within the context of secular institutions.

Finally, some of these questions are touched on elliptically, or very tentatively, or only in the most coded of ways. It is for the reader to make her or his own interpretation, find her or his own 'truths,' in this text.

This text is, therefore, a part of a broader process taking place across Canada, the contemporary cultural renaissance of Aboriginal peoples. Sundances, Sweat Lodge ceremonies, Fasting, Potlatches, traditional healing rituals, and other spiritual ceremonies – all are enjoying a revival. Aboriginal languages are being taught in language immersion schools as well as in band and public schools. Cultural-survival schools across the country function as alternatives to the public schools and are based on an Aboriginal philosophy of teaching and learning to provide students with an affirmation of their traditional and spiritual roots.

Over the past three decades in particular, Métis Nations, First Nations, and Inuit have placed themselves firmly on Canada's political and cultural agenda. In the areas of politics, law, and the Constitution there have been the struggles over the government's 1969 White Paper policy proposal, the Calder (1973) and Sparrow (1992) cases, and Section 35 of the Canada Act (1982). In the cultural realm visual artists of extraordinary power have flourished, as have Aboriginal organizations attempting to develop services and programs based on Aboriginal thought – the Friendship Centre

movement, healing and wellness circles, the Aboriginal women's movement, tribal councils, theatre groups, academic programs, communi-
cations societies; and cultural happenings such as Powwows, Elders'
gatherings, spiritual gatherings, traditional games, and other events. This
revitalization process has continued to grow and gain momentum.

In the 1990s, this process has been taking place in the arts, in popular
culture, in politics; it has been taking place among individuals, communities, organizations; it draws on ancient and more recent roots at the same
time as it embraces innovative technologies of cultural communication
and dissemination; it has involved spectacular and historic moments of
extraordinary symbolic resonance while its long-term accomplishments
may ultimately take place community by community and program by
program.

Emerging in Aboriginal communities are people with bicultural identi-
ties, individuals who have an identity firmly anchored in the cultural
world of their people while at the same time possessing the skills and
knowledge required to succeed in the larger society. This bicultural identity enables them to pursue the goals of both cultures.

While the realities – poverty, suicides, a vast range of debilitating problems – continue to give those involved in this process a fierce determina-
tion to make things better, it is worthwhile not to follow the media and
dwell on so-called social pathologies, but to remind ourselves of the
accomplishments. For political events, think of the constitutional meetings with First Nations, and the Royal Commission on Aboriginal Peoples.
For political leaders, Ethel Blondin-Andrew, Rosemarie Kuptana, George
Erasmus, and Ovide Mercredi. In architecture, Douglas Cardinal; in clas-
sical music, conductor John Kim Bell; in popular music, Kashtin and
Susan Aglukark; in theatre, Tomson Highway and Drew Hayden Taylor;
in painting, Norval Morrisseau, Carl Beam, and Daphne Odjig; in sculp-
ture, Saali Arngnaituk and Bill Reid. These are only a few of the many
Aboriginal people making significant contributions in their chosen fields.
In the sphere of scholarship and academic intellectual inquiry, a new
generation of Aboriginal scholars is emerging to challenge orthodoxies
and bring to discussion new ways of thinking about issues. And so many
others, in so many other fields.

We hope that this text will amuse and enrich and provoke you, that perhaps something in your system of values or in your mode of thought is
moved through your encounter with these pages. Elders are speaking.
Their words are strong. If we listen hard, if we listen in a good way, their
words will stay with us for a long time.

NOTES

1 Members of the Elders' Text Advisory Committee included Sylvia Maracle (Mohawk), executive director of the Ontario Federation of Indian Friendship Centres; Tim Thompson, Ontario Federation of Indian Friendship Centres; Vern Douglas (Anishinabe), Native education advisor, Toronto Board of Education; and from the Native Studies department David Newhouse (Onondaga), Shirley Williams (Anishinabe), Edna Manitowabi (Anishinabe), Paul Bourgeois (Anishinabe), Louise Garrow (Anishinabe), Peter Kulchyski, and Don McCaskill.

2 Joseph Couture, *Philosophy and Psychology of Native Education*, Society of Western Historians, 1977, 2.

3 Ibid, 3.

Eastern Canada Cultures

MARGARET PAUL (Passmoquady)

St Mary's First Nation, Nova Scotia

'Every song you sing just keeps getting better and better.'

Margaret Paul was interviewed by Emily Faries in the summer of 1994 at St Mary's First Nation. It was very hot during the three days Emily spent in the community, but Margaret Paul's energy was endless. She answered questions, told stories, cooked food, cracked jokes, and laughed throughout the interview. Margaret's stories stressed her commitment to the traditions, and to the young people in the community. Margaret lives with her husband and family, who were always around her during the interview. They are heard in the background with the sound of the television that she threatened to throw out the window.

Margaret Paul's traditional name is *Monimkeeque Bedug*, which means the 'sound of thunder,' or 'the sound the thunder makes.' Margaret Paul is known in her community as a traditional singer. Through her songs she expresses the traditional teachings and messages, especially to young people in and around the community.

Life History

I was born in Holton, Maine, across the border from here. And I was raised on a reservation, Passmoquady reservation, that's where we're originally from. The reason why I was born there is because my mother and my father used to go picking potatoes, so my mother was pregnant at the time so I was born over there. But I was raised on a reservation, in Passmoquady. I lived there fourteen years and I came over here, and I got married over here on this reserve. I married a Maliseed. I got married when I was fifteen [laughs]. Fifteen years old and I was married. I have five grandchildren. The fifth one on the way. I got married over here on my first marriage. I was married eleven years. Now on my second marriage, I have been married eleven years.

I went to school in Passmoquady, from grade one to grade eight. I think I got pushed out of there because I didn't really learn. I wasn't really interested in school. See where our school was, down at the bottom of the hill, and up on the hill I could see my home. That's where my heart was, at my home. And I was missing my grandmother, my mother, I'd see my grandmother coming out the door and here we were supposed to be doing something, here I'm looking to see what my grandmother's going to be doing. I could see it from the window where I sat. But I didn't really take interest in school, the only thing what I liked in school was music and spelling, that's it. No arithmetic.

I didn't go to residential school, no. Thank God. But my brothers did, my two older brothers did. Because my father came from over on this side, in Eskasoni reserve, Cape Breton. That's where he's from. So when he left, when he left my mother in Holton, he took the boys, but my mother didn't know he was leaving her. We lived in the woods in there, and when he left my mother he said, 'I'll be back with the two boys,' and he never came back. My mother didn't know where he went, where the boys went, and what happened. So back in '56 [1956], this priest came to the reservation, he got to know the families and he asked my mother if he could help her find the boys. And my mother said, 'I surely would, somebody help me.' So he only went on a tiny little picture about this small, so he found them in that school, Shiginany, Shiginany Residential School. So they came home. But it must be awful in those schools.

My grandmother was my main teacher when I was growing up, because my mother had to work, she had to get us food, she had eight kids to look after by herself. So my grandmother baby-sat while my mother worked in a fish factory, sardine factory, tuna factory, all those kind of factories down there, that's what she did. So my grandmother taught us a lot, how to skin fish and clean fish and dry the fish, and pick Sweetgrass for my mother. You see after the sardine season is over then she turns to braiding Sweetgrass again. So that's how we were brought up, through Sweetgrass. She did tiny little braids for the baskets, that's what she did. You weave the Sweetgrass in with the baskets. She did that for the ones who did baskets on the reserve. She sold these for half a cent a yard [laughs]. Even before she died – this was not too long ago – about six or seven years ago – I told her, 'Mom, why don't you raise your price, at least a quarter?' She said, 'I can't, that's too much money.' She only raised it to fifteen cents. She really thought this was too much too, but I said, 'No way, fifteen cents a yard.' She wouldn't dare go up to a quarter.

So when we were growing up, all I remember mostly growing up is we had to clear the kitchen, clear the bedrooms, you know our bedrooms, the only bedroom that was up was my mother's bedroom and the kitchen stove, tables, and chairs. Everything else had to be moved into the shed in the back. Sweetgrass all summer, hanging there drying, so we had to pick Sweetgrass for my mother all summer until fall, so that she'd have enough until the next season. So we'd pick it, we'd clean it and then hang it up, put it in little bunches and hang it up to dry. And that's what she used all these years, that's how she kept us in clothes and food. Was through that, Sweetgrass.

Creation Stories

I never heard those stories. I think it's because we were raised as Catholics. So the only thing we heard mostly is about Jesus Christ and the Bible, their kind of stories of how the world began, Adam and Eve and all that stuff.

Important Aspects of Native Culture

Language. Holy critters, if you didn't have your language, that's how I relate to Mother Earth, our songs, drumming, and singing. That's my life, singing and drumming. Before that, before I started doing that I knew I was always related to the Earth here. But I didn't know her as Mother Earth then. But I knew there was some kind of connection, and the moon I call her Grandmother Moon now, I never called her Grandma Moon back then. But I knew that there was some kind of connection, until I started walking on the Sweetgrass road, about twenty, twenty-five years ago.

And at that time, I knew I wanted to be something other than just being an Indian. Somebody asked me, 'You're an Indian?' 'Yeah I am.' You know, that's as far as it goes. I never knew anything that related to it. But I knew I wanted something else more than what I had. That was way back in the early seventies. And we use to sit around the table, us women, all the same age with kids, and sit around the table and say, 'We got to do something.' We had to, you know, we're Indian and that's as far as it goes. It's just 'we're Indian.' Nothing different, and when we put on our leather and feathers, that's the only thing they know us by. There goes the Indians with the feathers, even our own children on the reservation. 'Oh! there goes the Indians.' Gee, did that ever hurt! Because they themselves didn't know who they were either.

They weren't being taught that they were Indian or anything. And now, my grandson he knows he's an Indian and we don't even have to teach him, he just watches us what we do or what we say when we pray, and he does the same thing. It's just natural to him, which it should have been to us long ago, natural. He's lucky. Even when I started walking on this road, I used to help my mother with Sweetgrass, every year. We were true, true, true. Going there every summer to pick Sweetgrass and stuff for her to braid for the baskets. And when it came time for me to, when we are smudging, when we smudge with Sweetgrass, all of a sudden my mother knew that I was walking on some kind of road or other. She didn't understand, which I didn't understand myself, in the beginning. And I asked her, 'Mom, can I have the grass that you don't use?' Sometimes when we, as children, pick grass, we don't know which are good, there are so many different textures to them. Some are too sharp, she can't use them, they cut her fingers, all the way when she's braiding grass. And she said, 'What are you going to do with them?' I said, 'I'm going to burn them.' 'Ahhh,' she said. I said, 'Yes, I'm going to burn them, we pray with it, Mom' [laughs].

To her it was a waste going up in flames [laughs]. But she gave it to us so I supplied everybody over here on the reserve for anybody who wanted Sweetgrass, they'd come over to my house to get it. So finally she did, and after a while she started asking, 'You don't go to church anymore.' I said, 'No.' That's as far as it went. But after a while she didn't bother me about it or anything. I know she was peeved off when I don't go or that my children don't go and now it's my grandchildren. But she gave us the Sweetgrass and after a while she was asking questions. And she didn't mind after a while, when the priests and nuns allowed it in the church, now it's all right what I do because my mother felt that it was okay because this person came to the church and did the Sweetgrass and did the feathers. It's all right for us to do that because it was okay with the priest or the nuns.

Not too long ago, we were at a funeral. I thought to myself, I'm going to do this different this time because they make me feel like as if they have to give me the cue, then I'll have to do what I have to do. Well I ain't going to give anybody any cue. I asked that woman to tell me when they are done and I'll come down. So she told me when they were done. The priest looked at me, his eyes were getting bigger and bigger. I came all the way up, I walked up to the altar, he was still looking at me [laughs]. He didn't know what I was going to do [laughs]. So I told the women, this is what I am going to do here because those people always felt that they had to listen to that way.

It is because it has been five hundred years of Christianity! In this area, it's been five hundred years. It's almost like they're conditioned, and it's not their fault. But you see, I feel it, even that old man that was holding his crucifix when they walked the body out, he was holding that so tightly, I know he really believed in that. But when he was standing there and standing there and standing there, I was singing and I was trying to tell him, 'Go,' but he wouldn't listen to me. Even the guys that bring the body from the funeral home, they tried to tell that man to go but he wouldn't budge until he looked at the priest and the priest gave him the nod, then he went. He was in his seventies and that is too bad. It's going to take them a long time to get back there to be deconditioned.

Do you know Albert Lightning? Or did you know of him? He died not too long ago. He was the first one that we ever got down here that knew anything about traditional ways or anything. We went into it blindly. That was when we knew we had to go here and there to get somebody, to learn from something or somebody. So when we got him down here, that was about twenty-five years ago. He was telling us about Native ways, that everything is coming so fast now that not even the Spirits are going to wait for us until we're ready. They don't have time, they're just going to come. He said, 'Metal is falling from the sky.' I knew what that was. Those are planes falling from the sky. He was telling us that there were people who are committing suicide and we know that. It's here already. That was the first time a Powwow was ever held here. Before that it was 139 years before that. The last one!

Well they're just starting one now. We had one last year and they had another one here but it's just different people who are doing it. I would like to do that, but it's been 139 years before that and we didn't know what the heck we were doing. We knew we wanted something. So we got names from my cousin down Chibyga, past Wikwonay, Deanna Francise. We got names from her on who we could get a hold of, so we just did a proposal and we got a proposal for ten thousand dollars. That included plane tickets and getting people here and there to come down and one of them was Albert Lightning, Ernest Tootoosis, Vera Martin, Peter Martin, Albert Angus, William Dumas and we tried to get Philip Deer from down South but we had bad connections with the airport so we couldn't get him, but I was just talking to him on the phone. So we got all those other people that came. That's how it began around here in the seventies.

When the Elders came there, there were people coming in that had alcohol, and wanted to bring it in there and keep drinking and participating in whatever was going on. So the Elders told us that each and every one had to watch the camps and if they wanted to stay they had to get rid of their booze. So we did, and some young folks that had left were laughing and kind of making unpleasant remarks but they came back the next day. And they brought a great big truck with a load of wood in there to keep the fire going all week. After calling us names the night before, they realized what was going on and they stayed all week too. We had to do something to keep those Elders here. That was a beginning for a lot of other people. That's where we first met Gisatanomok. It was at our gathering, and he invited us to his gathering in Warnpanowgan, Cape Cod. I think he is not that old, but is seen as an Elder out here.

My life changed when I decided to walk this road. I quit drinking, but when I first started, I was still drinking. I was still tipping the bottle and coming home drunk. They had a meeting in town with this Aboriginal Peoples Council, I don't know who was all there. I wasn't even there! They had decided to make me the drum keeper because nobody wanted to keep the drum because you had to be clear of alcohol and drugs and keep it away from these things. It was just that nobody wanted to be responsible for it. Well, before that I used to look after the drum and I got used to keeping it at my home. Now it was just that nobody wants to look after it. This poor drum, my mother would take it home. You know, they leave it and so I kept it. I was thinking to myself, when I come home I can't even touch that drum, you know. What the hell am I doing drinking? Why am I doing all this stuff? I was thinking to myself when I lay there in bed because it was in my bedroom with me. What if somebody asks us to go drum here and there and I was just drinking and I can't even touch that drum. These thoughts were going through my head.

After a while I quit drinking. I had heard this man talking about his life and how he was brought up, how he grew up and how he is today. I was crying and crying because I wanted to say, 'It's all right, Chris, it's okay, come here, I'll hold you.' Oh my God, I was crying. That was the last time I took a drink, and that was when Albert Lightning was there too. That was the time they had him speaking, and this guy named Raymond Gold. That's how I quit drinking was through him and he helped me.

We started singing and I couldn't hold a tune, I couldn't reach the notes or anything and I was just a-puffing away. I smoked too much, I knew I smoked too much to hold a tune. It hurt my lungs to try to sing and everything. When you have to keep it up, you can't even do it because you are right out of breath [laughs]. So I thought about quitting smoking so I could sing. I wanted to sing, I wanted to sing my best, I wanted to sing the best for the Creator, I was thinking at the time. But I did the usual thing as I did all the time. I bought some cigarettes, bought a lighter, but I got some pamphlets and started reading, by the time I read all my books and smoked my cigarettes and I threw my lighter in the garbage and that was the last time I smoked. That was eleven years ago. I used to smoke three packs a day. But I love singing so much.

We started by singing everywhere, like around in town. Like when they had meetings. When Native people gathered, we would open the meeting by singing. So that's when we started and this was way back, I don't know how many years ago. And then they wanted us to sing at malls and some places like the RCMP opening, or the Rangers or Scouts. That's how we all started. We got money here and there. Then we started dancing, we started making outfits and putting feathers in our hair so we would dance for fifteen minutes, make six hundred dollars, enough to pay for our gas mileage on the bus. The Chief was charging us a dollar per mile. That sometimes wasn't even enough, because we had to put that in gas and to feed all of the kids because there was forty of us when we first began dancing here. I didn't like it. I didn't want that, that wasn't what I wanted. You know as an Indian person I don't want to be up there dancing on a show and everyone clapping, telling me I did a good job. I didn't want to do that. So I quit that until when we went to Mashbey. That was my first time really, really wanting to do something for myself. I didn't even talk to anybody because I was too shy. I would sit in the corner all day and listen to everybody talk as long as I don't have to talk. Then sometimes when people wanted me to talk my heart pounding fast and I would say, 'No, I got nothing to say.' I felt at the time that what I had to say wasn't important. Why should it matter what I say! It's not important what I talk about or nothing important in my life, nothing to say or nothing to share, but at that time in Mashbey. It was four years we went back and forth until I finally said something in the circle.

At that time my husband's uncle that lives over here, he was in his sixties, he said in a circle that he found himself through the Indian way. And it was at that time when I could hardly wait until it was my turn so that I could talk. I was so excited to talk this time. All of a sudden I wanted to share what I wanted because people were talking, sharing their dreams and I'm a dreamer. I could sit here for ten years and tell you about all my dreams. They are exciting and so colourful and they mean something. So that was the first time I ever spoke. I shared four dreams over there and ever since then I want to talk. Sometimes I might not understand the language and they sometimes talk big words that I might not understand so I lose interest or sometimes I get little pieces here and there that I can understand that will get me back there again, then when they use these highfallutin words again ahh, forget it. When it comes to simple, like simple, simple language, it's much easier because you can understand and relate to that person on whatever is happening, if they come down to Earth where we are. I speak my own language. I use the language most of the time.

I learned to speak English in school. I had a hard time, especially in first grade. I didn't know any English language. And a lot of kids were laughing at me because I couldn't understand. That teacher was talking to me, but I didn't know what she was telling me. I looked in this desk and I found nothing in there, so I told her in my language. And she just looked at me and everybody else started laughing. So I was still, I couldn't hardly understand English even when I was in the sixth and seventh grade. I still couldn't, I had a hard time with the English language. I did not go to high school, I went to grade eight supposedly, but I don't think I ever got there. We had to go to the White school for high school, then I started getting scared, I did not want to go up there.

Using Traditions Today

Through singing. That's the way I think, because that's how I think you can reach young kids is through songs, through dancing, through singing. I mean you can't reach them by talking, and talking about you know, Mother Earth and Father Sky or whatever. You can't reach them because we all see it, you know. But they don't see it that way. And I think that is the way we can get back to expressing ourselves, what comes from in here, your heart. And when you sing, you make that sound, and with that sound you're relating to the Creator through there. That's the way I look at it. Through dancing, you're dancing for the Creator. And through the drum, you know there's something to the drum. Because when I first started, you know, from way back to now, even the tiniest babies, what do they do when they hear that drum. They start moving already, they move, they don't even know whether they are dancing or whatever, but they move to that motion, to dancing.

Even month-old babies, their eyes perk up, or you could be so loud, you could have the baby right here and the drum is going and chanting, and he'd be sleeping away. Or a tiny baby, that does not even walk yet would be there standing making movement. And the ones that can dance, or even the most hyper kid like my grandson, he's so hyper, he's all the time moving all over, everywhere, but when that drum beats, he's right there sitting, he's sitting right there until the drumming is done. Through the heartbeat, through us, through the Creator, it's just that connection. That's the way I think we can get back, trying to get it again, is through song, is through singing. Because once you start singing, once you start drumming, once you start dancing, you don't think about how much money you are going to earn tomorrow, or that you have to make a payment, or I have to do this, I have to do that or that you are worried about my kids, or worried about my husband or my wife. You don't think like that, or you don't worry about what food you are going to eat next day, or whatever. You just dance, you feel good, for that moment.

Like when we first started learning songs, we only sang one song over and over again, maybe for a year or two. We learned it through down home. That song it's called 'Onewhode,' it's a welcome song, to welcome for everybody who comes to visit, when they gather and dance at a place. That's what we sang, we just use that, and then when we went somewhere again. We learned another song, this is an old chant. So we use that song for like an InterTribal, like where everybody dances the way they feel. So we use that song, but at first we only used one song over and over again. And then when we started learning songs from the Micmacs or Wapinogs or people from out West, they would say you know I want to give you this song, so we learn songs through that way, singing whatever, song, dance, whatever function.

Sometimes, when we all get together and then somebody would say let's sing this song, and then the way I think is I have to think fast or think which song to sing even though it might not be that song, but I think it fits at the time, place, and the reason, so I sing that song. Flag songs, I don't know any flag songs, but we're learning some now. Or Grand Entry, we don't know any Grand Entry, we know so many but they're given to us here and there because we don't know any of ours, hardly. Because they're not shared. There's some people that know and these people don't want to pass it on. It's hard!

Men and women sing together. We do that here. But it's from all over everywhere, I don't know whether people are saying, 'Why are women singing? Why are they using the drum? Women don't drum.' Why can't they just enjoy? Is it because so many people are putting rules on us? Are people making rules, or was it like that? Then I said to myself, 'I used to be that way too, I listened to this one, listened to that one, what are we to believe here?' I don't even know which way is the Passmoquady way or the Micmac way or Ojibwe, or whatever. To me it doesn't matter which way, your way is the way you feel at that time, that's that way. That's the way I feel. Never mind trying to say this one is right, everybody's right. Instead of saying you cannot do this, you cannot do that, it's the way I feel. That's how I do things because I've done making myself going nuts. Can I do this, or can I do that? We're going through that nod and nudge with the priest, again within our own people.

Traditional Dwellings

The only one that I have heard of is this woman that is still living today and she was born in a wigwam. She must be in her sixties so that wasn't very long ago because they were still sleeping in wigwams. They would probably be made out of birch-bark. Like the longhouses, lots of families lived together. They used to live all together. Even when somebody got married they all still lived together. It was like an extended family. The families would be closer if the generations all lived in one house. Everyone now all have modern houses and are more separated. It hinders our Native traditions, because we are being blocked off that sense of belonging and sharing. When I used to live down home, when I was a kid, there were rooms divided but there was a great big long room and we all slept in there, the whole family. Everybody slept on beds but it was that great big long room where everybody slept. I was brought up sleeping all in one bed, all eight of us, plus my mother would sleep with us, just like sardines, packed.

Wherever I have space when family comes over to stay, that's where they sleep. I love sleeping on the floor with my family because you talk, tell stories, and just be close. My son at age twenty-seven feels like he does not matter here in the society that they live in now, that there is nothing out there for them, people don't care, people don't ask them because it doesn't matter about what you say or how you feel or what you think. He told us that one night when he came home drunk and we were all sitting there, supposedly traditional people, and all of a sudden he comes in ... Quiet, just silence, nobody said nothing, they were squirming in their seats. He just sat there, then he came over and told us, 'What is this instant quietness because I walked in? I just walked in! And you are quiet already, and you are telling me you are supposed to be traditional people!' That's when he started telling us how he felt. Not just him, their whole group, how there is nothing for them, and it's so hard for them to live. Their peers are not strong enough to say, yet, 'I don't care how you think, I am going to stop drinking and I am going to do whatever I want to do.' It's so hard for them, they can't even say that.

They follow their friends instead of doing in their own heart what they want to do. We talked about that, when we, our own people, come in drunk, what do we do? We clam up, we don't even continue talking what we are talking about. Why is that, why is that block there? They are the same as us, just because they are drinking. He is my son and those are his people sitting there. There is a lot of young people that feel that way, that is why there are so many suicides around here. I don't know about out West but there are a lot around here. Even now our own reservation is starting. Two of them did and one was an older man almost sixty years old. He hung himself behind his friend's place and said that he would be right back. He went out the back door and that was the last time she saw him, so she went to bed. She thought that he must have left and then the next morning when she went out, he was hanging from her clothes-line. Not even a week later a young guy twenty-two years old shot himself, he even put newspaper all over in the kitchen so that he wouldn't get blood all over the walls and cupboards. He shot himself through the mouth and blew his head off. He was with some of his friends a couple of days before and he was saying, 'What am I living for? Why am I here?' He felt like he had no purpose on this Earth.

Elders

Even before the traditional stuff came about, they didn't even say Elders, it was old people that were wise, kind, that knew a lot. I think people considered as an Elder would be the older generation. The people that had wisdom of what was wrong and what was good and those that have been around. I don't even want to be an Elder and I don't even know how I got here. What the hell am I doing here? [laughs].

Heroes and Role Models

Gisatanomok! I like Gisatanomok. This is how I see him today and this is how I'll always see him as today, how he walks on Mother Earth. To me when he walks on Mother Earth, he walks gently on her, and he knows a lot. I don't know how many times I've cried and asked him why am I here, and he's the one that gets me through how I'm feeling.

Even that ball game we had here, we had National Fast Pitch here. They asked us to open it. They asked us, a week before we had it. That must be the way I am. They asked if we would open it. I said, 'If I am here I'm here, I will do it.' That's what I said. I told the organizer if I get a call this week I will let you know if I am really going to be here. I got my call, and I said, 'Yeah, we'll do it.' And we did it. We opened the thing with the national anthem for Indian people. We opened with that, and I sang a song for these two guys over here. And they loved it. Before that, when they asked us to do all of this I knew some of them were embarrassed about Indian ways. Or embarrassed about singing because they didn't know what singing was all about. And I said I was going to smudge too! 'Oh, that's a good idea,' they said, 'we're going to smudge the whole grounds.' We wanted to do that and we did.

We knew there was going to be alcohol there, but that didn't bother what I was thinking. I was thinking there was going to be alcohol there, and people that were drinking. I am going to smudge this area, I told this to my buddy that was doing it with me. 'We're going to smudge four times here, because there is going to be a lot of alcohol. We're going to smudge this whole place.' And I was praying. I was asking the Creator to look after the people that are going to be drinking, and look after them when they leave here if they are going to be driving, so that nobody will get in an accident. So when they get home they will not fight with their spouses or their children, and look after them. Look after this week, and I do hope they have a good time, and a good turnout. If it rains, bring the pour down. And that's exactly what happened the very first day, it poured. But give the girls a good day so that they can play ball all week, and they won't have to cancel, because it was calling for rain. But every morning I woke up early, it's a good day, 'Right on, the girls can play.' I am not even a ball fan. I have nothing to do with ball. But all week I was there [laughs].

But that morning I smudged the whole place. What is smudging all about? It is for reconnecting with your Creator. To think right and think straight. You want to say positive things, whatever comes out of your mouth and comes out of here, out of your Spirit and your body. And when we were smudging all around here there were men raking up the ball diamonds, men putting a nail here and there, and one of them said, 'It smells good, I wonder what that is.' They knew we were smudging. One came over and looked at me, and he said, 'Can I smudge?' I said, 'Right on!' So this other guy was standing there watching, and I went over to him and he said, 'No, I can't, I was dirty, I was bad.' I said, 'Bad? What the hell did you do?' He said, 'I was on alcohol and drugs last night, I can't smudge.' I said, 'Why not, if anything it will do you good. Smudge.' And he looked at me and he started smudging. He must have smudged for about three minutes, and I blowed it and a great big smudge came, and he was so happy when I did that. And it made me feel good because he really respects it, this guy. And after, he said, 'Thank you very much,' and I said, 'You're welcome.' We smudged that whole place. It must have taken an hour. We took a big bag of sage and we used it all.

Humour

That's what keeps us alive. You know like sometimes we don't have groceries, I don't have money, and then we talk about it and we laugh. I don't have any money, so what. Sometimes you wear sneakers like these, first time I bought myself a brand-new pair that costs that much in all my life. I'm almost fifty and I have a forty-dollar pair of sneakers. Or you never have a new jacket. When we were children sometimes my mother bought us clothes and all that, but sometimes she had to get second-hand stuff, but to us that was brand-new. We learned to appreciate what we got. I still go to them second-hand shops and that's where I do all my shopping now.

Role of Work

I think work is important. Like out here we have to have an education, you have to do what they want you to do. In the Indian way of life you work when you feel like working – if you want to make ten baskets go ahead and make ten, but if you only want to make one then that's all right too. And when you take a break there is always going to be a lot of people talking. That's what I remember when I was a little girl. Waking up early in the morning down home when you hear the pounding of the ash [the ash tree for baskets] and it would be echoing all the way down here somewhere. Do you know they would be pounding ash on one side and you can hear the echo way on the other side of the reserve. And then you can hear the men talking. When they are pounding the ash this man would be working away. Everybody else would be sitting there talking and laughing and then by the time ten o'clock rolls around all of the ash is done. They would be having a nice time talking and conversing with one another pounding the ash, having coffee.

These baskets. A really true basket maker can make a basket out of anything. You can make a lamp out of baskets, that is the kind of art we have here. Carving out of wood is another way, you have that right in you. You could see it in the people or in their art drawing. All my kids are like that, they are very creative. And what my husband does now is pottery. From the time when I first seen him do pottery and now, it still needs a lot of improvement but I told him, 'Every pot you do or every form or shape you make is better than the last one.' I said it just keeps getting better and better. Even in singing, you've got to sing every day. You know you have to hum a tune or sing a tune or whatever, as long as you're exercising your vocal cords and keeping that muscle the tongue going as to singing. Every song you sing keeps getting better and better, it all depends on how you feel, it makes you feel that way too. You could put yourself in that kind of feeling you are going to be singing for the Creator and you are going to be singing for the people and right off the bat you are going to feel it. I do, that's the way I feel.

Daily Routines

Well, the first thing I try to do when I wake up in my regular day at home is, when I get up in the morning, I look out the window. When I look out the window, I see another day. It's so beautiful, I say 'Good morning, Creator.' That's what I think. And then sometimes, more so nowadays, but I like the talks I had with Gisatanomok, he's always telling me, 'The Creator is so happy when we put Tobacco down.' So I try to do that, even if I don't remember early in the morning, I'll do it within that day. Maybe two or three times a day. I'm always thanking the Creator for everything, even for whatever goes on that day, I thank him. And then in the morning, this is the usual in the morning at home, people are all the time visiting me. I get visits sometimes from the time I get up till the time I go to bed at night.

So, there's hardly any washing dishes, or cooking or whatever, or cleaning up. But the way I feel, at that moment, I don't want to lose that moment with the people that come to talk. The heck with the dishes, the heck with the cleaning up, that can wait. It will still be there after. I want that time with the people. And then sometimes at dinner we will eat, we'll cook up something, hot dog, coffee, cake, ice cream, or whatever. Then sometimes we watch a movie, movies meaning the ones that my sister makes for me, like if there's anything going on down home, she'll make me tapes. She's the archives. She's the archives of that reserve. She has tapes on everything that goes on down there, anything and everything. All the weddings, all the traditional things, like the Indian Days or the traditional gatherings, or the Elder that we have down home, her name is Margaret, too. She's fifty years older than I am, so she's ninety-eight this year. She has a video of her and she has tapes of everything. Then you watch a movie, you put in a movie, well sometimes we'll be there two or three hours, sometimes you watch it and talk about it.

You know, we get the thing going, the wheels going. Then we talk about everything and anything, what things go on in our lives, and then sometimes we think we don't talk like that at home or nobody talks like that around here. They are learning at the same time and sharing and opening up and when you open up you can talk about anything, even the worst thing you did in your life. That's really something. Then that person might think I'm not really that bad after all, you know. Or they will think, look at this woman, she can talk about it. That's sharing, yes that's a way of healing, when you share experiences that's when you open up a little bit more. The more you share, the more open you get. I like to talk about all different kinds of subjects in my home because there are people coming there all the time. And young people, I got young people visiting me now from down home. They came about two or three weeks ago again and they were talking about what a good time they had. I said, 'You can come up any time and have a good time again.' So they come here again and they're out having a good time.

I love that, the drummers, this young man that had made his drum, it is ever so beautiful. And I told him that he has so much talent, 'You got so much within you, right in you, you could bring it out.' You know this is what he had in his thoughts and in his feelings. So he made it and he brought it out, and the carvings that he does, he's got so much on the go and he's got such a beautiful smile and he's only twenty-two years old but he reminds me of a older person that is so wise. He's got so much affection for people. He makes you smile, makes you laugh, and he can feel how a person feels like today so he's going to make that person smile. There's also other young people that come to the house. We all talk about stuff like that. We share, and sometimes I'll cook up something, macaroni and hamburger and tomatoes or whatever, while they're drumming and we devour it after. Just sharing, sharing is so important. And sometimes, Ned Bear asks me to go up to the high school and to share with the kids over there. We do a talking circle or talk about what they are doing, talking sticks, that's what they're doing now, talking sticks. And what little I know, I just share with what I know. I don't try to know any more than what I know, just share what I have or what I feel.

I talk to God all the time. I talk with him all day, all evening, when I go to bed I'm so thankful. When I wake up in the morning I'm thankful that I have my husband laying there beside me. I thank him that he's still alive, I look at him. I don't know why I have a habit of looking at people. Are they still breathing or what? I'm always so grateful, and I ask him to look after all my other children that are, you know, have their own homes. One daughter is far away. I ask him to look after them and their spouses, whoever they're married to, and all my people that are here. I used to think like that, what can I do for my people? They are so in need of help. Oh! I'd love for them to have what I have, I feel so good, and sometimes when you lay down in the evenings, on a weekend, you hear these sirens going or you hear somebody shouting or you hear somebody fighting. You just want to do something, you want to help them.

One night I went to sleep and I had a dream. I dreamt about this little fire person that was about this tall. I was going down the road, taking a shortcut. I was crying, saying to the Creator, 'What can I do to help my people?' And then I turned around and looked at the reserve and everybody was drunk, everybody was drinking. I wanted to go back but this little fire person would not let me go back.

Every time I wanted to go he'd go this way and that way, he just wanted me to keep going. But I didn't want to keep going because the man that lived on the other side of the railroad tracks is going to suck me right in that house when I pass right by there. So when I was going by there, I knew it was going to happen anyway, so when I went by he was sitting on the steps like this with a smile on his face. It was an old, old Chief that used to be on that reserve, that lived on that reserve. And I got sucked right in, as soon as I got sucked right in, there was a woman, a little fire woman that was standing there. Oh! She must've been about this tall. She had white hair and I was in the centre, where I got sucked in, and there was fire here, fire on top. I was in the middle, and that woman told me, 'The only way you can help your people, is they have to help themselves.' She said, 'The only way you can help your people, is if you are willing to die first.' If I'm willing to die, then I can help my people, through that way, but if you cannot do that, you have to allow them to help themselves, because I was burning in that fire, in the middle, in the centre. That's the message I got.

Ceremonies

The only thing that we do are feasts, like somebody that dies, we do the feast of the last supper. And we put out a plate for that person, and we do it ten days later again, and then a year later. That type of feasting we do, feasting for the dead. We don't do any of the other feasts. That's what Gisatanomok and I talked about, well, he was the one that was talking about. 'We are not practising our way of life, if we really practised our way of life we would be living it.' So that would be, the feasts and everything, we'd do the Corn Ceremony, we'd do the Berries Ceremony, the Bean Ceremony, all those ceremonies. It's because we weren't living it. And the places where I go visit, here, there, all over the place, they do their ceremonies like as if it's another meal. Because they practise, they were doing it, they never lost it. Around here, we never had those, not even in my mother's age, or my grandmother's. So we'd have to learn them again, learn them again, or do them.

Grieving

I don't know about teachings. The way I think is, I know they go somewhere. And I know that when they leave this life, they go into another life, but you cannot stop or choose how you're going to go. I've always thought that way. How am I going to go? What kind of a death am I going to have, since we cannot choose? But if we could choose, I would like to just sleep. I was thinking about some people that die so horribly, car accidents, burning or something like that, or get killed, or you take your own life or stuff like that. But I know there must be something else out there, there has to be. You know, in that other world. The other realm or whatever.

My cousin, Deanna, she does those kinds of ceremonies, when people are grieving. She did, they clean the house that they live at, and she gets that person to talk to the Creator, for the Creator to help that person so they don't grieve for that person anymore. And she gets them to speak, if they have an Indian name, she gets them to announce the Indian name, or if they or one, two, three, if they have Indian names, then she gives them Tobacco to put in the fire after they are all done. She was telling them to ask the Creator to get rid of this grief that they have, they don't

want to hold on to them anymore. Because when you grieve for somebody that long, you are only keeping them here. You're not allowing
them to go on. If you let them go, they don't have that feeling anymore.
Those that have left are happy over there, you don't have that grief anymore, like what we have here.

And then, we go all around the house, all around inside the house,
smudge, smudge everybody and everything and whatever clothing, whatever they own. She'll ask them to either get rid of it or give it away, or
bury it, whatever you want to do with it. And then that person who's out
there, that's still around, the one who you are grieving for, will be happy.
They will feel like they can leave, they can go on. She asked me to help
her, that's what she did. That's how they do it in Onandaga. She was
adopted over there, like they adopt you, I guess. The Bear is the only one
who can adopt you into their community, to their society. She was
adopted in that way. So that's the kind of things that they do for somebody who is grieving, because she belongs to the Okeway Ceremony of
the Dead and of the Living. There is not that many people who have
both, to belong to both.

When she built her house down home, she built it at a place where
there was running water, or a spring close by, and I guess where her house
was built, there was songs coming through the floor. And she always
remembered the songs, and she was singing them and singing them. All
the verses were from this woman. This old woman and this man were
teaching her. And when she went visiting over that way, she was humming
and singing these songs. Audrey Shanendowah was the one that asked
her, 'Where did you get those songs?' She said, 'In my dreams, this old
woman is teaching me the songs.' And she said, 'Those are the songs of
the living and the dead.' And so they're still teaching her through
dreams, the songs. And so she knows the grieving part, and how to help
people, and so she asks me to sing some songs, to sing whatever that
needs to be sung at the time when we are doing this. And that's what we
do. She and I do a lot of things together.

Relationship between Christianity and Traditional Beliefs

They are related in some ways. We tend to draw lines that this is your God,
and this is mine and this is yours. It's still the same, it does not matter how
or where because of the way the people believe in. That is their way, allow
them to believe and just have that respect on how they believe and how I
believe in and the next person. You don't have to do whatever they do in

their way or whatever, just sit aside or whatever, just respect what they do. If you do respect what they do and they ask you to come you go, if you want you go, if you don't you don't.

Prophecies

I don't know why or whatever, but there are these rock drawings down home. They say that the little people, the little ones drew them there, even before they had railroad tracks, they had drawn that on the rocks. They drew electricity and the boats that were coming. It was already drawn on the rocks. They already knew, yes.

Stages of Life

I don't really know. I know there are stages that you do go through in your life, you can feel it. You can see it in some people and what they are going through at a certain time. Like when you're a baby, you're a baby until you're an adolescent. You, or what I see anyway, you see a child when they are young and when they go through that adolescent stage, they don't know where they are or whatever. They want to go back to being a little kid again. They just don't know where, until that time, stage passes, and then you see them, they're all right, they went through that, as if it dies. That's the way I look at it, it dies. Then, you have another part in life that you have to go through. Then when you see them going into teenagehood, they don't want to be there, then they go back to being a young kid again. Playing with younger children, sometimes, or then they go again, dressing up and having lipstick or whatever they go through anyway. And they go back and forth, back and forth, or sometimes you see people stuck there. Maybe they're in their teens, almost in their twenties they're still way back here, because they just don't want to go or whatever. They don't want to let go, they are scared, too scared to get into this other life.

When they let go, then they go into a woman, they don't want to be a teenager anymore, they get scared as if there's a line there or something that they have to jump over. Like, when I was twenty-six years old. That's when I started thinking, life is so important, look at Mother Earth, and all this. You know everything started changing for me on how I looked at life when I was twenty-six years old. And somebody was telling me one time, I think it was my grandmother or somebody, they said, 'When you get a little bit older in your life, when you are in your thirties or forties, and there's going to be flashbacks.' Exactly. There is flashbacks, when I was a little girl, when I was young, I could sometimes feel it as if it was happening right then. Or smell, at the time, whatever, I seen this woodpile one day, right in the middle of the afternoon, all of a sudden, bang!, this woodpile appears, and those tiny little drops, I seen them, the way the snow was melting on the birch wood. And when I was looking out the window, I saw my mother's clothes hanging on the line, and the clothes pins were still a little bit wet, the way the sun was shining. And the spring air, I could smell it, just for that instant! I went back when I was a little kid.

Time

Before the clocks, I think it was the sun. That's how they were able to tell. That's what we got to get back to. Because in my dreams, the sun has a lot to do with my dreams, because sometimes early in the morning, I wake up and I don't know what time it is in my dream, and it has to do with the sun. I can pretty well tell the time. I know what time my dream was because of the way the sun was.

When it was going to rain, they tell by the way the leaves, or by the way the sun was or by the way the clouds were, they could tell when it's going to rain or what's going to happen. To predict the weather, they would look for this man over here in Armukto, that was when Jack Minamore or whatever his name was, he used to be the radio announcer, he would go down and ask John, that's John Sacolburg that lives in Armukto. He's still alive right today, he's a medicine person, he's the one that knows all the medicines. And he's the one who predicts the weather, every year he predicted the weather. He'd be on the radio, predicting the weather, and he was always right. He can tell by the way the ants, or by the way the moon, by the way the bees, how they have their hives, or the ground bees. That's how he told what the weather would be like.

Relation between Language and Culture

They are closely related, but I still feel you have to know your language. If you are an Indian, it's not your fault if you were not taught the language. But when you get at that age where you are on your own, if you want to learn the language or maybe sometimes you think it is too late for me or whatever, but sometimes in their life people really want to know because they have a hard time trying to bring it out in English when talking about feelings. To try to bring it out in English, you cannot. Because it's an entirely different meaning when you say it in English and it's similar, almost, but not the way when you say it in the language.

We're just starting now to get back our Indian names. The names that people get now are sometimes related to animals and in my family there are four that are related to the air. Something to do with the sky and the air. My husband that's his name, *Mosogeesk*, meaning 'The Spirit of the Air.' And my grandson related with the stars, that's his name, what happened when he was born. And my daughter is *Nebyobin*, meaning the 'Northern Lights,' and my name is related to the way the thunder came, when the thunder started and the lightning and when it makes the impact on the Earth, that electrical sound, that's my name, *Monimkeeque*. *Monimkeeque*, that's in Cree, it's in Ojibwe too. *Nimkii*, that's the way, thunder. That's what Liza Mosher said, she said, 'That's your name, *Monimkeeque*. *Que* is the woman. I got this name through my dream. I was watching, they were having a council up there, you could tell by the way the thunder, thunder beings.

There were a lot of them and I know they were talking about me, I was laying there and all of a sudden this one that's in the centre he turns and looks at me and he went like this, 'You are *Geelelleweezeen*,' and when he said that '*Geelelleweezeen*,' all of a sudden there was this great big thunder sound, and the sound and this great bright, bright, bright light. That was what he told me what my name was, but he didn't say it in there, but that's how he said it, '*Geelelleweezeen*,' and it woke up everybody. You should see all the lights go on on the reserve. In my house everybody was scared. 'What's happening?' they wondered. 'Is this the end of the world or what?' So that's my name.

Traditional Food

They ate deer, moose, muskrat, rabbits, and what they fished from the river was mostly bass. They used to spear bass down here. That was before they built the dam. And from the land, we got fiddleheads in May. Fiddleheads are from here. Fiddleheads last about a month in May. When they first come, the lilacs are starting to bloom, and when the lilacs are done, the fiddleheads are done, too. And in the spring, they get muskrats. And in the fall, they hunt deer and moose. We get ducks, pheasants, partridge.

Traditional Medicines

This area has what they call muskrat root. They use that a lot, and golden thread, they use golden thread a lot here too. You can get them underneath the moss, you lift and it's so gold, bright, bright yellow. That is the colour they are. And they use them for babies, when they have sores in their mouth. They still use it, right today. Muskrat root, they use it mostly for colds or it's good for singing. It's called bitter root. I eat it, I love it. It's hot when it's going down. All medicine is sacred. It's treated with respect, the beetle root, muskrat root, we consider that sacred, it helps you in every way you use it. I use it mostly for when I sing. It's good for you. You make a tobacco offering.

Life on the Land

If you are out on the land, you would be really connected with the Earth, when you are connected with the Mother Earth you are connected with the Creator and everything around you. I think it would help you to cope. You wouldn't have that same type of feeling if you are having a hard time. I think it would help you in that way. To get back to Mother Earth or get back to the Creator to help you in that way so you wouldn't have this hard time that you're having out here. That's why a lot of us people have to go back. I still think today you have to go back, not go back to living in a tee-pee, but you have to have a part of her anyway to help you to struggle with drugs and alcohol or whatever is going on out there. To me there's a difference. Mother Earth is all over, everywhere, it doesn't matter where you step or whatever, but when you live on the reservation and when you step into that White world it's different, quite different.

It's possible to maintain that contact with Mother Earth even though there's a lot of modern influence, but it's hard, you struggle with that because of competition. Sometimes I could throw that stupid TV out the window, maybe one of these days I will, but I'm working towards that. It hinders us from connecting to one another. That's a big competition, but someone said you have that option to turn it off and on, there's an off and on button there. There are a lot of people that use that for company. Like sometimes when you get up in the morning, you want to hear the leaves. Like in the summer when you have the doors open, you want to hear the birds. The sound from out there. That's what I like to hear early in the morning. Instead somebody turns the TV on, gee. They might as well slam the door, shut the door in your face or something.

Education

I don't like residential schools, from what I hear. I've never been there, I haven't been in a residential school, period. But the way my brother, he didn't hardly talk about it until just lately, he talks about it, like what they did to him, not just him, to all the kids that were in there. If you did something for that nun or the priest, whoever was looking after them, you might be the favourite one, and you might get all the attention and everything. He was telling me one time that he and his brother, my older brother, had to scrub the stairs. I seen that stairway. My brother said they used to have to scrub that with a toothbrush, scrub those stairs with a toothbrush, on their bare knees, they'd have bloody knees because it's all cement. They used to have to scrub that, it was part of their punishment.

These people need to get together. You do feel better after you talk about whatever is bothering you in here. You feel better each day. You might not have to bring it all out the very first day, it might take you years to bring it all out, but each time you bring it out, when you get up you feel a lot lighter whatever it is that's bothering you. They need to get together, they need to talk about it, or even if they can't get together with someone they should talk about it with somebody they trust, whoever they can connect with.

They didn't learn how to be a parent, because they were raised in these schools. I suppose we could talk about it, so they can learn how to be a parent. They have some of those Native parenting workshops, I've heard. This guy, not too long ago, I hear him saying, 'I got to go to my, how to be a parent.' Which is good, I think. Even the ones that haven't been to those residential schools, I think it could be used by somebody to learn how to be a parent because after a while the parents do lose it because of all of the rest of the other things what comes, like TV, and bingos. Some want to drink alcohol so they're not worried about being a parent and the kids bring up themselves.

We could have our own school. We don't have our own school, the only thing we have here is a Headstart and kindergarten. And they are going to try and bring a school in, they're going to build a big building over here and they're going to put maybe from grade one to grade six. It's been so many years down the line we've been asking for a school, but it's always been put on the back bench, they say. They said that when they build this building, which they said it's not too long, but I'd be able to see it, because I was one of the people that took the petition around the reserve.

I talked to people about what it would be like to have a school on the reserve. That's what it is, a survey. And it took me a long time to do it, because when I went to talk to people, you're supposed to only spend fifteen to twenty minutes with them. I spent a whole day or half a day or till that night, twelve, one o'clock in the morning, talking to them about if we had our own school. We'd get all excited and we'd talk about it. Then I'd come home with preserves or meat or bread. They'd tell me, 'Come back, come and visit.' They said they never laughed so much in all their lives. We need people like those around us, that can talk to people, that's all they need to have that connection. Over there at the regular schools, all they have is the language, they are limited to fifteen minutes or ten minutes, that's all. The kids can't really learn anything in that short time, and to punish them, they are not allowed to go into the language place if you're being bad. They punish them that way.

Even on parent-teacher days, people don't go. I never hardly went. When I went, I had to drag myself there. I didn't feel comfortable with it out there. I didn't like what they did with kids, I didn't like the schools, the way they teach them. I didn't like it. When I started walking this road, my daughter, who was growing up, would tell me that she gets a hard time because she's out of school lots. Well, I said, 'I don't care, when I bring you out of school, this is to teach you something, this is what you should be learning instead of being in there learning something that you really don't understand.' Sometimes, when it's just offhand, when we're just going somewhere, well we just go and get our kids from school. 'We're leaving, we're going to this place, we'll be back such and such a time.' This is part of their Native education. If we had a school here, I know it would be better, I know that.

Attaining Balance

It would all depend on the individual. I don't know much about that part, I don't have anything to say about education, period, because I think that's what happened to me. I don't know too much of the English language, but at the same time, I feel that it's not important, to me. But sometimes, if I don't understand a person, then I ask myself why didn't I go to school, and learn all these words. I'd be able to understand what they're talking about. The little bit I understand, and I say to myself, ah, it's not important anyway. I'd sooner get in tune with my language, and the importance of it, as simple as I can live. You can understand anybody if you interpret what they said in that language, you understand it in Indian anyway.

The history is important. I would like to learn about my history, if they taught it in school. Their history doesn't mean anything to me. How else can a child feel proud of who they are, when they don't even learn about themselves in school? If they would put it in school, then the kids would understand. Some of them, even right today, are ashamed or don't want to be Indian. It's because what they portray on TV, or what the people say nowadays. And right today, people are still prejudiced, you teach that child not to go play with one, because that's an Indian, don't play with an Indian. I don't want you going to the reservation, you'll get beat up, or something. It was not too long ago, the young man that came up here, didn't want to come up here because he thought he was going to get beat up. And he went off the reservation on his territory, and he got beat up, he almost got killed by his own people. And that's what I always say, these university people, there was one university person that came here to live with us, his name was Michele. He was a White guy. That's what he thought himself, how else am I going to learn about these people if I don't live with them? So he came and lived on the reserve. Things that we ate, he said, 'I wouldn't eat that, that's what we feed our dogs.' All this stuff what we eat, they don't eat at home. He lived with the people.

Relations with Non-Native People

People should know or be proud of who they are. Allow that mother, allow that father to teach that child who they are, about their background. This is what I think happens to these children. You know, all of a sudden I want to be Indian, or I want to be that, or they don't even say 'I am Indian' or I want to be that way, and they don't even think about their mother is White or Indian or whatever. When I was a kid, when I was at that age I never thought who's white, black, yellow, or whatever colour you are. I didn't even know that I was Indian. All I knew was that I existed. I didn't know that I was a Passmoquady or what. And when somebody asked me what my mother's name was, I didn't even know my mother's name because all I knew her by was Mother. And they all laughed at me and I cried and I cried because I didn't know my mother's name, or I didn't even know if I was Indian. I didn't even know what white, black, red, or yellow was. I think that's what's happening to our children. Nobody wants to be White because of what they did to the Indian people, so these children are stuck in the middle or something. How do you teach your child what your ancestors did to your dad or to your mom? I wouldn't know how to teach a child that way.

Traditional Justice

I don't think people should be going to prison because those prison walls are just not for us. They should have more healing places for our people. There's a lady in Saskatchewan and her name is Norma Green and she's the warden but they don't want her to be called the warden. They want her to be called 'mother.' She comes to visit us when we go to visit the prisons in Kingston. She comes in whenever she can, and she wants to come in when we're there because she likes it when she comes in with us. We are getting to know the girls that are going to be coming to the new healing centre. She says that there won't be no prison doors, no locked doors, no stuff like that.

The main differences between the prisons and these Healing Lodges, is the Healing Lodges care! I know that the difference will be that they care and that they trust them enough. How else are they going to be normal people when they are locked up? All they do is sit there waiting for the locked prison door to open. They still even do that right now, right today, because they are institutionalized waiting for the door to open when they could be opening it themselves in the Healing Lodges. I even get that when I go back and forth to the men's prison and the women's prison.

In the Healing Lodge, they would ask the Creator for help by giving them cedar baths and using that kind of stuff on them to purify them. The prisons should be allowed to have healing men and medicine men come in to work with people, that way you would be dealing with the problem instead of locking them up and making it worse. That's punishment enough when you lock somebody up and keep them like a caged animal. They keep punishing them in there and start to play head games with them, so there's no healing whatsoever going on there. They should have things in there like parenting or economic development for people to learn something while they are in there.

While they are in prison they don't have anything to look forward to. If they don't have people coming in there, not just only the medicine men but the rest of the people that they have out there that can help. You have to utilize them while you still have a chance. A prison should have help like counselling or whatever they need. Before it was the people themselves or the family that dealt with a person who did something bad or wrong, whatever they thought the punishment for this person should be. That's how they used to do it.

Dreams

I think the role of dreams in my life had to do with when you sleep, when you dream, it's got to do with your waking state, how your life is, what your role is or whatever you have to do in life. It has to do with your dreams too, so you can not forget about your dreams. Your dreams are just as important as visions. When my grandson was born there was still a big lump of mucus caught in his throat that nobody knew about and he was always choking all the time and spitting up some stuff and we took him back and forth to the hospital. They would say, 'Here comes the Paul baby again,' the nurses would be saying at the hospital, and I was getting angry because I don't care what they say, the baby was choking and he didn't breathe from the time we left here till the time we hit town and the baby was gasping for air and before that there was nothing. The baby wasn't even breathing.

So finally we got one doctor that was on call that one night and I think his name was Dr Hart. He's the one who heard the nurses whispering, and he said, 'What's this I hear about the Paul baby?' He was angry and he was telling them, 'When you see that baby coming in here you don't say, "Here comes the Paul baby again." What is this place where we are? What is this hospital for?' he was asking them. 'It is to bring in patients and save lives. That little baby could be dead while you are saying "that Paul baby is here again."' That was the first time I ever heard a doctor talk like that. I said, 'I like this doctor, he's human.' He turned to us and said that we could bring that baby twenty times tonight and we'll still have to accept that baby. This is a life, he said. 'Come on in right now,' he said.

He told us to come right in because the reason is the baby is choking and we went right in the room and he asked us about his name and do we still use your language. And he said, 'Right on, you teach this young fella.' I still talk English but I'm still plugging in there with our language. The next day when we were there, this big clump of mucus came out and I went straight up to the hospital and I said, 'That's why the baby was chok- ing and you say, "Here comes the Paul baby."' That's what they do to us. It is awful up here sometimes. To hear a doctor say something about that was really something.

I think the baby was only three months old and I was dreaming that this great big bear grabbed my foot to wake me up. 'Go see your grandson because there is somebody trying to get at your grandson.' And when I woke up my daughter, I said I just dreamed about that and I jumped up and she came into this bedroom and went back to bed. That's why I say, it's so important because that was right direct and right then. And I had to get up and she was sleepwalking and then when I put her to bed she snapped out of it and said, 'What are you doing?' I said, 'You just came and told me what was wrong with the baby, it was choking.' I grabbed the baby and that's what came out was that big clump of mucus. And that's why it is so important for your dreams. Sometimes your dreams are telling you something. It is so much a part of you, it is a part of everyday living.

Later on in life you find the meaning of your dreams. You relate back to your dream again. This word kept coming into my dream. I was thinking and I remembered it so well, what it is that word, that don't sound like our language, I wonder whose language it is or whose could it be. I didn't know what it was but when I woke up I grabbed my tape recorder and I tried to sing the song. But in that dream, there was this young woman, young dark-haired woman. She's the young girl from the South, that's the one that comes to visit us. When we do things, we can smell the flowers in the spring, that's what you smell when she comes to visit you. When I was trying to learn the song in my dream, I was thinking to myself, I have to mark it down, because I'll forget it. And I tried to get this paper, and I tried to get this pen, so when I grabbed the paper, but she was already handing me the pen. I didn't grab it, 'cause I wanted to grab the paper. And when I turned around, the pen was gone, she was gone. And so this grandmother said it was all right, she said, 'I'll get up and I'll teach you this dance.' And her little granddaughter got up and they were dancing this dance. And I looked at them, I thought the dance looks familiar, could it be the round dance? I watched her, and watched her, and she said, 'Watch,' and she said, 'Listen to the song.' I was listening to the song and I was watching her. She had on this bag, and then I looked at her and then this word again, somebody said this word again, so I woke up.

I don't know if I marked it down in my dream book or not. But when I woke up, that's when I grabbed my tape recorder and I started singing, but I remembered it. I was telling my dream, telling that to somebody around home, I was telling that dream to Deanna. And when we were down there this summer, it didn't even dawn on me, this was so many years, but it didn't even dawn on me what this woman was trying to show me in my dream. Sarah, down home, she kept on trying to show me this booklet, 'Look at this book somebody gave me.' It's small print there, so I couldn't hardly read it, because of small letters. I don't like reading a book with small letters. Then after a while again, she asked if I read it, so I picked it up and looked at it, put it back down again. Before I left she asked me to pick it up again, so I did, so I read what was in the book. What's that with all the stories in the book? And I read this 'How Grand-father/Grandmother Peyote Came to the People.' I was looking at it, so I read it. When I read it, I seen this word, the word, I dreamed about.

And when I read it, it was the same thing that the grandmother told me in Lakota. It meant the love of the people. And that dance she was showing me, it was the woman dance, in the *Weechill*, grandmothers' way. When we dance all night, we do this dance, that's what she was teaching me. And that bag what she had, she was taking the peyote medicine for the people because they were starving or something, they were hungry, and she put all that medicine in that bag. That's why, today, they wear those bags. That's why I say dreams are so important. She was showing me already. And that word, that word I did not know, then I found it in that book. Henry Crowdog wrote the story. There are so many dreams that I dreamed that are provided direction or were telling me something.

Those kind of dreams that mean something. There's another dream I dreamed a long time ago when my son, my middle son, he was at this place where he lived in Guelph. He was sitting on the side, by the water, by this bridge and there was this man away over here. It was on a Sunday morning and all of a sudden he went sliding down, and I was way down there, and I said, 'Somebody help my son, he's sliding down, he was going to go in the water.' I said, 'Somebody, somebody help.' I was running and running and falling down, and getting up and falling down and getting up and falling down. By the time I reached there, this guy that was standing away over there, you see he lives right here on the reserve, Frankie, he saved me, he grabbed him before he went into the water. And that's the same thing that happened to him that day. He was lying down and he almost fell into the river and some man saved him. And I dreamed about that. I don't like those kind of dreams, but I guess I must have saved him in that dream, then somebody saved him, I wasn't there when it happened.

I dream about animals talking to me. I used to dream about bears a lot, grizzly bears, black bears, grey bears, brown bears, and white bears. I dream about bears a lot, and eagles, and whales, I dream about them a lot, they talk to me. I dreamed about an eagle a long time ago, he was flying from on the other side of my mother's house, which was in the morning, the sun would be about right there, and he went down. And my sister and I were sitting down on the side of the road looking up the road towards my mother's house. I told her to wait here and I'd go and check and see, did it land or what happened? So when I was on my way up the hill, it came up again. This was a great big white gigantic eagle, and it came flying right down, and I was looking right at it coming, coming at me, and it must have been a forty-foot span, it was coming down, coming down, and all of a sudden, I seen his talons. They were right here in front of me. And I seen him with these pair of white wings. And he put them right down on my legs, and I landed back on that rock where I was sitting at. It was so heavy.

And I looked at these wings, they were just draped right over my legs, and I picked them up and they were heavy. But I picked them up anyway. And I looked at the eagle and he was talking away, and I couldn't hear what he was saying. But the last thing what I remember him saying was '*Niscu.*' *Niscu* in the language means God or the Creator. That's all I heard was 'God, Creator.' Then I picked up the wings and I went up to my mother's, to go show my mother what the eagle had brought me. I was so happy and crying at the same time. My mother didn't care, whatever I brought, or whatever the eagle gave me. I turned to my husband and he was standing by the doorway, waiting for my mother, to take my mother to town. He didn't care what the eagle brought me. I was crying and crying. I looked at everybody and everybody was busy in the house. So I turned around and walked out with the eagle wings, that was the end of the dream. I really don't know what it meant. It could be, whatever I carry is going to be a heavy, heavy load, and that there'll be nobody there, all alone, that's just exactly like the way it is right today. And that word, what the eagle was saying is that it is going to be with the Creator. I turn to the Creator. Nobody, nobody else there for me that I can talk to, just the Creator. It's the Creator that's going to be there and will always be there, no matter what.

Closing Thoughts

I feel sometimes that the teenagers, and people that are young, at a young age, like my son's age, the twenties, late twenties or when they reach their twenties, and within that space, twenty and thirty, they are all alone, they feel so alone. I don't know why they have to go through that or is it we as parents who tend to forget about them? They act as if their life does not matter, that's how I think what they are thinking. I don't even matter, nobody even cares if I'm around, or even the community, they don't even try to do anything for kids at that age or something. But what I would like to tell the kids is that they do matter. They do count. Your voice is as important as the little one, up to the old, their voice and what they have in their hearts and what they have in their minds is so important to share with everybody. It matters whatever you have to talk about. Young people might not think that they have anything important to say. Anything that you come out, whatever comes out of your mouth is important, it was meant to be said. And it's meant to be shared with somebody. Pick somebody in the community or whatever, your friend, all these thoughts in your head that you are not sharing, you are not verbalizing it, verbalize it, share it, take the load off you. All that garbage that's inside of you, throw it out, dump the garbage can, then fill it with good stuff.

After you dump all that, after you get rid of the feeling, whatever is in here. How else are you going to feel good, how else are you going to communicate with your mother or your father, tell them what happened today or why did you feel that way the other day? Make it, bring it back to community again, community wise, bring it together the way it used to be. Everyone is talking to one another, laughing, and if they have a problem, let's help, talk about it, maybe we can do something about it, all of us, collectively, instead of one person carrying it, and not saying anything. That's what I think. And listen to the kids, listen to the children because they got so much to teach us. Even these little ones, the tiny ones, they don't even have to talk, all they have to do is do something. You can see it, that's what I think is missing sometimes in our ways.

We tend to lose it, and we don't show our people, show them face to face, not just talk about it, show them. That's how we visualize things. I mean, you can tell me until you're blue in the face, how you feel, or telling me something I don't even see, well show me, show me. You can tell me you love me for the rest of your life, you can tell me you love me, but to put your arms around me or to rock me, or to even just to touch me, that feeling has to be there, we tend to forget about how to touch one another. That's what's forgotten, that's what's missing, that touch. Children, teenagers, young children, adults, they do matter, they do count. It's just that it's been lost or gone, or maybe they feel no one is listening to them.

I had a dream about that. My son, Harold, he was in a community building, or in university, somewhere in between the doorway, crossing at the doorway. And he turned around and told me to keep on saying what you are saying to the teenagers, don't stop whatever you're telling them. Whatever I'm telling them must be what I had just finished saying. That's what I think that he meant. Don't stop, don't stop listening, don't stop verbalizing with them, tell them how you feel, and they tell you how they feel, don't stop. I love everybody. I communicate with teenagers and young people very well. I communicate with anybody and everybody.

Music, I love music, so they love music, so we all communicate with music, sing together, dance together or whatever. I tape for them. The little ones, from the time that they are in here, when you're carrying them, when you bring them up, teach them in your language and culture, so they'll be proud of who they are. A lot of kids are not even proud because they don't know nothing about themselves. Teach them who they are, Indian, Ojibwe, Maliseet, Passmoquady, or whatever, so they'll start talking about it. You hear people saying, 'Are you an Indian?' They say, 'No, I'm not an Indian.' Right away kids say, 'I'm not an Indian.' They don't want to be Indian. Why? Because they still see that on TV, or they hear people talking about Indians are bad, Indians are no good, Indians are lazy, so they hear all that stuff. When you can teach your child to be proud of who they are, tell them what your grandmother or your grandpa did, like your grandmother beaded, your grandfather knew pottery. That was his life, pottery. You know, your grandpa made drums, was a drum maker, and he's a basket maker, he's a bead worker, and he also sings. So they have that to share with their friends that my grandmother sings, and she plays the drum and she dances and she goes everywhere to talk to people. So they grow [up with that] as part of their life and to be proud. Gee, my grandmother does all that, my grandpa, or my uncle, he's a good dancer. He's a good fancy dancer or stuff like that. To be proud of who they are, to be proud of their own individual self.

You know, when the Elders look at a little one, they can already tell how they are going to be like when they growing up, because of the way they are when they are small. Even when we do our ceremonies, when we do Sweetgrass and smudge, they want to learn. So I go with them, or sometimes when he sees a sunset, he'll run to get me to see it. To be proud, look at Creation out there. That's what we have to teach our little ones. Birds, birds are beautiful and the animals, everything. Sometimes, people only introduce the older folks, never mind the children, nobody introduces children. Everything went bad, but we all count, everything counts what we do. All the kids that are into music, keep on singing because everybody has a voice. A lot of kids think they don't have a voice, we all start that way, when we start singing. Oh, we're too low or too high, we don't sound good, we think we don't sound good, if we don't, we don't. So we get better in singing every day. Or in singing as much as we can, we get better just like in the language.

If we can't say the words today, we keep at it until we can say it right. Know the language or whatever. Just like singing, because the more you sing the better you get. That's what I tell my husband, the more pottery he does, the better he gets, each pot he does is better than the last one. Each basket you make is better than the last one. Each braid you do, that's what I do too, I braid these big braids for smudges. That's what I do too, that's what my mother gave me, the Sweetgrass. That's how I was brought up, with that tiny little braid. Then during some stage in my life, I'm still with the Sweetgrass. I still gather the abundance of Sweetgrass every year. We still do that. We're still in the Sweetgrass family. I used to not want to go to school because I smelled like Sweetgrass, because the kids would tease us, 'Here comes the Paul family, Sweetgrass, do you smell Sweetgrass?' You know, I used to hate it. But now, I could die in it, bathe in it and everything, to smell like Sweetgrass. And I'm allergic to it, but I still braid it, I still use it.

Singing, keep singing, learn to sing, drum, connect with Mother Earth because it's our Mother's heart. The drum is our Mother's heart. I felt that in the Earth, I don't know where it was in the Earth when I was laying there, when I had my hands like this. And I felt something beating, and I said, 'Must be my hand.' But when I went back down there again, I could still feel the beat, it's beautiful. You just have to connect with her. Sweats, Sweat Lodges, connect with the Earth as much as you can, picking Sweetgrass, laying on the grass. There are so many people getting messages from the Mother Earth, showing us how she feels. Or what she can give us, if we go with her. We should lay on her, she misses that. My cousin went fasting, and she was told to talk to the men, that is what the Mother Earth told her. Go tell the men to come and hug me because the Mother Earth is lonesome for the male touch. Deanna told the men you just go out there and go lay down on Mother Earth and just hug her. That's what she wants. Mother Earth will connect with us. There's a song Mary Louise gave me, she loaned me the song to sing. She said you sing that song wherever people need it. And I think it's being needed more because I sing it more. And that's how people connect how they feel.

I'm proud to be who I am now. You show that to me, I heard it in the song. And Mary Louise, the one who that song was given to her, and she allows me to sing it wherever. And so I sing that song, and when I sing that song a lot of people connect with that song. A lot of people say I am proud to be who I am. And I'm part of it, I'm part of Mother Earth, I'm part of the Native person. That's why I say music and dancing, that's what's going to connect us all. The drum, the music, the dance, it's going to connect us all. That's what we have to do, that's what we talk about. Mary Louise, Liza, and myself talked about that, how are we going to help our people to get better, and to realize who they are. And we can't do it all, because there's not too many Peter O'Chieses around, there's not too many Gisatanomok around, Harry Laports, Maggie, or Liza, or Mary, or whoever else comes in within the medicine field.

There's not too many of those people around, so we have to do it massively, in mass, to try to heal people. For them to know who they are, and to feel good. That's how I feel, is through music, chanting. That's how you're expressing yourself to the Creator, you're singing for the Creator. You're singing for the people that are healing with you. And everybody has that, everybody, I'm not just talking about Indian people, I'm talking about the four races of colours, everybody has that, black, white, yellow, and red. Everybody has that, everybody has that key, it's just that we all have to get together. We all got to do that. And sometimes when I'm singing, I can almost just lose it, because that's how good it feels, when you see somebody dancing around with that gleam in their eye or the moves that they make with their body. I just get chills, I just want to keep on singing forever and ever, that's how it feels. That's how good they feel, we're connecting. Dancing, music, the drum, that's my way, that's how I feel I can contribute to the people is through my songs, my singing.

ALBERT WARD (Micmac)

Eel Ground First Nation, New Brunswick

'I have seen a real beautiful thing.'

Albert Ward was interviewed by Emily Faries in the summer of 1994 at his home. Emily spent four days in the community and was 'welcomed, fed, and taken care of.' She described his home as very comfortable with lots of traditional medicines hanging on the walls. Smudging during the interview was very important, and was done frequently. Albert Ward's traditional Micmac name is *Gisageweek*, which means 'Grandmother's helper.' He has eleven children and eight grandchildren, and spends most of his time travelling and teaching traditional culture at his home in Eel Ground First Nation.

Albert Ward's interview was one of the longest in this collection, and one of the most difficult to put on paper. Very little editing of the interview took place in an attempt to capture the rhythm of his speech. Albert speaks very quickly, and his words flow for many minutes without a break or change. This resulted in some very long paragraphs. We recommend that you read the words quickly, and attempt to savour the rhythm of the language. The ideas that Albert put forth are very complex, and require many rereadings to be, at least partially, understood.

Life History

I had a really hard life when I was growing up and we have a large, large family, about seventeen of us in one family. The house that we had was pretty poor, and you could see right through the cracks, makes it really cold for the winter. Us kids when we were growing up had to get a lot of wood for our parents and had to do a lot of things like that.

Right now, my old man and my mother, they are gone now, but they left us the real good teaching behind and they taught us that before they left, they told us 'not to feel sad of us because, because we go someplace where there is not going to be suffering anymore.' This is called the Spirit World. So they taught us not to cry anymore because the suffering is over.

But the life that we went through, well, I have to say that my old man was an alcoholic, and I am not ashamed to say that because they gave us a hard time. That is why today I know about alcoholism and people what they went through – about the life. So I understand about life and I have these special gifts that belong to the people, which I didn't know I had this gift. But there was an Elder, and one time they came to me, he told me to sit down, sit down with me, and he had a Pipe with him. I didn't know anything about a Pipe to begin with and I was kind of afraid of it, but the old man could see something in me, and he said, 'You should start helping the people out,' and I said, 'I couldn't even help myself, to help the people.' 'Yes,' he said, 'you could do it.' 'How am I going to do it?' And he said, 'There's a Fast coming up in February,' and that was in '85 [1985].

So I didn't know anything about it, but I went through that Fast and four days later I seen something that I wanted to know about myself, I wanted to know about the Indian ways, the Native way of life. So I told my other friends what happened to me, what I seen, and he called this old man again. His name is Albert Lightning in Alberta. So that old man he said, 'I am getting on a plane tomorrow and I want to see this man. It's very important to me.' So the next day, that following day, that evening and the old man came, and he started talking to me. And I didn't understand, but he kept talking and he said, 'One day you will understand.'

So what I seen at that time when I finished my Fast is about a Native people, what happened to me. I have seen a real beautiful thing. I seen the Grandfather with the Sweetgrass in his hand. And he told me, 'This is what you asked me. This is who you are and this is everything for you and this is what you really should do about this Sweetgrass and this is what you asked me.' So that – still I did not understand. I seen all kinds of different things at that time. I seen water, lights, and all kinds of things, but it was a Spirit, he told me, that said, 'You see that light shining down and that's how far you are going.' So one day a second vision. I was on a canoe going to the east and I was gone. A third one I see I went through that light, and the fourth one I see I went up there, the light was all red and beautiful colours and it opened up and I went there.

Then I beginning to see the Indian life, what is this all about and everything. And I beginning to see other different things. I beginning to see a lot of different things. How the people are, the hard life, what they are going through. I could see that. But again, you know, it is not up to me to say to anybody that you have a problem. It is up to the person to come and ask me or something is wrong with this person. So this is how I work today, and I can go back today. I can go back to the beginning of time of Native people. I can see that.

So, sometimes I run a Sweat Lodge for the people. I heal people with my Sweat Lodge, and sometimes we have us what they call a peace because people need peace in themselves once in a while. So we go to the journey. I talk about the beginning of time. Today, we are not going to say it's '94 [1994], we say '90 [1890]. We look all around today, we have everything we need. We don't need anything else anymore. And I tell the people that you take a good look at yourself. Look all round and see what you have. But let's work back, let's look back a bit more and try to see what our Elders used to have many years ago. Many Elders call these buildings we have today a square box. That's where the people live today. As we go back a little further and there is a trail going to the river, there's a river and there's a canoe right there. We put our children on there and we put women and the men to steer the canoe and we are beginning to go back to see what we had. We beginning to go back as far as the river. We could talk about this here. We are beginning to see the teepees. We are beginning to see the Native people. We're still going back and back and back, animals, all kinds of different birds. Early in the morning as we are going back we say, now we say we are in 1600s, still going back and back and back. And this same river. We are going back and back. And one day our Elders start beating the drum. Not the drums we have today, they use stick, hollow stick from the ground sticking up. And they start sending the message and the song, they beginning to sing the song to deliver the message far distance, and they were saying, 'You prepare yourselves because we see something coming way out in the ocean. You prepare yourselves.'

Later on they begin to see that ship coming towards them. One day they come ashore. People on the ship they are sick, they are starving, they need water. Our Native people, they gave them a new life, they gave them water, they gave them bread, they gave them medicine, and they brought them back alive again. Later on in life the people, when the people are getting straight and back and everything they tell them to go back where they come from. They gave them the food again, fresh water, and they send them back. But later on in life they came back, again the drum starting to beat. They are beginning to send a message to all of the villages. And then again the sailboats come in. When they came they came more than one. They came ashore, they wanted piece of land, they gave them a piece of land, where they are going to stay, and the confusion begins at that time.

They are beginning to take more land. They are beginning to fight, beginning to bring in the book which is the Bible we have today, and today, that confusion is still with us today. That's why our Native people cannot understand who they are today, because they are mixing it up too much. They want to take a little bit over here, a little bit here and they want to put it together, they want to bind it together, they want it to work, but they cannot see it, they are not going to make it work, because that's not ours, it belongs to somebody else. When they brought that Bible the first time and that confusion is still here today. Our Native people crossed the North America, they don't have a religion, they don't have, should have nothing to do with [Western] religion because that's not ours, it belongs to somebody there that came from far out in the ocean there.

And then this here is so much confusion today that now if you take a person which takes the Sweetgrass and the Bible on one hand, again you go down to the river, and you say that to yourself, I want to get across that river, but I am going to use two canoes. I want to put my foot here and another one over here. And I am going to paddle these canoes across the river. As you go along you cannot hold these canoes together anymore because they are going to go apart like that and you are going to fall into the river. So you are not going to get anywhere with that. And that's the same thing with people taking their Sweetgrass into the church and mixing it up. All you know is what you know from the Bible or what you see there and that's all you know. You can say, 'That's the Sweetgrass there, yet what am I going to do with it? I'm carrying it. I don't know why I am carrying it because I don't believe in it.' The same thing with the Bible you are stuck into that, and you can't go anywhere with it.

You see there is so much to learn about the Native way of life. You see once I get into this kind of life, it's like when I told you I can't tell you that I know anything about people, but I sure know a lot. I know a lot. Even Elders that have problems with their lives because they had a hard life when they are younger and they want to go back to their own tradi- tional way of life and even my old man he was Catholic, he was strong, and my mother. But there was one day my father came to me. He said, 'I want to know about the Sweat Lodge.' So I told him a little bit about the Sweat Lodge and he wanted to come in. He did come in more than once, but he had really bad arthritis. He had sore knees and he couldn't crawl anymore into the Lodge, but he told me, 'You are doing good. You are doing really good and I like what you are doing. You keep on doing what you are doing, but for me, how I was taught, I am going to take it with me and I am going to leave you a clear path. I wouldn't interrupt you any- more. But the things I learned I am going to take it with me and I am going to give you a clear path and nothing is going to get in front of you.' What that means is that my brothers and my sisters today, I got mostly my brothers and sisters going into the Lodge and doing all kinds of other teachings. So these are the things that we can go on and on and on.

Residential Schools

I went to a regular school, they had a little school. There is few people here, as far as I know four, that went to residential school. And they have a hard time today. Their younger ones, they lose their language and they try to get it back and when they try to say something in their own lan- guage, but when they try to say something the words do not come out and the other kids will laugh at them. So they stick with the English, but today they are a little older and they are trying to get back the language.

Now, you have to look at it as the beginning of time. And the sailboats when they came and the Native people were here as one Native people. There was only one language at that time. I don't know which one but there was only one there. And when the White man started coming to interfere in our lives and this is what I said the confusion begins at that time. And when the White man gets in-between the Native people and the language is beginning to go apart. We see a little patch of people over here and over here and they are separated like that, and that is how come the language is so different today. But the beginning of time of Native people they have only one language and today you go to other different communities and listen to the people when they talk the words they are saying is related to you – almost sound the same.

And you know that if all the Native people go back in their tradition and work together and the language will come back as one and we will understand each other again. This is what I see. I travel many different places, and the Native people they want to know more about it. And the White people also they are into this kind of life now, because when the people have problems, because when you go to the church you cannot talk about your problems. You just sit and stand up and kneel down and go like that and listen to the same old thing every each week you go there.

But this way of life you have a chance to talk about your problem or maybe the family or something like that and let the people hear how you feel about it. You can help and that way you can solve your problem because there's the Elders sitting around like that. They listen to you very carefully and once they close their eyes and put their heads down then they can see you. They can see what kind of problem, when this problem begins, maybe your problem begins when you are a child and today you are a big woman and some people have this problem and they don't know how to solve it. And when you go to church you don't talk about these things because you just sit there, but when you go to see the Elder and the Elder tells you all about your – the things you want to know about the life.

This way of life, I didn't know the Native way when I started out and I didn't know nothing about it. But I was just going real slow about it and I am beginning to find who I am and other Native people they should go on their own in this way of life, tradition and like. If you really want to talk about the beginning of time we could talk about that also. These are the things that we could do.

People they talk about a Creator. The Creator, all the time. I do not want to get in deep because you would not understand. So I am just going to talk about these things which you can understand. Who is the Creator? People don't know who is the Creator. Okay, when the Creator left us one time he said, 'I shall be with you always.' Which I understand today. The blood, it belongs to the Creator. Now the man is the Creator. Every man is the Creator because he created you. That's why I'm sitting here and you are sitting there. You are created by your own father. Now the Creator is a man and is creating the little ones. So we can go into this in the beginning of time. Now you take the Creator that said, 'I created all of this for

you. I created everything here. Beautiful land, beautiful earth, everything. But there's no people. I have to do something about people.' And
he came out and he called upon the Grandmother of the West, and the
Grandmother came. And they talked about the creation. 'What we are
going to do?' So they created the love. They created the love at that day.
They made love to make a baby. Later on in life there was a little child
that came to this world. And there was another one. There was a boy and
a girl. And the creation begins. Later on there was a whole bunch of little
ones. They are looking after them, the Grandmother looking after them,
the Grandfather looking after them. All the food and water you want.
Everything and there's more and more and one day those little creations
become man and woman, and they taught them again. 'This is how you
are going to share your love with the other one and start your own
creation.' So one day there was too many people and the Grandfather
Creator said, 'I want you to take your family and go to the South. Don't
come back until I tell you! There's another family here. Go to the West
and don't come back until I tell you!' There's another patch of people
going to the North, and to the East the Grandfather said, 'I will look after
the doorway.' And one day Grandfather came out and he called on the
people. He look at the West, the South, he seen a man and a woman and
all the children coming down. He look at the West. More people and
more people, whole bunch of people all around. And he gave them the
teaching. He gave them the teachings, he showed them everything and
the life begins, and that's why we are here, the Native peoples.

They have fire, one thing, and I hear even Native people saying that
don't do anything wrong because you are going to burn in hell. Well, I
didn't want to burn in hell 'cause I didn't want to do anything wrong but
I still do something wrong. And then when I was little older, when I got
my vision, and I asked the Creator, 'What is the fire? Is it really a fire is
hell, are you going to burn in hell when you die?' And he showed me. He
said, 'I made this fire for you to keep warm, for you to keep warm, for you
to cook your food. There is no fire in hell.' 'What you asked me,' he told
me, 'you asked me about hell. I show you a little bit of it,' he said, 'and
there is hell – is a tunnel, it's cold, there's no fire there, it's nothing,
damp, it's nothing, and that's where evil lives,' he said. 'And when they
take you, they take you there and they are going to suffer there for a long
time because there is no fire.' I don't want to get any deeper into that.
Just a touch of what I am telling you.

Only one thing that you people, Native people really should do. What
helps mostly people is talking circles with the Feather. They sit down and

talk about alcoholism and drugs, and that's what. We talk about this here all the time. When I treat somebody with alcoholism or drugs, maybe I talk about alcohol or drugs for two days and after that I don't talk about alcohol because I do not want to educate anybody what alcohol can do for you, and another thing the drug, what the drug can do, maybe I talk about that a little bit, what drug can do, and after that I do not talk about that alcohol what alcohol can do. If you talk about alcohol all the time you educate a client like I say. You educate them people. Maybe a lot of people want to do alcohol or drugs, and you start learning them how to do the drugs.

Learn more about it, and after they leave they are going to decide to try that, eh, because they like to know about it. And next time around maybe somebody's pushing drugs and they say, 'Well, I have to go to the treatment centre again and learn more about a drug,' and after they come out there and they start practising how they are going to mix it together, and that's what is happening to treatment centres, and these people, White people, they come in and talk about drugs and they show that film and the other ones sitting over there they try to cure alcoholism or drugs, and the other ones are educating. That's what happening in treatment centres. Well, some of them they are okay. Some of them they go back on drugs again and alcohol because they had a really nice education from it.

Like once you start doing the drugs and alcohol and he says, 'Okay.' But the main part of it you never dealt with it. It is still inside. You feel okay, you look fine outside. What about inside of you? And that, I could say that that little thing inside of you, and that's got to come out. You know what that is? That's a little evil in there. A little demon? That's got to come out to purify your body and everything, release everything, and start off a new person. But treatment centres you go there, you talk about alcoholism, every day you talk about that, and after they release you, you got a really good education about it. You see? What I do is I kill it. I kill it. The way I kill it, I tell my clients not to talk about it, if anybody wants to talk about it you just walk away from it because you don't want to hear about it because you went through that kind of life. That's how I treat my clients that are on drugs and alcohol.

Traditional Decisions and Roles

I had a grade-four education only myself and there was a little school, and there was a Chief that used to come in our school and talk to us. We didn't have anything. We had Indian Affairs, I remember Indian Affairs, but Indian Affairs never done too much, except Indian Affairs always tried to destroy families and they tried to take all the culture away from Native people.

As far as I know, like Chiefs today that are more into the White man's world. But I remember that time that there was, if there was an Elder in a reserve, the oldest one, and that's the Chief. And that's the Chief making all the decisions he should make and councils are sitting all around there and they do whatever they have to do there. But today is different. It's ... I don't believe that White man education, that a man can do too much with that today, because our Chiefs today, they see money, they go for it, they don't think about the people.

Now we go back into tradition. Women's work is a hard work also. As a woman has a lot of certain things a woman can do in spiritual life. A woman, for one thing, that Sweat Lodge, it really belongs to women. But the woman doesn't know how to take care of it. Because there is too much alcoholism and drugs women are taking today. That's why the Sweat Lodge was left behind a long time until the Elders started to do something about it. Now today I am beginning to teach many women how to respect a Sweat Lodge because that Sweat Lodge is part of you. You are the mother and you are the mother of the womb of the Sweat Lodge.

So a woman should really look after the Sweat Lodge, learn how to build the Sweat Lodge, how to put things together and everything. And the Elder comes. When the Elder comes he looks all around everything is here that is needed and you have to start doing the Lodge for the people and that's a woman's job, but a man has to do that. To more like bringing a woman, making a woman see again. You see. And that's why many women are doing the Sweat Lodge today, they don't know exactly what they are doing. That Sweat Lodge. Again that, if you don't have certain gifts belonging to the Creator, easily someone else can take over your Lodge and the teachings become strong in there, people wouldn't be happy in there, there is something wrong with them and they will want to leave and not come back. So that's a woman's job, make sure the Sweat Lodge is smudged good. Make sure everything is in order and the people come. People come with their healing or whatever. And that's the woman's job right there.

They have women Elders, they have their own women, and they talk about it, and the men over there and they get together. And when they all get together they talk about it again. Okay. This is how it is going to be done today or next week or whatever and everybody knows what to do when the day comes. What to do, eh?

There is a lot of people fighting over the water. You know. Now we have to look at the White people. If the White man gets the best front of the river, the best land, beautiful, all that. He lives along the land and starts putting up the cabins and stuff like that, and nobody can go through that water. They try to own the water. You can't own the water because the water got to go free, and if you go on somebody else's land like the water passing through there they say, 'Get out of my, leave my water alone!' You see. So that's another thing that White man don't understand. You can't own the water. That water is going to go through anyway. You can't stop it. And the land, they can own the land and still all the land really, like I said when I started, right across North America. Native people, where they live, that's their land.

What the Elder should do is, the Elder should go around visiting people, or somebody comes over and might have a little problem here or something like to do and won't know how to do it. And the Elder goes there and they talk about these things to make it work. And that's the Elder's job. That Elder is a Spiritual Elder. There's all kinds of Elders. There's some of them are very special Elders like they have gifts that belong to the Creator. He knows all about the people in the world, and sometimes that people comes over they need a Pipe Ceremony. They don't feel good about something and the Elder do the Pipe for them and they pray for them and everything and these sort of things like that. The Elder should do really and we have everything we need, we have everything but people, Native people do not practise their own culture like baptize for one thing and marriage ceremonies and last rites and burial and all kinds of different things and I do all of these things but not enough people ask, they would rather go to a church and get buried by the church and the Elder has all that because I was saying we have everything we need, we don't, all we want now is just to practise our own culture and everything will go back together as one Native people, and that is how we are going to get the language back to work together. And to the culture together and ceremonies together because there's the Dead Feast you can do and there are other different kinds of feasts that people really should practise. And I do all this now. Many different kinds of ceremonies and people should really practise it. Maybe some Elders they don't even practise but still they want to know.

I look at people sometimes when I go in their houses and visit the people and I be seeing an Elder laying on a bed there and they're not really taken care of as they should. And they don't respect them that much because they look at the Elder because he is old and they don't want to and they say he doesn't know anything because he is so old. And that's how they look at older people. The reason why that Elder is laying down and resting is he is getting ready to go home. Because the Elder knows this and the Elder will say, 'Well, nobody listens to me anymore and I am not that strong anymore, I am so helpless I am going home, I am going back to the Creator, my father is waiting for me at the Eastern gate.' You see, and the body stays in the earth, but the Spirit goes back to your father. You see, and that's how when you talk about the creation, and that's how everybody goes back to his father at the Eastern gate, that's where the creation begins. And you have to go back there and go on beyond heavens, and you live there again, and you never get old there.

I am beginning to notice over here people want to know more about their Elders. And they come over and maybe they stay ten or fifteen minutes and they ask about a little bit of Sweat Lodge and you tell them about it. You have to share a bit, and don't give them too much because if you give them too much of it they wouldn't come back again. So you have to make them wonder, you have to make them wonder so they come back for more. And again sometimes what I do with the people that I feed them little bit, half, so that I don't feed them the rest of it because I want them to understand, think about it so that they will come back for more and that's what I do. And sooner or later they come back and they want to know more so you feed them some more and you don't feed them anymore. And then he leaves and he comes back for more and after a while he has a real long story about it, and he is beginning to feel good about himself, and after a while he is in the talking circles.

Responsibilities

A man's responsibility is hunting, getting food, bringing the food to homes and after they bring the food home the woman comes in there. The woman divides the food and cuts it up and whatever has to do. I remember that time many years ago that my father used to hunt. And deer and moose and beaver and muskrat and all kinds of different things I used to see when I was a boy. I remember one time a White man tried to starve us, telling us we can't hunt anymore. You can't have this and you can't have that. But what my father done is he had plenty deer and he hid it in the snow and the game wardens will find out about it and they come with their sticks and they start poking in the snow looking for deer hiding in the snow. And they never found it and today I understand why the White man wants to do that because they want to starve us because we had a hard time that time. That's all we do – we had fish, and deer, and moose meat,

and stuff like that. And you can't have any more than what you have. And
that's how I see it when I was a young fella. And I remember the time when
the White man's fishing down the river and the Native people couldn't
fish. And the White man is fishing across the river. And my father used to
go across the river and buy fish from the White man. At that time I remember you can buy salmon for maybe a dollar. Or twenty-five cents for other
kind of different fish and my father used to buy that other kind of fish. My
father used to poach with the net to get the food, because if the game wardens knows about it they are going to take the net.

I talk to the people. We have talking circles. When I go out there it
doesn't matter to me what colour a person is, White man or Black man or
Yellow man or whatever. I sit down with them and I talk with them and I
try to talk about the culture, what kind of life we Native people went
through. These sort of things I talk about and I try to make them to
understand and talking circles. I heal a lot of people with my words or
Sweetgrass that I use and another thing, that it doesn't matter to me what
colour a person is, who he is, it is my job to look after all the people.
They're humans too. And that's how I look at people, it doesn't matter to
me what people are, I still help them. It doesn't matter to me so they gave
us a hard time, but even today I see a lot of people are changing. The
White man is changing, a lot of different ways I see changes. I hear one
lady, White lady, saying that I just want to ask your apology, what my ancestors did to you, and she cried and cried, and said, 'Yes, I give you apology.' So these sort of things, what people went through, they have a hard
time, these White people. For one thing there was an Elder man that told
me that 'if a White man let the Indian people teach many many years ago
then this wouldn't have, we wouldn't have so much problems. If the
Indian ways of teaching that's the right way of teaching. But our way is not
working anymore,' he said. And I hear that many times. White people saying that.

Elders they don't write anything down. I never understood that before,
but today I understand that, that's why you never see the Elder writing
anything down. And if the Elder start writing things down, what happens
in the Sweat Lodge if you make a nice beautiful prayer and it's all written
down, the other one comes in and looks at the prayer, and 'That don't
sound right.' You know when you start writing something down the Elder
that made that prayer that day, it's ruined. Every day you want to say your
prayers it comes out differently. You are not going to say the same way as

yesterday. You always talk to the Creator right directly. But the White man's way, well, you have to say all these words in the book, and the right way they say. But the Native way any problem you have, something you don't understand, talk to that man directly and he will give you answers.

Well, we have to go back a little bit, of people with the alcohol problem and drugs. Okay, that's what the people one day sit there alone by themselves in the room or with people with drugs or alcohol and that's the time they are up to something. They start to say, 'I am tired of living this way. I can't go on with that anymore,' and something happen to his mind and he starts to think of suicide or something like that. Maybe they want to do something else, kill somebody or something like that. And that's why when people are all alone like that, that's what they are creating themselves. Okay, when you feel like that then you should go out and wander around in the bush, or go down to the river or something like that to keep your mind going, not to stop in one place like that.

The only time an Elder will sit all alone is when he is thinking about something or praying or asking the Great Spirit what he is going to do or what the Great Spirit wants him to do. That's the time they are all alone, and when the Elder's around the Lodge, when he sits all alone and he is thinking about the people and he is going to look after the people into the Lodge and nothing will happen to them.

Traditional Ceremonies

The Dead Feast is just like you lost a loved one, we say you lost a loved one six months ago and you didn't have time to say, 'I'm sorry. I was going to tell you this, I couldn't tell you this because I was too busy. And I was too late in doing these things.' So the family got to say, 'I want a Dead Feast. I want a Dead Feast for maybe my mother, or my father or my brother or sister because I feel I have to do something. I am not happy. I am not happy the way things are.' So the Dead Feast and the Elder prepares that.

The Dead Feast if you can have it in the teepee is much better or on the ground is much better, but it works at the house too, but it is not that strong. What you do there is you ask the Elder, 'I want the Spirit to come back and I want to talk to that Spirit.' Okay, you put out your ribbons and the Elder brings out the Pipe and the food and everything and there is going to be a special little plate, everything you put in there and that's for the Spirit when it comes. And the Elder will ask you, 'Now you stand beside me and when I call on the Spirit, the Spirit will come.' Maybe you see him, maybe you feel him in your heart. And the Elder will say, 'Now, say what you have to say now because it's here.' And when you start saying whatever you have to say at that time you are supposed to say, when he was alive you couldn't say it. So we are bringing the Spirit back in the feast so you are going to start eating. Everything people eat they are going to eat with their ancestors. But the person asked them for this feast. That's the one that left you and that's the one that's going to come back to you. And he's going to talk to him and he is going to say until the feast is over and the Elder brings the Pipe, he releases the Spirit, goes back to heaven and everything all calm down and you won't even think about your, what you went through, the loved one you lost. You wouldn't think about it anymore, you wouldn't feel like nothing else happened. But many people are holding that inside and every once in a while they think about this and they get hurt by it, and that's what the Dead Feast is all about.

There's many many reasons for Sweat Lodge ceremonies. For one thing people come in for the healing. People come in for they will want to know more about their spiritual life. They want to know maybe their ancestors. They want to know how they used to live many years ago. They see visions in the Lodge. And when they see a vision they want to come back again. They want to learn more about it. Sometimes people they don't see anything for a long time and the sort of things that we do in the Lodge, many, many other things.

Besides the Sweat Lodge there is the Pipe Ceremony, and the Pipe Ceremony is just strong, like the Lodge because the Pipe could be open and the Spirit be there and sometimes the people they don't know what's wrong with these people. They feel so happy and they starting to cry, and all things come out and everything.

How the Spirit works is maybe a year or so when the Spirit is left. When he comes back to the earth he wouldn't land on the ground or on the floor. So you got to put Sage where he is going to stand, and you might see him. How you might see him is like this: the Spirit is over here, it went in you like that, it leaves the message there and goes back out like that, and you see a Spirit here. And you look at him like that. He might tell you, 'Okay, now the message I left in there for you, you will understand it so.' And the Spirit leaves, the Spirit is here for such a long time, but he left a message in there. He went in to come back just to tell you how it's there. And you are going to wonder about it a long time, and the more you going to wonder about it, the one you lost, the stronger you get, because it's pure. And whatever the message he left it in there you are going to be able to read it after. Wouldn't come right away, but that's how the Spirits work.

If you follow two cultures, like the White man's way and the Indian way, and when you die and go to a certain place, and there be a Spirit there waiting for you, and is going to tell you what's your name, what's your culture. And if you can't answer him then he is going to send you over there. That's Catholics there and Protestants there and so on. And the Spirit will tell you, 'Okay, you go over there then and learn and then come back to me.' And you go there, well you say, 'I don't like this one,' and Spirit won't say anything, just you go over there and try that one. And you go there and you try that one there and you don't like it and you come back again. Finally the Spirit tell you, 'Who are you? Are you Native? Yeah? What's wrong with your culture? How come you don't learn about your culture?' 'Well, I didn't know anything about my culture.' And the Spirit will tell you that 'okay, there's Indian people over there. You go over there and learn.' And you will learn and learn and learn. And one day you will go back to that Spirit, and the Spirit tells you, 'Well, did you find what you were looking for?' Said, 'Yeah.' 'Are you happy with it?' 'Yeah, I am very happy with it.' That's yours, that's where it belongs. That's how you learn about your culture. But otherwise you are learning other things that aren't going to get anywhere with it. You know how a child is born again, because today many children they don't learn about their culture. And when they are born again. They are born in the same family, he is going to be born in your uncle's or maybe your aunt's. And that's how come that child looks like you or your grandfather or grandmother. And that's how they come back. And they have to learn about their culture. They sent them back. And when the Spirit is sent back, and that's why today you hear children ask about the Sweetgrass, 'What is that?' And you tell them what is a Sweat Lodge. And these kids are saying today because they want to learn about their culture. Because just like I was here before, but I never learned nothing. Today I learned a lot of good things about myself, about my people. You see. And that's how we are going to bring these things together. Like what you are doing now you are trying to put everything together. It is true. It is true what you are doing.

I tell you about the Grandfather Eagle. When he came to me one time I seen his little light coming a long ways, but it's getting bigger and bigger, a little bird I am beginning to see. Just bigger and bigger and beginning to be Eagle coming. When it was an Eagle it began to land, my foot, where my foot was and turned to a man. As Grandfather Eagle said, 'I brought you something, I brought you something that belongs to the people. Would you accept it?' 'Yes, Grandfather.' 'I want to show you a ceremony, and this is for the people.' And he said, 'You go like this, you go real slow with your people. Walk slow with your people, teach them slowly. Each time somebody falls down you wait for him until he gets up. And you go very very slow with your people and you teach them like that. Until one circle complete like that,' he said. And that be one circle. He said, 'It's going to be another one, but this one is going to be the final one. It is going to be the inside one. And the inside one here it goes almost the same way. Right there. But this one here will be in at the Eastern gate. This one. And from east to south, that's going to be a doorway.' And all the people now they want to know about it. People are coming in everywhere. They are coming in because they want to know, every thousand years something happens to Mother Earth. They beginning to notice this going around like that. But the inside circle. All the people they follow their own culture. The good way of life. When the Mother is starting to leave us again one more time and this circle we are working on today, all the people will go in there and that's going to be a Spirit World, and everybody going to be in there, and when the Mother is starting to leave we wouldn't know anything about it, but we will be all in here. We be safe in the Spirit World and the Mother will leave. And a new one will come, a new Mother will come. And this is how what you doing now, doing like that, and everything coming together now. The way you travel now you want to know more about it, everything. And that's what it is. And the more you talk about it the more people will try to understand more about it. It's a very good thing what you are doing, and the message will travel to many different cultures.

Our own way is everywhere you go on this earth. In the woods or in the bush, and many years ago they used to travel with canoes all the time, and there is a certain day, you say that today we are going to this piece of little ground here and we are going to smudge it, and we are going to have our Lodge or whatever we have to do there, and this is our church today, that piece of ground. And after they used that piece of little ground they closed it again, just like it wasn't touched before. And that's their church.

Traditional Clans

I know a little bit about clans, but over here they lost that many years ago. Clans that, like the Bear or Deer or Beaver or Eagle or all kind of different birds like that. If you really want to start your clan over again, say you have to have a man and a woman. They don't have to be young. If they ask for a ceremony, like a Name Ceremony. So you give them the Name Ceremony and you maybe call them an eagle, Grandfather Eagle and Grandmother Eagle. And other little children, it doesn't have to be children, it can be other people, they go to the Grandfather Eagle. 'You want to be in my clan?' The ceremony comes and I use as clan, Eagle Clan. And the clan's starting to grow and grow and grow and grow. And how the Eagle clans are, they want to do something, and they have to see the Grandfather Eagle and the Grandfather will go and tell him, 'Okay, go ahead and do it.' If the Grandfather is not there then they go to the Grandmother Eagle and the Grandmother give them the okay to do certain things like that. And the clans they are living in a circle like that and it's all clans. And that's all set up like that clan. But nobody really used that.

I have one prophecy. We're going to lose a lot, we're going to lose a lot, and not just the Native people, all over, all over the place, well, one thing that is going to happen, that I know is going to happen, is going to be another civil war. People will start fighting over something that they don't even know what. They are going to fight over and that's going to come, and after that comes and the starvation will come again. It's going to be another drought. We're going to need water, the land is going to be so dry and nothing will grow, and trees will be starting to dry up and that's the time we will, everything will beginning to come to the end, and another thing that I seen in my vision is the civil war again, the people will fight. I see women and children running up the hill with the barbed-wire fence and everything like that and get caught on that. I seen people are shot down get killed by guns everything, and you cannot say when that's coming but it's going to come one day, like it's so true the visions that you see, like for one thing, like Oka, I seen that before that started to happen, and it happened, but this one coming is going to be a big one, because people are going to fight.

What you're doing now, you're getting people ready that when the day comes maybe all the Native people right across the country they are thinking about their culture and they are going to go back to their ways because they know that something is coming close and the only way I can say to myself is to go back to my grandfathers and grandmothers then what I used to have.

Stages of Life

This, it's like the people use colours, like rainbow colours, like prints, they call it prints, colours, and those colours that it's all it is a symbol. It's a symbol of the Creator, and those are levels of life and the stage, the last one would be the red and it opens up like that, and it goes through that and beyond that nobody knows beyond that, and as far as we can go is the lights of levels that people go through. And the colour of black and people are scared of that colour of black. It's the colour of black is only the Native way, you see many years the North direction has been closed, you know it's darkness over there, a long time and that's the colour of black that people use to open that direction again, the colour of the North. But the stages of life and that's what it is. In my experience of stages of life, when I seen this lights of going up in heavens there's so much confusion about those colours of life and I don't like to talk about these things that people don't understand. And to my experience of spiritual life, and this is what I seen, and there is, there was one man up in James Bay, I believe it's Fort Albany. He has a hard time with people over there, he's an Elder, I forgot his name and he wanted to know about the stages of life. He is an old man now. So I said, 'For you that if you really want to believe in something then you got to go there,' and I looked at the Elder. His life is very good. He has his living, he is good and a very honest Elder. So I took that old man, I smudged him and I said, 'I don't know how far we are going to go but we are going to go someplace.' And he had a humpback because he was working hard his whole life and I manages to straighten his back a little bit and smudged him, so we went someplace up there. And he seen all kinds of different things there, and I told him this is the last place when you start to see the red and that's where we are going to stop and we did stop there. And this is what he seen: it's the symbol of the rainbow. The rainbow, the flowers all around, and beauty, and the Creator. And the Elder is talking in Cree and he was talking to the Creator, and when I brought him back and that man was just changed and his face was changed was younger looking and everything. And he never said nothing, we just sit there. Well I didn't have nothing to say then. There was Archie with me there that time, and I said, 'Archie, you talk to him.' So I went to the other room and sat there for a while and sat there, and that old man just opened up in Cree. And what he seen, he didn't want to come back. He wants to stay there, he was so peaceful over there and he didn't want to come back at all. But I told him when you're bringing back something here it doesn't belong to you it belongs to the people. You are just going to deliver the message to the people. That's what happened to that old man, the stages, the stages of life. And the stages of life depends how you conduct your life when you are young and older. Then one day you will ask about the stages of life, how far you are, and those things that you'd see, and you conduct your life the right way then it means you are going to go for further stages, four stages of your life.

Predicting the Weather

Well, there's, I hear Elder people talking years ago that I never understand. They use beehive, and those ones in the field, you see in little bushes in the field sometimes, and if there is a beehive on top like that, and it means that it's going to be a hard winter, there is going to be a lot of snow. If the beehive is down below like that there is not going to be too much snow.

Language and Culture

Okay, now, for me, this is how I do it. Before I start to change my language to English, and I have to talk to my Grandfather. That's the Grandfather Creator. So I tell him what I want to do. This is the way I want to do it today, I want to speak in English, and I want you to understand so we can work together. Like today before we started this morning, I light up the smudge and I told him that I don't know what I am going to do today, but I want you to understand to help me to speak the right way, so that I can answer the questions. And if you don't so that then it means you don't really care about your culture or your language you see. Your language has always got to come first. No matter if you are in White man's world, it's still in your mind and you start with your ancestors first, and then you understand and you understand also and they help you out with that. See, your language is important, your language has always got to come first before the second language comes.

The Indian names is, okay, is another thing. It's easy to give a child a name when he is small, walking around, the child comes with the name when you are born, and he comes with the name it's easy to find the name. But when you take an older person and try to take a name and it is awful hard for an Elder, so you have to sit down with an Elder and talk about your childhood, as far as you can remember maybe two or three years old starting to remember these things that, how you used to play around with your toys or something like that, you're pretending this is a little animal or so on like that. So we really have to find that, and say what's wrong with that little girl over there talking to herself and, but it's not really talking to herself, it's talking to the Spirit, the one she is pretending. And that's how you have to try and find when you get older it's hard to find the name.

Native people should learn about their culture. We don't have too much left about culture so we really have to start bringing it out again in the surface. When you said that the drums were burned and all kinds of things were throwed in the fire, now it's time again to bring it out in the open and let people see it. No more hiding, it's time to bring it out on the surface and make it work and people see that.

When I was starting to grow up and understand about life I was starting to see. I used to go to different reserves and I was beaten up many times because I am different from other ones so that part that, it wasn't good at that time, but today everything is going back to where people are beginning to understand, and the people have the colour of the skin is your identity. You cannot lose that. No matter where you travel you see your identity there. That's your brother and your sister or whatever because in the beginning of time the Creator gave us this kind of skin to recognize your brother and your sister and it's still happening today that's why so many different languages today, again we better understand each other yet to bring that together again to get along together to understand that again. You see the reason why we get along together now is we are using the language of the White man. That's another thing that we call the White brother and if it wasn't for the White brother we wouldn't get along at all.

Dreams

Okay, we have to get into a spiritual life. There's two Spirits of you, one good, one bad. It's always like that, it doesn't matter who it is, the other one is always following this one around, and a good Spirit of you he stays inside, he is protecting your body and everything. But the open chance, when you start doing something wrong you shouldn't be doing you open the door for him. So the bad one gets in you and the other one gets out. Okay, now the mind, okay. The mind is different. It is different because your mind is, we could say, it is black magic. If you let your mind do all kinds of things for you and your mind takes over your body and your heart is not telling you anything and it's just using your mind. Okay. Now people have different kind of dreams. When you sleep at night and if you don't know how to pray or ask your Spirit to stay with you, not to go anywhere, okay. Now when your Spirit leaves at night and it goes to the other Spirit. There are all kinds of other Spirits there at night. And your Spirit leaves, your Spirit wouldn't leave until you fall asleep and that's when it leaves to join other Spirits out there. So you get into trouble, or doing other things, or scared or something and your Spirit is running back, and your Spirit runs back into your body and jumps in there and you wake up.

And sometimes you have a real bad dream like that. So these kinds of things that people always really ask me about, and that's what going on into their lives. Now if you dream about water or Sweetgrass, or Sweat Lodge, or anything like that, these spiritual things, or maybe you dream about your father, or your mother, or something like that. That's a spiritual dream. That's a good dream, and there is something there. Something, but if you been dreaming about this over and over and the Elder check on that, maybe the Elder will say, 'What are you doing to yourself anyway? You don't even pray or do anything for yourself. You don't talk to the Spirits before you go to sleep, that's why things happen to you.' And that's what the Elder will tell you. And as this goes on you get scared and scared and you have to tell somebody. But the spiritual dreams are very good things.

And when the Elder put his head down and looked at you and put his head down, that's the time they could see about your dreams. And the Elder said, 'There's nothing there, just a wild dream.' The Elder will tell you to say your prayers at night and the dream will go away.

Now we talk about dreams just like I was growing up I had this gift that belonged to the people. It ain't mine and I am always having these bad dreams and I holler at night and my mother keeps telling, 'What's wrong with you, you should go to sleep. Stop making that noise.' But I never understood what was happening to me at that time until the Elder. I talked to the Elder. And he told me that 'Yes, you got something for the people.' That's why the gift you have now is just like I was telling this to him, like I was fighting okay. Now good and bad they were fighting over me, not for me they try to stop me before they understand about my gift. I always have bad dreams and I could see things and I never understand that was just a dream of some kind. I never understood this until one day and the dream stopped. Everything just changed and everything is so real. And I never understood why this was happening to me. Every time I go to sleep at night they fight over me. Good and bad they are fighting for me not to understand. They always blocking me, blocking me and at that time I didn't care anyways. After that I beginning to understand the people. Understand where the medicine is at and everything, and this is for that and alcohol that. So I don't carry medicine around. Because I was told every place you go there is medicine for you. There is medicine there for the people. It's all kinds of different kinds of medicine. Okay, now the gift. You take the gift and you go, maybe you go to that grass or any kind of plant over there, and you touch that and you give a little bit of tobacco and you talk to them what you want it for. And you tell him what you want it for. And that plant or that tree will turn as medicine, and you put it in the water, stir it up and give it to them. It doesn't matter what kind. It's your gift to be able to do this. A tree when you look at the tree, especially the trees that size and they are healthy, they are strong and they can survive in winter months. And you can go talk to that tree because that tree is alive and you talk to him and tell him that, 'I am here today, I want to ask for a little bit of flesh from you for certain person I want to help to heal them. You should share me some.' And that's what you do and the plant or the tree will listen to you because you touch him with your love and the plant will do it. And that's the gift and that is how you, and that's the same thing with the Sweetgrass over there. I see a lot of people they try to light that Sweetgrass, but it wouldn't burn. And sometimes when you take a new braid and talk to Grandmother, and tell her I am starting a new braid and the Spirit of the grass will come back.

It is very important to do that because everything we have, it come from the land. Everything, that material, everything, that communication with Mother Earth, and that's where everything come from because if it wasn't for Mother Earth we wouldn't be sitting here and that's the connection you have to make each day.

It was an Elder that told me every man-made thing on this earth is going to go back one day. And everything will fall apart, and everything, that's identity. Now you take that iron that comes from some kind of stone in the ground, and I will grind it down to make a metal like that and that metal it be looking for its identity one day and it's going to go apart and that's going to back where it come from. That's the same thing with human life.

Land and Boundaries

Nowadays I am beginning to see that, especially Native people they want to claim a piece of little land, a land where they can build their camps or whatever they want to build there, and I am beginning to see that, the land belongs to all the Native people, you can't buy the land. But now the law says you can own that piece of land. The Indian law is you can't own the land you can live on the land. You got your freedom to go anywhere you want to go.

Traditional Education

There is Elders, they sit around maybe outside with the fire and the

Elders and Elder women they sit around and tell stories. All kinds of different stories and they make children laugh and all kinds of different things like that. They go on for hours and hours just to learn their kids.

Residential Schools

They shouldn't even do these things that they try to change the Indian to a White man and I hear people talk about it. They beat kids if they speak in their language, they beat them up and they lock them up or cut their hair right off. When I was, I hear people talk about it and it's very confusion whatever they try to do there – to do something like that, to torture them really. And that's no need to do that. They treat our people many years ago just like animals.

Abuse and Healing

Abuse in, especially women, they don't come out of it easy. Because something happened to the Spirit when that thing happened. So she takes a long time to bring it out, forget about it. If she can forget about it for a little while, not a little while for a long time, your life will be much better, and if you can forget about it, your life goes on there will be one day you have to deal with it, not here, but up there, whatever the problem is. So she is not going to be all alone. Whoever is causing the problem is going to be the one punished about that, because I work with women that have been abused, many many women, and I worked on them and I take them to the Fast so their life is much easier for her and that thing that is inside leaves, and life is much better. So these sort of things they have to deal with these things.

Some of them come out of it quickly, some of them don't. When they are too small when that happened, more like a different Spirit is inside and the different Spirit it has to come out, and sometimes you see that thing it comes out and the person gets better. There's all kinds of different people has problems about that. But different way of happening to them. Some of them were tied and some of them were just happened, just happened.

You have to learn yourself. You have to be a little girl again. The beginning of time, whatever that thing happened. The beginning of time, the age you are now and this as far as here and there this is a waste of life. You don't know anything. Then you have to go back here and try to make the person focus on that. Okay, and you start bringing them back as a little girl. Just go along slowly like that, until you get them that age. And that's how you get them back. This is waste of life. Do you know what I mean? We got to find this here, so they can understand about the teachings today. Because this one never had a chance to be a little girl. Becomes a little girl and a big woman and that's a waste of life.

Living in Both Cultures

Yes, it is very important. Now these people I see one time. These Native people are so smart with their education and the White man can't teach them anymore because they don't know anything anymore and the Native way and they say what I could learn now a White man can't teach them. The Indian takes his own culture from where he stopped and keeps on going because he wants to know more about his culture.

Culture is good to learn in schools because maybe someday that is all we are going to have is our own culture, our own Native teachers. We got our teachers here, are teaching Micmac language and they have half-breeds. They don't really know that much.

Warrior Societies

That's another thing that I would say warriors shouldn't learn how to destroy anybody. There is the Sweat Lodge they call a Warrior Sweat. Many years ago they never used that Warrior Sweat. Only certain times they used it. And Warrior Sweat is awful hot, awful hot, because the Elder will, is training you how to sneak and attack without anybody seeing you. They call that a Warrior Sweat. And these days people are learning how to destroy life. But many years ago they don't even, Native people they didn't even know how to kill until the White man starting to kill people and the Native people wonder why is that man over there killing people? So they never did understand that until the killing starts.

Traditional Justice

What I hear from Elders in Nova Scotia, when somebody killed somebody or they don't know how to prove it and some people say, 'Yes and yeah, you did wrong.' So they don't know how and they don't want to kill any-body. So they told him the only thing they can do. 'We have to tie you up, and on a certain full moon tide, then we tie you up to a rock where the tide comes in. If the Mother kills you and you done wrong. If you survive then you didn't do anything wrong.' So they tie him up, and the full moon tide comes in, comes into that whatever that person might be and the water comes in. If it doesn't cover him up then he survives. The Mother will punish him, Mother Earth. And that's what I hear about how they used to punish.

The Elders sit around in a circle again and they talk about it. They talk about it and what's going to happen. If they decide, well, maybe they take him back in the woods someplace, and they just give him an ax or whatever material they have and they just leave him there, and that's your punishment, and you can't go back in a village, and you can't see your family for a certain time. And that's how they used to do these things.

I worked on people, like come over here, and if they don't come over and see me about their problem they have, they go in jail. So I treat them here and we have to report back and forth like. And if I treat him and he gets out of it he's okay. But the other way around he goes into jail. Another thing is attempted suicide. You can go to jail with that too. I treated attempted suicide people and the whole family I deal with one time. About a hundred miles from here, a man and a woman and his children, they all try to commit suicide because of the drugs and all kinds of things. So I treat them there, and I put them in the Lodge.

Your own culture is a lot stronger than a lot of people believe. All you are doing is to make other culture strong when you use somebody else's culture. You make him strong and nothing happened really. But your own culture is different things happening all the time. But these sort of things, if we can use our own culture, it will be a lot better for people everywhere. When I travel I try to tell people to go back to their culture. To learn your own culture. And the culture you are supposed to follow. That's where it happens, your own culture, your own people. But you go over in towns or cities. You can't find no happiness there, you are more like second-class person there. No matter what you are trying to do you don't fit because you don't belong there. But you are trying to fit there but you don't. But when you are trying to get to your own people, and you find a lot of happiness, and you don't have to have a whole lot to be happy. That's another good thing about our culture. You don't have to have a bunch of other things. What's important is your Spirit. What's happened is you got what's in you and that's what makes you strong and happy. But you cannot buy anything like this, your own culture and your own love. You cannot buy that. You got to earn that. You got to start doing your own culture and make it happen and see it happen and that's where the happiness is. Just like a lot of people make believe, 'Yes I am following my culture, I went in the Sweat Lodge one time.' Just saying that I done that. But when they go into the Lodge they don't put anything into it. They don't want to learn anything. That's why they don't learn anything, because they don't want to give up anything. When you go into the Lodge you have to really give up something and the Elder will tell you, 'Whenever you go into the Lodge you have to smudge yourself and go into the Lodge. And once you are in the Lodge now it is time for you to give up something. Whatever is bothering you leave it go. Leave it in the Lodge. Go free.' That's the Elders talk about all these things. You go free as a new child. See again people come into the Lodge. I tell them this. You sit like this, they hold tight and they don't want to let go of nothing. You have to relax so the Spirit can get into you, and you are going to Sweat whatever is wrong inside you. You are going to sweat it out, it goes back into the ground that sweat. The sickness or whatever is wrong.

Now the White man is so much lost we don't know what to do anymore. He turns to the Native people again because the Native people's teachings are so real. Everything is there for them because many many years Native people they don't want to recognize their own culture. They don't want to even recognize their own medicine around like that. But today the White man he wants to recognize that. How are you going to make it work? The Elders have their way to see it work and everything like that, but I believe that the Native people if they put everything together and start using it and you can teach the White man to listen to us. Once they make them listen to us then we can able to do something.

That's another thing because too much greed of a White man, one million [dollars], if he has one million that wouldn't be enough. But if you take a Native man, even if he has twenty-five, thirty thousand dollars, he's happy because that's a lot. But the White man once he see a pile over there, he wants it all, never mind the other one. 'I want to be in control of that,' you see. And that's what the White man is. And you start giving little bit to the people over there. Just a little bit. And that's how the White man is. The way of explaining this here is your mind. You have a little bit of water in your brain. You got to learn that to balance that. Take your left foot and right foot. When you walk and this water tells you that you're balanced so you wouldn't fall. And the White man is not. The White man is different way of thinking. Okay, if it's too much balance over there and he is off balance it's going to take that more and more until he is up there you see. He is off balance. And the same thing with the human here. Human is, if he's using his mind too much he comes black magic. And nothing comes from here [points to heart], it all comes from here [points to head], and your mind is creating that over here [points to head]. That didn't come from here, you see [points to heart]. So if you want to make a big pile over here it is not enough so you are going to create some more how are you going to stockpile some more. That's your mind. That's what mind can do to you, the greed. It's two different ways of looking at these things. It comes from your heart or it comes from your mind.

Concluding Thoughts

For one thing, what I like to see more is about a culture of Native way. Have parents to teach more about the Sweetgrass. Sweetgrass, people should learn about Sweetgrass. There is lots of teachings in that Sweetgrass and people don't use it. The first medicine the Creator gave us is the Sweetgrass. And that medicine these people don't know how to use this medicine, but there is the medicine right here. That's the seed right here. And you take that seed and maybe that much you start putting into the water and that's your medicine.

And another thing is that people should go back to their own culture. Like we talk about that two canoes. That will give you a lot of answers about that canoe you talked about. We are talking to Archie Bishop there up in Haughten Bay. Last winter we had breakfast together and he asked us about, how about mixing two cultures together, and how about bringing the Sweetgrass into the church, and the Pipe into the church? So I let Archie to answer that question at that time and that's what we came up with that two canoes and he told him that, 'Well, if you follow two cultures then you are not going to get anywhere with that. You are going to fall in and you are not going to get anywhere. Like two roads going this way, and that's your road there, you should follow that. And this here is another road here going different directions. And this one here is going down instead of going up.' You see, you don't learn everything here because you are going down. But your own path like our Creator gave us this path to walk on many people call it Red road or Sweetgrass road, or whatever they want to call it and that's the road we should be all on that road, what the Creator gave us that culture, just like I told, you can learn a lot of things from that tape, those things I told you about the circle. And if you can really understand what I am talking about you can learn a lot of things from it. And that's how you educate these people that don't understand about culture. It's so many different cultures and I seen different experiences of coloured people. They have their own culture. I worked on one person, he's from Jamaica, and he wanted to come into the Lodge. I said, 'You are welcome to come in.' I am not going to turn anyone down, and I asked him to sing, and he said, 'I don't know how to sing.' I said, 'Try to sing something.' And he is starting to sing, and his Spirit came to him and he is beginning to sing real good, and he brought the jungle into the Lodge, and he is beginning to cry and sing louder and louder. And he said, 'It is unbelievable what I seen. I never seen anything like it in my life.' He said, 'If I tell my people what I seen they are not going to believe me.' So it is so important to learn about the culture. Indian culture, there is no two ways about it. There is only one way to learn that you go back to your own culture and then you learn a lot of good things about that. And that way you will find a way of life and there is a good life there.

Central/Great Lakes Region Cultures

TWYLAH HURD NITSCH (Seneca)

Cattaraugus Indian Reservation, New York

'My heritage was so ingrained in me that I knew I would never lose it.'

Twylah Hurd Nitsch, a Seneca, was born on 5 December 1912 on the Cattaraugus Indian Reservation at Irving, New York. Her parents were Maude Shongo Hurd, a Seneca, and Raymond Perkins Hurd, of Oneida and Scottish descent. In 1935, Twylah married Robert Arthur Nitsch, of German and Prussian descent. Their children are Janice, Louise, Diane Elaine, Robert Arthur, James Raymond, and Marcia Ellen (deceased). Twylah has two grandchildren: Daniel, Robert's son, and Jaime, James's daughter.

Twylah was educated at the Normal School of Practice, South Park High Human Dimension Institute and Snerial's Secretary School, all at Buffalo, New York. Twylah and her mother founded the Seneca Indian Historical Society, which holds a permanent charter issued by the State University of New York, Education Department, granted 16 November

1972 by the Board of Regents as number 10,894. Twylah is the president and James Nitsch is the vice-president. This society is located on the family property at the Cattaraugus Reservation. She has retired from her position as recreation supervisor for Erie County Recreation Department, located at Buffalo, NY.

Twylah has lectured in Canada, England, Mexico, South America, and throughout the United States, on the Wisdom, Prophecy, and Philosophy of the Senecas. She conducts intensives for students who wish to become teachers of Seneca Wisdom. The Senecas have been known as the philosophers of this ancient Wisdom. Twylah has co-authored *Other Council Fires Were Here before Ours* with Jaime Sams, her adopted granddaughter. She has written the following resource books: *Entering into the Silence, Language of the Stones, Language of the Trees, Nature Chants and Dances, Handbook of Prophecy and Philosophy,* and *Mythological Philosophy.* Twylah, her son Robert, and Joan White have compiled a curriculum called Native American Studies, released in Canada for the 1995 fall semester. Presently, Twylah is writing a book about her Seneca ancestor Red Jacket. This book includes an overview of the Seneca from the sixteenth to the nineteenth century. Plans are underway to make this piece into a documentary film.

Twylah's interview is much different from the others in this collection. Each Elder was given a copy of his or her interview to edit. Many made changes, but Twylah completely rewrote her interview in the style of her teachings. Her revision has not been edited, and although strikingly different from the rest in this collection, it contains wonderful teachings, as well as many stories and personal reflections.

Introduction

History has been recorded as human progress on Planet Earth. This history has overlooked the First, Second, and Third worlds of earth's existence. Recorded history has its beginning after the Great Flood that ended the Third World. To feel comfortable about what happened prior to the Great Flood, we can look upon these events as a myth.

While Earth had been drifting in darkness, Earth birthed love, truth, and peace as a natural instinct for survival. At that moment, Earth became the Mother of Love, Truth, and Peace. Next, time awakened the seeds of all living entities called clans. Therefore, Clan identified the species of Motherearth. There would be no division between Mother and Earth because she was one and whole.

Motherearth birthed all kinds of clans. These clans learned their identity and ways of living in harmony with other clans. Thus, the clan system became a harmonious way of life responsible for establishing the sovereignty for self-survival.

Then, humankind emerged from Motherearth, of which there were five races; the black race, the brown, the red, the yellow, and the white race. Each human race had an Earth Mission. The black race perceived the hidden gifts of Motherearth as sounds of rhythm and harmony known as the Music of the Spheres. The brown race perceived the gifts of growth hidden as nourishment within Motherearth. The red race perceived the blood lineage hidden to perpetuate the future of the clan system's survival identified as 'Seven Generations into the Future.' The yellow race perceived the Rising Sun as the dawn of each new day for healthy living. The white race perceived the hidden gifts of Motherearth to perpetuate discoveries for personal achievement through self-learning. Each of these races would experience success until the Fourth World of Separation and Control, at which time the brown and red races would unite due to the lack of nourishment and the fracturing of the clan system for survival. The Fourth World would collapse due to illness and greed.

The Fifth World would be called the world of Illumination. Love, truth, and peace would be the banner of the Fifth World. However, noise would become the disease of the Fifth World, causing the sound barrier to collapse. The major disease of the Fifth World would be deafness.

The Sixth World would introduce revelations of great intuitive gifts. However, a vast number of people would be afflicted with a disease of recalling the Truth (liars). Thus, their voices would lose resonance, resulting in a lack of communication for survival.

Why The Seventh World would be called the World of Synchronicity is beyond anyone's knowledge. Perhaps it unites all the gifts of the former worlds into a State of Wholeness, to enter a wider dimension of awareness healed of the fears that plagued the six previous worlds.

This introduction gives food for thought of what purpose humankind offers to perpetuate Love, Truth, and Peace in one's 'way of life.'

Creation

The plant people were the first to emerge from Planet Earth and firmly established a way of life for their survival. Next, the animal people emerged from Planet Earth to live off the plant people. Then the plant people taught the animal people how to survive by learning how to live and where to grow to achieve a feeling of comfort. Through this process of growth, all the creatures of Earth eventually established their own survival methods and found that living depended upon a balanced cycle governed by a predator system. Living progressed in a harmonious way of life for each creature. A feeling of comfort made life compatible for all Earth's creature beings.

When the two-legged emerged from Earth, they were totally dependent upon both the plant people and the animal people for survival. The two-leggeds were not aware that comfort was achieved through being compatible with all Earth's entities. They sought only self-satisfaction. In the meantime, all Earth's creatures had developed a life of shared responsibility among all Earth's manifestations. The two-leggeds did not realize they needed to take on some responsibilities for their own survival.

Every creature being honoured Earth for her nurturing gifts. Thus, Earth's creature beings respected the lifestyles of other creature beings, except the two-leggeds. Reproduction of all life forms was honoured by every Earth creature. Each creature had a mission that was adaptable for survival. Soon, the two-leggeds became aware they had a place in this overall survival responsibility. As a result, all creature beings also had a limited time span while being sovereign entities that emerged from the Earth composed of living Earth Energy and ingredients. When their life cycle was complete, their bodies would return to Earth for her nourishment. Thus Earth's evolution was eternal.

There was one more gift the creature beings wanted to share with the two-leggeds. Soon, they realized the two-leggeds were not ready to learn this great gift. This gift referred to the Magic Circle as the Shape of Harmony. Every lesson had a beginning place and when the lesson was learned the circle became whole. Truth lives within the circle and provides the living energy to create the Spirit of Wholeness.

All for one ... one for all.

Field of Plenty

Let's talk about the Field of Plenty. Our Elders have said, 'Long before Planet Earth became a living entity, there was a place in Infinite Space called the Field of Plenty.' The Field of Plenty contained all the seeds related to a living force. However, some of these seeds were dormant waiting to be awakened. The original TRUTH had been encoded in these seeds to maintain and sustain their living energy. All seeds were gifted with wisdom, integrity, stability, and dignity. The symbolic North maintained the wisdom. The symbolic East sustained the integrity. The symbolic South ordained the stability, and the symbolic West contained the Dignity.

TRUTH is a magnetic energy that attracts and releases all life forces. The North maintains a continuous flow of living energy. The East sustains the quality of energy in its flow. The South sustains the TRUTH ENERGY as a support system for stability. The West contains the Dignity to energize Self-Esteem.

These seeds also entertain a balance of male and female energy. The male energy protects the female energy by uniting their pulse in relation to Earth's rhythm.

Each seed is encoded with a mission called timed energy. Thus, each seed becomes its own agent and is responsible for reproducing itself. Each seed chooses where it will express its life force and the length of time it wishes to remain earthbound. At which time, it releases its Earth body, which returns to Earth and the seeds return to the Field of Plenty. This process completes the cycle of Earth connection.

Migrations

The Five Nations were a small band of Native Americans surrounded by the Algonquins. These Five Nations were spiritually gifted people. They were called the Mohawks, Oneidas, Onondagas, Cayugas, and Senecas. They were sensitive to Earth Energy. They knew when it was the best time for planting and the inner-knowing of survival instinct. For these reasons, the Algonquins held the small nations in bondage. At last, the Five Nations escaped this situation and set up residence in the central part of what is now known as New York State. The Mohawks were the Keepers of the Eastern Door of a mythical Longhouse. The Senecas were the keepers of the Western Door. The Onondagas were the Fire Keepers. The Five Nations hold these roles to this day.

When the Five Nations arrived at their Chosen Place to live, they found great unrest due to the constant raids among the people. During this time a man who called himself the PEACEMAKER approached Hiawatha, an angry, human-flesh-eating man who had lost his wife and daughters. The PEACEMAKER helped him heal his great sorrow and both men left on a trek to awaken Love, Truth, and Peace in the hearts of the people. The two men met a woman at the Crossroads of Life and told her about Love,

Truth, and Peace. She was the first to hear this message from Hiawatha, who was the spokesperson for the PEACEMAKER since he had a speech impediment.

'Words are empty without form,' she remarked.

The PEACEMAKER answered, 'There is form. The form is the Longhouse to which each additional home is the extension of the original Longhouse. Also, there is a CLAN FAMILY living in each Longhouse to retain a pure blood line. I shall call you Jagonsaseh. From now on, you shall be known as the Mother of All Nations.'

The three people set out to visit the Mohawks, who are credited with the founding of the Five Nation Peace Confederacy. Next, the Peace group visited the Oneidas, Cayugas, and Senecas, finding these Nations in full agreement with the PEACEMAKER. People from all the Five Nations converged upon the fierce Otadaho to convey the Peace Message to him. He roared and ranted with snakes writhing on his head when he heard the Peace Message. Presently, Hiawatha approached Otadaho and commenced combing the snakes from his head. After the snakes were removed a Peace entered the image of Otadaho as the PEACEMAKER HELD HIS HAND OUT TOWARDS HIM. All the people crowded around him were overwhelmed with his great transformation. Suddenly, someone said, 'Where is the PEACEMAKER?' The PEACEMAKER was nowhere to be seen. But everyone knew if ever he was needed, he would return.

Sign Language

One of the lessons the PEACEMAKER taught was body language. We often think that body language reacts only to movement. This is not entirely true. Our bodies react to inner thoughts. The PEACEMAKER tapped into the hidden thoughts nestled deep within the brain. These thoughts respond to feelings centred like a core biding time. This spot has a colour that identifies thought images. These thought images we could not grow. Sign language is directly connected to this spot in the centre of our heads. This spot never rests. It's our aware centre.

When we are not busy with everyday activities and happen to sit quietly, thinking he was busy at all times. This activity comes from that never-ending desire of attention. Our Elders say:

Sign is attached to questioning thought
Why, how, who, when? Wherever it's sought

Sign is a symbol that can be taught,
Sign is the truth that can't be bought.
KEEPER OF THE HILLS (*Ha non dia suh*)

Keeping Track of Events

The runners were responsible for coordinating all events. These activities
were regularly scheduled through the seasons for easy recall. Social activities coincided with the various games, competitions for all ages, physical
fitness, dances, singing societies, ceremonies, and craft sharing for everyone.

Traditional Villages

Within every village was a special location where the people could meet
for council gatherings. People from other villages were invited to share
their ideas for all to hear. Everyone has their time to speak, even children
were asked for their opinions. Decisions were made after everyone had
been heard. Listening was a major characteristic in the Native society.
Everyone honoured the speaker because they wanted to have the same
attention when they spoke.

At large council meetings a 'talking stick' was used. In some cases a
'questioning stick' was appropriate, especially when several issues were to
be discussed. This intercommunity dialogue was encouraged. When representatives met in council, they listened and then took the subjects back
to their own councils for discussion. This system gave an added dimension of strength to prepare for a Grand Council. Grand Council made the
major decisions when the issues affected more people.

The women took a significant role in the governing of their people.
The Clan Mothers selected most of the Chiefs. There were a few Chiefs
who had inherited their position. The reason behind this practice is that
the men were the protectors and the women the nourishers. Often,
women were chosen as representatives.

It has been said that originally the Native people observed a wolf pack
and recognized a structured survival technique that worked. They had
many people, both men and women, observe the society of the wolf and
found human ways to adapt these ideas into the lifestyle of their people.
The bear, beaver, hawk, deer, heron, snipe, turtle, and wolf became teachers to the Native people. This is the reason they identify with birds and

animals as acceptable members of their own family. Native people eventually adopted these creatures as family and honoured them as family clans.

After the clan system was part of the Native heritage there was no division between the animal, birds, and other creatures of Motherearth. Living was one big family relationship. If an animal was eaten, its gift was needed for the survival of all creatures. This idea changed the entire survival structure of the Americans long before other cultures came to the Western Hemisphere.

The Clan System

Every Nation has its own Clan Families. The number of clans depended upon the population in each Nation. The Seneca Nation has eight clans. They are the Bear, the Beaver, the Hawk, the Deer, the Heron, the Snipe, the Turtle, and the Wolf. When these clans were placed around the Medicine Wheel, Bear was the Medicine Clan and taught about the use of herbs. The Beaver Clan was about honour and taught how to be industrious and thorough in assessing the truth. The Deer Clan brought endurance into the lives of their people by teaching patience. The Hawk Clan brought pride in whatever they did and taught their people the importance of Feather Cleansing. The Heron Clan brought healthy thoughts to their people and taught the importance of good nourishment. It is said the Heron taught the people how to fertilize their crops. The Snipe Clan brought one's mission into view through self-understanding and obedience. The Turtle Clan brought purpose into one's life by being fruitful and considerate of others. The Turtle Clan teaches the Moral Code. The Wolf Clan brought listening into the lives of the people. The people of the Wolf Clan brought survival instincts into the people's lives. They were the message carriers and were gifted with inner knowing. The Wolf Clan taught the importance of dreams. The Great Black Bear was the consolidator of all the clans and was responsible for setting up councils. There were four directions. These directions were not clans. The Buffalo represented the North and brought wisdom into the minds of the people. The Eagle represented the East and brought lofty ideals into hearts of the people. The South was the Porcupine and brought the gifts of transformation into the lives of the people.

Few of these traditions are practised among our people since the foreigners blindly entered the Sacred Space of our people. Even though much of our culture has been erased from the people of today, it is still here and soon will be returned to our race. The White society is clamouring to know how the original races have survived. They are seeking to understand how these clans were so strong and valuable to the original people in this great country. 'Living in truth is the reason.'

Tradition

People sitting in a circle ... the Shape of Harmony ... the Council

The Council Ring

The most important tradition is to recognize we all have a value system based upon Love, Truth, and Peace. We also have an awareness that all our gifts are within us and in order to practise these gifts we must learn who we are and how we feel about ourselves. First, we need to recognize the feeling of self-esteem. Self-esteem includes self-respect and self-responsibility. From this source, we can learn the basis of Truth. Truth has twelve components. We place these twelve components on a wheel called the Wisdom Wheel. In olden days this Wheel was called Good Medicine.

Ceremonies

Ceremonies were activities to be honoured. Achievements were activities that honoured rituals and ceremonies that brought together not only villagers but neighbouring villagers as participants.

Vision quests were personal ceremonies and were considered a natural part of everyone's quest for self-understanding. These ceremonies were part of a growing ritual for both boys and girls at the age of puberty. Boys would be with their fathers and girls would be with their mothers.

Death and Grieving

In some Nations death was looked upon as a completion of one's mission. The grieving was not for the loss as much as for the completion of a sharing of one's contributions. Some nations conducted a Ten-Day Feast, at which time special gifts of the deceased were given to special friends of the deceased. Food was served to everyone present. A plate with samples of all the food stood on the serving table. This plate was taken by someone who needed spiritual food. No one really knew who took this plate. When survivors honour the achievements of the deceased, there is a greater sense of Love, Truth, and Peace at these Feasts. If the person was a dancer or singer, a demonstration was included because the deceased entered the Happy Hunting Ground.

Burial Grounds

Burial grounds were decided during one's last days. If the deceased wanted to be interred near a favourite tree this was done. Actually, everyone had his or her choice. If one wanted to be buried deep into the Earth, or if one desired a shallow grave the wish was carried out. It was not until graveyards were suggested by the White society that Native people followed this custom. If the deceased wanted special objects to be buried with them, this wish was carried out. This is the reason, when Native graves are exhumed, many sacred items are found. Elders had the sacred bundles buried with them. It was thought these sacred items might identify the spirit should it return in a dream or in a spirit visitation.

Traditional Lodging

Skin-covered lean-tos were used for travelling from one village to the next. Often these lean-tos were found along the trails between the villages for others to use. For long-distance travelling tree houses were found. These tree houses were merely platforms constructed between tall trees upon which one could rest unnoticed. Runners who carried messages from village to village used these tree platforms.

A travois was used to carry lodge poles. These poles were placed in a circle and tied together at the top. When covered with hides, they were quite suitable as a place to sleep for a short span of time. Today, we call this a tent.

Native people travelled extensively. Even Longhouses were used for only ten to fifteen years. It was thought better to move from this site to restore the surroundings. A new site was only a day's distance from the old site. The people in the village moved together, thus no one was left when the former village was abandoned.

Europeans

After the Europeans entered this virgin land, trees were cut and entire forests were burned to make way for a new culture. These people raped the natural beauty of the earth, trees, fruit, and medicine by wantonly destroying the tradition of an ancient race of humankind. The Europeans feared the Native People of the Americas and made every effort to obliterate them from the face of the earth. Even though these people were not wanted in their homeland and came to a new world, they carried the same mind-set of their European culture. It was a sad day when these outcasts set foot on the Land of the Free. Unfortunately, they brought all their fears with them and without an awareness of their trespassing laid claim to a virgin land that was not theirs.

Our Elders said: 'They are children of the Earth just as we are who brought new thinking and new ways of life. But a day will come when they see that their ways spread disease and loss of inner peace. Then they will wonder why we, the Native people, have survived. Their rope will have frayed and will have loose ends. They will ask, "How have you withstood fear?" We will answer them ... Our answer is this:

Truth is our watchword
Truth is our key
Truth is our password
Truth sets us free.'

Treaties

Treaties are a written promise made between Native people.

Every treaty the U.S. government made with the Senecas has been broken by the government.

It is important to make a promise with a group of people before making it with other groups on the same issue. To make such a treaty, all concerned must establish their own wisdom, integrity, stability, and dignity. This philosophy sets the mould for a sound foundation of truth and satisfies the respect and confidence needed to carry on a successful reputable transaction. These actions of inner confidence create the tests upon which we rely for making a valid decision. When others are standing in their truth, we can intuitively sense the right decision for both of us. This judgment has a survival essence attached to an inner feeling of truth. This thinking has a definite pattern that is part of indigenous teachings. The more stable one feels the more integrity one can exercise. It is this feeling that develops self-esteem. 'Self-esteem is truth supreme.'

The Role of the Elders

The role of the Elders is to help open the door to the person within.

The Elders act as role models for Native identity. They speak softly, listen quietly, reach out in a friendly manner, offer ideas when needed, make people feel comfortable, and use humour as 'good medicine.' An Elder does not give advice without first being asked. They would say: 'We don't know the circumstances under which you live, and for this reason we do not solve the problems.' They might say: 'If we had this problem we would sit alone and ask ourselves the question within. Because all our questions have the right answers within. However, if you want to have someone to talk to, Elders are ready to hear what you have to say. Whatever is said between us is never repeated to anyone else.'

It is appropriate to tell the Elder how long one wishes to confer. The Elder usually agrees and the friend excuses himself or herself and leaves. It is not appropriate to overstay the time allotted for the conference. The Elder always closes the conference by saying: 'Thank you for being ... all for one; one for all!'

People still visit Native Elders for various reasons. In most cases, the Elder will give the client a word to help them centre themselves. This word is private and never repeated to anyone else.

Heroes and Role Models

Definition of a hero: A man of noble qualities who performs brave deeds for others without self-praise or glory.

Definition of a Model: A person whose behaviour is honourable enough to be imitated.

Red Jacket is a historical Hero and Role Model of the Seneca Nation. During the cultural misunderstanding between the foreigners, the Senecas, Oneidas, Onondagas, and Cayugas were stripped of their Sacred Homeland and placed on reservations by strangers of their race. In spite of the wrong accounts recorded in the history books, that Red Jacket, Corn Planter, and Handsome Lake were enemies, these three men were friends united against the separation and control of the conquering people. These three men met frequently to assess the dying situation their people were suffering. However, Handsome Lake did not live long enough to achieve his part of the role. But he was an important part of Native society. We give honour to Handsome Lake for creating a code that is valid to this day.

Tricksters

The role of a trickster was to release stress and open an avenue for change. Thus, the reason for Elders and teachers supporting humour. Laughter offers a different point of view because it stretches thought patterns into a wider dimension of creative awareness. We must really enjoy the situation, remembering not to bring teasing in that can become distasteful. If a person is too serious, we must find out why they are so serious. Giving compliments to a serious person is a good way to make them smile.

'Laughter brushes the cobwebs from the mind.' Our Elders have said:

Laughter comes from the Light within.
Darkness hides joy where it's been
Smiles are gems of the inner self
Sparkling eyes release that SELF.

The above four lines can bring a smile to anyone's face especially when we say 'Sparkle your eyes.'

Recreation: The Lacrosse Game

Lacrosse is a well-known Native American game played by both men and women. Both teams have a stick to carry a small hard rubber ball. Lacrosse sticks are unique in design. They are made with a net strung to hold a ball. The handle is short and easily manoeuvred to catch a ball in the net. Lacrosse sticks are light in weight. Each end of a Lacrosse field has a goal, one for each team. To score, points are made by getting the ball into the net without the goalie stopping it. Years ago, anyone could play. Now there are a limited number on the team. It's a fast game with great teamwork. There are fouls for roughness that cause time out. Getting clobbered during the game is not unusual even though unfair hitting is a foul. No one can sit still during this game because of the excitement it arouses in the spectators. Box Lacrosse is played in an enclosed space. This is much safer for the spectators.

Following are other forms of recreation the Native Americans enjoyed. Snow snake was one. A narrow trench was dug with higher sides. A long narrow stick was thrown down this trench to see who sent it the greatest distance. This was a favourite winter sport.

All kinds of competitive sports were devised for physical endurance. The more creative it was, the more fun the participants had. There were many games played with a ball. Kick ball was a favourite sport. It is a note of interest that the Native people introduced the ball to the Europeans when they first came to this country. Remember, the circle was the shape of harmony. Any game based upon the circle brought people together as one body to share the gifts of Motherearth.

Music

Anything that makes a noise is music to someone's ears. It can even be coughing because it moves the body in a rhythm. Any item can become a musical instrument. Native people make whistles, drums, clappers, or anything that creates a sound especially if it is a part of nature.

Singing and dancing are an expression of one's personality. Actions often require strange sounds to enhance the dramatic meaning. Singing, clowning, mime, and plays were happy experiences for both young and old. Music was also used to elevate the energy from tragedy to joy to exert healing. Music was an appreciated expression for the talented. There were travelling acts that included talented families that were part of every celebration in the villages of long ago. Talented people often joined roving actors and musicians during the summer months to direct one's thoughts towards peace of mind.

Art

Native people encouraged the artistic expressions of their Nation. Art is an innate activity that requires a time and a place to develop this desire to share one's joy through entertainment. Every child was given encouragement to develop self-expression. One way was to give youngsters all kinds of projects to help them build a useful item or trinket to wear. These projects awakened the sleeping genius in the minds of these novice artists. Games were devised to awaken the creative ability of every woman, man, and child.

Dances brought 'good medicine' into the villages for seasonal activities. Ritual and ceremony held these artistic functions into a 'way of life' making social functions ways to grow into the feeling of wholeness. These activities bonded the people to Motherearth's survival rhythms. Laughter cleared the cobwebs from the mind to enrich unity as one body, one heart, one mind and one spirit.

Memorization: Honouring the Memory Bank

Messages were sent from place to place through a system of memorization. Every student memorized the wisdom they heard. Legends were memorized with the meanings added at the end of each legend. This system secured a cohesive energy within each legend. Thus the lesson within the legend remained unchanged.

People carried names they were responsible for, using human examples to reinforce the memory: such as, He who cares, *Honosdah*. She who listens, *Ghotonedah*; He who remembers, he sees; She who thinks, *Yenoday*; He who helps, *Hahjadagayhus*.

Colours had their meaning; Red is Faith; Yellow is Love; Blue is Intuition; Green is Will; Pink is Creativity; White is Benevolence; Purple is Healing; Orange is Touch; Grey is Taste; Brown is Scent; Rose is Sight; Black is Sound; Crystal is Wholeness.

Feathers had their specific meanings. Any feather represented lofty ideals. Feathers were the symbols of Love, messengers of Peace. The colours in the feathers were expressed in the above colours. Feathers also meant organized personality. How the person was organized was represented in the colours of the feathers. Thus, the reason for wearing colourful regalia.

Stone Reading: Cycles of Truth

Learn, honour, and know the Cycles of Truth, which are called mentors. At each mentor is a month. Look at the month of birth and place that month at the South. The month directly opposite the birth month is one's wisdom. The East is one's integrity. The South is the stability and the West is the dignity. The truth line goes from the wisdom to stability. The Earthpath is from integrity to dignity. This is the traditional chart. Therefore, a person born in June is a speaker and speaks through the gift of wisdom. The Earthpath is from March to September, integrity and dignity. This is the form from which all months are taken.

Select a small stone that has a feeling of comfort when held in the left hand. Give the stone to the reader, who places it on the Cycles of Truth chart. The marks on the stone tells a person about themselves, also the stones have colour that represents the Pathway of Peace. The circle is the shape of harmony. The centre is the vibrational core or the centre of our being. It is also our feeling and comfort centre. The vibrational core expands into Sacred Space and Sacred Space designates the months. The month of birth of each person indicates where is their gift of faith as they enter this Earthwalk. The lines that run from the stone to the monitors indicate the gifts and directions a person can take to accomplish these gifts. It is not wise to select more than one stone for this stone reading because the energy of the first stone is the most practical for this reading. This first stone should be placed in a small pouch and worn or carried by the individual because it is an extension of their energy connecting it to Motherearth.

Daily Routines

Every day was a happy day because there was something unusual occurring. 'Let's make this day special,' our Elders reminded us. We seek the energy of each day to accomplish four projects. Children were told to put them into a thought form. Listed are some of these ideas:

- Thank someone for what they have done.
- Find a place for an item that has no place of its own.
- Tell someone why you like them.
- Do something for yourself and feel good about it.
- Tell someone in the family you love them.
- Sit alone in a quiet place and thank the creatures and grass for being.

Each day there are daily routines that need to be done. Observe how being helpful can make life easier for everyone. Take on a daily responsibility to build self-respect. Listen to the surroundings. Feel that you have a part in the achievements of others.

'Sharing is caring.'

Energy/Ego

Native culture in the past was not as it is today. We like to look at what energy the ego used in those days.

We'll suggest that energy is power and the ego is how we use this power. In addition, let's use our psychic gifts to interpret the ego. Our Elders told us that the ego uses a motivation instinct to emerge from spirit into the physical form. Then energy allows us to change from spirit form to physical form in order to learn the lessons during our Earthwalk. Pure ego has no needs. It only has wants. An Elder recently said, 'Look at our ego as a vacuum.' To satisfy the ego, we fill its vacuum with energy. We can look at this empty space as one of our greatest teachers: OURSELVES.

Now, we can fill this empty space with thoughts and see the value of our teachings. This is where wisdom, integrity, stability, and dignity have their beginnings.

Self-identity replaces low self-esteem by knowing who we are and why we are here. Some people think the ego is a negative force that needs to be reckoned with like a naughty child. If we think this naughty child should sit in a corner, she or he will retaliate and grab onto the first thing that passes by. It is important to see our ego as a symbol of energy, growth, and opportunity. A good definition of the ego is the expression of our image, philosophy, compassion, and process that must be honoured and utilized to become productive. The ego is the striver. Guiding the ego takes us on a guided tour of self-growth while offering us positive direction for self-achievement. The ego directs our inner knowing to complete our mission through wisdom, integrity, and stability so that we leave this Earthwalk with dignity.

This is a Native American concept of the ego.

Energy

The first time energy was identified with an image, it introduced an ancient symbol called a circle. We learned that wisdom, integrity, stability, and dignity sit at the four directions on a circle known as the Shape of Harmony.

We sit in the South at stability, looking down and up the truth line to wisdom. Where we sit has a strong impact of energy in relation to where we sat and whom we sat next to. This was the way Native people dealt with energy.

Native people look at energy as a living Great Mystery. We cannot see the Great Mystery, we cannot identify it, but we can feel the Great Mystery within. The Great Mystery is in every place and in every manifestation (in a drum; in a stick), as a life-giving force. Because the Great Mystery is that kind of reflecting energy, it creates its own wholeness. This wholeness is being lost among the people of today.

This lost energy is still being manifested and we can do something to return it to its usefulness. Listening within recharges this energy stored in our withinness. Our withinness is called truth. Schools don't teach the truth withinness; families don't teach it; religions don't teach it. All teachings are outside. When we feel comfortable, we are feeling our truth within. Sit within our own circle and be grateful for our energy of truth within.

Work

Work is creativity. When we work, we are creating a flow of our energy.

Imagination and ambition define work. The more we work, the more we develop enthusiasm and ambition.

Clothing

Clothing keeps the heat out and the warm in. Foreigners brought cloth, we grew cotton and wove cloth from the cotton. Cloth was not new to Native Americans. European cloth was more easily obtained because they had material in bulk and it became 'trade cloth.'

Christianity and Spirituality

Native spirituality is connected to the heart and Earth. Foreign spirituality is connected to the head.

Prophecies

In the case of truth, some people feel the truth is inherited due to its inner feeling. If the feeling of truth is absent, people do not have the desire to question it. Changes that occurred have been brought down and passed on. Long ago, people made prophecies of how many children would be born in a particular area, if they would be boys or girls, and how long the area would be productive.

Time

Time was measured by the moon. Time, in relation to seasons, affected Native lifestyle. Weather was predicted by inner feelings through the physical body. Older people were sensitive to weather changes by saying, 'I can feel the changes in my bones.'

Language and Culture

Language identifies the truth and growth of a person. Language is an expression of one's culture. Language tunes in to the culture to describe situations. Language portrays the communication system of each culture. Language expressed names. Native children did not get assigned names until there was an appropriate time in their growth. A name was given by the Elders when the child expressed some particular characteristics that would earn a qualified name. Geographic locations earned their appropriate names. Buffalo, New York, as an example, received its name because long ago herds of buffalo once roamed the area.

Role of Dreams

Dreams were interpreted by the dreamer because if someone else interprets the dream, it will not suit the dreamer. Dreams are personal experiences. Dreams draw material from past experiences as well as dream of prophecy. Dreams are cleansing experiences.

Traditional Medicine

Medicines are sacred. Medicines have a specific energy that unites with body energy to release blocked cells. Medicines do not heal; they help the body heal. Medicine gives the body an opportunity to speed up the healing. Native people used herbal medicines. The medicine people practised sleep therapy, walking therapy, running therapy, and rest therapy. They told their patients that thinking strong and well was the 'best medicine.' These fine medicine people were both men and women. Usually where there was one, there was the other. They taught that male and female worked together because we have male and female energy within, the male energy is the protector and the female energy is the nourisher. A complete healing needs both working as one energy. When these energies are not in balance the patient can have a relapse.

Temperature has a great influence in exerting proper healing. To have the body temperature feel comfortable to the patient produces faster recovery from any disease.

In ancient times broken bones were the major health hazard. The patient needed to remain still in order for the bones to knit properly. Splints were used to keep the patient immobile.

Native healing depended upon ceremonies to enhance the time for recovery. These ceremonies were conducted as thanking ceremonies. The patients were asked to see themselves 'Healed and Whole.'

View of Territory

Native people did not feel ownership of land or homes, they felt the responsibility of preserving it through caring for it. They maintained the area for future use and productivity. Land was a shared, living entity. Years ago, tribes followed the animal paths between watering places. Today, the highways were once animal trails between watering sites.

Economics

Native people made various clothing items and set up trading posts. Food was the industry. The Native grew the staples: corn, beans, and squash. They hunted for the meat and smoked it for preservation. They dried all the vegetables and herbal remedies. They used all the parts of the large animals for hides, ceremonial items, and craft supplies.

Transportation

Horses were used after being introduced from Spain. Most transportation was by foot and boat. Boats were made from birch-bark. The rafts were made by lashing logs together. These canoes and rafts are used today.

Relations between First Nations

There was little competition between the Native people. Survival was the greatest issue, thus cooperation was the major focus. Trading was the greatest effort practised by all the nations. What one nation had was traded for what they needed.

Traditional Healers

There were definitely traditional healers but they did not heal anyone. The misunderstanding of medicine men or women is that they heal. All they do is help the person who comes to them to help themselves, by giving them what they need. If someone had headaches, that meant that something was clogging their system. Medications were given to clean and cleanse their systems, so the system could function in a whole way. The process of healing was to become whole.

Living on the Land

Regardless of what we have, automobiles and homes, the culture of today is exposed to the Earth, environment, meaning we are still connected to the land. Everything is still earth connected; it's just that we must honour this connection.

Education

Education has moved from the heart to the head. If it is heart connected, it must be truth connected and peace connected. That's where comfort comes in. If there is no comfort in education, then I think there is something lacking in the educational system.

The Native education system of the past recognizes that there must be Love, Truth, and Peace present, in all learning. People will recognize it as something that is wonderful for us to be involved in. Because everything we look at is teaching a lesson; a tree is teaching a lesson; grass is teaching a lesson, everything is teaching a lesson. We need to recognize that we are able to grasp that lesson if it is brought to us in an interesting way. When we can feel comfort we are part of its whole.

A reserve school has an opportunity to integrate the surrounding nature into the school system. Every school that has this particular environment will reflect nature. The city schools are reflecting sidewalks; they're not quite connected to the Earth, they are more connected to a physical feeling than to a spiritual feeling. There should be a balance of both to become whole.

Some Native people have attended residential schools and have been affected negatively, because the teachers were not Native. The teachers were generally of a different culture, thus, didn't have the same connection to the Earth. This is why Native people felt unfulfilled. The feelings were not there due to competition with grades; they did not tap into the real core of the individual who was there to learn.

Personal Balance

I can only speak for myself. When I left the reservation as a child I was placed into the homes of white families. Their lifestyle was entirely different from mine, yet my heritage was so ingrained in me that I knew I would never lose it. The lessons that were taught by other families were not compatible to mine, so I only took what I felt would reinforce my Indianness.

Many things have happened to Native people that were not compatible to their inner feelings, consequently they had to accept some of them and integrate some even though it felt uncomfortable. In other situations we did not conform, react, or deny.

Native people have been exposed to all kinds of religions. For example I have been baptized four times. I didn't say to the people that I had already been baptized. I said nothing, so they felt they were saving me, by baptizing me into something that would last my whole life. When I lived with a Catholic family, they were eager in having me baptized again; what difference did it make as long as it made them feel good? I complied with the rules and regulations that were set before me. It made the family more comfortable because I had to live with them and go to their church. 'Do what they expect of you while living in their home,' my Elders advised.

Warriors

Originally, the warriors were responsible for keeping peace and were called Peace Warriors. But when the dominant society looked at warriors as conflict, they immediately made a different definition of these people. They figured they were the ones who started the wars. The major focus of war today is that there will be peace, but in the meantime there is a lot of killing. For the Native people, it was not necessary to create killing because the environment was harsh enough as it was to survive.

Traditional Justice

Traditional forms of justice had worked well because they were based on truth. When people understood the meaning of truth based on an inner comfort; they felt comfortable when truth has been exercised. The minute we feel discomfort, we know that there is something wrong with truth, thus there is a lesson for us to learn. In the distant past, a person who committed a crime was taken to the centre of the village and publicly stripped of all their possessions and sent from the village with only what he or she wore. In a year's time they could return and bring gifts to the person or people they had committed the crime against.

Bridging the Gap with Other People

People from all over the world feel there is something lacking in their society. They want to know during all these years of destruction how the Native way of life, the Native stability, especially the dignity of the Native has survived. When a Native person is seen walking along the road, others can see their dignity because it stands out in the way they carry themselves, also the way they face life. Other people want to know what a Native person has that they don't have – we say that others lack a feeling of truth within. If a person doesn't have this feeling within, they do not feel comfortable. They are looking for something to happen that brings them comfort. The moment we enter this Earthwalk, our main desire is to seek comfort. We want to be warm and we want to be fed. Natives feel everyone seeks this comfort within.

Other cultures look for comfort in having a car, having a beautiful home, a lot of clothes, and people around them who can do things for them. That is their idea of comfort. When these comforts are gone, they don't know how to survive and some even die.

Native teachings and values can be shared. The people come to the reservation and find that there are things around us at all times that can provide a support system. Oftentimes they are blind to it. The greatest feeling is to stand up and feel tall and straight, by giving over to the strength that comes from within. So the whole difference is that the Native people function from within; that is where all their gifts are, and other cultures had to have something outside whereas a Native person will look at the outside things as adding to whatever comfort they have. Also being grateful for it is important and also to know that when it is not there, they still have comfort within.

Closing Remarks

I think that the greatest thing that is not addressed is that every person is different. Every person has time frequency that they need to understand within themselves and this time frequency helps them determine what kind of jobs they get into, what kind of environment they want to live in, how they dress, how they look at themselves, how they feel about their surroundings. I think the education system should look into that and they will find that all children's energy fluctuates from a very wide dimension of energy. I think if the education system of today would take a hard look at energy and know all perimeters that it has and to see where we stand like in that circle. The vibrational core is a feeling centre, that's where the energy is and we can use it to attain what we want out of life and how to understand who we are and why we are. We need to know all these things and I feel that in the past the Native people knew this. After being drawn into the dominant society and after a period of several generations, the Native person has come up with the same kind of background as everyone else. But I firmly believe that these are the lessons we have to learn.

We ended the Fourth World, and that came when all the planets were lined up and also when Jupiter was hit by a comet, so we have no control over that. But as Native people we understand what is happening and we understand that when that collision occurred suddenly the time frequency increased. So we planned to do something, and all of a sudden the situation has to become a reality, some of those fast-laid plans go down the drain because we have reached that reality, and that's the difference between the Fourth World and the Fifth World. No one knew about the different worlds, and so we started to talk about it. That's another thing, this culture knows nothing about what happened in the First and Second Worlds. All they knew, there was a flood and they didn't know it was the Third World.

In the First World, people communicated by sign language. They didn't use their mouths, however they communicated with the animal world, and the cohesiveness was far more refined. In the Second World, communication became more divided, the people of the Second World developed a feeling that they were different from the animals, and they could do things the animals couldn't. But they still depended on the plant world and the animal world for food, which we do today. The Third World was an expanded world of expertise, due to inventions that would enhance their capabilities. We built aeroplanes, automobiles, boats, buildings for human use and developed a mental process to increase the capabilities of what we had.

The Fourth World was a world of separation and control. Separate and control by the people is still being practised. Governments, schools, work, cities, and everything has a controlling system that sometimes prevents people from growing, by keeping them boxed in. We are just emerging from the Fourth World into the Fifth World. The Fifth World is the world of illumination. People are beginning to do what they were born to do. As the world progresses, people will be developing their own gifts and find that with these various gifts, they can share them for a while. But as we enter into the Fifth World, it will become very noisy because the noise is now beginning to increase. At the end of the Fifth World the sound barrier will be completely shattered. People will be completely deaf. Deafness will be the main disease of the Fifth World. Look at the world today, people are deaf or just not listening so they have to depend on their eyes and their noses and learn how they can communicate without speaking. Obviously, sign language will be a very prominent way of communication in this Fifth World.

The Sixth World is the world of revelation. The Sixth World will be a revelation and people will see that there are many wonderful experiences that can be enjoyed. It will reveal the wonderful gifts of all creatures, since only creatures know who they are. The animals have not changed. They don't need churches or governments to live. They can survive with all the gifts of Motherearth. They know how to survive. Humankind has become dependent on other people's expertise, and when it comes right down to hard facts, each person can survive, even if they just lie on the ground and eat grass.

Any person who looks within their environment will connect to the Earth. People will recognize that it's the Earth that is really the Mother. They will notice that Mother and Earth are one word – Motherearth. These teachings can help in developing a way of life.

Parenting: It Takes a Mother and Father to Become Good Parents

There is a place every parent occupies called Sacred Space. There is a Sacred Point of View that every member in the family must respect each other. There is a feeling every family member wishes to enjoy and that feeling is comfort. Every desire of achievement wants to satisfy that sense of comfort. Parents offer this space.

The home offers protection. Parents exemplify this protection by the way they speak to their children and to each other.

Everyone is born to become a parent
With inner gifts of a true chosen talent
Parents are the only ones who can make this choice
But the children are the ones who enrich their voice.

THE PEACEMAKER

We do not call him by his name
So Sacred are his teachings
And Hiawatha earned his fame
By helping with his preaching

He brought peace into the world
And truth began to unfurl
Love had healed the fragile race
When Peace entered its Sacred Place

We do not know when the Peacemaker was born

Some call it ancient history
We only know when hearts are torn
It's healed by the Great Mystery

The PEACEMAKER's Message

Sometime during the middle of the fourth world of separation and control, the PEACEMAKER entered the lifestyle of the Native Americans due to
their memory loss of Earth connection. Many times during the history of
Motherearth, this loss of memory has visited humankind. Memory identifies the Truth within as wisdom, integrity, stability, and dignity is for eternity. These characteristics of Love, Truth and Peace are the qualities of all
life. The PEACEMAKER had said, 'When I am needed, I will return.' The
PEACEMAKER has returned. He advises as follows:

1. *Faith*: Embrace a fertile mind that looks at present conditions (or situations) to see what is missing and needed.
2. *Love*: Envision councils that encourage discussions for establishing
   practical programs to satisfy basic wants and needs for growth.
3. *Intuition*: Co-create a way to live that envisions a form of rational justice for all the programs for healthy growth to make whole everyone's
   body, heart, mind, and spirit.
4. *Will*: Explore patterns already in the creative mind of being through
   open-minded discussions that inspire social and individual growth for
   transformation into a feeling of wholeness.
5. *Creativity*: The most important message is to build a home for protection, which will have a fire for warmth, a bed for comfort, and parents
   for the children. Thereafter, from this Longhouse each addition is an
   extension of the original home.
6. *Sharing*: The council fires shall continue to burn and be as unquench-
   able as Love, Truth, and Peace.
7. *Healing*: We bind ourselves together by taking hold of each one's
   hand so firmly and so strongly that if a tree should fall upon it, this
   bond would not break.
8. *Touch*: Peace is founded upon the sovereignty of a common law of
   Truth as statesmanship lies in the will for peace among *all* the people.
9. *Taste*: Our strength shall be united in Truth and our way, the way
   through wisdom as reason, integrity and stability through righteous-
   ness, and peace through dignity.
10. *Scent*: We court courage, patience, and honesty by thinking of 'advan-

tage' as the future welfare of all the people that extends seven generations into the future.

11. *Sight*: The portal of peace is *loving thoughts* and *truthful actions*.
12. *Hearing*: Health means soundness of body, heart, mind, and spirit.
    'ALL FOR ONE – ONE FOR ALL'
13. *Clarity*: Should these ever become an indifference to the League of
    Peace, call upon me. I am the PEACEMAKER and I will return. We
    called, and the PEACEMAKER has returned.

Special thanks to the following people for their expression of both their
physical and spiritual energy: Mark O'Connor, Rainbow Weaver, Linda F.
Smith, and Kathy Fife.

ERNEST BENEDICT (Mohawk)

Akwesasne, Ontario

'I would say when you search after truth, truth is that which you will find that is dependable and is of use to you.'

Ernie Benedict was born in Akwesasne in 1918. His traditional name is *Dwalygwonda*, which means 'goods gathered together' and he is Wolf Clan. Emily Faries interviewed Ernie Benedict at his home in Akwesasne in the fall of 1994. His wife, Florence, made baskets during the interview and helped by telling stories and remembering events in the community. Ernie and Florence have four children, and in 1994, nine grandchildren. Ernie Benedict received a bachelor of arts degree from St Lawrence University in 1940. He also started the North American Travelling College, which promoted Native cultures, and has taught in various places, including the Native Studies department at Trent University, where he received an Honorary Doctorate of Laws in 1994. He opened the conference on the Royal Commission of Aboriginal Peoples in Montreal, and has spoken at many gatherings across the country.

The interview with Ernie lasted three days, and is included here with very little editing. The life history portion is fascinating, and incredible stories and teachings are interlaced throughout the discussion. The use of words differs greatly from the other interviews, and reflects Ernie Benedict's way of speaking. Ideas and images flow from Ernie's speech, but he speaks tentatively, quietly. As he explains in this interview, he seems almost wary of the English language, and one must listen closely to divine his meanings. This is also true of the printed words that follow; one must read carefully and patiently to understand their teachings.

Life History

I was born about two miles away from where I'm sitting right now. And it's directly south, straight south from here, across the south side of the St Lawrence River and on the other side of the Racket River, which has its mouth emptying into the St Lawrence, directly opposite where we are sitting now. My birthplace was at Ogdensberg, New York. That's what was put on my birth certificate. It was on the St Regis Reservation. The Indian reserves in the United States are called reservations. Where the St Regis Reservation now lies, its headquarters, council hall, health centre, there was also a bookstore and Traditional Mohawk Nation has recently set up an office right there, close by the elected council. The Traditional Mohawk Nation has its office right at the site where I was born. There was at that place a log house, and my family, my father and mother had moved their family in, they were occupying part of the house.

At that time we used to have sometimes two families living in the same house with perhaps a wall between. I was born there, so they tell me. I lived there perhaps three or four years, three and a half maybe, and then my family moved to another location a mile away, out to a farm. That's where I spent my happy years between the ages of four to nine or ten years old. My family moved again, quite a few times, but during that time, also my grandmother who lived on the very outskirts of Ogdensberg, needed a bit of help. The young people to do little chores, so I was selected to go and help her out. So I stayed with her a number of years, five or six years perhaps. Then I moved back with my family, my grandmother moved in with the family within the village of Ogdensberg, and that's where she died.

From Ogdensberg, New York, I went to school at a small village about six miles away, the little village of Bombay. Since then, Bombay has withered away, the high school no longer exists there. I was there for two of my high school years. Then I decided to go to a larger high school that was at Massena, New York. I went to high school at Massena and graduated with the class of 1935. I went to a university a year after. Even though I had graduated from Massena High School, I went for another year. Because for one thing there were no jobs for me, it was still during the Depression years. I was physically pretty small for any kind of a job. I don't think I was strong enough for any kind of labour job [laughs].

So I decided I might as well go to college or in Canada it's university. The class that I graduated with from high school had a few Native students from this reservation. They had talked quite a bit about going on to university, and I guess we had others, a second cousin of mine, who also had his, part of his family was on Cornwall Island too. He went on to university in New York State and he had been a role model for some of the students. And his father before him had gotten quite a good college education at McGill University. And so there was quite a bit of interest among the students that I went with to high school. So some of them went on to various colleges, but most of them didn't get through, they quit. Since I had started, there was no sense in stopping [laughs], since I wasn't getting any bigger. I was told, when you get a diploma, that the world opens up, and you can pick your job anywhere. I found out it wasn't true either [laughs]. When I finished, maybe I did get jobs because of having gone to university. But they weren't high-paying jobs, nor were they long-term jobs, they were summer jobs. I got jobs in summer camps. As camp staff, I got to travel to West Virginia, then to Indiana.

Now the Indiana job was among the really high-fallutin kids, very upper-class place. It also came at the same time as the American peacetime draft, and since I was roaming and lived in the United States I was eligible for the draft in the United States. That's what I was doing in 1939 when the peacetime draft was instituted. The United States went to war in 1941. During that time I protested against the draft as applying to the Native people in the United States. I had gone to Indiana and had come back and practically within a few days was taken by the United States Marshal to go to jail. So I stayed for three months while I was waiting for a trial. The reason why I was there and the bail wasn't all that much, however I guess justices of the peace and the United States have an option of setting bail in a form of a lien against a piece of property and since nobody on the reservation could pledge a property, then there was nobody on the reservation that could put up my bail. It wasn't all that much. A hundred dollars or so! Then there was a hearing at which then the judge then set the bail at two hundred and fifty dollars, even that of course could not be put up by anyone on the reservation.

And so I think eventually a business in Fort Cobuton, which was another small village, a businessman there put up the bail and I came home for a short time, long enough so that I was then able to get a job as a labourer. Building what they call a defence plant, a factory. It still exists. The work was at Massena, New York, outside of Massena not far from the St Lawrence River. That plant still exists and has enlarged quite a bit there and I earned enough there to pay for the lawyers for the next stage in the actual trial, which was to begin.

So while I was waiting for the trial, war was declared with Japan and I went and so I thought, the United States is at war so there's no reason for my protest of the peacetime draft. And so I allowed myself to be conscripted. There was something that I did gain from that, one my conscience was clear and I did not allow myself to be conscripted by the United States with which we had a kind of a treaty I think. Yes there was a treaty saying that if the United States were to go to war that the Iroquois were bound to help them out and so up to that time they were supposed be peace and so now that the war had been declared and I felt sort of that I should go and I gained a little bit in that in registering they gave me a number that corresponded to a volunteer. Rather than a conscripted one. So they could not claim that I was drafted. That was my big purpose there.

That also goes back to a promise that George Washington was to have made and it was in the teaching or the traditions of the people that he would never require the Iroquois to do anything that he would recognize their independence and so I felt pretty comfortable there as a volunteer. That was not more than one year after I had been what they call drafted, and so then I was taken down into New Jersey. I went to a school at Fort Momoth and there I learned radio repair and they sent me out to California, from there to Australia and from there, there was a need for someone or in fact I was briefly up to New Guinea and they and I was supposed to be a replacement for somebody that had become a casualty. It wasn't a very happy trip up to New Guinea. Meanwhile the whole unit was brought back to Australia but up in New Guinea I got sick for a while and I had to come back and join them afterwards, back in Australia. A few months later then we went up to New Guinea and kept going and there were various landings and there are engagements with the enemy and so finally we moved up into the Philippines, most of the time at Mindanao in the city of Zambowanga. From there I came back to the United States and was discharged out of Fort Dix, New Jersey, so that was the end of my army career. That was the end of the war.

During the war my grandparents had died and my father had come and had been given the old homestead here on Cornwall Island. So when I was discharged and came back I was met by my father who brought me back to the old homestead here which I used to visit when I was a child, and it is the place we are in right now. And so I stayed for a while here and helped out my father, he was steelworking at the aluminum factory in Massena but soon quit his job there, I guess he was old enough. He was also doing fishing out on the river, sturgeon fishing. I helped out that for a while then the Indian agent came and said come and teach a class in St Regis Village. Now to get to St Regis Village from the house here I would need to travel somewhere around eight miles by the road and about three miles by boat. So it was quite a ways away and I could not commute every day so I rented a place down there and so the pay one hundred dollars a month, this was in 1945, and my rent came to about eighty-five dollars a month. Out of the hundred dollars the government took five dollars for something called superannuation. Something like social security maybe, I don't know back in those days. It was not part of the regular social security plan I don't think.

So I had sometimes at least ten dollars a month to eat on and to buy my winter clothing and so on. My discharge money there went that way and so at the end of the year of working for the government I had used up all savings. So I went back down to our road building job as a labourer and I made a lot more money than I did working for the government [laughs]. Finally at the end of the summer of working as a labourer on the road I had toughened up quite a bit so that when a friend who was doing masonry work building cellars mostly using cement blocks and building chimneys and all, needed a partner and I went and worked with him and so some buildings that are still around Massena are the work of my partner and I. So from that I went into work at the Alcan plant and worked there for about seven years perhaps then they were having a layoff but at the same time they were having a layoff there was a Reynolds Metal plant which had just begun and so I came over and worked at building it as an electrician and then when the plant opened up I worked there for eight years.

Meanwhile my family was growing and I had tried to do some farming here, eventually settled on raising cattle, beef cattle. Had some nice white faces, Herefords, not very many because the farm was only sixty acres, and considerably smaller now because my kids have taken three to four acres each. However the farm did not make any money and the beef cattle were eventually affected by the pollution that especially the Reynolds plant was putting up in the air. The pollution was not just chemicals like fluoride, but they were also sending clouds of dust and the dust was very abrasive and that wore the teeth of the cows quite a bit. Now somehow or other there may have been some other bits of pollution because the cows were having calving problems and one spring the calves and the cows were so much affected they were weakened, so I sold the entire herd that year and decided that I would never be able to make a living from or make any profit from the herd except the beef was very good [laughs]. Anyways, that was my experience with the farming.

During that time also there I did get interested in serving on the, on what is called the band council, and we still had the Indian agents in charge but the council was getting a little bit more stronger more self-assertive, this would be perhaps in early '50s, and at that time also was St Lawrence Seaway was making announcements that they were, in fact they did start in 1954, and since I was serving on the council then I saw the maneuvering that they were doing to get permission to use not only the river but to raise the levels of water because of the dam that was put across the St Lawrence. And the bridges had to be replaced and new bridges and quite a bit of the land was expropriated and the council put up the best kind of self-defence that we could, but much of it was what you call dirty dealing by certain Seaway authorities and so we were very much at a disadvantage. But we did the best we could to save some properties and to get the best deals possible for the people. We just couldn't think of every-thing.

So also at that time the Seaway was changing lots of things, the way the river was flowing, they were doing dredging, and the currents were changing so we didn't know the river anymore, and it became clouded with silt and dirt and so on and it hasn't cleared up even to this day. At that time education was one of our big concerns and I think we were in the mid '50s or so. The government or Indian Affairs invented a new the-ory of education called integration whereby the children would no longer be educated on the reserve and would be taken out to be inte-grated in the White population. They said, 'Well you have to deal with them sometime so we might as well get started early and then you would know.' That way also the government would not have to rebuild more schools on the reserves, they didn't want to do that. For some reason they didn't want to spend money on the reserves, they would rather spend it outside the reserves and so when some of the students were taken to Cornwall for schooling, well Cornwall had to build more rooms onto the schools. So the government, the Indian Affairs were paying for that they could have put that onto the schools on the reserve but they didn't. So in a very short time they, because of the Seaway the city of Cornwall was growing, their population was growing and pretty soon they didn't have enough room for our students there so the Indian Affairs had to improve the schools on the reserve and built new schools. But meanwhile we had to have the experience of a few years in the Cornwall school system and we didn't like it. I don't know if there was any benefit that was derived from that experience.

Well, let's see, we're still talking about me, aren't we [laughs]. I was in the council at that time and I was working at Reynolds Metal Company just across the river on the American side. It is directly opposite of the western end of Cornwall Island, and can easily be seen from the international bridge. So it was very convenient, it wasn't very far to go to work and of course I was given, it was a good job with an electrician's pay. And there were good working conditions, I really enjoyed it, but eventually I was put in one place where I was exposed to some dangers and I have some scars to show for that. Anyway, I thought that because of getting older, that I was becoming more accident prone. Well, there was so many things that could harm somebody there in the factory like that.

So I was thinking a little bit about how much longer I would have to stay there whether perhaps I should find some other job somewhere. Of course you have been to Trent University. You know about the name Charlie Wenjack.* That was in the newspaper, I read his name and story and that was the big influence at that time for me. I said, 'What am I doing here? There are kids that are the same age as my kids and they need some changes in their life.' And again there was another influence at the same time there was a man here who had been hired as a community development officer by the Indian Affairs. And the Indian Affairs bureaucrats thought that community development was of course an economic development. That's what they thought and this young man that came had other ideas and said that people must be given encouragement to think for themselves, to plan for themselves, to be courageous. And that was part of his program of encouraging people here whenever they wanted, he would say, 'Okay I'll help you out as much as possible with all my abilities.'

And he was researching history because that's what the people said,

---

*Charlie Wenjack was an Ojibway youth who died on his way home after running away from a residential school in the 1960s. The main lecture theatre at Trent University is named after him.

'We want to find out where we have properties still out there, claims areas.' And so he dug into the archives and said, 'Yes, you have very good claims here, here, here, here, and here and so on.' And so the people very much had a certain goal there and researched these things and the Indian Affairs didn't like that. And they fired the man, but then they fired him at the same time that there was a program in the government started by the prime minister. Prime Minister Pierre Trudeau, who started the program called the Company of Young Canadians. And so our community developer just moved into that one and kept on going there, stayed here for a while and was making a real big difference in the self-confidence in the people here.

Now, this was at the same time that I was wondering what could be done about the situation of that was exposed by the Charlie Wenjack story. Somebody had some conferences about it there amongst the neighbourhood and we thought well let's do something, why not revise the whole attitude of the education system. We are not to be anymore like empty bags that need to filled by the White man, let's decide what it is that we want to know and find out what that is, let's find out what skills we need to practise and so on. Well, let's make the education system work for us, not us for the education system. So then we had to think about it for somewhere around two years and we were thinking about one plan after another and writing down reports. This happened in the mid sixties.

During this time also there, a local agency was based in Cornwall, then he had an office over there, in the government buildings. Then they moved farther away, about a hundred miles away, to Kingston, then I think they went to Peterborough. And I think it was a general movement among the reserves to be more and more independent. So there was a time when the people were really asserting themselves, more and more. And this one about the education was the one that occupied a lot of my time. Eventually, in 1966 I quit at the Reynolds plant and took a job with the Company of Young Canadians. They didn't pay very much but it was full-time and it involved my wife, and even the kids were halfway involved in this Company of Young Canadians. We set up an office right in my back yard and volunteers of the Company of Young Canadians came here for instruction. And they did a little, and we planned this new idea in education which we called the Travelling College.

Most of the time we were trying to raise money for it, writing letters. We were looking around for ideas, mostly local people, so an idea came, if our people are so isolated, and they were at that time, where we didn't know very much what our neighbour reserves were doing, and only the people that came from them and travelled to the city, or something, and met up with others, then they would talk there. But the reserves, communities, were pretty much isolated from one another. So in order to break that down we'd have to go from one to another, and so that's where the idea of the Travelling College began. We'll call it a college because college means that we're looking for a better education, bigger, or more than what's available. Our ceremonies very often mention putting our minds together. And so that's generally the basic idea that we have.

They talked about the idea of travelling. 'How do we travel?' Well, you have to have a whole university, pick it up and put it in trucks and go to various reserves. Well, that was one idea. Eventually one of the volunteers said smaller vehicles are better and we can depend on them upon the people that would be in the vehicles would provide knowledge and inspiration and skills or whatever they needed. And they would be able to stop for short times and then go other places. If there's some more work needed at the first place, well they could always come back or another unit could come in. We need lots of communication though. So that's how we settled, but even small units also needed lots of money and of course the government agencies weren't too receptive about funding the whole new experiment and especially in Native education.

So we had to do our money-raising ourselves and after these people went their separate ways, well, we were left to do all the work of trying to get somebody to donate some money to this cause. Well that was hard, it's hard to convince people to part with their money. Eventually, we were able to put together about thirteen thousand dollars and were able to buy a Volkswagen van, one Volkswagen van. So all the ideas had to be scaled down to one little thing, but, again at that time, it was 1970, there were very few, or '69 actually, and there were really very few books of any worth with the Native point of view and very few books about Native people, generally. So whatever we found we put together. We built bookshelves in the Volkswagen van. At that time the National Film Board was training a film crew and one of the people in that film was Willie Dunn, the singer, he had already shown lots of talent in composing songs. Then there was Noel Star Blanket, who was a filmmaker, and our own man Mitchell, and there was a man, his last name was Daniels, who told us about the Native films that were in the National Film Board film library, perhaps we could obtain copies, loans, and so that's what we did. They even lent us a projector and a few other little items. We loaded that onto the van.

Some of these young people, Company of Young Canadians, they would volunteer, they were here and they wanted to go along and so some of us toured Ontario. We went to almost every reserve in Southern Ontario even as far as Thunder Bay and we visited and of course gathered as much information as we could from various reserves and while we were going along, we took part in Powwows and if there was no Powwow then we would put it on ourselves. One thing that stays in my mind is going up to Pic Mobert where a little party was going on in a school, of course it was a one-room school, small reserve, and so when we offered to put on our little program, I gave a speech. Then Dicky [laughing] was one of our volunteers and he could sing the Iroquois songs and played the Iroquois water drum. So we sang and danced there, the Indian dance in a place where they haven't had an actual Indian dance for a whole, at least a generation, perhaps more than that.

And then so many of the young people that were there had never seen or taken part in an Indian dance and they did it that night, that was a big thing. I have since heard that Pic Mobert has their own drum and they even have their own Powwow, beautiful. They've taken control of a lot of their own affairs. At the time that we were there, the entire reserve measured one-half mile in each direction or a half mile square set in the middle of the bush. Not a tree on that half mile square, because it had been used long ago for fire wood, and fuel for the winter had to be brought in by tank truck through this little small roadway going in there. They were in the middle of the bush. They were very much detached from the bush, perhaps some of the people there still did a bit of hunting, but had lost very much of their culture and with that much of their Spirit. And I like to think that maybe we brought a little bit of change in their attitude back to them.

So that is what we were doing here, and there at Garden River near Sault Ste Marie we also showed pictures there and it was an afternoon thing. We did do some demonstrating of songs and dances with the people. And since that time, Native values have grown there also, at this Garden River and also at Nipissing Reserve, near North Bay. Anyway, there was a very good response from many places. And it was a really great experience to go around to all those places. There was a little bit of a down side, in that I was driving this van and I was doing all the driving because all these young people did not have driver's licences. They didn't dare drive without a licence because it would have ruined everything. But anyway, when I was doing all that driving myself I developed a really bad backache. During that one summer, during really heavy activity, I met up with a professor of Trent University, Dr Kenneth Kidd, and he said, 'You should come to Trent University as a member of the faculty. We are making plans to turn Native Studies from an institute to a department, and we will need to enlarge our staff.' And so I said, 'Okay, we are running short of money on this project, so I will consider your offer, and be a member of your staff.' So, in September, I went to check in.

It was on my way there, to check in at Garden River, I had a very bad spasm in my back, it really hurt. So we did build a little fire down on the beach and the heat from it I got really, warmed it back up, so we came down the rest of the way down to Peterborough. And just as I came into the Admissions Office, that spasm hit me again, I folded up, right down there on the floor. Dr Kidd came by, and he arranged for me to be brought home [laughs]. But on a mattress in a van. So after I got back home and got ready and I went back to Trent at the regular time the semester began and luckily I was able to get a room there and I would be able to come back on a weekly basis, on weekends. And I was there for two years, then I was offered at home a job as a counsellor for Post Secondary School and so I worked at that for two years. Then came an offer as a faculty member at Manitou College and I was there for two and a half years. Manitou College was in Quebec. It was up in the Mount Laurier region of Quebec, sort of north-east of Ottawa.

That was a big experience there because of the student body and almost entirely Native, there were a few that were non-Native there, but very few. Then there were from various different tribes, some from the James Bay region, and even a small group from the Inuit country. Many from all across Northern Quebec, Innu people, Labrador from around Northwest River, the North Shore of the St Lawrence. There were about two hundred to two hundred and fifty students, they all lived there as well. Anyway, they were from every place you could imagine, now one thing that, there were a few things that distinguished them I think. They were from extremes, as I was able to judge. Some were extremely bright, extremely competent, with high standards, and then there were some that were just a jump away from the sheriff [laughs]. One reason for that, I think, was that those with a very high ideal or high regard for their own Native heritage they picked that because they said Indians are there, Native peoples, Native student bodies, Native venture, lots of Native staff people, teachers. That's what we want, they thought. Then there were some others that were referred there by their counsellors, post-secondary counsellors, because they were pretty risky candidates for regular university.

Some were drunks, some were pretty involved in thievery, I guess, things, I guess when you start at an early age it gets to be a habit with them and so they were sent up there because it would be out of the way.

They would not be young, so they sent them up there and they did come with all their very difficult, very bad attitudes, some of them. But during the time they were there and associating with those that had all that talent and that encouragement from people there as to what could be done with what they had. I mean quick turn-around, and came out really good. Some had problems right to the end of course, but then it was a very short time that the college was in existence. The reason for closing it up, they had, was that it was running into too big of a debt, but we found out later that any debt that had been incurred was easily erased if the money that was promised had come in, but I think that somebody was trying to make the college look bad, they wanted the student body to look bad and thereby make all Indians look bad, and they did. However the student body of course, quite a few of them, they were so loyal to the school itself and to the principle of the school that nothing fazed them there. Those people that were there would probably praise the thing to the skies. And their only regrets that were there was that it had to close. They didn't even get a chance. So that was that.

So that's when I came home. I got involved a little bit more with the council politics. That was a very short time. Then there was a proposal from the American side at the time, a group of nurses, Native nurses, had come together and said, 'We would like to have a community health facility right on the reserve,' reservation on the American side it was. So they had a committee set up and they selected me as chairman of that committee. So we studied and learned all we could on how we could run the health facility and we had a staff, a group that got a bit of money just to plan, just to make the plans, met with the people, we met with government people and took training sessions. And finally, we got that medical facility approved and they began as a rather small way as part of the American Tribal Council, they had a building that was going to be a library so they put it on the upstairs of that library, they made that health facility there, and moved the library downstairs or someplace. Anyways, it was a start and now they have a building, a regular building just for the health program. Dental and well the whole thing there as within that one building specially built for it. Then of course, the Canadian side also wanted their own, but I wasn't a part of that.

Anyway, I was then invited by the National Indian Brotherhood to come up to Ottawa to give them some spiritual direction and so I was up there as a resident Elder. That would be about in 1975, six or seven years there. During that time the Elders were, we began to be pretty active. I know that since the last three or so presidents of the, the National Chiefs have not given as much recognition to the Elders as they were doing in those very pleasant years of, especially of the time of Noel Star Blanket. And of course the highlight did come with the Brotherhood's lobbying effort in London, England. Now, so I spent a few days there in London getting to know all those people there. And the ordinary history, well that's available every other place there. We came back fairly well, disappointed that since the queen was not available and for a direct meeting and that the Parliament of England was not going to make a pronouncement on the treaties that were involved in that.

However, we did meet, and had some effect on the present Earl Grey and one other member of Parliament, a Labour member I believe, named George, his last name is George, both of whom came and toured throughout Canada, within the next years, so let's see now. I don't think that it was an entirely wasted effort to go into England at that time, and the Native people then began talking of Nationhood and so the idea of the First Nations was born then and the idea of more and more sovereignty, of taking over the ownership of much of our own racehorses [laughs] and our own future. Much of that was given the law a big boost by that trip to England, so rather than get our help from outside, we found it in ourselves and I think it is much better.

I think that was 1984 when I left the AFN (Assembly of First Nations), up to that time there was an effort by Chief Ahenakew I think to take a look at the structure of the AFN to see if it could be more responsive to the needs of the people across the country. At that time some of those in the Prairie Provinces had left, there were some that were thinking about leaving and so there were some bits of dissension. And so they were going to revise the structure of the AFN. But I did give my report to a meeting, the next annual meeting, and then I was not and then of course since I had left there was no need for me to stay anymore. I had no more contract with them so I came home and I was never asked to go back. This I think was 1984. But while we were, while I was with them, I think it was in 1982, at the annual meeting when the Elders proposed that our big concern would be the natural environment around us. Then that we should make a big effort to deal with it, to make recommendations to study, to make recommendations to take some, you know, to take some kind of leading role in the saving and perhaps helping our environment. We were going to have a great big environmental conference sometime later in the 1980s. It never came about. And from time to time some one or another of the AFN leaders would dig up this old resolution and bring it back out and say, 'Hey, how come nothing has been done?' and so nothing continues to be done, except some certain projects, they have one or two projects going about having to do with the environment, but nothing with the kind of clout that was asked for by the Elders. So now I came home and so really tired and so I got invited out quite a lot and of course while you have been here of course I got an invitation by two phone calls. So that's how things have been.

Another project that I have been spending quite a lot of time with is the FNTI, First Nations Technical Institute. Their staff is mostly Tyandenagah people. The other directors are Tyandenagah people, their staff are some Native, mixed-Native, and non-Native university people. And we've been working mostly with social workers that already are working on reserves. And so we're training them to do the job that they are already doing. It encourages their special abilities and to give recognition of their accomplishments. And if they have some needs as far as information or skill then we arrange to provide that for them. Meanwhile everything we try to do is use the Native culture in the instruction and in the content and the program itself. Some of the writings that are coming out now are, I think, are very good. One book especially that impressed me, with the staff, it's called *Dancing with a Ghost*, and that's one that we use a lot and all the praise, he [Rupert Ross] recognizes that the Native people, the Native culture, is different.

Rupert Ross concluded that the potential of the Native culture has not been fully explored as it should be and it would be useful to know all those elements of Native thinking, spirituality, and other gifts. Well, he's interested in mostly law and the justice system as it applies to Native people. He thinks that there should be more recognition of the special needs and attitudes and special gifts that Indians have. We at FNTI we are also on the lookout for things like that and apply them as much as possible. We've had some pretty good compliments and feedback on those things. Unfortunately I'm reaching the age when I guess I'll be, what is it, senility, as I get forgetful, absentminded, and just plain blundering, well that's now when these things are opening up [laughs]. I am a little bit disappointed. Everything is starting to look good now and I'm not participating anymore like I should.

Creation Stories

These stories came from the teachers from other reserves. They were the ones that remembered, they told us the story of the Sky Woman and the people of the sky world who apparently were the only people there was at that time and probably were a super-race of people. They weren't very clear as to whether the one that we call the Creator in our days was in that sky world and frankly they don't mention it and so I've never asked. Did you want to hear that story?

It's been a long time since I heard it last and I'll probably leave out very important parts of it but generally the story is that in that sky world, which was kind of sealed off from the world underneath. The world underneath was just a large body of water, all ocean, and the sky arched above, and above that was where these people lived, who had lived there forever. Now there is a story among them they had a ruler, they called him the old man or sometimes they have a name for him, *Henook,* I don't know what it means. And he had a daughter and they lived together in one house beside a tree. Which was a very special tree, it had very very bright flowers always growing on it, very bright, and it gave light to all that world up there. The daughter, however, he was watching his daughter very closely, he didn't want her to get away, but one time she did get away and one story is that she was then impregnated by a Spirit creature that was sometimes called the West Wind, *Enagah.*

The girl then told her father and he became very angry, but not necessarily at her, he was just angry. He pulled up the great beautiful bright tree with the bright flowers and threw it down on the celestial ground up there, the heavenly ground, and it still shone bright but it was there laying down, the girls came over to look and wondered about the tree laying there, and suddenly found their selves falling through the hole that the tree had made when it was pulled up, when she fell through in the hole, the hole had gone all the way through the crust of heaven and made a hole in the sky and she was falling through. She had made a grab going down, at the earth in all direction there, and came in her hands she had brought Strawberries and the other hand Tobacco and she came sailing down through, in this ocean below there were animals and water creatures and water birds. The birds looked up and saw her falling down through, and when the council among them saw as to what was happening, they flew up and intercepted her fall and brought her down very slowly. Meanwhile the animals had counselled together and they had gone down to the bottom of the ocean and had brought up, tried to bring up a piece of ocean bottom, but only the muskrat was successful and as he floated up dead he had in his paw a bit of dirt from the bottom on the ocean which he put on the back of the great sea turtle. The sea turtle began growing, the earth began growing and it became the continent, floating on the water. So then the Sky Woman was able to land upon this newly created earth, her first thought was to have something growing about her and so she planted the Strawberries and the Tobacco and they grew. They are called the heavenly gifts.

Then there are two kind of stories, one says that she gave birth to a daughter who grew up and again was impregnated by another Spirit and gave birth to twins, boys. The other story is she herself gave birth to the twins. One was sometimes called the left-handed twin with some other stories, and then sometimes one would call evil minded and good minded but the words in the Mohawk are not that way they call them the *Taleywondo*, holder of the heaven, supposedly the good one, and the *Saweskadow. Saweskadow* means more like no good, no account, not necessarily bad, but just not of any use. But both of them had these magical qualities, so they went about creating things and the good-minded one created humans, and we don't have any story as to creating just one, he just created humans. I don't know perhaps there are some of the old traditions talking about other, how the humans came in. The stories I know are just that guy who created humans and all natural things around, the grass and the trees, flowers and vegetables, the rivers even and lakes and there's *Saweskadow* however come along with you and if you would try to make a river and he would have only rapids and maybe waterfalls and things like that for the river so you couldn't, it wasn't really practical to do any travelling along that river. *Taleywondo*, with a good minds would create a nice flower and *Saweskadow* would put the barbs on it or make it poisonous or something 'cause he couldn't do things right and so there's all those things there that he just wasn't up to creating.

Eventually though that they, the two, they just keep out of each other's way, they just had to fight, in the fighting the *Saweskadow* was defeated but, so he was given charge of nighttime and the other one was in charge of the daytime and all the good things around. But *Saweskadow* was always coming back into the daytime and messing things up every place he'd come. So that's, that's the spiritual creatures. Then, I guess that's pretty much as far as that creation story goes, it comes to those two actually were the two Creators, but they were the ones that did all that work of putting the things on but at the same time the Creator that is worshipped is not those two, we don't think. *Taleywondo* doesn't seem to have the kind of characteristics that we put to them as recognize as the Creator of all things. So there must, there's another figure, another figure somewhere there in the background.

Migrations

Well, of course the Ojibwe have theirs of, beginning, their stories began
on the east coast somewhere and then coming up towards the West. The
Iroquois have sort of a story, we used to be very very vague about having
coming from the Southwest. Now we look at a map and it looks possible
that they had, sometime or another, had been on the great plains and
they had come up the Mississippi River up to the Ohio River and up followed the Ohio River up close to the Great Lakes, some of them went
north of the Great Lakes, became the Hurons, some stayed on the south
side and came into what is known as New York State and then divided up
to five different Nations, they are all related, their languages are all the
same, we just stretched out, what is now New York State. And others sort
of broke off, they all have names that are somewhat similar to the Five
Nations. There's Suskawneks down in Pennsylvania and some in Mary-
land and then below that there are the Cherokees and the Tuscaroras,
and I think there may be other Nations down there, small groups that
were also offshoots from the main body of Iroquois.

Well in historical times, in colonial times the Tuscaroras got into some
fights with the White European settlers and they fled up through the
mountains and then came up and joined the Five Nations and became
the sixth Nation, their language, you could find lots of words in there that
were, that were like the rest of the Iroquois, but lots of their expressions
are really way out there, where you can't understand them at all.

Important Aspects of Traditions

We are, of course, descendants of the Aboriginal people of the country.
There is some purpose in mind and I think that the Creator had some
plan in mind when he placed us here on this continent, and the ancestors
said we are supposed to be here to take care of this continent. The continent we figure is our mother and fulfils all the attributes of a mother. A
loving mother at that. So, if there is a mother and we are her children
then we have certain privileges and lots of responsibility to take care of
our mother. And so that's what we are here for. And I think that's some of
the things we can do much better than any people whose roots are in a
different continent. They can go and take care of their mother, where
their mother is. But we don't want them messing around with our mother
[laughs].

That is something we have to remember. Not only is it a responsibility, but it is a kind of privilege, which means that we, now that we recognize our responsibilities to our mother, we also have to have those, some tools, some benefits, some real gifts from our mother to use for fulfilling our responsibilities. Now, what are those gifts? I think there are a lot of material things that we have been cheated out of, and that should have been ours, but somehow we have lost that so now it is the newcomers who are now taking possession of all the material things. And then telling us that they will give us a little bit of that if we stay good in their eyes. Now, that should not be enough, that we should have not only those privileges that are allowed to us but we should also have some rights, what do they call it, prior possession? Well, so we may have those rights but we can't enforce them, we don't have the force. There has been various proposals whereby we could get force. Now I don't think we should. For one we proposed us to get some control over what we were dispossessed of is by, we could get some force or strength by joining them and so that means that we would then be able to use whatever privileges they have, like voting is one, all kinds of other things, like paying some kind of taxes, would give us some privileges, or some claim to those things. But I don't think that is necessarily so.

Now, if we were to use those privileges that they will allow us to have then it would also mean that we would be, have become a part of them, which means that we would become accomplices. So if we don't like what they are doing, if we think that they are thieves, villains, then we are joining them, we would also become that too. And we would be thieves of our own resources. How can that be? It just contradicts itself right there. Sometimes they get mad at us, or scoff at our efforts, we say, 'We own all the land, you took it from us,' then they say, 'Well, you get all these benefits, free education, free medicare, and all these other things, and getting welfare,' but again we are still the victims and if we understand that we are okay. Even if we are going to be receivers, all these other benefits to us, we are still, we still consider ourselves the victims. But when we join them then we are helping to, we are helping these to take away, we have been asking only for little bits of stuff, education, welfare, that's only small stuff compared to what they have, behind their walls. It's really little enough, and if we are asking for it, begging for it, to keep ourselves going then that's okay. But when we move over to their side, then we are in possession of all that loot that has been stolen from us, or our forefathers, then we would be put in a position of stealing from our own parents and grandparents. I don't think that's right, I don't think that's what we want. Okay, that's one little point of view.

The first part of our culture is our appreciation of life and all of the good things that are still surrounding us our, again, Mother Earth, of course, and all of the products of the earth and that's some of the things we enjoy, everybody enjoys, the environment around us and also there are some certain things. I believe that we are more spiritual than, as a people, as a Nation than anybody else. And as such we are, I think, in a very fortunate position, we can claim that relationship as a part of our family relationship. Now there's some other things also, because of maybe they're all related. I think that, naturally we are more honest, and I think we are also more willing to share, which means also that we recognize that all the good things we enjoy come from the one Creator. This is something that we recognize naturally without having to have it taught or drilled into us. We believe also, and much more likely to believe that we should be able to sacrifice ourselves for others, well that's part of that sharing, I think generosity they call it, which is a little bit different than the White men define as generosity. Generosity to him means something that you have enough of and, then you can give it somebody that you favour, that you have a certain power of giving and withholding that gift. I don't think that we recognize that, I think that when we give it is a full gift with no strings attached, we don't recognize that we could withhold it. Now that, I think is a very fundamental difference.

Using the Past Today

Of course our past is important. One thing is that throughout the world and it is the world that is recently called the western civilization, of course that is the wrong name for it. But it's something that has caught on. There are an awful lot of privileged people that have contributed, but actually use a lot more than their share of food, clothing, shelter that the biggest part of the world needs to keep themselves going. And we're still sitting on it and hogging it even though we know the need is still out there. And it's showing up more and more, and of course the big thing right now is Rwanda, now it's spreading over to Zaire, and while even into the northern part of South Africa, a great big part of Africa has really been in shambles. Now why is it? There are a lot of reasons been proposed as to why it's happening. Obviously they don't have anything. How come they don't have anything? Where the country has rain forests, and all those riches that go with the rain forests. Well, because the people that have lots of money have been buying up all this and just shipping it out and so they're sitting on top of a lot of it. And the people over there that actually owned it for generations don't have any use, don't have the use of it. So they keep cutting it away, and cutting it away and shipping it out, more and more just to keep living. Well, there's got to be an end to that too, so the people, the world today is really building up a big catastrophe for themselves. Somebody is going to be figuring it out pretty soon and they're going to begin to take back what is theirs, at least enough to live on. Anyway, I think that kind of responsibility is more natural to Native people, I've never found anywhere on the continent where our Native people have been taking things away from somebody else and holding on to it just for spite.

Traditional Birthing

I've heard of some, and of course, they were in the neighbourhood, I think in my own family my grandmother was one in charge. The younger woman would learn from the older woman. There were some where you had to have somebody with a little bit more experience, or courage to do the officiating there and whatever was necessary.

Traditional Dwellings

Well, a long long time ago, traditions are, there are two types of stories that were told, one is that there were villages, people were concentrated in villages, sometimes with some kind of stockade or wall around, and houses inside, these were longhouses with framework and big pieces of bark on it, there was bark on the outside in two layers and in the inside there'd be a lot of furs, skins, and corn, corn husk mats laying around on the floor or in the beds. Then there was also these smaller parties, sometimes hunting parties, sometimes there was an institution, Luondusaloon, where a family group would go away from the village, by themselves to a deep part of the forest and set up a kind of hunting, trapping location there. They would build a single family building sometimes out of bark, sometimes out of leafy boughs, evergreen boughs.

There was a story about the Spirit of the cold, icy cold, he would come to visit, they were out this one family, one family dwellings, lots of adventure out there. There was one there where the Spirit came in and sat by the fire, shivering, they didn't know he was a Spirit or was a person, he complained about being cold, so they built up the fire and kept him warm. It was in the fall, while this fellow was building his house as warm as he could, especially with the framework with the leafy boughs around it and another layer of bark around it on the outside, then this stranger came in and he helped even to lay in a big supply of wood, they put a big supply in. So all winter long he'd sit beside the fire and putting wood on the fire, making sure that the fire never burned out. As the winter wore on, he kept on getting smaller and smaller until finally, they went to look, it had already gotten spring outside, they went to look where he was sitting and he had disappeared entirely, there was just a pool of water sitting there. He was called *Oto*. It's the first two syllables of *otolic*, the cold weather. There were a lot of stories about the 'Spirit of Winter.'

Traditional Self-Government

In the old days, the people were organized in clan units, a clan was very important, so in those big longhouses, the story is this one house would belong to one clan, maybe a whole village, in their prosperous years would be mostly one clan, but of course it would be mostly the women who would be in charge, and take on most of the responsibilities and the work. Usually, they were organized in that the older woman would be called the Clan Mother, and she would have lots of influence as to who marries whom, generally the moral teachings of the whole clan come from the Clan Mother, the old woman. And some of the decisions and the ceremonies, when they would be done and how much work would be needed to get these ceremonies going.

But the men would be from other clans or other villages, because they would have to be married into the clan. They would serve that clan, they would always have their own clan, that's a part of them. But they would go to another village for their wives and serve that clan, the other clan. They would have to leave the village and go and hunt and bring in their kills and they would build that house. If new villages or houses needed to be built, they would do it. They would be building for their wife's clan. Meanwhile, the main judgment who runs the family, the husbands would have very little to do with it, mostly any decision or discipline within a family unit is left to the mother and enforced by a mother's brother. Or if there is no mother's brother then it would be some other male member of the clan. And the kids would all recognize that older man and call him *Lungunohowa*, 'He Who Takes Care of Us.' So that would be the authority, he would be the authority figure and enforcer.

Clans cannot marry each other, a person of the same clan cannot marry another person of the same clan. It wasn't allowed, but the head woman was in charge of that, and she would be careful. There might be some difficulty, sometime, when a Wolf Clan father would be married to a Bear Clan mother, and there would be children and the mother dies, then the father would have the responsibility of taking care of all these children, and maybe there would be difficulty, what's he going to do with them, take them back to his own clan, because he would still be under quite a bit of loyalty to his own clan? But if these children then were, if they were girls would be Bear Clan and they would be going to a Wolf Clan village, it might be different, it might be a little bit difficult. I think that the old custom was that the clan had greater relationship among the clan than the father. The father could maybe make another selection in the same clan or not or might go to a Turtle Clan. Maybe look for another girl among the Deer Clan, who knows, but he would have to leave the clan. But the kids would have to stay with their own clan. The other clan women would take care of the kids.

Treaties

There is no treaty that has been for Akwesasne, there is that Royal Proclamation, 1763, also the Treaty of Utrecht of 1713, they were included in that but they weren't signers. It was the British and French between themselves and they just mentioned the Five Nations, that happened also with the Jay Treaty of 1794, when the United States and Great Britain signed the treaty and mentioned Indians in there, crossing the border line. Indians were called third-party beneficiaries [laughs]. The Native people interpret the Jay Treaty to mean that they can go across the border and not have to pay any duty. That's right, that's the theory, now Canada breaks that, or the customs man at the border, he will put himself in greater authority than the treaty itself, when he refuses to recognize the treaty, then the government backs him up on that, and we don't very often have enough money to question it.

Well, Canada is much more prone not to recognize the Jay Treaty, they say well, we never signed it, it was Great Britain that signed it. We haven't been able to make them recognize that they are what they call successors, like supposing I have a house on which some money is owed to a bank. Then I go and sell the house, then whoever buys the house still owes the bank, besides paying me, still owes the bank. And we figure Canada bought a house which has a little lien, they took over a debt, and Canada doesn't recognize that, but I think they will. They're pretty much embarrassed by it now, that's why they set up a little special thing there that says that we give special privileges to St Regis. And so they set up a different lane so that when we come from the States and we go through this other lane and there's this very little hassle, they just wave us through. Only once in a while they will get a tip that somebody is bringing dope through and they'll look through the vehicle.

Elders

I've never heard of an Elder being defined or anything. Well, in my case, I've been called an Elder long enough so maybe they know what they're talking about. But there was never any cut-off or starting time, or no time when I qualified, or time like that [laughs]. It was just that they kept on saying it and eventually they got me convinced.

Role Models

Something that role models should not be are drunks, they should not be. Some would say, 'Oh that's too much to ask.' How much drinking is a person allowed before they become a drunk? I don't think a person should be a drunk or an obvious drinker. Too much harm has come from drinking that we can't afford. I don't think, as a people, we can afford that luxury, we can't afford to indulge. He has a higher standard for himself than anybody else. I'm saying 'he' because that applies to women, I was taught in school in English that 'he' includes or applies to women too, only in some cases. I'm still uncomfortable with it because the Mohawk we have a certain gender, which would include both sides or would include or ignore the person. Too bad they had to pick English as a model language. But it seems to be catching on all over.

The only example I can give is when this old man was telling about his life story when I was a kid. And he said something about when he was born, not very long after, a few years after the Civil War. He said that the old soldiers returned. Very few years after that, and he said, 'That's when I was a young fella,' and he said he was sixteen at the time and he left the reserve here and walked and he got out onto the plains [laughs]. This would've been in the late 1860s. So then a few years after then he was sixteen years old and he, I have to pin it down a little bit better someday, maybe looking in the history books because he said he was, he got out on to the plains and they were building a railroad, he said. And he watched there for a while, he said. I think he also said that he worked at that railroad building and got friendly with some Indians who were on horseback and came to watch also. And they invited him, so he left his job on the railroad and he went with the Indians, and I don't know what tribe they were, he didn't know, he was just an old-timer from here and he couldn't talk English, and of course they couldn't either, and so he didn't, he learned, he picked up the kind of sign language that they were using on him and he learned it and so, of course he used it therefore when he travelled with them for a little while, he didn't say how long. He said we got into some swampy region, here he was on the prairie and he went with these young fellows, two or three of them and they lent him a horse, they would give him a horse or something and they went and wandered down and the only swampy region that I can think of is on the border of Texas and Louisiana.

Somewhere in there, the guys got homesick there, his Indian friends, and they left him and he made his way back. So he was maybe eighteen, nineteen, maybe more before he got home. This was Big Tree. What was his first name? I forgot, it wasn't John, Noah maybe? Well, anyway, this fellow, he was a ninety-year-old when he was telling me this story and he was, after he got back, somewhere he was still a young man and somebody came around recruiting for a Wild West show. If you remember stories of Buffalo Bill, who made up a Wild West show after his own life on the plains and he had gathered some other real big names off the prairies. I never did find out yet what show this Big Tree was on, but they especially liked him because he could talk the sign language of the plains and they had Plains Indians with them and so he became sort of an interpreter.

Anyway he got over to England and got married over there and the show was travelling little village to little village over in England and so he got married and had one child before he left there. He brought a wife and child back with him and that child, I knew him when he was an elderly fellow and became the elected chief of the American side for two or three terms anyway, and his sons also were, but he, because his mother was an English woman, didn't have a clan and so he, in the old traditional way, he was not even Indian. But he looked like his father quite a bit, but he had bright blue eyes, pretty dark, real dark but with bright blue eyes. Big Tree, I have to remember what the fellow's name was, because he was kind of a hero to me there when I was a kid.

Traditional Games

Well, of course, lacrosse is the big one, of course, that goes way, way back.

The only other real Indian game that survived on through, it's been called the peach stone game. It is kind of a gambling thing using stones, markers that are black on one side and lighter on the other and throw a handful, I think that there are six of them that are thrown out on a blanket, count how many comes up black and how many red.

For children's games, well, there is one that resembles lacrosse and they call it *dagonnoodel* and that, you take two objects, sometimes corncobs tied together with a leather string and you use that and you throw that to one another, you use small sticks and you can toss it and catch it with a stick. There is, of course, the usual things there of throwing either stones into a hoop or throwing sticks, I suppose, at one time maybe they say it was spears but I think that it was just straight sticks that you throw at a hoop that is rolled along, around. At one time children, when I was a kid, children almost always had a bow and a bunch of arrows. And you know, never saw it really build up into archery. I know that there are some archers on the reserve now, but of course that is a whole lot different now, you almost always have to have a compound bow nowadays and aluminum arrows.

Celebrations

Yeah, well, they are still going on over at the longhouse, different celebrations or Thanksgivings right from the middle of winter to the General Harvest Festival there in the fall. In between the Maple Festival, the Strawberry, the Green Bean Festival, and Green Corn and General, let me see now, the General Harvest and way back in the fall there would be Dead Feasts. Again when I was a kid they, the Catholic church, had a certain, had two elaborate ceremonies, which involved a parade, parading out of the church with flags and special clothing, I guess, and there are priests going out and praying at various stops in around through the village there at St Regis. I think there was crosses put up various places and then there was one which was called the *dajogayagay*, in Mohawk, 'they shoot at the fire.' What I saw though was not a shooting at the fire but there was a flag-pole, at the base of the flag-pole a fort was built, but at the top of the pole there was a little sprig of evergreen, spruce I guess, and it was this high and two branches on it so it looked like a cross. There was prayers by the priest, there was a parade around and then there were booths, little something like gardens set up, with lots of flowers on it and maybe a religious object in the centre, and a priest would stop there and pray at each one and these booths were set up.

Family Responsibilities

In the olden times, the father, actually, was sort of, he would be expected to bring in the food, in the old days, to a certain extent while I was growing up there was a little bit of that left. And the running of the household, mother and even the grandmother of the kids. My grandmother, she would come in and she would make sure that people were going according to the moral standard she had set for them. Then, of course in my case, she wanted to be sure that I would learn some of what she knew. She tried to teach me some of what she knew of Native medicines. We would go out in the woods around, and she would know where to pick various kinds of medicines. And she kept a stock of medicines in her attic and once in a while she would send me up and pick out a bunch of these roots and bark, and I'm going to need a bit of cherry, black cherry, and I would need some white ash bark, even aspen, especially those certain kinds of barks and certain kinds of roots. I can't translate into English directly what the roots are. And so she would translate the 'roots that crawl,' well that's the name of the root. It was kind of hard to translate those thing. She would name off these things, and I would be expected to find these things in that pile of storage, where she had them drying out.

Well, there were those kinds of lessons, there was a certain idea too that came out from being with my grandmother. Something that I didn't realize at the time, but I've been thinking about it quite a lot, she was probably over sixty and had done a lot of sitting down in one place in her last ten or so years, because she had been supporting herself by making baskets for a dealer in Ogdensburg, in the village there, and that kept her pretty still. So it was a bit hard for her to walk long distances. So when we went to visit my family, my brothers and sisters who were living a mile or two away, she'd say they probably live about 'two look backs.' So we'd walk out and I guess she'd get tired, we'd find a place for her to sit, a rock or maybe a stump. And we'd stop and she would look back, from where she had come. And I think it had a lot of significance in the way she lived her life. She liked to look back and talk about the high points in her life, I suppose that helped her get along with the next section or year. I think it's a very interesting concept, she would say, 'Maybe it would be three look backs to where we are going.' And then I find in the old-timers in that same age group, they would say that was a kind of measure of distance.

Some of the men around there did know about medicines. However, according to my grandmother, they were not so effective because they were prone to drink. And she said medicines won't heal in the presence of alcohol. And she couldn't understand why, in the stores, the drug stores, you would find some kind of medicine that's suppose to be good for colds and it would have alcohol in it. She could never understand that. So she said, 'Well, it says so right there on the bottle.' I used to have to translate what it said on the bottle. And she would say, 'No that's no good, put it away, I'll have to find something else.' She wouldn't even use cough medicine that had alcohol in it. I knew the names, Mohawk names of quite a few weeds, what we would call weeds, that she used. During the wintertime we use a lot of evergreens, especially spruce for cold medicines, but I used to know those things, and scrambled up in the attic, they were in a dry state. And sometimes she would send me out into the bush there, to gather some, that was after she had shown me where they were.

Arranged Marriages

My grandmother tried to get into that, a matchmaker, and she stayed pretty much with her clan members. But by that time, the real formal authority just wasn't given to her. And the way of living had changed so much but there was still a little bit left. Traditionally, the older woman of the clan would have authority for the women of the clan. Especially the women, they would choose the men out of the other clans by talking to the women of the other clans. 'Who is this man there?' [laughs]. But then in this reserve the clans weren't isolated in various regions anymore, so the elderly women did know each other's clans, and the women would know the people of their clan, most of whom would be related anyway. That was pretty fun, I used to have a lot of fun listening in to their conversations [laughs]. There was one man who was a widower and had been single for a few years, and my grandmother matched him up with a woman who was visiting from Kahnewake. She knew very little about the woman, except that she knew her clan, and she invited this woman to come and stay with us, I was there too, as a child. So this woman did come, and so my grandmother's nephew would come and visit there too, and he courted her there. And eventually they did get married and the man moved away. I guess the Kahnewake woman took him back with her.

People did not always stay together, but looking back, people did stay together for long periods of their life. I don't remember too much about it. I know that there was, when I was in school, grade school, a girl of thirteen to a man who was almost forty. And they stayed together, and they had about eight children from the same father. I guess he lived to a fairly ripe age, and her too. I don't know if she's alive, she may be still alive. But that was there, across the river.

Homosexuality

There were some right in the village of Ogdensberg, who were White people, but on the reserve I think there was one, that we know of. He was married to a very beautiful woman and they lived together throughout their life, and they died within a very short time of each other. She outlived him by a couple of years, I think. But he had, I guess it was known that he had the tendency of trying to befriend young men. In this one case, it was, well, the couple looked like a normal couple except that they didn't have children, it was only through rumours. I never heard of women only. When I was growing up, they almost declared them that, almost declared them lesbians, women living together outside of the reservation, but they were not Indian. I never really heard of it or couldn't understand it. Well, we never hear of it on the reservation, well, I never heard of it until we watched the White people.

Tricksters

People as clowns, well there were some that were always, they didn't really, that were not really working at it, appointing themselves as such, there were people there, laughing. Even if you just heard their name, then people would laugh. That person would eventually, would go along with it, and do funny things, or play jokes or something like that. I never hear of anybody declaring themselves a trickster.

   Again, people would gather together and tell stories. And the one that, the first one I thought was close to what you say, is a fellow there that was always telling stories about his various adventures. When I was a child there, about 1926, this man had a Model T Ford, which was ancient, it had to be about six to eight years old from right directly after World War I, 1918, he probably got it in 1919, and various funny things about it, and he was regularly going up and down the road there because he was working his father's dairy farm. That was about a mile away from our own house. That man would go up there and milk the cows up there and then go and tend his own, he had a little small farm himself and he had his own family living there. And once in a while he would stop off and tell us a few stories. He told us about going off the road, when he was carrying a full pail of milk, which would be twelve or fourteen quarts, very shiny pail. 'I was holding it outside the body of the car and I hit this pothole and the car went off the road and I had this pail and it got thrown away up and I got out of the car to see what was going on and the pail came down and covered me all with milk' [laughs].

Music

Well, as a child we didn't know any of the old, old chants, or any of the old, old ceremonies. During the early part of the 1900s just before I came around, got around to knowing things, before that, there had been quite a group of show people who had been recruited by various road-show companies. They had recruited people here, and taken them away, and toured the country. Come to think about it, this woman that married my grandmother's distant nephew, she had been a show person when she was young, and had been a sharpshooter, and displayed her shooting tricks on stage for these tent shows that were going around. My neighbour down the road, about a half a mile, he had come back to the reserve after having been in show business for a few years. He had been a contortionist. My grandmother had a picture of him as he was going through these twelve-inch rings, silver rings, very shiny, steel rings. And he had a whole bunch of them around his body, he must have been really thin and agile. I met him later on, and we talked for quite a long while. He was talking about the shows that he was in, one of them was quite famous, which he called the 'One Hundred and One Ranch.' That was quite a show, of some note.

Anyway, there were a few others, I guess, who were in show business. There was one man around the village of St Regis or *Gonaugadoom*. *Gonaugadoom* is the name they've given it recently. His claim to fame at that time was that he had built a hotel which was right on the boundary line, international boundary line, so they called it the International Hotel. It had a few rooms in there anyway. He had been a trick rider in the west shows, the Wild West shows I think were trying to get a mix of western people, and eastern people because they figured the eastern people could relate better with the western ones, and perhaps influence them. Because the western Indians, when they were out of their element there, and they tended to drift into the cities and go out and get drunk [laughs]. Then they wouldn't show up for the shows, well the eastern Indians had a little bit more self-control, because they knew what the cities were like, so they were able to be more at ease in the cities.

And of course this fellow I told about yesterday, the fellow whose last name was Big Tree, who could talk the same language as the Plains Indians, relate to them, and I guess when he was a young man, he could ride the horses like the westerners did and he, by his influence, showed people too. So he was quite an influence. And so they were able to go and stay in these show circuits, they could generally stay sober [laughs]. So that was the only contact they had with some, they knew they could pick up a little bit of these western plains songs, they had forgotten completely the songs that were part of our own distant heritage. There may have been a, just a few little snatches of tunes that we still knew.

Now that was the old-timers. In the late 1930s there was an Elder, a blind man who came from Onondaga, and his name was Alec Clut, and he came here and began to teach the prophecy of Handsome Lake, *Scuneadabco*, and he gathered a bunch of people around him, and after a while they were believers. So then the revival of these ancient traditions began. Those old-timers that began, didn't know the songs, couldn't sing, couldn't dance, so they invited more of the people from the other reserves, the Onondaga reserve, and others that had preserved it and had I think one of the first preachers of this prophet's message. And so for about five years, this one teacher was here teaching the elements of this, of the prophecy and the teachings of Handsome Lake.

They were lessons on how to live, and the prophecies were really like, 'If you continue in this way, this is what's going to happen.' And so the prophecies that this one prophet gave were choices and involved this prophet who has supposedly entered into the world of vision, and certain spiritual beings took him around and showed him various things about what the future would be, in relation to the 1800s. Up to 1813 was when this prophet was preaching. And from 1813 on, there the converts remembered his sayings. So the songs, dances, and most of the traditional teachings were sort of shared or imported. Some say they were brought in from other reserves, but basically they were the same people. Senecas, you can understand them, if you open up your mind pretty good, a Mohawk could understand them. Generally it was the Senecas who could understand Mohawk better that the Mohawks could understand the Senecas. For some reason, I haven't figured that out yet. Anyway, they were able to come and teach their ways, the old ways, so other people accepted it, and eventually we're running our own ceremonies here, and singers, the young men are singing songs, more songs, more songs than any of their predecessors. More songs than I ever thought would exist even. And of course, they are also composing new ones in the old way, just like Powwow singers are doing all the time, new songs, borrowing from one another. Well, they have, you can pretty well recognize the Iroquois songs, even among the other songs.

Traditional Art

Well, basket making is a very big variety, you see that pack basket over there, then the little picnic basket my wife uses and then there's other baskets. Let me think, well, the graphic arts, I think there's a few cliff paintings somewhere in the area, but that had been abandoned long time ago. We did have one man who mixed up a bunch of house paints, and he had already passed on when I was growing up. And this old man he was in his older, when he was old, he had painted quite a few paintings they say. And I used to walk a couple of miles when I was just about eight or nine years old, with my older brother, come visit with me, some friends he had across the river, and I would go along just to look at those paintings [laughs]. And that man is, he is, his paintings did outlast him, but his grandson, I think, was the one that sold them for drinks. So I don't know where they are now, and another granddaughter is looking for them now. I don't know if she'll ever find them. But there was this one painter. Then again, if you think some athletes, that those lacrosse sticks are works of art, they made lots of them here and sort of, and had to develop the design of them, pretty much here.

Clothing

Just generally, 'course my grandmother said *Dagonaweehoe*, leather that was, the word itself means 'leather that is split,' but it doesn't, it's not really that accurate, what they were referring to were the fringes on garments. My grandmother said all the dress used to be with fringes on it. It would have to be deer hide.

Spiritual Ceremonies

They had the Strawberry Ceremony, Midwinter, Green Corn, Green Beans Ceremonies, and the vegetables there that are the end of the planting, General Harvesting. Each time a harvesting season was finished they would have a ceremony, and they still do, this is something happening now. So these ceremonies would be, are mostly held, in thanksgiving, what they've received from the earth, that kind of thing. In fact, even in early spring when you get the first thunder, when you hear the thunder, first time in the spring, then a certain, sometimes they'll have a meeting, nowadays it's over the telephone, and somebody would be delegated to perform a welcome, would welcome and give prayers and burn Tobacco, and welcome it to the Grandfathers, the Thunder, because now they would be bringing in a new planting season. So almost everything is related to their connection to the earth, what they receive from the earth, a kind of agriculture, I guess we have a few dances, but these are all social dances that are in honour of animals, but they don't have any ceremonies specifically for any of the animals, there may be one for the eagle but that's delegated to only one society. Not necessarily one clan, but a society, a group of people that get together and dedicate themselves to the eagle. And probably the Eagle Society is connected to a clan.

Burials

Well, I guess, well archaeologists are pretty happy about it, they find out all about it, we've heard of times when a dead person was wrapped in bark and placed maybe in maybe a tree, but that's, I don't know if that's ever happened. With the serious stories we have, deal with them being buried in the ground. And the traditionalists today, they have their ceremony that goes with the burial, with the wake before the burial. On the island the one that is supposedly non-denominational, but right beside it is a longhouse cemetery. I think the gate is side by side, but I think there is another one on the American side, and that one is used too, and I don't know if it is only for convenience.

Grieving

It's kind of hard to say, it's kind of hard for me to know what the old traditional way of thinking, but there is an expression there, that such and such a person is, he or she has left to go pick Strawberries, out picking Strawberries. That goes back to the legend of Sky Woman coming down and bringing Strawberries from up above. The Sky Woman came from a Spirit world, and she brought Strawberries down to earth, and so now they've gone to pick Strawberries, and this would be at any time of the year, that they died and so they would go up. Now there's another story, of kind of an expedition that went and kept going west, and eventually found the place where the sun would come down and the sky would lift up to let the sky out. And so, they went there and followed the sun as the sun went out, these fellows went and rushed in before the sky came back down again. That story, and they got into the Spirit world and they saw lots of wonderful things there.

And this one story is that one of that party, a young man, fell in love with one of the young women that was there. But she wouldn't have him and she sent him back, sent him away. 'Cause she said, 'I died long ago, and I may be one of your ancestors.' So there's no question of marriage then. And so, the story is that he, what was that, and she said, 'We are

Spirits up in this area and you are a human being so you can't stay here.'
So the story goes, the next time the sky lifted up, they came back into the
world and, but this young person that had fallen in love back there, he
stayed and looked back into the other world and the sky came down and
crushed him and so he went back into the other world as a Spirit.

Traditional Beliefs and Christianity

The usual virtues are pretty much the same. Honesty, and of course the
best ones of sharing and caring for one another, and I think that many of
the Elders across the country all have settled on those virtues, they call
them gifts I think. Caring, sharing, and respect, and what's the other one,
thankfulness! And so, all of those are in the Mohawk tradition, they have
supported that all along. Very confusing however was when they, even
when I was a kid, they were talking about when a priest or clergyman who
was supposed to be teaching all these things the people detect something
missing there. He is not virtuous as he wants us to be and he was supposed
to be our leader and show us the way and if he is showing us, then he is not
showing us the right things. Well we have all that kind of confusion there
and so I think it's pretty amazing that we kept as much as we have.

The other one, the big item of confusion is, most of the Christian sects
talk about the special day of Sunday. Well I fix up to that now and everybody observes Sunday as being a day of worshipping, rest, and so on. Well
the old-timers there were and I think to a certain extent still do question
that because when they look at the White people they see them, especially
the merchants that came here went to the church there to learn honesty
and when they come out they cheat people. So that was the source of a lot
of confusion.

The thing too, well, with Christianity you have to have clergy, who are
appointed or self-appointed into the clergy appoints other clergy and
they oversee the spiritual needs of the people. Well with the Native
people everything just about, it's built in. They, the people, appoint their
leaders who pick the singers for the ceremonies and the singers of the
songs. Everything is amongst the people and they don't have clergies that
will declare this day as a holy day and you must act and behave in this way,
must be someplace special that the clergy presides over. Now, so that's
one of the big differences, it is without force, no that isn't quite the right
word I was looking for, coercion, that sort of thing. Well, with Christianity
you do have coercion if you don't believe certain things you, if you want
to change the church doctrines you can be excommunicated.

Time

Well, of course, throughout my life we have used the clock, and of course we say, one stroke at the bell, the bell was hit once, is one hour, in our language. Most of the clocks had that bell. But of course we always had sunup time, and afternoon, and the time of sunset.

Seasons

Oh, course, you had to go by, had to order your life according to the seasons and weather. And another thing to that probably affects much of our politics, is that during the winter the village gets to be kind of impractical, in the old days they used to leave the village and go into the bush, I think I mentioned that yesterday, mostly for to be sure they had enough fuel, and hunting might be a little bit better, you do take a chance, but whatever food you have, well you can, well, pretty much take care of yourself that way, more easily than in the village. So here, the village would be somewhat deserted in the winter time. The people going off, but during the time of, that the government placed the Indian Agents, superintendents, these superintendents would pretty much have free rein to do what they wanted, and we lost quite a bit of land that way, because there was nobody here to put up a good protest or any kind of opposition. So I think that it was very important that we remember that it was an important part of our life and it affects us today. Now, we have so much less land then we had before.

Relationship between Language and Culture

I think that the biggest component of a culture is the language and in Canadian politics that is what Quebec relies on most, they want to preserve the French language and I think that is the most important part. Even though most of the people [from Quebec] are living not too much differently from the rest of Canada. They figure that it is the big component of culture, I don't believe in their conclusion but I think that it is true that the biggest part of a culture is the language. For one thing, if you get certain habits in there that are in the language itself and certain ways that you use the language is what would be different from any other language and of course all of the Native languages point to is that there is no way of cussing, in the English language sense of cursing and damning and that sort of thing, you don't do that in Indian. So in a way you have higher moral viewpoint there in Native languages.

All kinds of other things there too that you might have, well, a whole different thought, vocabulary. Some things you can express in many ways in Indian or ways that make you feel good and it's built right into the way the language is built so I think that is an important part too. I suppose that I should give some sort of examples too. We have a wider range of distinguishing between he and she. In the English language animals are not given a gender, unless they are a pet or something, it is always it. In Indian you are always referring to something as people the way you would refer to a person, he or she. Animals are people to the language, that makes a difference to the way you actually treat them too, which means also, when a hunter perhaps prays before a hunt he will ask that the certain animal will be kind to him, allow himself to be killed because he needs that, and as the books say, that is the way of all life, he will give his life for another. That is very often mentioned in the old prayers of the old-time hunters.

Now with the coming of the European philosophy and it seems to have influenced a lot of people and that part seems to have not been given as much importance any more, it is not important to pray before a hunt any more, but if you do, sincerely, well that is the way that you look at it, you give them a personality, of course you have gratitude afterwards and you thank that animal for giving up his life and that is in a way, it is a much truer kind of politeness than what is generally the habits of the White man.

Traditional Names

We have Indian names, that is one of my favourite topics. My name is *Dwalygwonda*, which means 'goods or possessions, which have been gathered together.' That happens in the ceremony in the midwinter when they have a ceremonial game and people bring various things to bet one another, the purpose of the game is to establish which clan or which group of clans will officiate at the ceremony for the next year, so that is done in the winter time and it is a very happy occasion and people bring all these things and so it is part of an exchange of what you value the most, handicrafts and things, so that's *Dwalygwonda*, which means 'all of these possessions are brought together.' Now that, well it is one meaning, the other is that it could mean that it is 'firewood that is brought together in a pile.' That is part of another observation that I've made, you were reading stories there about a people of the plains probably are given names like 'kill straight' and 'shot on both sides' and things about warfare. I have never heard of a Mohawk man's name having to do with warfare.

Warrior Societies

They would have warrior societies I suppose, long ago. According to one fellow, Jake Thomas, who reads the wampums and recites lots of the history, he says that warrior societies were banned at the time of the establishment of the Five Nations Constitution. The word *warrior* is an English word, they were applied to all the young men, of course, and even if they were out hunting they were called warriors by the English writers, so that is where the confusion comes in, and it has made confusion with Indians now. The other part is that the young warriors were also expected to serve the community and serve all of the disabled people.

However, as time went on the Natives lost touch with their own background and so they accepted and thought the same way as the White man who said 'warrior,' and then the Indians said, 'Yeah, we're warriors' [laughs]. So that is kind of a thing that has happened, I think we've adapted the White man's translation. The other thing that you hardly ever hear anything in the Mohawk names having to do with war, you have great manly hunks of masculine power there who would have the name of a flower perhaps [laughs], sometimes that is really strange. One of the fellows there that used to do tough talking, and he was elected to the council because he was not afraid of the White man, he never said anything very clever or anything, but he talked rough and his name was translated to scattering flowers.

Another thing, there were some I think of the other tribes that used some animal names. Mohawks hardly, I can't think of any animal names. But you would have the Bear, Wolf, and Turtle clans among the Iroquois and some Snipe, but they didn't take the names of, you know, you have the clan membership in those animals, animal figures, but you would not name yourself after any of those.

Places with Mohawk names, it is changing back to where now around the reserve, this is called *Gayowangono*, 'on the island, or the island.' New apartments are *Gayowangono* apartments down there, island apartments, and then you have health facility down there, *jeegwondjsekew*. It's 'see, our house or our building,' and *wayjeegwondjsekew* and that means 'our new house' and that is a shelter for adolescents I guess. Down there, there is an old age home where my niece lives and that is *ukesota*, that means our grandmother. So names are coming back, there was attempt one time to change Ogdensburg back to Akwesasne, and that didn't take, but the whole reserve now has called itself Akwesasne, 'One of the Partridge Makes His Noise,' sometimes they say 'Where the Partridge Drums.' There is a name for the St Lawrence River, it is almost been forgotten but it is *katawequi*, it means 'full of clay.' The river used to be a green a very very green, clear, so they thought or somebody figured out that it was because of little bits of clay, or clay on the bottom of the river.

Economics

Fish, agriculture, corn, beans, pumpkins, squash, tobacco, sunflower, I think that was the old-time, traditional food, and they ate fish, and deer, too, some raccoons, and down east of here in the marshy areas, there's muskrats and of course there's rabbits around there. They preserved food to last them the winter, in their traditional ways, mostly dried and smoked. With vegetables and corn, you dry it. With corn, they'd usually braid the husks and you'd have the cobs of corn sticking out of the braid and then you could usually handle it, drape it over the beams of the houses, so that it would be up above the floor where it's hotter and drier.

Traditional Transportation

Long ago, you walked or used canoes. If they could get it they used the Ojibwe birch-bark canoes. And eventually, I guess, they did make some themselves, but the old, old canoes were either dugout or basswood canoes, or they were elm bark. Elm bark is kind of heavy, but they scraped it and it was, I would say serviceable, it lasted just as long as birch-bark and it was just as tough.

Modern transportation, well, the good things in that life is easier. You can get around faster, and in some ways, your life is longer because of better improvements over medicines and health care and less danger, so your life is longer. Well now disadvantages, morality is breaking down, and I think that's one of the important things in life that you live a good moral life and that's no longer, no longer has the respect that it should. An actual enjoyment of life I think is less known than it was perhaps because life was a little bit precarious, at one time, then you had to enjoy it more. The stability of the family is not as great now and there's less, less willingness to accommodate yourself to others' needs. Furthermore, people are encouraged to be selfish now and that's what's being sold to us as a virtue when in our days it was, it was not ever a virtue, not a good thing. Well that's all I could think of right now.

Relations with First Nations

Of course most of the visits that we got from other tribes were from other Iroquoian tribes so they were always time of great rejoicing. Well, the history books, they talked about all the Iroquois were warring against the missionaries and went and raided this Midland mission over on Georgian Bay, and of course the Iroquois did that and that was supposed to be very, very bad of course. There are a few things that the history books leave out, historians leave out. One is that it was a time of war and so people in those days, raids were carried on both sides and Indians were raided probably either as often or more often than they raided. I point to the efforts that the local people here of St Regis of Akwesasne made in the war of 1812 to stay neutral, and they tried as best they could, well they could not stand up to the persuasion of the White man's whiskey bottle, which was the usual quite often a big clincher there, come and join us and you can have all the booze you want.

And so they, off they went these young men. Still, the people that were in charge of the council, in charge of the whole community, they tried to stay neutral all during that war and at the end of the war, were confronted by both sides, the United States and England, saying, 'How come you supported the other side?' This was both sides talking to us here so, so that's what happened there. I can't see too much logic in the way these so-called enlightened countries in how they think. I got a big grudge against them there. They want to fight but they want someone else to do the fighting and then after that they wonder why it was that they were not supported as much as they, it's just unreasonable. But anyways people did hold on to their identity here, their oneness and so that even when the United States had a kind of a policy of pushing all Indians out across the Mississippi River, and they even had a place marked out for the people of Akwesasne way out there, in Kansas. The people here didn't go, would not go. And so they had to stay, they had to be recognized as being here. I don't know all of the background for that but we managed to stay in one place, managed to keep our identity.

Dreams

We did have a certain person that I remember who was called, well they say that she was in communication with the Spirits and she could locate people who had drowned and she would point out the spot and you look over there and that is where it is and other things that could only be coming to a person that had this extra perception. I don't know very much about that, but there had been people like that and were recognized for that. Now since that woman died she hasn't had a successor.

Medicines and Healing

We have had them here too, but after one person died he was the last one. We haven't had any since that time that I know of. Yesterday we talked about traditional medicines, people must still know about the medicines that the traditional healers are the ones that the people would go see. I think that it would be, a lot of it would come a result of those dreams or visions, otherwise why, who would have thought to go deep into the marshes there and brave all the mosquitoes there and pick out which ones out of all the thousands of different kinds of plants that there are and so there had to some kind of extra help there.

Balance in Two Worlds

I think so, especially somebody, and I would say when you search after truth and truth is that which you will find that is dependable and is of use to you. There may be a lot of truths out there, but if it doesn't affect you, then it doesn't matter whether it is true or false. So, you have to go searching it out for yourself and I would say whatever is of use and you can depend upon for good things, that is okay too. To obtain to and to take it up and put it to use, so there is only some concern, perhaps we would call universal truth, and that would be morality, which would mean the various use of honesty and generosity and caring and sharing and so that, and gratitude. If something in the present world will help you achieve those things then you would be very beneficial, very good to pursue those things.

Division of Land

I think in the old days there was a house of course that belonged to clan, sometimes a whole village would be a clan and the husbands of the women that were living there were of other clans, but they were subject to the rules of that house, subject to the rules of the Clan Mother. That was generally the old way of operating. Outside of those houses and outside of those villages there would be the gardens, and the gardens would be owned by the women, even if the men had gone in there to clear it out and work at it and still the gardens would generally be just assumed that they were the property of the women, and mothers were careful to keeping up with their families so they were given all that responsibility. So, there would be some markers, they would know where one garden ended and another began.

Now very early, it seemed as though the influence of somebody, perhaps it was a White man's influence or else maybe it was a White man that came and lived here, marking off a certain piece of land that he wanted for himself, and so that began the idea of personal property here and I've noticed that there was some other reserves where there was no personal real estate and so they, and only people occupied a piece of land with the consent of everybody else there and just assumed that they would be there. Well, here, claiming of land, specific boundaries you staked it out and put fences on it and it started quite a long time ago, maybe in the early 1800s, perhaps around 1810 or so, even before the war in 1812, and there were quite a few White settlers on the reserve itself.

Education

There have been some experiments in putting the culture directly into the school. There is one little school operating now that is a total immersion Mohawk school and all the language is in Mohawk. There are still some needs there, they're having difficulty using this knowledge say, in accounting or higher mathematics or study of geography in other countries, studies of classic literature, so there are some weaknesses. I think the strengths of total immersion are pretty well accepted by the people here. One of the reason for not supporting that school more by sending more children there is that perhaps parents are a little bit afraid of the outside world, of disapproval by the authority outside. They are afraid that maybe they might miss out on maybe the Dick and Jane stories or something like that [laughs]. Or they are a little bit embarrassed that they did not themselves carry enough of the language to teach their children to be talking the language fluently before they go to school. So it might be a little bit of embarrassment in there. But I think that things at that school are going well and total immersion is a good idea, especially in the younger grades. Well, it's something for the future. I think it's going to come and it will, among the people here, Mohawk will be the main language again.

Traditional Forms of Justice

You have to have alternative systems because even to the White man that invented the way the justice system, is, it still doesn't work for him. So how could it work for us? And so we ought to devise our own. We have had some consideration of it, there have been, have been, when was that, two years ago when there was a series of meetings in Ottawa and I guess around the country dealing with alternative Native justice systems and I think it was, well I thought it had been very well decided that the best thing for us is to devise our own, make it fit the local culture the best of the ideals of the local people, make it flexible, administered by the local people so that it can be all of the circumstances can be looked at not just the act itself and the punishment for that act and all over here on this side. Bring them on this side, bring them together and therefore men be sentenced. Make, it must be, the idea of justice is to adjust the behaviour of people so that they will live in more harmony with one another. If a person makes a mistake in his actions and it hurts somebody then there should be a chance for the victim to be a part of the process of getting satisfaction, and the satisfaction would not be revenge, it would be real satisfaction in that if something is stolen then the equivalent is given back. If it is a hurt and a person is physically damaged then there must be some adjustment on the perpetrator's part to help that person to heal. And it would be flexible, each case would be, has to be accepted by both parties so that sides would be working towards the same common goal of, for instance a man may, well this might be a common event today, a man will get drunk and beat up his wife, then the community will step in to protect the wife. There needs to be negotiation as to whether that man will promise and make some kind of adjustment to make sure that he doesn't get drunk again if that is what the danger is, if he does that when he gets drunk then he doesn't get drunk anymore. If, then the whole community must be told about what has happened that, then that one person is going against the community by his drinking then the whole community must help to prevent that person from drinking again, as well as that person make it his promise. So there must be community effort whenever the, whenever possible and personal effort on the part of those thought to be the ones making the mistake or crime, and they must all be a part of it as it is the, I don't know what they call them, not, well a criminal, well if you want a better word than criminal, after he is given, made his, committed his crime then sometimes he doesn't do nothing until the police come to arrest him. After the arrest has been made then everything goes according to a plan of which he has no part, the criminal then will, is just riding along on a structure that has already been made and sometimes he doesn't even know where if he has changed his mind or determines to live a new life. I don't think that there is no place where he can show it. They say that you are going to confront accusers, it's not true, the accuser and the accused are put in different sections in a court-room, a courtroom has certain rules of behaviour, so he is not permitted to shout across the courtroom to the other side and say 'I'm sorry.' He is in contempt of court if he does that, so where is he going to get his, going to be able to show his, a change of heart or whatever he might have, well if the justice system was correctly made then the both sides would be accuser and accused would talk together then they would then settle upon, either, discuss their differences, they would settle upon a solution.

The people would also be represented there and they would, there would be a settlement that all would accept and the accused would accept whatever sentence or punishment that he's supposed to do and if he accepts then what is the purpose of a jail? Jail removes him, for short time or certain length of time, sometimes a long time but during that time he is of no use to anybody, he is a burden of everybody. So the sentence is against the people actually they have to support him or her. So that has to be addressed and I think that the Native communities have a very good chance on insisting on putting their own justice system in place.

A panel of Elders could be selected to sit on, sort of sit in judgment, they would not be judges handing down sentences, as I say, the accused and the accuser would discuss the matter they would in front of the Elders. The Elders would bring out all of the details, but they would not allow the two to actually fight each other, they would be, they could only talk about what had happened, not what they felt. The Elders would then say where the crime was, where the mistakes were made by persons, and so they would talk to both sides. 'This has happened to you and you are having, you have great anger in you, now that is bad.' And to the accused they would say, 'You have done, appears to have done this so, did you do it, did you, and how much of it did you do, then you have noticed that this other side is very angry and that they have been very hurt now you have made them hurt. You are, what do you say about that?' You say, 'Well I was drunk and I didn't know what I was doing' or something like that, then there would not be, then there was the drinking that did it, so you've made your mistake when you first swallowed. But all those things aren't, so the accused then would have a part in his own sentencing or decision. He himself would say, 'I will do this and that to make up for this,' in fact he would sentence himself in one way. Then since it is a community thing, a community matter, then the community makes sure that this sentence is carried out by that one person, he stays in the community, the community has not lost his services or his whatever, and probably has still some good in him.

Non-Native People

I don't think I like the White people making all the decisions for us, the big decisions. And there's another thing too is that somewhere back there the government has given to itself, something, a kind of an overlord, a lord of all things, kind of a power over people, in other words, let me see, I think the law says that they have underlying title. So that if you have a car and want to drive somewhere, they will not allow you to do it unless you have their permission to do it by owning the form of a licence. And so that kind of attitude goes into everything, you have a piece of property, you have land, the government will not allow you to sell that piece of land to somebody else unless they give their permission through their bureaucrats. Now who that other one is, suppose you want to sell it to an American, the American comes in and he will say, this is now a part of the United States, I bought it from [laughs].

Well the federal government will not allow that so they, but the thing is they have gone much too far in claiming that dominion in Native lands and Indians have to get some of that back. Now for one thing, one example, over in Alberta the Lubicons [First Nation] have been proprietors, they have been recognized by the Canadian government as owners of a big piece of land, which has all kinds of goodies in there, the forest and the mining. They are not going, the federal government is at the same time determined not to give it to them, not to let them use it until all the forests are gone the mine, the gold all come out of the ground and the oil and the, everything, gas and anything else they could squeeze out of it. So that is what they call a sovereignty or underlying title and I don't think that Native people should allow them to do that. I think it is theft, thievery, pure and simple, and Indians have to get that back because if they were here during the time they were here they believed and all of the evidence has shown that everything that was here of material value was a gift from the Creator, and if everything was a gift from the Creator, how can an earthly government proclaim itself to be the owner? So I don't think they are right to do that and I think that we've lost a lot, we've lost a lot of our self-respect, just that way because it was taken away. We are justified in trying to get back as much as you can get.

Anishinabe Cultures

LIZA MOSHER   (Odawa)

Manitoulin Island, Ontario

'We have to go back to the original teachings.'

Emily Faries interviewed Liza Mosher at her home in the spring of 1994. What stands out in the interview with Liza Mosher is her laugh. It is a deep, infectious laugh and it usually follows a joke or an embarrassing anecdote told in her stories. Liza discussed many serious topics in her interview, including sexual abuse at residential schools, alcoholism, drug abuse, and suicides in Native communities. But at the end of these stories, there is always a joke, and her great laugh is shared to relieve some of the tension.

Liza relates the problems in Native communities to the loss of the stories and traditions of the Elders. There is a lesson in each story she tells, and these stories are emphasized by Liza's personal life. Liza is from the Bear Clan and her Indian name is *Gosahkii Kwe*. She was born in Wikwemikong 18 April 1932. Liza was raised in her home community except for four years when she was in residential school. Liza is second degree Midewiwin, and she is involved in women's circles and works with children of alcoholics. She lives outside of the community of St Charles, Ontario.

Life History

I was born in Wikwemikong on Manitoulin Island and I knew my language. My language was first. My mother never spoke English, she couldn't read or write. She never went to school so the language was spoken in the home, the Ojibwe language. It wasn't until I was seven when I went to residential school. The life we had as a child I remember as that, was really, I really had that closeness with my mother and father, I hardly remember my older brothers and sisters because they were already in residential school. I don't even remember them actually when they used to come home for summer, summer holidays. It wasn't until I was, I guess six, I began to remember a lot of the things, but I know we had, it was a very close family. I never knew of getting a licking but there was always a willow stick by the door hanging on the wall and if we did something wrong, I remember there was some Tobacco on top the stove, the wood stove, there was always Tobacco there, I remember that. And my mother used to get that Tobacco and she'd hand us the bowl and we used to have to take a little of that Tobacco and go in the bush and get that willow stick if we did something wrong because we always threw that willow stick away, we burned it or got rid of it [laughs]. So we'd always have to get that willow stick anytime we did something wrong but it was never used. But we knew it was there all the time.

One time my grandfather came in and was sitting there and I did something wrong, and my mother gave me some Tobacco and handed me the bowl to take some Tobacco to go and get that willow stick, and you would talk to that willow stick and go and offer that Tobacco. And one time I picked the smallest one, and I came in and my grandfather was there and he said, 'That's the one that hurts the most,' so I threw it away and I told my mother I dropped my Tobacco so she gave me some more Tobacco, but she already knew, so I went back out and got a big one and she said, 'You were talking to your grandfather, the grandfather's been talking to you,' so I brought in the willow stick. I really remember that, I guess I was always the quiet one.

One of the things is my, what I notice as a child – I never noticed it until I got into residential school and when I came back for summer breaks – is on my father's side was more Catholic and my mother's side was more traditional. My grandmother on my mother's side, she taught me a lot. I remember a lot of things about her. I remember the fields of her garden was full of Tobacco, she'd have racks in her bedroom, hanging over, she had a great big huge bedroom, there was a wood stove there in her bedroom, a heater, a box stove, and she had all these racks with all her medicines up there, drying up there. I remember following her and helping her to pick the Tobacco and helping her dry the Tobacco. I remember the old spinning wheel there. They used to have sheep and they'd make their own wool. I remember all that. I remember helping her clean that wool. There was a certain way of doing it: two boards and you'd put it on that wheel.

I remember all that. I really felt good. I used to always be with her, my grandmother. I used to follow her around and they used to have an old hollow log, a great big log, and she'd have corn in there, she'd make corn flour. I know how to do that, because I watched her and I used to do that, pound that corn. She never told me anything, she never talked about this is what you're supposed to do. All I had to do was follow her, watch her and she used to make her own hats, we used to go to these bazaars, fall fairs, rummage sales. She'd buy all these old hats, men's felt hats, and she had boxes and boxes of these fancy hats and she'd make her own hats. She'd wash these and she'd dampen them and when they were still wet, she'd shape them and then she'd decorate them with flowers and ribbon and everything. She had beautiful hats. I used to love being in her bedroom because I used to play with her hats.

Residential School

I was there for four years and that was enough for me. I never really learned anything but I think what happened was that's where all the abuse started. That's where I got my first licking. And one of the things is, I couldn't speak a word of English when I went there and I think the second week we were there I got a licking because one of the girls lost her candy, somebody stole her candy, she blamed someone, I was the one who was blamed. Just the way I was raised we never had candy at home and I am still never one for candy. Because what we had was mostly dried fruit, my mother would dry apples. They would be hanging above the stove, and that's what we had. Dried apples and figs. I remember those figs, I still buy those figs. I was raised on dried apples, dried fruit. So I always go and buy them. I was never one for candy, chocolate bars or anything. I don't recall ever, I never liked pop.

When I was in residential school, that time I was blamed for that candy, I couldn't defend myself. I couldn't speak English but they had one of the older girls to translate for me. That was my first licking I ever got. I was really hurt about it. I wanted to run away. I was seven years old. I guess that's where I began to rebel. I began to withdraw. Another time, I ran into this supervisor, we were playing tag, he and another girl in the play-room, I bumped into her.

When I began dealing with myself, working on myself, that's what I seen, because I had blocked all this, all this what I went through in that residential school, I had blocked everything. And the one thing I saw when I began working on myself was the authority figure. What do you say when you bump into her, and I didn't want to say. I didn't know how to say, 'I'm sorry,' so she punished me. I was kneeling facing the corner of the wall, she made me kneel there. I must have been there for about an hour.

That was new, different to me, and because I never had contact with White people until that bus came to get the children to go to residential school. And here I thought I was going for a ride because I'd never been in a car before. I never travelled off the reserve. So it was really exciting for me, but I was wondering why my mother was crying when we were getting on the bus. I didn't know where I was going. Another thing I remember is my aunt. My mother left one time and my aunt baby-sat us and my hair was really long. It was past my knees, and my aunt, my hair was braided and she just took one braid and she just chopped it off. I never forgave my aunt for that. I was so hurt. I went underneath the bridge and I stayed there and cried and cried until my mother came home. I felt so naked when my hair was cut, but I never understood that until I began healing myself. Because all my life I had no use for that aunt just because of that and it wasn't until later on when I got out of residential school, my mother has a cedar chest, and she had a lock on it, and she had all her good stuff, her embroidered stuff, her treasures in there. It was like a treasure box, and none of us would ever get to see what was in there. One time she forgot to lock it. So I thought I have to check to see what's in there, so I started looking around in that trunk and there was a red cloth there and I was drawn to that cloth. It was rolled up, I was wondering what was in there, so I undid it, and that's where I seen my hair. She kept my hair, the braids were still on them.

It wasn't until I came out of residential school that I had seen my hair in the cedar chest. I must have been sixteen or seventeen years old. I rebelled against my mother, I withdrew, because I blamed her for my hair, not really, but I blamed her mostly for residential school, sending me to residential school. When I used to come home for summer holidays, I'd speak English to her. I was paying her back, that's how I lost my language, because I just blocked it. I understand but I can't speak it. I can just speak slang words but I understand all the words, but for me to speak it I can't do it, it's really hard. My mother wanted to cut my hair because she knew that they would cut my hair once I got into residential school, and that's why, she knew if she did it that I would never let her, so she got my aunt to do it. That's why she left – for my aunt to handle it.

It's part of the tradition, keeping hair. Your ties are with your mother and when you're away from her, you still have that tie, that connection, the mother and the child. I remember when my dad went overseas (he was in World War II), he always took pieces of clothing of the children, so that child will not miss him. I remember that. Even when he used to go in the bush to logging camp, he would take one of the kids' shirts.

Creation

We come from the Creator. Usually when I go out and do workshops that's one of my teachings that I give is that Creation story, also when you give it that's 'cause so many of our young people are lost today and that's where their identity is and their spirituality, what they are searching for, that's where it is in that Creation teaching. To tell it, I would have to, it takes a long time to tell it. I usually need to smudge to do that, to clean your mind, your Spirit, to give those teachings.

The stories are passed on orally. Some people write it like drug and alcohol counsellors at treatment centres, they use those oral teachings, where I got mine is in the Lodge, that Creation story, but you can combine it and put in what you have learned in the treatment centres, because they have missed quite a bit when they do that, that life cycle and the four directions, they've missed the Creation story. So you have to go back to it. I usually go back to the Creation story to be able to give those four directions. Even everything of the Creation because the seventh Creation was the original name so that's where most of our identity comes from, right from the Creator, to that first man is where Mother Earth and all of the spiritual realm that's where we came from.

Importance of Culture

For me, I've never known my home yet, because I went through that wandering stage, I wandered all over looking and searching, it wasn't until I walked into that Lodge that I found what I was looking for and then I finally came home because that Lodge is my home. And that's where my teachings are for my life and for the first time, hearing the teachings. I was raised in a Catholic home but I never could feel anything, it was prayers, you'd memorize those prayers but they don't mean nothing. But when you go into the Lodge, when you talk to the Creator, just like I'm talking to you. You feel good because it's coming from the heart, not from the mind, you don't memorize, when you memorize there is no feeling, there's no connection, but for me to talk to the Creator from the heart because feelings come with that, the tears come of happiness, of joy, of peace of mind and the respect of all creation at all times.

Reaching Back into the Past

By finding our identity, by going to ceremonies, going to Sweats, going to fast. For me, fasting is where most of my teachings are. Going out there and sitting with my Mother (the Earth). I abused alcohol. I was an alcoholic. I abused alcohol for thirty-one years, since I was fourteen, and I didn't quit until I was forty-five. That's a long time to abuse alcohol.

I just didn't want that life anymore. I used to work on Great Lakes, used to cook on the Great Lakes for seven years. I made good money but I used it on drugs and booze and thinking I was having a good time. But you never realize until you sober up that you know it's not a good time. But that's how I went to my first ceremony, and I was drunk on the way too. I had said I wouldn't drink anymore, but we had to leave from Sudbury that night. I was on Manitoulin Island, so we went to Sudbury and I said, 'Oh my old friends, back to the bar.' So I was up all night drinking and partying it up.

I was feeling okay but I got scared as we were getting there. I thought, 'What am I getting myself into,' because I was terrified of these, because of the way I was brought up. How our teachings were pagan, they were witchcraft, bearwalking and all this, and I was scared. But I wanted so much to leave the drugs and alcohol. I wanted to get better and I was willing to try anything and that was my last resort. And boy, that was the best time of my life, the best time of my life was when I first went into that Lodge.

Even my first Sweat was a healing Sweat. I was terrified, I thought that the man that was conducting the Sweat that had the powers to do that.

Here I was thinking of going back to bearwalking, that's what he's doing. But the feeling that I got was there. I just cried and cried in there, when I came out of there I was just floating on air, I wasn't even touching ground. I felt so light, that was my first experience. When I came out of that Sweat is when I first came home. I never drank but I had booze because I had all kinds of money to buy it. When you're out on the Lakes, you're there for nine months, you come out here, you have all kinds of money to buy booze. That's all I did, I had all kinds of booze in the house. I'd go and pour myself a drink in the morning, try to drink, spit it out.

That's how I quit, every time I tried to drink, it was just like someone was grabbing me by the throat and was choking me, I spit it out, when I swallowed it I got sick, I'd bring it up. Then I went crying to one of my Elders on the reserve. I said, 'I can't drink anymore.' I felt so alone, so lost. I didn't know what to do with myself, so he said to me, 'So what happened to you when you drove there to Wisconsin for ceremonies?' I told him what happened in the Sweat. He said, 'You were helped, if you want to follow this way you can't have alcohol in your life.' So I quit and that'll be eighteen years ago. June fifteenth will be eighteen years. It's been eighteen years since I first walked into that Lodge.

Since then I've been following the ways, I have never taken a drink since then. Mind you, I had a fall-back, a relapse, that was from burn-out. I was working at the treatment centre, that's when I went and drank. But that old man told me, 'One more and that's it, you'll never touch it again.' We had got into a car accident, my girlfriend and I, and just from the after-shock I just went, I had to have a drink. I drank one evening and that was it, that was my last drink [laughs].

Raising Children

I think it was important for men in child rearing. The way we taught, I really respect my father, my grandparents. My grandfather on my mother's side was a real tease. He played with us a lot. I really liked being around him. My other grandfather was more into politics. One of the things is when he used to tell stories, he'd never leave the table, we couldn't leave the dinner table until the story was finished. The stories, I never kept those stories because I was too busy thinking of going out to play – that was all that was on my mind. So I never really kept those stories, but I guess today when all of things happen, I think, 'Oh that's what he said.' It comes back.

Elders

An Elder is one that knows their teachings. I don't consider myself as an Elder, the one that I see as an Elder is my Elder that I have very high respect for is Peter O'Chiese and Mary Roberts, those are my two teachers that I have. They are the ones that I see as my Elders. I do not see myself as an Elder.

To approach an Elder the Tobacco, the Tobacco offering always comes first. An Elder is not going to tell you anything until you offer that Tobacco and you pray with that Tobacco first, you don't just go and buy it. You can feel that Tobacco when you're holding it when a person comes and gives it to you, you can feel it if there's no heartbeat in that Tobacco, then that person did not say their prayers for that Tobacco, on what they wanted it for. Because they see it done, they don't understand so they just know you're supposed to give Tobacco to an Elder but they don't know the meaning of it. The meaning of that and what they're supposed to do.

A lot of times that person wants their dream interpreted or their Indian name, when that Tobacco is given, we're human beings, we haven't got all the answers. When a person's dream is being interpreted, grandmothers and grandfathers of the four directions, that's who we bring that Tobacco to. An Elder is a vessel or instrument with that Tobacco. So that Tobacco helps your words, they just come out. So it's not you that's doing it, if you really concentrate on that Tobacco you don't try to use your own mind, you have to do it from your heart, from your centre.

Heroes and Role Models

I have no heroes. I have lots of role models. My mother was my best role model. My grandparents were my best role models, so was my father. Because your Spirit chooses those as your parents as your Spirit leaves the greater side. You learn from those parents, that's what you came for. It's good even though you go through a lot of pain.

You're always learning, positive and negative, you balance them. Always try to walk in balance, that's why at the time of going through a lot of pain, you're building a lot of anger. When you begin to deal with that pain you begin to let go of that anger, you see the other side, that balance, when you see the other side of the dark side, you begin to have that respect. It is a powerful teacher, so is the positive side, it is also a very powerful teacher, so you balance that. That's how you let go of that pain, you're able to see and you recognize that. When you start working with people you begin to see that. You try to see balance to see where that person is coming from, because you have dealt with your own issues, your own pain, so you can help others. A lot of times when you're talking to a person that's dealing with a lot of pain, usually they can't see, they can't feel, but it isn't until they've worked on their pain, then they could see it.

One time they cut one of the big trees at the house, my little brother was small, and he still has that scar on his head. We had no ball or nothing – some of the other kids would have a ball and we didn't, so I was pretending it was a ball – it was a block of wood and I was standing on that stump and I threw it and my sister was supposed to catch it, but my little brother ran by her and it caught him – it landed on his head and he passed right out, knocked him out. I was never so scared, I guess the cut was so deep. That's the first time my father ever took his belt off, but what happened was I was backing away from him and he had a little bench there with a basin and a bucket of water to wash for us kids. I was backing away from him and he was going to come and give me a strap. I was backing away, and I must have tripped because I fell right into that basin of water. And it was cold. That was the end of my licking. My dad just burst out laughing. That was my punishment. That was as close as I got to getting a licking from my father. My father has never laid a hand on me.

Homosexuality

They had a special role. They were not outcasts, people knew they were different, that they were born that way, that balance was not there. Their sexuality and their spirituality was, I know one at home, he was never an outcast. He was always the one, they were given a role, for example, if there's a woman on their time during ceremonies, feasts, gatherings, or namings, I remember that person had to do the cooking; or if the woman is on her time at home it is that one that comes in and does the cooking. And also if the parents had to go somewhere, usually if it's the mother. I remember my mother was helping as a midwife and she would go and be gone so it was that person who would come and baby-sit. That was their role. They were respected. They were known to do different things.

Tricksters

It's to put that balance again. Lots of times we get too serious in ceremonies and it's always that trickster that comes in and puts that balance back, to bring the balance. They do everything backwards. I danced in the Sundance for four years, every time we finished one Sundance, because it's really, it's one of the greatest, 'cause you're up there. I guess it's to ground you to come back down from that Sundance, because most of the time, you're taken right to that Spirit realm. So when the Sundance is finished, it's the clowns that come in, and you laugh, and they do every-thing backwards, they come in backwards in the Lodge. Their pipe is upside down, they have little wee arrows and you have to give them some-thing, throw something, Tobacco or money or something, and that arrow has to touch that gift. Sometimes you don't have time to do it but they come and tease you. It's really a lot of fun.

Traditional music was already banned. I'd never known what a Sweat Lodge was until I first went to my ceremony. But really I had seen it before, but the first thing that came back was my flashback as a child. Because we spent a lot of time at my grandparents' on my mother's side. I think that's where most of my learning came from. I remember even my mother every 1 November or All Saints' Day, they'd call it, she'd have cooked and made a big feast and she'd leave all that food on top the stove overnight. We'd have feasted that day but those pots were left open all night. I'd seen the Sweetgrass, medicines and Cedar. She used to smudge all that food, Tobacco was put in the stove, I've seen that. Even at Christ-mas time or Easter, they didn't have a big meal but they really cooked on All Saints' Day, that's when they'd feed the spirits, very big feasts. All those pots would be opened, that Tobacco was always put in the fire, but I never knew what that was. All I remember is saying thank you for that, *miigwech*, because I heard my mother, my grandmother, my grandfather saying that to burn the Tobacco.

They all take a dish from any house you go to on that day, maybe it's that person that had gone on from that house, you'd offer that, so you'd go to different houses and do the same. I remember my mother always smudged the house with Cedar. She'd put holes in the pail and she'd go around and smudge inside the house, outside, all around she'd walk around with the smudge.

Art

There was not really much art, but I've seen picture frames my grand-mother used to do them, and she used to make canoes, those great big canoes, not dugouts, she'd use the outside of a tree. That's the kind of work she used to do. A lot of them they made their own sweaters, mitts, gloves, toques, and they would put little men in a circle holding hands in a circle, even my uncle used to make those, they had a pattern and they used that. They used to make a star on your gloves, on your sweaters. It's from their own wool and they dye it. The last one that I've known to have done that is my mother, but one of my cousins still does that, it's being carried on.

Routine

I get up pretty early, my best time is in the morning. I always enjoy my morning, it's my favourite time, just the quiet, I don't like anybody interrupting me, I guess that's why I like living alone. I like my mornings and I get up before even the sun comes up. I get up for that woman (*Beesim kwe*) and it really feels good. You have that connection and you see that light, the day coming, that's my best time, my favourite times.

Importance of Work

Being a role model is a contribution. Being a role model, you're teaching your children. My grandchildren do not abuse drugs or alcohol, they've never seen me use alcohol and drugs, so I've been a good role model for them. My youngest granddaughter is already going on her first degree. I've put all my two grandchildren in the Berry Fasts and looked after them. It gives me life just helping them and they have that respect for me. I'm very fortunate. But I had to go through a lot of pain for my own growth. A lot! Like I had to fast a lot to find myself. For me that's hard but that's where you learn. So I sit out there. Everything even what I do today, that's where it came from, the visions that were given to me, because they're really strong, they never leave me. Everything that I've went through, when I am out there, things I have to let go, letting go, that's where I've been able to let go. Psychiatrists, all my life I've been going to psychiatrists and never got anywhere, but my answers I got through fasting.

When I began working on myself, healing myself, my vision began. I go out and do workshops on Native perspective on child sexual abuse in communities. In communities I do an outline of it, but I don't go into a lot of detail because they don't have the support there. What I've been doing is going to treatment centres and doing workshops with them on that topic, so that's where it begins, people have to heal themselves. How can you help someone when you haven't dealt with your own issues? You're still carrying that incest and sexual abuse. You still carry it if you haven't dealt with it, so how can you help a child that's been sexually abused? So you have to deal with your issues, accept those things that have happened. It's the same with me, the pain that I've gone through is all worth it, we're here to experience and to grow, because sometimes we are sent here for a reason and we have to look for the reason why we're here.

For me, one of those is to help incest and sexually abused victims and dysfunctional families. You have to have gone through it and dealt with it, in order to help that person. How many times when I was going through all the pain, I never knew why I was going through so much pain and carrying all this anger, I end up going to psychiatrists and therapists, they've never helped me, they don't understand. They've took it up in universities but they've never experienced it, so how can they help that person? They understand what's going on but they can't get in touch with that person's feelings, so they can't help. For Native people, it has to be a Native person to do that. They're making money to pay psychiatrists and therapists and they don't even help us.

It's just a waste of money. Now it's time for us to help ourselves, we are Native people and we know that the White system doesn't work for us. We have to do it ourselves, we have to go back to original teachings, in order to understand ourselves and to help other people. You can't help them with the White way of teaching, the White way of helping people doesn't work, we have to do it our way.

I was terrified the first time I did a Cedar bath. It was a grandmother who came to me in a dream when I was fasting out there. She asked me to help her pick some Cedar. There was a young man lying there, his back was full of wounds, he was whipped, his back was just opened with cuts. She said, you're going to help me help that person. So we got the Cedar and put it on the stove to simmer and she strained it and put it in a bowl. She made me watch everything, she told me to watch. She washed that man, she said, 'You help me,' and when I first seen that man he was a little boy, a baby, he was about seven years old when I saw the lashes on his back.

As we started washing him, he was a young man then. He was in so much pain and when she began to wash him he threw up and what he was bringing up was green. He cried, it was just like a new baby crying, a newborn baby cry, that's the kind of cry that came out. She just kept washing him, her hands were just black and the medicine water was just black. The smell was not good. After she finished washing, she had sea salt and put it in the water and everything just washed off. She wrapped him up in a bear wrap, there was not a mark nor a trace on his back. When she finished, she said to me, 'Now I've shown you what to do, now it's your turn and you go out and do that. I've shown you what to do.'

I was scared, boy was I ever scared, [in a very loud voice] I said, 'I couldn't do that, it's too strong, too powerful.' It wouldn't go away. But eventually a man called me and asked for my help. It wasn't until I got over there, he was in Toronto. He didn't meet me at the bus.

He kept me up all night, he could not sleep. What happens is their mind races and he was just going. I tried to help him but I didn't know why. He told me, 'The voices are telling me that it's you, you have to help me, you're the only one that can help me.' He couldn't even find his car. I called his father to pick him up. I had to do a workshop. He was taken home and his people put him in a Sweat. His wife called me and asked me to come to help her. She said he was calling for me to help him. I went to see him and looked after him for a whole week. It finally dawned on me what was happening to him, he kept throwing up, getting sick, that green stuff coming out. I began to clean him up with Cedar water. Everything that grandmother showed me is what I did. Everything she showed me. That was the beginning, he slept all night, whereas before he hadn't been sleeping. Now he was getting a few hours' sleep during the day. He was okay when I left, I had to keep giving him those baths during that time. That was my first Cedar bath, I didn't want to do it, I was scared to do something wrong.

The Cedar bath is getting rid of the abuse as a child, to let those go. It makes you see where it's coming from and what's happening and you can deal with it. That's what a Cedar bath does. Sometimes some people take four Cedar baths. I actually have to give them four Cedar baths in approximately five years, which is how long it takes to deal with sexual abuse, maybe longer. I know with one person who'd been sexually abused by her father, it took seven Cedar baths to open that door. When you go through that severe trauma, your Spirit leaves your body and sometimes that Spirit can't get back in. So when I clean them, I know their Spirit is not there, it's on the outside and that Spirit wants to come in. It isn't until you hear that baby inner cry is when that Spirit returns. You begin to heal that inner child, then you have to nourish and feed that inner child, look after him or her. That's why by going to ceremonies, hearing your teachings, going to Sweats is how you heal that inner child.

The Healing Lodge here will be opened in July. You can't bring that whole family together because there'll be withdrawals and anger towards the family. When I began to heal, I began to get angry with my family, I began to get angry with everybody that I called family that's close to me. It's best that the family heal themselves first. The Healing Lodge will be in cycles, the men for thirty days, women for thirty days, children for thirty days by themselves. When you feel that they have reached their growth in accepting, then the whole family is brought together and they are healed as a whole.

I can only handle fifteen to sixteen people there at once, in order for it to work. Most will be dealt with individually, a one-to-one basis. Group therapy will be done every day too, Sweat Lodges, there'll be fasting. Elders that do healing will be there to help. We hoped for four counsellors, right now we have only two counsellors, so we're looking for other resources for funding to at least get two more counsellors.

Every thirty days when we finish one cycle we will take a week break, to be alone, to rest, and we will have our own sessions and workshops with staff, just to build them up, keep them strong, because this is very heavy so we need to look after ourselves if we want to work. I've been burned out before and I know what it's like. It takes every ounce of energy out of you and takes you about four years to get back.

Ceremonies

Ceremonies are held during the four seasons, Mid-Winter for four days, Spring for four days, Mid-Summer for four days, and Fall, for four days. We have Naming Ceremonies, we have Memorial Ceremonies, Young People Ceremonies, young boys when their voice begins to change, same as young girls when their cycle starts, they [girls] are put into Grandmother's Moon Lodge and they're given teachings too. When they come out a ceremony is held, because when they come out they're bringing life to the people. Those young girls fast on those berries for one year. They pick them as they come in season and that's what they feed people when they finish their fast. They can't pick up newborn babies for one year. So it's a treat for them, some of them just look for a baby to go and take one, and hold. At all ceremonies, there is a feast. We have Sweats all the time, we have Full Moon ceremonies.

Grieving

Once I've known my teachings I've never really gone through that grieving. You probably go through the grieving process for about a month after they're gone. Not even that for your loved ones. But you know where they are because of the teachings, it's a more beautiful place where they've gone, there's no worries. This world is a growing place, where there's a lot of pain. It's pure where they are. From the teachings we know, when the Creator blows his own sacred breath and gave Original Man his own Spirit, we too have the Creator's Spirit, we carry his Spirit. So how is he going to destroy, that's what really bothers me. When I was a kid in residential school, I'd been told that I would burn in hell. The Creator is not going to destroy his own Spirit. We're here to learn, so we go back to him when we leave here. So why should one grieve? You know that Spirit is happy where they are. They're at a good place, they're true with themselves.

Traditional Beliefs and Christianity

When you read the Bible, it's similar. We were given these teachings in the beginning. We can relate to them, we can feel them, we can identify with them. For me that other teaching [Christian], I can't relate to it because it's not mine, it wasn't meant for me, but I respect it. Even my own abuse as a child, your own Elders are strong Roman Catholics, it turns you off. How come they couldn't see the abuse? My grandmother was a very strict Catholic. I even got tangled in her prayer beads one night [laughing]. She never went anywhere without her prayer beads, even when she was sleeping.

Clans

I'm a Bear Clan. Usually Ojibwe people go by their father's clan, usually Cree go by their mother's clan, same as Mohawks. That's why we have clans, we don't marry into your own clan. If you marry your own clan, it's your family. A lot of times when you see that since we've lost our clans, children are being born deformed or something is wrong. That's why it's important to know your clan. Also your clan is your helper. Clans sit in different places in the Lodge, they have different responsibilities. Like the Bear Clan, they are healers, they protect the community and the people, they also do healings, it's that bear that does the healing. With me, I know I'm a human being, I have no powers to heal anyone, but that bear is the one that has the power to heal. There is nothing, no sickness that he cannot heal. If you pray to that bear when you're helping someone, it is the bear doing the healing. Those four directions, they take all those resentments, that eagle takes it away and those Grandmothers and Grandfathers throw it away. That's one of the things I can't see in the Catholic church when you go for Confession [laughs], you think it's going to go away. You have to deal with it, you give it to those four directions.

Prophecies

[Long silence]. I'd have to reflect on that. [Another long silence]. I believe in the prophecies. Everything said in the prophecies has come true. Right now today I believe we are the seventh fire children, we are the ones who are struggling, we're the ones who have to go out to fast to get our answers because the Elders, nobody knows our teachings, we have to go a long way to find our Elders. Our Elders are asleep and don't want to talk about them. For ourselves, we had a hard time when we began to search. My father nearly disowned us, but when he began to come over here, because he was very close to my daughter and she'd go and get him to stay here for a few weeks. He would go to ceremonies, he'd feel the difference of the place because it's a sacred place. That's when he began to talk to us, he began to see where my sister and I had left the drugs and the alcohol and we were trying to live a good life.

So he saw that. It took a while and so he began to tell us things. He gave his youngest grandchild, my niece, an Indian name. He gave her his grandmother's names, that she was a medicine woman. He's told us about medicines and told us about our grandmothers and grandfathers and what he remembers. Even when he died, he wanted to go that way.

Stages of Life

There are seven stages of life. That first stage is Spirit life, when mother is carrying that vessel. That first stage is up to seven years and there's even a break there and we have a hard time to go into each stage. At the first stage, the child is half Spirit and half human. It's more in the Spirit world than in this reality, that's why in the first stage, what you give to that child is the learning, they've learned everything about life already. The mother and father are the teachers, whatever we give them is their learning, good or bad. Because the child is closer to spirits, it's open to knowledge at that time. The mother is the first teacher to give life, everything is given freely, all physical and mental needs, love, affection, example, it's very important how the mother is. She prepares that child for the life path. Child is affected by all that goes on in the home even before birth. When the child is seven years old, they should have all the foundations for a good life. Around seven, boys should spend time with fathers, and girls should spend time with mothers and women.

Discipline is based on reason. The mother loves unconditionally. Father places conditions on love and tries to do what is best. He sees where life could go wrong. That's why it's so important for the mother and father to raise that child. Because the mother gives that unconditional love, the father gives that discipline. Here again you see in the Creation, in that fire, that Grandmother Moon, that water, so with unconditional love, you have that balance. Father places conditions, he's the one that disciplines, he's the one that has that fire, that voice of thunder, even when that child hears his raised voice to discipline that child will run to that unconditional love of the mother. It's important that the two parents raise the child, he needs both parents. It's important to bring that child into the Lodge when they're born. One time I did a Moon Ceremony when a young girl had finished her cycle, there was a little boy, and he was crying and crying just before the ceremony, and the mother wanted to take him out, saying he'll disturb the ceremony, and I said to leave that child here, he'll go to sleep, he'll take those teachings, his Spirit will carry those teachings. Sure enough as soon as the drum started the little boy fell asleep. He didn't wake up until after the ceremony was over. Just the way he was, you could tell he was taking those teachings.

The second stage is that fast life. They should have everything they need in life. Everything starts coming at you fast, you want it right away, cars, arcades, changes all around you, physically and emotionally. Children begin to move away from their parents, but parents' responsibility is not over. If you have given them everything for a good life, all you can do is keep reminding them. Child doesn't want to listen to their parents. Parents can prepare the child by telling them this is going to happen. Children will turn away from parents, they must prepare to fast, parents must understand what the child is going through. When the parents prepare the child from the first stage. Like with me I took my grandchildren to fast for one night, one day, when they were five years old. My little granddaughter, the youngest one, ran to go fasting, she had all her stuff packed by the door, she was all ready.

Second stage is between seven years to sixteen or seventeen years, it's the fast life. With the break-ins in our communities, a lot of times it's that child calling for help, saying listen to me. That's his way of asking for attention. A lot of times you can talk to those children, you can repeat yourself, you have to keep talking to them, you can't give up on them, because they're going through that fast stage. They'll go and try things, that's why it's so important for mother to be there, it's the hardest time for parents, children don't want to listen to you, they want to go and try things. For instance, I had one of the kids that I raised, she went downtown and I told her not to hang around in the mall, and she said she's going to the library. Sure enough she didn't go to the library, she went to the mall. She stole a card. I've never know her to steal, yet she went downtown and stole a card for me. She got caught so the police brought her home.

She was so ashamed, two of my students boarded there. She called them uncles because in my home we're all family. She was ashamed because her uncles had seen the police bring her home, she stayed in her room, she wanted me to bring the TV in there, wanted to eat there. I kept telling her I'm glad what's happened and she was so upset, she said, 'You don't love me, you hate me.' I told her, 'I love you, that's why I said this.' I told her, 'When you're ready to listen, I'll talk to you.' So later on she got tired of staying in her room and she came out and said, 'Okay, Auntie, I'm ready to listen to what you have to say.' I explained that the reason why I was glad this happened, you got caught, because it was your first time. I talked to her about that second stage, that fast life, what she was experiencing. I understand that she had to go and try it out. 'That's why I'm glad you got caught, now you won't do it again. What would have happened if you hadn't been caught? You would have just done it again and maybe do it over and over until it gets so big that you could end up in the Correctional Centre, and then in jail and then in prison. Do you want that? I don't want that for you. This is why I'm glad you got caught the first time.'

You have to explain, you have to keep talking to them, you gotta explain, don't just say, 'Don't do this.' A lot of our kids commit suicide at that stage because there is no one there to talk to them. Parents are too busy working. Our families, in order to survive, two parents have to work, so where's the mother, where's the father? They don't have time, they're too tired when they are home to pay attention to their children. So that's why there's so much violence with our youth today. There's no one there for them. A lot of people now today don't know their teachings, the young people are asking, 'Who am I, where am I going?' And the parents have no answers because they're lost themselves, so that's when suicide comes in, they give up, they think, No one loves me, no one cares for me, no one pay attention to me, no one wants to listen to me. That's what happens.

The third stage is the wandering life, wandering all over. What are you looking for? What is the meaning of life? What is the point of going on? This is the time to seek answers. He looks behind and sees nothing, he sees no value, he looks ahead, he sees nothing, he sees no value. This is the time he may choose to step out of this life. What they had been raised by influences them, they seek out their own teachers, some are good, some are not. Parents should keep talking to their children.

They can be on that stage for a long time. I was on that wandering stage until I was forty-five, until I found the Lodge. That wandering life is where you wander all over looking for different answers and teachers.

The fourth stage is truth life, it shows what gifts and talents are. You are your own person, helper of one another. Now you do for your children what has been given to you. You should have that truth life, those four directions in your life, you should put those four directions in your life and you should be living it. Your Spirit comes into reality with those four directions and you have to put it into your life.

In that first stage, that child should have that belief. The second stage is the freedom. The third is wandering. The fourth is truth. The fifth stage is planting life, having your family, taking responsibility as a parent. The sixth stage is doing life, practise what has been given to you, your teachings. The seventh stage is looking behind, you are the Elder, you must do it alone. Teachers are key people for beginning of life, your grandchildren. The Elder passes on knowledge.

So those are the stages that we go through life. There's a break in everyone in those stages, we go through a very hard time. Like if you haven't gone through all those stages, you might pick it up later on like in your planting life when you're older. All of a sudden you're forty and you go through that fast life [laughs], because they've never experienced that second stage. There was too much discipline in their life, they never experienced those things. That's why you allow those children to go and experience, so they don't have to go through it later on. If they go through it later on, they'll find another partner, they'll start running around on their mate. They haven't lived through that before, they go back to those stages. Some go back and forth in those stages.

Even a child who leaves [dies], that child's Spirit decides to go back to the Spirit world, especially if the family has violence, drinking, that Spirit does not want to stay in that environment, so it goes back. There's different ways of looking at it, maybe that child just came to do something, to bring something to that couple, had one purpose and went back.

The seventh stage is the wisdom, the Elder has the wisdom, that's why children are drawn to Elders. It's not all Elders that have the wisdom, it's your traditional teachers, it's who you see as teachers. There's a lot of Elders out there who are still growing, that haven't dealt with themselves and those are not the ones you go out to seek. You'll know which Elders are the right ones. Doing life, practise what you're given, that's where I am today. That's where the knowledge is there. I'm planting life. You should have respect for one another as partners, respect each other, work together. Wandering life is looking for that truth.

Language and Culture

Native language is very important because our teachings are in the language. You miss out on the meaning when you talk about it in English. I have a hard time because I can't speak it but I can hear it, feel it and understand it, but for me to talk, I still have to work on that because I had blocked that and I had blocked it when I was in residential school. That's one of the things that I've never dealt with. What I understand is when I hear the teachings in the Lodge, how beautiful and how sacred it is when it reaches people in the language. I can't even describe how it feels. But when you talk about it in English, it's not the same, you don't have that feeling as you have in the language. We have to get back to our language, it's important.

Traditional Names

Usually you go to someone who gives names and they find that name for you and that Tobacco always has to go first. That person cannot find that name unless the Tobacco was given because Tobacco is to the Spirits, it is not to the person, it has to come in a vision or a dream or just hear it, you can hear it in the trees or in the wind, you could hear that name up there, you'll see that person.

Economics

My grandfather used to go out on a boat in the summer, as soon as those blueberries come out. We always had plenty of food, we had blueberries, raspberries, and strawberries, and those that are in seasons, we had dried apples all year round. They were picked and were dried. My grandfather always picked cranberries. He'd be out on a boat all the time. I went out with him. As kids we'd be gone for two or three weeks or a month, just camping, picking blueberries. They also dried fish, they smoked fish, smoked meat, we always had smoked meat. We had no freezers so most of the food we had was smoked fish and smoked meat, dry meat, good food.

Dreams

Dreams have helped me through my life, especially when you're fasting. Dreams and visions, when a dream comes and it doesn't leave you and it's so real – it's telling you something. Sometimes those dreams don't come, they don't work right away. With me, I just told you my experience of going to the centre of the world and look how long it's taken me to realize the meaning of what I was being told [the tape recorder was turned off when this dream was told to Emily]. It's just affecting me now and that's probably ten years ago. Sometimes it takes a long time before you understand it.

There are people who have the gift of interpreting dreams. When you go and ask someone to interpret your dream, they will not tell you about that dream until that Tobacco is given because that Tobacco is always first when you go ask your traditional teachers, you have that respect. A dream cannot be translated unless that Tobacco is given, because you pray with it to the four directions. That's where it goes and you're only the vessel. You can hear some people sometimes talking in the Lodge, that are praying. You can tell that person it's not them that's praying, it's a Spirit. Their voice begins to change, like in a trance state, so you know it's not them talking, it's the Spirit talking through them. They are only a vessel, people don't have the powers. Like with me, when that grandmother showed me how to do those medicine baths, it's her who does it, it's not me. I'm only a vessel. I haven't got the power to do that.

Traditional Medicines

Yes, there are different kinds. But it's not the healers doing that healing. They're the vessel. We all have a Spirit of that and some people can use it better than others who haven't learned how to use that gift because you have to have balance in your life to be able to use that. If you abuse it, it will disappear. You can see what is wrong with that sick person and you can see what kind of medicine you can use. It's a gift certain people have.

Education

Residential schools really damaged our communities. I think it affected all the families without realizing how they've been affected, like today, they're more possessed with material things like they were taught in residential schools. I know for myself, the cleanliness and perfection was what I was taught in residential school. When I got out I was obsessed with clean. I got really upset when I go where people can't clean their place. I have to have everything in order, in the drawers neatly. That's one of the things I learned. The teacher used to come and open the drawers to make sure everything was in neat order, your bed had to be made a certain way and your nightgown had to be folded a certain way and your shoes had to be a certain way under your bed. That's learned behaviour. I learned that from residential school. I'm trying to get away from that and I've really had to work on that. When I was married, my house had to be clean, everything had to be shiny, no dust around, everything was in place in the drawers.

I raised my nephew Dwayne. I used to get after him to be neat and in order. Later he went to live on his own next door, so everything was in its place. One time he asked me to look for something in a drawer and everything was just perfect in that drawer [laughs]. So he picked that up from me because that's the way I raised him. My daughter is the same way and I'm still like that today but I've learned that I've missed out on a lot of things because my house had to be so clean, dishes, floors, beds made, before I could leave the house and because of that I've missed out on a lot of things. I spent a lot of time cleaning, that's a learned behaviour from residential school, because that's the way I was raised, I was brought up to be a perfectionist. It's awful. I have one friend that I've been working with, she was in residential school. I was telling her that if I want to go someplace, those dirty clothes are going to be there when I come back, those dirty dishes will still be there when I come back, the floors will be there [laughs] so that's all right, I'll have something to do when I come back. All those behaviours have to be let go and you have to see it.

Hanging on to Culture

As long as you carry your medicines, your bundle, if you have one,

Tobacco, that bundle that's been left, scattered on the trail, that's what you need. It doesn't matter if you're in the city, you can still use that medicine to smudge yourself, you can make offering for that water with Tobacco. Some people go to Sweats, like I can go to Saskatchewan and there'll be a Sweat over there, there'll be a Sundance, and I can go to that. If you look, you can find it. If you're really looking, it's there.

I went to a justice meeting last week in Ottawa and there's people from all over across Canada there. That's what they were saying, you can go anywhere and find my culture, a Sweat Lodge, women's circle, that I can go to. All you have to do is look. Teachers are all over. If you can't find them, you're not looking in the right places.

I went to northern Saskatchewan, La Ronge, one of the girls who ran the workshop was taking me to the airport in Saskatoon and on our way she said that she knew some traditional people on the way. So we stopped at their house to say hello. They have Native radio systems and these people had heard about my workshop, when we got there they were just getting ready for a Sweat and they invited me to go into their Sweat. It doesn't matter where you are, there's always culture there.

Traditional Justice

Even if they get locked up, they go back into society, there is no one there for them. This society is so fast and people are in their own little world and they don't have time for anyone else. These people who are locked up and then freed, they always end up in prison. Even these halfway houses don't always help, because they're not dealing with the real problem. Some halfway houses have Sweats and circles.

When you go into prison, you carry a lot of anger and you come out with a lot of anger, you're still carrying that garbage around. So when you get out, there's no place to go to deal with that anger. They always end up back in there. When I do work on anger management there's a way of doing that, you take them into a Sweat and they let out that anger in the Sweat and you talk to them and give them the teachings in order for them to let that go. The spiritual realm and teachings is where you begin, only then will they have real understanding. Even with how to deal with sexual abusers, they used to cast them away from their communities, usually that person is a loner out there, they go to another community and people there know why he's been cast away from his community, they were the only ones cast away and they are not accepted into other communities either.

These sexual abusers wandered. Today you don't cast that person out. I guess that was a way to teach a person not to abuse. I know a lot of communities who have said, we don't want this man here who has sexually abused a child, so he's cast out of the community. So what does that man do? He goes to another community and picks a woman with a little girl the same age and does the same thing. It continues, it's not dealt with. That's why men are in one session at my Healing Lodge, because those men have been abused as children and they've blocked that and they don't feel the child's pain when they abuse them. It's the same with women who abuse. You have to look at all those things and see where that abuser has come from. You just can't cast them out, the violence will just continue. You have to break that violence, so it will not be passed on. That abused child will just go out and do the same thing when they're adults, it's a learned behaviour. You have to treat that person, help that person, by making them see where it's coming from. Help them see how they can deal with that problem. They go to Sweats and medicine baths, fasting, they can't be cast away or locked up. The only ones who can't be helped are the ones who go out and sexually abuse a child and kill them. Those cannot be helped. In prison they can't hurt anyone. I've done workshops in prison on family violence, and I know they say they can't help it, and they feel safe locked up.

The one who sexually abuses a child will just continue to sexually abuse children because they haven't dealt with their own issues because they've blocked all feelings and cannot feel that child's pain. So he has to get in touch with his feelings. That's the only way he can be really healed.

Relations with Non-Native People

We have to make them understand who we are. That's the only way we can work together. It's just like with corrections people I told you about earlier. Their gift is movement, they move very fast and we move a slower path. It's like the Original Man, he was the last one to leave the Creator's side, and the White man was the first one to leave, he didn't even look back to the gifts he was given and look at them now, he's lost all his gifts, he doesn't know who he is and he moves very fast. He gets all over the world and wants everything, he wants to control everything because he has lost all those gifts that the Creator had given him. But the Anishinabe was the last one to leave the Creator's side and many times he's turned around and looked at the Creator and the Creator had to coax him to go. That's how slow he's walked and that's how we are, like that Original Man. We walk very slow and examine what's there and we don't jump into things right away, as soon as we jump into things right away, we try to go real fast and we fall flat on our face. The White man has to understand that and not to push us, he's always pushing, trying to make things happen right away. But with us, we have to examine, we have to move slowly.

Closing Thoughts

As a person that's been going to different communities, what I see a lot is abuse of Elders. I even see the government abusing Elders, they take them to open ceremonies and that Elder has to travel a long way, they give them the cheapest flight rates and they don't look after them properly. They put them in a fancy hotel but don't give them enough to survive, to eat. All of these government people don't give Elders anything for honorarium, they are being used. Because White government doesn't understand us and the Native teachings, they do things their way.

Government wastes money on commissions, they travel first-class and at the end they ask for a conference with Elders. They get all those Elders there and didn't pay one cent in honorarium, yet they did all the work. There's a teaching on that, on how they cried for that Native brother to get what they want and they're still doing it. I see a lot of abuse, same as the Elders, sometimes people classify themselves as Elders and abuse people in Sweat Lodges, it's not right. You have to see and know who your teachers are. We're so conditioned to that movement and jump into things. Go slowly!

Young people should have respect for those teachers, should know how to treat their teachers and Elders. I see so many being misused and are so tired out, they are so demanded. They don't know how to say thank you properly. They just see what they want. That is why it is important for us to pick up that bundle and learn those teachings. Know who you are. To carry yourself with respect, that's why the Creator put you here. Carry your gifts. Sure it is good for you to have all those material things, but all those material things are not for you to follow.

ALEX SKEAD (Ojibwe)

Rat Portage First Nation, Ontario

'It's just like reading a book when I am talking to you.'

Alex Skead was born on 9 March 1922 at Rat Portage First Nation in Northern Ontario. He is from the Sturgeon Clan, and his traditional names are *Nopcumeeganung*, which means 'following footsteps,' and *Mishakeyaskege*, which means 'lightning.'

During Emily's interview Alex Skead was still very busy. He was rushing off to Sweats, talking about meetings, and looking after the training centre. But he dedicated numerous hours to the interview and patiently answered all of Emily's questions. He thought the work done by the university was very important, and he took the interview very seriously. In the discussion with Emily he stressed respect for all cultures, and an intense knowledge of Native traditions. Most notable is Alex Skead's description of his Sweat Lodge, and how it related to his teachings, and his philosophy.

Alex Skead passed away in the spring of 1995. He is survived by five children and, in 1994, three grandchildren. His Elders–Youth Training Centre still operates at Rat Portage First Nation. At the centre Native traditional values are taught so that they can be passed on to young people.

Life History

First of all I'll introduce myself. I'm Ojibwe, my name is Alex Skead. I was born in Rat Portage Reserve, in 1922, and I was born and raised here, I never been any place until I was about thirty years of age, and I started to do some travelling and started to see the country. And then I began to see a lot of things that is very important in this country, and I've been almost coast to coast. I've been up to as far as maybe Montreal, and I didn't quite make it the other way, but I hope I can make it sometime. But I been all the way down to Vancouver, down to Mexico, and the northern parts of Canada. It's very interesting when you learn the travel, how important everything is. And when I begin to see the people I learned a lot.

I've been involved with people for quite some time. I can't name the dates because I don't remember, I never wrote them down. The time my kids were very small I raised them in a Native way, and I had people come down to my house a long time ago, they called themselves the song of Asia. They are all nationalities. They are Black people, Yellow people – Chinese – and we also had some White people in there. So that's made the four colours of the people. So I kind of learned a big thing out of that. When I learned there are four types of people in this world and I began to realize when I sit in the Sweat Lodge.

The Sweat Lodge teaches me a lot of things. It comes from the Mother Earth. How everything gets to be together, how important it is that the great teachings of Mother Earth – the things that are growing, the trees, water, and the birds and the animals that are four-legged. Even the bugs, everything, everything in this life. We learn, I learn that I am not any better than all these things. They are all equal, that's life. Some of these things like bugs and animals, they got shorter life, and something else that have a longer life, like a turtle has a long life, and us people we are just about in the middle. Some of them die young, some of them die old, and I think it's part of our fault to why a lot of our young people die off because the Creator didn't plan it that way, for people to take their lives and all these things. We were very flexible, that's why the world is so interesting, being so flexible.

There's a good and bad and always take people that are really bad people that are doing something wrong – always pity on them and pray for them, because I learned that I have the same feeling for a poor person that has problems, and I feel that I am part of those guys that are having problems all the time. I went through it myself, but I caught myself one time. I used to experience the problems, the things that a lot of people are facing.

Now when I start talking about people of four colours, the Native people always follow, that's four directions. That's my own opinion, I am not picking it up from a Bible or from any kind of a book, but through a Sweat Lodge I began to realize there are four types of human beings. The White people, there was a man that came down to teach them how to live.

Okay, I'm telling you the story and it comes from inside of me, but I don't know if that's going to help you, but anyway that's just the way that I see things. It's just like reading a book when I am talking to you. But if you have any problems with it just let me know. I think this is the most important thing, because I use this when I am training people here. This is the way we start.

Like the people. People are very important. It doesn't matter if it's black, yellow, red, and white. Now I'm talking about White people now. The White people, from way back, like I talked about when I started.

Okay, I drew something in there, of a circle. I was working for a sacred circle and I'm not there anymore. I am over here. So that, a Sweat Lodge, is a sacred circle itself. The beginning of life is from the East, because you rest at night. When you wake up in the morning then the sun comes up. That's the beginning of life. And then you just go forward with the sun. The Earth keeps moving, the sun always. That's the teachings, the sun is moving. Just to make a better understanding. So, actually maybe the sun doesn't move.

Anyway, the way of the teachings is to keep the understanding because some people got me all confused, because the world is round and it's circling around the sun and changes everything, and the weather and all kinds of things. So the teachings of the Native people is the reason that we always see the sun moving. We don't know we're moving. These people down south, they're Earth people. You know that they follow the Mother Earth. And us people here up north, we have the birds. Like the eagle. The eagle is flying around. So that's the way the clan system is down there. The clan system up here is the father, and the mother is down south. So that, those are the teachings. So that's why, a lot of people don't believe in that because they are so confused, but when you come to a sacred way of living and thinking you follow the sun, and you will get down and it's just like we are sitting in one place. I used to think that when I was a kid. 'Where does the world end? Everything is just flat.' I used to wonder that a long time ago. Before even I went to school. I didn't know that the world was round. So this is the way I always thought about it, you know, I thought that the world was flat, and there comes to the end what's in there. It's a big wonder.

Anyway, when I talk about the people, they are, what do you call the White people, the Red people, Yellow people, and the Black people. Now my Sweat Lodge works like this [Alex Skead draws on the ground]. Okay? Now when I talk about White people, there must be some teachings that Jesus came down, how to live, and teach them how to make medicine. How he made miracles. He did all kinds of things, healed all the people that were blind, impossible things. I believe in that because everything went through. And they also had a feast. The food never runs out when you have a feast. You know, so that's the way Jesus worked in here. It's only a little part that I am talking about.

Now when you come to the Yellow people, they have their beliefs. Buddha whatever you call him. But anyway, I asked the Chinaman, 'Why are they putting fruit on that statue?' It's an offering for that. We do the same thing as Red people. We're up here. Sunset people, Red people. And we had our teacher, how to make medicine, how to live, the legends, everything. We still see a lot of things here. That man he never dies, he went back sitting there with the mighty God. Same thing with this guy here, Jesus. He is sitting over there, he didn't die. And the Yellow people also. He must be up there, with mighty God. There, right there in the centre. And he is the four corners, the four doors of the Sweat Lodge. And there are also Black people. They must have had, the White man wasn't there all the time to teach them how to pray, how to dance, how to sing, how to perform ceremonies. Who did that? It must be somebody in here, the mighty God.

Now when you come to these four directions, we're all related. You probably, I don't know, your grandparents, great-grandparents, maybe there are some intermarriages. Red people, Black people, or Yellow people. This is all cross-marriages. Love is there. Love is there in the centre, God. And this man here worked hard, he got killed. That's like what's going on here in this world right now today. And this thing here too. I don't know. It's wars and killing one another. That's what happened to Jesus here. And here, even worse, they had slaves because they didn't want to follow these people.

That's why our people are so silent. Because we don't practise what this man taught us to do. We're lost. Look at our people, young people here, up north, suicides because they are not following what God wanted to teach these people. He taught those, but it's our own fault as people. We don't believe in something we are taught to live in harmony with this guy, with these guys, with these guys, to respect the culture in all those people. I respect the White man's culture. Religion, I respect that. I don't know how they do that, so many religions in that White man's religion. I believe in Chinese and Japanese. They have a flag, a sunrise flag, and they see the sun coming sunrise, and that's what they believe in.

What about the Black people? I don't know I've never been there, but I'd like to see what ... but we had a workshop with these people. They have the same thing what we have here as Indian people. They say they're fasting. That's what I did. I went on the island over there and fasted to learn about myself. The very first thing I realized, there was a little tree that was standing in front of me, right in a crevice of rock. I looked at it and that represents the tree. And here I was sitting there representing the people. I was thirsty, I wanted to drink water. What about this little tree, how does he get the water? I have to pray because of the thunder. I asked thunder storm, 'Please I want a rain.' In no time the rain came, a thunder storm. And the little tree was happy and I was soaked and wet [laughs]. You know. That's the way it is.

And we get sunshine, and that's how we learn by doing things. This is not a lie I am talking about. It's true by my own experience. That's why I am talking this way. How do we find these things? How do we learn? We move to a Sweat Lodge. Tell the young people to move to a Sweat Lodge and go fasting and then you know who you are. And understand that you are a Native person. Maybe we all crossed like this. Everybody has blood of every type. The Sweat Lodge has four belts on it, and this four, there is Mother Earth, that's the prayer. So that's what we learn from the Sweat Lodge.

It's pretty hard to understand. I cannot understand, but I believe what the prayers are saying, and the same thing with the four layers of universe. So that's just the thesis. I don't know, sometimes there are things that we do not understand. Is there a land over there? That's something we cannot understand. Our minds cannot deal with that far. When someone dies, there is no end. He doesn't come back again. So that's something that's impossible to learn. That's why we just have to take whatever you been told, just like Jesus said, there's a heaven up there. Who knows that eternal life, maybe there's no end where there's heaven. But I don't know where the hell is. Maybe there isn't none. Maybe there is limbo in there. But there's a lot of Indian people tell me that they have dreams of someone taking them down to the darkness, until they age, the limit of age, and they come out to the Happy Hunting Grounds.

This is something a lot of young people have to understand, what are, what are the teachings. Even the Bible says eternity is something that we cannot understand. When we die we know. I don't know. I haven't been up there yet. Pretty close. So does that enter something in your mind?

I went to residential school, St Mary's School here in Kenora. I was there five years, up to grade five. I learned something out of that. I can't say that I did learn patience. I gave it a good credit, but the only thing I didn't like about it is trying to stop us from using our language and our culture. That's the thing that I'm talking about, off balancing, because we didn't start, when you start thinking about the White man's way you don't have no respect for Native people. I used to think that they, when they say working for the devil, when you're doing Native culture, and that's exactly what people are doing now. People they don't like Indians because they are a bunch of savages and they are working for the devil. Because they think Catholic religion is the only one, or Protestant. But there are other cultures or you could call them religions. The Black people, the Red people, the Yellow people, they have rights to understand and lives of their own.

So it's there and that's the reason why there are four different colours. Now we are getting back to a number of them are White, but a number of them are Indians, but we shouldn't, because we are brothers when we come together. That Sweat Lodge here. You see this is the West. This is the East, and the Red people are sunset people, in the West. It's just a diagram that, it's just a picture. We're not sitting that way. It's just the way the thing is just to make people understand.

I was involved in Treaty Three. I did a lot of travelling. The very first thing I did is when I begin, I used to have a problem with alcohol, and then I got into an accident. Then I sat in a wheelchair, and I began to think more about myself, feeling sorry for myself, and thinking about the people. I was in the hospital for about four months, and that made me think because when I saw people, they, the doctor told me, 'I am going to put you outside so you can take some sun.' I couldn't walk because I was in a wheelchair. So then they put me up and I used to see people drinking. I see them sleeping outside, all that kind of things you know that wasn't fit to look at. And there was another young man he was in the same way. He sat beside me, he did the same thing, he had binoculars, and he said what's going on down there? So it was terrible, you know.

Anyway I began to think if I was ever going to walk I prayed. I asked the Creator, that's the time I prayed hard so that I can walk again. Because a lot of people said I would never be able to walk. So in time I had in four months I was able to stand on my feet with the crutches. So when I came out I took a job on a street patrol. I was there for seven years and hard times, my legs were sore, yeah, and I put up with it. I wanted to help the people. And my boss told me, 'I'm not going to tell you what to do. You took the job to look after this.' I was there for one year and three months. I was walking at night. But the next year I had to again apply for that job, and the boss told me I should put myself in for supervisor. Well, I said, 'I'll take you up on that.' But then I had to go through an interview. And then I started talking about my life again. Where I worked I did all kinds of work at that time. I was plumbing, and all kinds of things, and guiding, fishing you know, hunting and fishing. I went through a lot of work, carpenter work. Anyway the interview came through pretty good. I didn't have the education to run the office, but I had a lot of help from people. I formed a committee I needed, Native women there, Treaty Three, and I had a man working in the courthouse as a police sergeant. I had seven of them. So they threw all of the responsibilities to me to help and just to make the arrangements, and the boss said, 'I am not going to interfere you have to form the committees,' and I got to go through orientation to help the people. It was kind of difficult because I didn't have the education. But I had lots of knowledge of other things, how people should work.

Anyway, there was a guy that worked in the courthouse. He was a policeman, and that's how I got this how to patrol workers, because we were not policemen, but we had to work on twenty-four-hour reports. Every incident we don't have to stand in front of and write down like the policeman, we had to catch everything and then report what you see at night. We had a lead pencil, and we had uniforms and mitts, and shoes so that you can stand the weather if it's a hundred below zero so that you can work, no excuses. You have to pick up these people and you have to walk. They were passed out and you put them in detox and they were locked out and thrown out from detox, and then they go drink, and we saved a lot of people. And then that teaches me a lot of things about what's happening. When I came as a supervisor I got the job that I had these people and I had to tell them what to do. They don't carry no money, they don't carry no cigarettes, just a pencil and paper, and then you walk – slow, don't run, just do it together. Any incidents happen there you witness. You might find someone dead, you might find someone fighting, you might find someone stabbing someone, an eyewitness all the time. And then don't start chasing kids saying get the hell out of here, try and make friends with people. And don't give them cigarettes if they going to bug you all the time. So these are all my responsibilities, and then I start writing letters to committees, every one of them. I sent them out. At the time and the date, I phone them. Even the day before 'O' phone them, let's have a meeting. Every two weeks we had a meeting. And all those reports that they made I just put them on top of the table. These peoples from the committees are all questioning, 'What is the matter, why did the detox centre not come to the committee?' I asked them. 'Come on over.' He was kind of hesitating for a while because he was scared. I told him, 'There is nothing to be afraid of because I opened all the meetings, and I don't want no arguments, but let's straighten out all the things that are, where the problem is.' So that's what we did.

That's how I learned to work with people, and I knew exactly what we need, and after that I became involved with Treaty Three, and they put me to work. First I worked in the band office and they wanted to learn something about culture. There was some Elders in there that I worked with, and then I went up to Lake Ontario, Manitoba, all these places, all the way across Canada, and then I became involved with national Chiefs, met all these Elders, I got involved with a lots of these Elders across Canada. And then people start to find out the Chiefs. A lot of people asked me to do those workshops in those communities. And all these places like Armstrong, all the way across to Peterborough, and I've been involved in a lot of these schools, sharing the culture.

I didn't run a Sweat Lodge at that time, until I went fasting and I learned, that was given to me. There were a lot of things that came up, the teachings, the Spirit tells me a lot of things. And that's how, what I shared to the people, even the Treaty Three. When they have a problem they ask me and I go and help them straighten the thing. And that's my job to help people to straighten out. And then I had visions and dreams that I had to build this place, the training centre. I had the ideas of using Treaty Three, so that I can build something like this training centre. And all these twenty-five reserves. But it didn't work that way. When all the money came in, ninety thousand dollars, they all took it to all the twenty-five reserves. So we went down in the hole that much money. So the band took over and that's why we're still in the hole.

So it didn't work out the way we planned, and we have been having a hard time trying to revive this thing. For all these cabins we have to buy gas, you know that propane, and electricity, and the roads, and the septic fields that we built and everything like that. And that's why we had a hard time to get employment because we don't have any money. That's why my family is still involved here. We all worked for nothing. That's why we want to keep this thing going so that nothing doesn't freeze. Anyway, that's how things began to use. We use this place here to teach the resource people what is the Native culture. We had MNR [Ministry of Natural Resources], we had doctors, and we had police, and we had schoolteachers, and we had board directors of education. So the hospital got involved also.

There's also kids that came in a yellow bus there, from the States, that are having a lot of problems with the law and all kinds of things. They were picked up from all over, from all kinds of different states. And a man that's teaching over there, he used to Sweat. We had a Dream Quest together. And also the lady that works with this guy. So that's where they are in North Dakota. And it worked out very good and with those two bus loads that came in. I think that would be something good for these kids that are troublemakers, and they turn out to be pretty good. So we had a call from these people, now these kids they want us to go over there next Friday, they are going to have Powwow, take my two boys here that are teaching also.

This is what this is made for, this training centre, to encourage the young people to go to universities and go to school. And yet, learn the culture. This is what my teacher said to me, it's very hard to believe that, to understand. And I wanted to share that with you also. Years ago when my nephew was still alive, his name was Douglas Skead. A man came from the south to teach him to run the Sweat, and then they had Sweats in there, and that's when we started to, when we went to a Dream Quest. It's a long story I wanted to tell, but I wanted to make it short. Maybe some day when we have a little more time I can explain how things started.

Anyway, I dreamed that I was going to my nephew's, to a Sweat. Before I entered this house I dreamed that there was a big turtle, a big one about that size. He had his head stuck out, great big head. And he started talking to me in Ojibwe language. And I never made out what he was saying. I don't know, maybe that was the purpose because it's a message for the people. So I went in there and then I woke up. I didn't, it bothered me. What was he saying when he was talking? So one day when they had the Shaking Tent over there I heard that turtle talking over there, I heard the small voice. I wanted to go over there very badly, I wanted to ask him what was he saying, what was he telling me? So I got some Tobacco, and I went in there when there was just a little opening. Just to make a short message, a question.

So I put my hand in there and I offered Tobacco. I said, 'Mister Turtle,' I said in my language, I told him I asked him, 'I dreamed about you. I was talking to you and I didn't quite understand what you were saying.' Right away with his small voice he said, 'You people are very stupid, and very ignorant,' he said. And he gave me hell! And he said it wasn't me, but I know the one that came down. I am going out and then that one stopped, and went some place I don't know where. In a few seconds again it came back and started shaking again. And two turtles came in. You can hear the shhhwooo, shhhwoo, inside that thing. And it started to go like this and it was really going. And then it was singing, and then there was more singing and then one by one. And then he said, 'The one that was talking to me, here now I brought this turtle that talked to you. And he is over here now,' she, I think he said. And then that turtle again started saying, 'I am the one that came, and you didn't listen. You guys are stupid and ignorant.' And that's what he said, the same thing. And that's the picture of a lot of people. Not only me because I was just carrying a message and he said, 'I was going to give you something, but you didn't listen. You hard people to listen to teach something.' I said right away, 'I accept, I apologize, I am very ignorant, I am stupid. I wanted, that's the reason I am asking, I want to learn something.' 'I was going to give you something but you got to work it out yourself, and be very very careful,' he said. 'You are going to get a tree, the one like you're holding. It's a little tamarack. You are going to get it in bush and put some Tobacco, and a prayer what you want him for, then put it alongside your bed. When you go to sleep he is going to tell you something.' And that's all they told me and down they went again and started singing.

Well, I had to keep that in mind what they tell me. So I went and got a little tree, I put Tobacco and I hung up one little piece, and then put it alongside my bed. I was laying like this facing west. And I was thinking and thinking and thinking, and all of a sudden I must have fallen asleep. I saw two young men coming. I was still in bed. There was a big table there, this way, it was just like my room it was so big. Those two young men were dressed in blue suits, had long hair, they were Native. They were Indian people. And then they were going to give me a flag just like that. It has golden letters and silver letters, and all kinds of designs, like all this lake, everything you see. It was so beautiful, a big thing about that size. And it was lying there and I was going to grab that thing just like that and this thing here, it turned out to be a man, and he said, 'Hey don't touch it yet,' he said in the Ojibwe language. 'Don't you touch this yet. There's a few things first you have to learn, before you do that before you touch those.

'First of all is your language,' he said. 'And the way you speak, even language. And then songs, those are important things. And then dancing is another one, and then your culture ceremonies, and all kinds of things like that.' I never got to touch that thing and I woke up. And I got up and I was laying there, and I filled up my Pipe and I started praying with my Pipe. Something came just like light in my head. What does that mean the language? Yes I was born with the language, and as Ojibwe. I can learn Cree, I can learn English. I can learn French, and I can still hold my language. That's important, so I can't criticize the other languages, I can learn a lot of languages. That's the part, encouraging our young people to go to universities, they can use this Lodge to learn, to learn their language, to learn their ceremonies, to learn their songs, to learn to dance, and yet be a doctor and maybe be a psychiatrist, and yet you can be working in an office, but that puts the package together.

Same thing with the songs. You can dance, all those beautiful things that you wore, feathers. And show off what you are. You are a Cree, or maybe you are Ojibwe. Your songs comes in with it, with your tribe. So that respect, you can sit there in the dance hall with the music. With the fiddle, guitar, or any other kind of, what people are offering. You cannot refuse that. It's part of life. People have to share, just like the thing I do here, share everything together. And dancing, singing, these are the things that are very important. Now the culture, we got to Sweat Lodge. I have White people come to Sweat Lodge. I can go to church and listen to the church. I don't have to pray like him, but those are the things that has to be put together and balance these things. That and the four directions.

So this is a big thing I am talking about, that relates to our Mother Earth. Relates to the whole nationalities. To be proud of who we are and to respect one another and love one another. We are all equal in life. Mind you they all are different, cross-marriages. But you can see you still have a blood, whoever it is that shares, there's a lot of that coloured people, Chinese people, the White people, the Native people. I don't know who I am, but I respect who I am, Anishinabeg. That's why that language is so important. When you pray. You have all kinds of languages in there when I go to my Sweat Lodge. I have people speak English, I have people speak different languages, Blackfoots, Crees, all kinds. We all belong to this Mother Earth. So that's my part of teaching.

How the World Was Created

This might confuse a lot of people. It's so far off because a lot of these people they want to share. They say Whiskey Jack made, built this world. He might've bring it back to life, the same as Jesus, he didn't make this world. And also the Chinaman, and the Black people did not make this world. We know there is one God who made this world. I think this is where the answer is, right there. Because he is the one. He is everywhere. He has no body, in the whole universe he is there. And then the world, even the stars and the moons, and if you put those things together the sun. We never know. Maybe the scientists, some people will know.

But anyway, all these people that I am talking about that made this world. Why are people saying there is four layers of the universe? Why the world has got four layers of Mother Earth? Now when you look at the world itself, it has a lot of problems. It had earthquakes many many years ago. It flooded many many years ago. And it got hot many many years ago, that's where the diamonds show you where it really got hot. So that's, those are the four things that happened. How did that happen? Maybe the four layers of the universe, that's how close that came to make this world new again. We don't know. These are the things that some people should think about, where we came from.

And the moon and everything like that the believers of Indian people. These are the ones that are responsible for your woman. She is our Grandmother. And the stars, there is something in there that helps us to be able to survive in this country. Why is the sun up there? Way up there. That's how we survive. God made it there. At first what I heard in the Bible, so that's why the people should work together, like the White people. There was Adam and Eve, and there was only one race and somehow must have went haywire some place, why this Mother Earth turned into disaster, so maybe God changed us into four types of people to be able to get along.

But the world is so flexible, the greed came in. That's what off-balanced everything, the White people. Why did they, how did they kill Jesus? There was money involved in there. So that's why all these teachings that flag I didn't tell you about, that young man was giving me. I didn't take it, but after a while I began to think when I went to these big meetings that you had to start talking about money. That's what the gold is and the silver. So there will always be some money involved in what we do. If you want to eat you got to have money. Even if you have to go to a hotel to sleep you have to have money. You are going to run your car here, or my truck you have to have money. Now we start using money everything. That comes last. We have to build a house first before we can have these. It's a long story, but it's very small.

According to what I hear from a lot of people we came from the heavens. That's why they call them Anishinabeg. I don't know too much about those things. Anishinabeg, we brought it down with some kind of string, an imaginary line, they put a man here, a man that came down. And then the woman, I don't know where that thing came from, maybe from Mother Earth, water, I think that's what I hear, but I won't speak on that because I don't know too much about it. There is some people that have knowledge about that, but I will upset everything if I start talking about something that I don't know.

If you don't believe in nothing then you go haywire. You get lost. You got to keep that circle of life. You got to be thankful, that's an important part of it. Whatever you see, you think, you wish, God is listening to you. That's why you say that God is not a body, he is everywhere. And that he put these things here for helping us people like the trees, they have the duties to do like the birds and the animals, and bunnies and everything. He put these as helpers, we call them Spirits. That's what controls our bodies, controls our thinking. When you go to a Sweat Lodge it's dark in there. Then you got a chance to pray whatever you got to say. There is nothing that interferes or look at, no clock or nothing. That's why the Sweat Lodge is a very effective thing to follow the way of life.

Like a Sweat Lodge again, there's a hole in the middle here, and you got four doors, okay. When you crawl in there's an altar here, and there's pipes in here. Anyway, you crawl and you say all my relatives, identify yourself, your name and your clan. Okay, then you start crawling and then you sit right here, and the other people they start going, and anyway that's the start when you start here, is life okay? And there's doors here, okay? And then there's another one that goes right across this way, it's supposed to be right in the middle here. And you start life about here you are a teenager. You're a baby here, a teenager, and over here you become to be a parent, and that's a soft door, the children, you're a baby, and an adult here. Then that opens the doors, and another bunch come in the rocks, and you go again, and you begin to become a grandfather, a grand-mother. Right to the door and then you get out again, and then you come out and there will be a grandfather again, and great-grandfather, and a great-great-grandfather, and then you got a white snow your hair as a grandmother and a grandfather. Then you start moving and you are really really old, a hundred and ten years old, and you start crawling, you start crawling back like a baby. And you can control yourself, and then when you complete the job, and then you go out, your Spirit carries on, sharing. That's all you think about is your grandchildren when you come to there. So that's the circle of life. That's what you're looking forward when you sit here, you know. And we all sit around here and we go around the circle and pray.

I am not a medicine man, I am just a messenger. I do some healing for some people sometimes. I run a Sweat Lodge, and drums and eagle bones, and sometimes someone gets sick and I bring him back to, from the coma I bring him back sometimes. It all depends, I am not a holy man or nothing like that, I am just a labouring man.

Homes

I was raised in a log cabin, a one-room house. I didn't have no spring bed or anything like that. I had a deer hide for a mattress. I tell you I was pretty sore whenever I slept in a bed. I was so used to sleeping on the floor. That's the way I was raised. And my feet were so strong I could run around here with no shoes on barefooted. But now you have sponge shoes, the heavy socks. You get spoiled. I can't even hardly walk now.

People lived in teepees, birch-bark teepees. Just recently they used to make out of logs. All of it was just logs, and it had a hole in the centre. We used to have that. They were warm. You just make a fire in there and it just heats. My mother used to make bannock in the open fire and it was so delicious.

There were some really strong women that had that respect, because it was the women that stayed at home to look after the babies, I guess that was the way it was meant, and the woman was gifted. They have a lot more patience than the men. Strong, strong people the women. Because otherwise, and today they are getting spoiled. Some of them they don't have to look after their babies they put them in day care. That's what makes it harder because they lose that love. If you have your baby with you all the time close to you then you can't lose that love it always stays with you. Even the men they cannot get away from their mother, like me, my mother was so close to me, all the time. I even work with her when I was a boy. Getting wood, it was part of my place. We had a dog team and worked together. Once she made hide and I was to work with her. Even grown up as a man I used to prepare the grounds for a garden for her.

That's what she liked, to plant a lot of vegetables. We used to live out here, just on the other side of this point here. I was raised right around this area.

My mother used to say when she was a little girl she was always home, and when the woman did all the work around the house, and the teepees, when they had these teepees, they cut wood, and my mother used to say, 'One woman would say let's have some tea.' They used to drink tea, but there was no sugar. My mother used to say, 'But I didn't know what it was, I tasted it once. It was so good and sweet, but there was no sugar at that time.'

I had a dream, one time, because I think I really respect that Treaty. That's the only thing we have left. A Treaty is something that is very spiritual, because our Native people when they had this problem fighting and killing one another they had to do something to have peace, and make that relationship with the White people, because they were really going off the track. So that's why they sign the Treaty. They were very careful. They prayed, they used this as spirituality, like the sun, the water, and the trees that you see and the grass. That was their signature. As long as it is there, that thing will never, that promise will be there. That's why they shook hands. You know, to promise, because those people couldn't write or nothing. That's what our Native people use is the land. That's why it is strong, we don't want to sell nothing, we don't want to break nothing. When they meet the law. The law is right there outside. That's where it is. That's the law, and the sun, the water, and the trees, the grass. As long as sun shines and rivers flow. That's the law. That has to be respected because the Creator, we used the Creator for that.

They use Shaking Tents. That's why they said never break the law. Now today everyone's breaking the law. The government says he owns the land, but where did he get it? It never been surrendered. That's stealing. It doesn't belong to us it belongs to Nature, to the Creator. You want to ask the Creator, can I sell this land? There is no way! They have their piece of land that was given to them in the old country. All Indian people here, all different tribes. A lot of different tribes here in this whole North America. This is ours. Nobody can say the Creator didn't tell them that you can't buy this. No way!

Elders

The reason they call me an Elder I guess is I may be old. I don't know. I have very little that I can share that I learned. Some people might not agree, but it is every man's opinion. I feel that love for young people that they should lean a little bit, whatever we can share. I don't like to see this suicide thing going on, and that's not love you know. A person has got to love himself in order to love other people.

I can't share just to White people because I am not a White person. I can share them only my culture because that's where I belong. If a White person wants to share, he has to share to his White brothers and we kind of have to respect that. You can't say that White man should come to me, no, you got that White man to go to. But they need respect. We don't mind having White man dancing at our Powwows. He doesn't ... I don't want a White man to make big money out of the Powwow.

If you don't know what you are talking about never mind being a teacher or an Elder. You may be an Elder, but you can't teach nothing. He's got to have that love, who he is. That's number one is your identity. They call that love. If you want to love someone you have to love yourself first. Love who you are and what you are and you can share these things and whatever you learn from nature, the nature itself. It teaches a lot of things. Like that seagull over there. The seagull is cleaning the lake, cleaning the dead fish, everything that's dead here on the ground. Some of those animals, that's why they eat those sticks, the medicine, because the moose eats the sticks and their bodies are all medicine. When you are eating that animal you are eating medicine. That's why it keeps you strong. Same thing with water. If you don't drink water you get weak. That's why I like water.

Offerings

Maybe you want to get a name, maybe you have to pay for it, you have to pay food, or something so that there is an offering to the Spirit that gives you the name. Sometimes people will just give names out of anywhere. It doesn't work that way. I give names to the kids sometimes, but it's got to come through my experience, the Spirit. Sharing that Spirit name. For instance there was a man called X, he wants to get a name. Then he gives you Tobacco and sometimes after a while you dream of an animal or a bird. And then he calls himself who he is. Maybe he calls himself, well, Running Wolf, or something like that, and then the wolf wants to be called every time you call this little boy. Every time you call that Running Wolf, you are calling the wolf. That's his helper.

That's like me, I had a bear. I had to follow his footsteps. And then I got another name from the Thunderbirds, the lightning that come down to the ground. So those are my helpers. When I go to the Sweat Lodge and I pray and I ask them I need some help, I pray and I ask them, and then they come. That's how the thing works. It doesn't come to like Tom, Dick, and Harry. Sometimes you love kids and they call them all kinds of funny names and then the names are usually carried that way, but there's no spiritual thing. It's just like what they call nicknames.

Role Models

I listened to my mother and father. I still think of them as role models. And the spiritual teachings come to me. I don't listen to people to tell me things. I will listen, but until I understand what they are talking about it is still the Spirit that shares. That's how I get it. There's lots of Elders that are speaking, and then I picked that up and then I got to straighten it out myself. Sometimes you could maybe use it the false way. You have to be very careful how you use these things. Just like the interview here, we might, if I make some mistakes they might say this guy is throwing it off the track. That's the dangerous part.

Traditional Games

There was all kinds of games in here. Canoe racing, and I don't know what they call those things in English, lacrosse, and there's a place down there, just across here where they used to have this lacrosse on the big long sand beach there. People used to live there all the time. There was all kinds of things like running, and there was moccasin games, and all sort of different. I can't remember much of that because this residential school kind of put me off.

When I was a kid we had lots of games in the snow when we played. And there was all kinds of activities. As far as I can remember we played hockey too. Everything was getting down to modern way in my time. But the only thing is my dad probably had still, my dad was in band, orchestra. He was in a long time ago, I guess, I wasn't born then.

Powwow was the feast. One in the spring and one in the fall. They had Powwows and celebrations. It's a thanksgiving, but there was no dates, and there was other activities, picking blueberries and picking rice, and that's when they had the celebrations, and that's when they all got together and had Powwows. And there was all kinds of games, and card games and moccasin games.

I think the teachings were more about a danger, where ice is dangerous, fire is dangerous, and guns are dangerous, all kinds of things like that, that come in the teaching of our children. So they don't, so you try to avoid accidents. Walking on the ice you have to know where the current is and avoid there. Paddling a canoe, and how to handle a canoe. Supposing you are out on the island and you have to tie up your canoe at the same time that you pull it up. Otherwise in the fall there's an ice that forms on the waves and when the boat is rocking like this it will pull away the canoe. Then you will be stranded or starved to death on the island.

There's a thesis too, when you kill an animal you take a certain part of the animal and you put Tobacco and ribbons on it. So that when you kill an animal you don't actually kill it, it comes back again. That's the thesis that we have. I can't tell you very much about the woman because I never was that close with the woman in those days. The only things I learned was from my wife when what she says about something how to be cautious, not to step over a traditional man's cap or clothing. You know you cannot step over them. And not to go into ceremonies when the woman has her time, and those are the things. I cannot speak very much for the woman because I was not really into.

I was ten years old when they put me in school and I was there five years, and all that time I was brainwashed. I am starting to realize that I had to look to the future, for my children and great-grandchildren. I have to look forward because years ago, that's gone! We can't go back to teepees or anything like that. So the culture is the main important part. The belief of Nature that was created by the Creator. It is the only thing that we are really looking at now, the respect for growth, and respect for Nature, and also the teachings of respect for woman. A lot of people don't have that respect. The woman, they think the woman is just a human being. It's not only that, the women are life givers. And that's the main reason that people respect that, because that's our number-one teachings that the Elders should always carry, to respect the woman because without no women here there would be nothing left alive. So the woman has to listen too to the Elders on how to raise children, why are they women, why are they so and so. I can't speak to that myself. But the women have those teachers there and they should follow that custom.

Humour and Music and Art

The reason for humour is it's part of the medicine to keep a person his lungs working. You can't always be crying and have your head down, you have to laugh. Even at the same time when you have ceremonies and Pow-wows there is always some jokers that come and make people laugh and that's the way these people are. All over across Canada I see that.

We always had the Powwow drum. I have a drum here that I carry from my grandfather. I didn't even know my grandfather, he was a medicine man. We had what you call social dances. You dance with the girls like they have a waltz. We use that for drums a long time ago. The drums always been that way, half and half. For entertainment and for praying.

They have all kinds of artists around here. All kinds. Even my boy is one of the best, but he doesn't practise that anymore. I don't know why. Maybe not enough encouragement. Maybe he is too busy at something else. I don't know what. Work is an important part of life. You have to keep moving in order to live long. Just keep the blood moving.

Like I said this morning, you look outside and that's our culture, and then there's time that you have to have thanksgiving. Like the change of the season, like it is going to be winter pretty soon and there is going to be snow and ice on the lake. And then the fall, like in the fall we have leaves that are falling. Everything is changing into colours. So that's why we have to give some thanksgiving. And before the hibernation, some of the animals are hibernating like the bear, and the chipmunks and snakes, what have you in this living world.

When people die, I hear they go to the Happy Hunting Grounds. For about four years they hang around near the grave and then they go, I don't know where, they go. I never been there.

The people that committed suicide they take their lives. I hear that a lot of these people go underground. Some kind of a Spirit calls them under the ground to stay there until the time they are supposed to go. Like limbo, it is dark and there is no happiness there until they reach the age, the year, when they are supposed to go, because when you are born the time is set for how long you were supposed to live.

A lot of people think our traditions are related to Christian teachings, but I don't think that's right. I think one thing at a time should be suffi-cient. Because I can't be praying here and here is a Bible, and here is that traditional healing. I get myself into trouble, all mixed up. They are sepa-rate, but there is only one God.

I can't seem to sit down in one place. I am always on the go. I move around to different places, wherever I am asked to go. Sometimes I go to Fort Frances, sometimes I go to Eagle Lake, or I go to White Dog, Grassy Narrows. I don't really pray all the time. The only thing I always do, I say I am going to meet the sun in the morning and I am glad to be alive again. I thank him that I am alive and he looked after me at night, and then I am out again all day.

There is another thing I was talking about Sweat Lodge. In the door, and there is this West door, South door, North door, that's the same thing I was talking about. This line is going to go this way to reach for each other. And then this one again, and they reach each other again. And then another one goes here and comes out to reach again here. Go together, the same with this one. Okay? And here is the centre, and we start out from here and meet again and they meet here, and another one in the centre here they go and meet again. Okay. Now supposing I take this East, North, West, and South. Okay, the time of the ice age, there was a white bear here. This White Bear, he is the North animal. This is East, this is where wolf, White Wolf. And this is White Eagle, and this is West, this is White Buffalo.

When the ice age came, right here. Maybe a lot of people don't believe in that, or maybe it's just a dream the people have. We don't know what happened, and nobody can tell the truth until you witness that with your own eyes. So there is nobody that will say what happened, but according to the legends then you see that in the painted rocks. Or sometimes people will say that when you are walking on any of these rocks, all these rocks are aligned this way, North and South. Maybe a little bit Southeast. Anyway that's how there's those tracks in there.

Clans

So the North Spirit came after that ice age and the ice went through here and pushed everything. This was the thing that I often wondered. I use that in my Sweat Lodge when I sing this White Bear song and it comes to White Wolf, and then it comes to White Eagle, and then to White Buffalo. And these relationships came in. The Spirit Bear came in and said, 'I like to have this Native in here, that's standing, to be my brother.' Or he said, 'I'd like to have this one as my sister.' So this one came along said the same thing, the White Wolf. 'I want this one to be my brother and sister, and this one too,' White Eagle. He says he wants this one here to be his brother and sister. Same with this White Buffalo.

So those two people can't be married together. The same clan, those are same clan, you have to go to this one, or that one, or that one. To be able to be married because you can't marry the same clan. So there's all clans, and those four clans came in at that time. That must have happened over years and years, it didn't happen overnight. But as the people started to develop and the children started to grow, and these Spirits here they said there should be more, like they have a meeting here, and more Spirits came. Me too, I'd like to have a brother and sister, these Native people. So it came, some of them came, the Bobcat, the Moose Clan. Some are Fish clans, all kinds of things here they want to be brother and sister. So that's why there are so many clans. In one reserve there are a dozen or more people because of the intermarriages there. You cannot marry the same clan. That's why the marriage was so sacred at that time because the clan system was working real good. Now today the people don't understand, they married their own, same clan, just like a brother and sister. So those came in to help the people, all across this way, animals. And that is how the clan system came about.

Prophecies

Prophecies are what you see on the painted rocks. That's to tell you that some day a White man is going to be here, there's a big boat and a Bible, and a priest. They already knew that was going to happen. It's coming. It's not the end of the world, it's a clean-up. Mother Earth is being disrespected, there's pollution. And people are going nuts. That's what happened years back, many, many years ago they say there was a half-man, half-horse, but that's not the way the Creator wanted it. That's why you got to clean it up. It might be worse in the future. I see some really bad things, TVs and not only killing, but there is a lot of sex life. It's very very bad. I never heard about anything of homosexual people. Since the movies and the stuff they smoke, drugs, and the people start to go out of control and their minds.

The Sweat Lodge is what teaches you what the life is, because we are only here for a short time. When you are twenty-five years you are at the prime age, when you are fifty you are going downhill, you are not a hockey player anymore. When you come to a grandfather and great-grandfather you can't even skate, period [laughs].

The Weather

The people they knew the weather. They knew better than we do, because they were well prepared. Even now today, the birds know. The animals and birds they know. Like the ones that fly by here is geese, they know when they should start and what time to arrive there when it is nice and warm. You never see them in the middle of winter to come over here. They sure know when the weather is going to be nice to travel. And then the way they travel. For instance there is some geese that fly here, and they are way up, you can hardly see them. That means it's going to be a very nice warm fall. And because that weather is not there yet. But if you see them fly almost to the trees, there is a bad weather coming to push them out. Some of them read the stars to tell the weather.

Language

Language is the most important. You can't translate the things. It entirely changes altogether. You get Indian names by giving Tobacco to an Elder and then he gets that message, maybe that tree says okay, just like I'm talking about here. A clan, same thing has a name. Maybe a tree will say, that tree is a poplar, we call it *Azate*, there was a man that was called *Azate* here. He was named after a poplar tree. And then the poplar tree, that's his brother working together. As babies is the best time to get your name. And then when you get those names you do that early in the morning before the sunrise because that's the beginning of life. That's why when people pray to the sun, never pray past noon, because this is the end of everything, carries everything out there.

If you know this country you will never go hungry. There's all kinds of shelter. You can make a fire. That's why we have these teachings. Teach them to get lost and how to survive even if you don't have no tent or nothing. You can make a fire out in the bush. People got around by dog team and horses, and walking. I've got snowshoes over there. Modern things like snowmobiles and trucks have been both good and bad. Bad in that it kills the labour. Your physical movement, you don't have that exercise. I have that beautiful car here I just bought that two weeks ago. And that kills me. I can't walk anymore like I used to. Of course I am getting old, but I could have still done a lot of walking. But I don't, I don't have a chance. I get a call and I am zipping over there in the car. But you never get anything done without the car. It is good, but it's not good for health. Same as this thing here. You can't use your brain here anymore. This thing is working for you [points to the tape recorder, and Emily laughs]. Sometimes you have to call home and then you have a telephone. I am out there in Vancouver and I am talking to my family right here. That is good, but that's why I say good and bad. If there is a meeting in Toronto and all the people are getting together, it's good that you will be there in two hours. I want to go to Vancouver I am there in two hours. So that's the best part of it. And still, that doesn't give you much exercise for your life. When the people are sixty-five years they are already crippled up and they can't walk, they don't have that exercise. Years ago when my dad was alive, sixty-five or seventy years of age, he could run out, thirty, forty miles out there. As a young man I had a hard time to keep up with my dad because he moves all the time. Like a boxer or a wrestler you have to train your body all the time. But when you start using the car you don't have that kind of exercise.

Traditionally there were wars. I think it was the cause of the White people, and then it came to a traditional thing, you know who's got the powers. That's the way it developed. Medicine people were never involved with the wars with White people. The White people started the war, but the Native people started to fight each other because they were using medicine. They used their medicine to show how tough they are.

It's very lonely when you are out there in the bush by yourself. Years ago you did not feel that way. You got to be alone there with the nature. Things has changed way different right now. I don't think I could stand it there myself if I had to be there by myself, because I have already been brainwashed. It's hard to learn your own ways. It gave me a hard time to learn to be able to understand a lot of things.

Dreams and Visions

It all depends on the person, some people don't pay attention to them. For example, you could be paddling a canoe and all of a sudden you are walking on the ice. Sometimes they don't mean anything. The Spirit dreams are when a Spirit talks to you. It is up to the individual who wants to learn, sometimes dreams are warnings or teachings, but the dreams do not tell us the facts, they do not explain, but we have a brain to use to understand and after a while you realize that is what a dream meant.

There was a girl one time that said she saw an eagle in her dream, the eagle was drowning, struggling in the water. She was trying to help this eagle and finally she pulled it out. So this represented the human being, sometimes you have to help them, but they also have to help themselves. You just have to help them but not do everything for them.

I do not have visions at just any time, but I have visions in the Sweat Lodge, like I see something coming in like the bear, the wolf. The visions are not always good, sometimes you see something that may happen, such as someone that is going to die, drown, those kinds of visions are not good news.

While fasting I have had visions. Sometimes you will see something and it disappears. You could see something beautiful and then it is gone. It gives you a chance to see it. I saw an eagle and looked at it so close. It was beautiful. It looked so shiny. It was a big eagle and I was just going to pick up my Pipe to give an offering and it was gone. So I prayed anyway. As long as you see them, you know that they are still around. The visions do not come all the time. They only come once in a while.

It is up to individuals if they want to understand their dreams. They can use the Shaking Tent to find out about dreams and what they mean. They tell you what to do. Just like the turtle I told you about. I could not understand him, and why did he tell me I was ignorant in the Shaking Tent? That is the whole picture, people in general do not pay attention.

In the Shaking Tent the Spirits come in there to tell you what to do. They investigate. For example, if a person drowned or if someone is lost in the bush, the Shaking Tent will tell you where this person is. Spirits can see everything, they travel so fast, at the blink of an eye, they are there. Only certain people can run a Shaking Tent, it is a gift.

Medicines

I know of the main things such as medicines for high blood pressure, cancer, kidney problems, miscarriages. The medicines have to be mixed a certain way, all what you see outside is medicine, even the water is medicine. There were medicine men who were gifted to heal. Some people today act like medicine people, but it is just for money. Not just anyone can heal people. A real healer doesn't charge money, but will accept anything they give them like Tobacco. It is up to them on what they give.

Medicines were used. You have to know what to pick, just like mushroom, some are poison, you have to know what to pick, you have to be careful, you have to know what you are doing. Just like how a doctor practises for years, a medicine person does the same, practises for a long time. A lot of traditional healing and medicines are lost now, young people did not want to learn from the Elders, they depend on doctors and hospitals. The hospitals cannot do a lot of the things Native people did, that is the way it was.

Living on the land is very important. Even scientists do this, they study and go all over the place. It is the same thing with Native life, you have to search to learn, if you don't, you will never get ahead. It is like going to school, you have to exercise your brain to learn. Those that are serious will be the ones who will learn. It is the same thing with Native life.

I was at a gathering at a high school one time. People were preparing, writing down notes and getting ready for their speech. I was sitting by the window looking at the nature. A policeman came and he asked, 'Why are you sitting there?' He thought I was lonely and sitting alone. I told him I am just looking at my agenda right now. He laughed.

I can stand and talk all day about Nature and what it is. Always be close to Nature. It is possible if you want to have that connection, if you have a good mind, concentrate on learning. Then at nights you will start dreaming about those things. It is the same for a man who wants to sing a song. I have some songs that were given to me through a Spirit. Think about the things you want to know. Your dreams will start to come.

Years ago, when my boy was five years old, I dreamed we were walking facing north and I was holding his hand. All of a sudden I saw a white horse standing there, he looked vicious and I was scared. I said, 'I have to go back, that horse is not very friendly, let's run back.' I started running down the hill and there was a big high ramp and I threw my boy on top and I jumped on top, then the horse stopped. The horse started talking the Ojibwe language and he said, 'I didn't come to scare you, I am here to teach you something.' He started to sing a beautiful song and after he completed the song, it turned out to be a white Pipe. That was all I had. I always wondered what that meant. As I travelled I always looked for a white Pipe. After about fifteen years after the dream, we had a sobriety Powwow here, we usually have that every year on New Year's Eve, lots of people came to this particular Powwow. When we finished at twelve o'clock, everybody shook hands and kissed one another. One of the traditional dancers told me that he had heard a voice singing from the top of the Powwow building in the centre where there is a hole on top. I think I may have heard the song before I would recognize it.

The next morning a young man from Thunder Bay came in and told me that he had tried to make it to the Powwow the night before, but he got lost and turned back to the hotel. He said, 'I have something for you in the car.' He went out and he come back with something wrapped in a towel. He handed it to me, it was a white Pipe, exactly the same as the one in the vision I had with the horse and the song that came with that Pipe. I told the people at the Powwow that day that we will have an honour song for our guest. I told my son to sing a song to honour the Pipe. Everybody got up and danced. After we finished, the man who had heard the song the night before came up to me and said, 'That is the song I heard last night, from above.' That is the way it is. I had to wait fifteen years for that Pipe. It takes a long time before you receive the gifts in your dreams and visions.

Residential School

Grandparents were teachers, this is the circle of life that I talked about. When you reach the age of grandparent, you have lived many years and have experience on how to live. Your hair is white. Our greatest teachers have white hair, the oldest ones. They have gone through bad and good things. Good and bad is a part of learning, learning from experience. That is why we have our grandfathers and grandmothers as teachers. They have learned a lot in their lifetimes.

The residential schools are the reason why we are lost right now. They tried to make us one nationality, one people, but they cannot do that because it goes against God's will. Residential schools throw off the balance. Parents can no longer teach their children, some grandparents cannot either. They have lost their way of life.

In residential school, I didn't pray to live. I used to pray to die so I could go to heaven. We do not teach that way in our Native way, we pray to live. God put us here to live, to work, to respect, to love yourself. When God gives you food, you have to take that life of that animal, some people do mean things just because they don't like something.

It is pretty hard to balance that life once you are brainwashed. Suppose you have been brainwashed to be a Catholic, how can I move you? After all you are a Native and you have no business being a Catholic. It is pretty hard to change someone back to traditional ways.

In residential school, we were told that if you follow what your mother and father are doing in Native culture, you will go to hell with them, because they are going to hell, and that hurts a child. Then we were told if you follow the church, you will have eternal life. That is the way we were taught, we could not even use our own language, we were slapped around, kicked around for doing so.

My brother was in jail in residential school, they had a jail with bars. He was there for seven days with just water – they used to tell us that we were working for the devil if we do wrong. That is how tough and hard these people were. Even if a boy looked at a woman he got slapped in the face. He would be told that he had bad thoughts. There were lots of things that kids did. My brother ran away from school, the Mounties went to pick him up and he was put in the cell at the school, I don't know how he did it but he got out of there. He never went back to school again.

To heal they have to go to the Sweat Lodge, let the Spirits take away the bad. You have to ask the Spirits to put you on the right track. Otherwise talking to them doesn't help, they don't take it in. But when they go into the Sweat Lodge, not only once but several times, they change. Even those youth that were sniffing gas, they changed. They learn the teachings to help them.

The worst part is that these people [that went to residential schools] do not know how to be parents. The Native teachings are lost. There are now lots of single mothers, before it was very embarrassing not to have a partner or husband, but today it doesn't matter. Those things have changed. It is hard to talk to young people like that. They get mad if you try to talk to them.

Wars

Wars are bad. I think it started from the old country overseas. I had a daughter who was with a man who decided to join the army to learn all kinds of things. He took off and joined the army, they had one little boy. My daughter was suffering, trying to make a living. She wanted to have love and she met another guy. The man came back from the army and they started fighting, she went back to him and she got beaten up, this man had learned to be a fighter. The kids came back after they had finished school, the boy recently came back, he is nine years old now, we have him now.

If Native people practise and follow their own teachings and culture that will not happen. We will not be lost, but it is a very hard job to do. The government does not want to give you any money to help your people, like this training centre. I have no government funding for this place, I get a bit of money from people using this place to hold workshops. This money is used to cover maintenance costs, food, cooks, snowplough, electricity.

If we got government funding, at least we would be able to help our young people to learn their own culture. And we would be able to teach White people about our culture, so they would have a better understanding of each other. This is the reason why we set up this training centre, but it will slowly come into place.

The wars were revenge, testing powers of medicine men. In the Grand Entry, a man enters with a flagstaff with eagle feathers. This man is a medicine man that is gifted, one that has powers even to kill people. He is not only associated with living things as we know, but also Spirits. A Spirit cannot kill. This man has powers, the number of eagle feathers means the number of warriors who will fight. Those feathers mean that, for example, eight warriors will get shot and never get hurt, because they had this Spirit that cannot be hurt. They could be shot and not get hurt, that is the way it was a long time ago. The flagstaff represents a man, it is good stuff, but could still be used for bad.

Some people used these feathers also to get animals, trappers would use it. Sometimes bad medicine can be used and it is very strong, people are encouraged never to use bad medicine to get what they want. This is what bad medicine is about. There is good and bad medicine. Eagle feathers were used to fight, to make them strong. They could also use the Spirit. We Native people did not always have good relations. Just like the animals, they fight, sometimes you could hear moose fighting in the bush, sometimes they kill each other. Medicine can be used for bad or for good.

A long time ago the feathers [flagstaffs] were many, still used today, that is what makes the Powwow successful. Sometimes you have such wonderful visions. As long as you use it for good, not to make money out of it.

What really helped the people were the teachings of our Native people. Our Elders were respected – that is what we were taught. What controlled people is medicine – it scared lots of people because they knew if they disobeyed, that medicine would attack them. I would not want to do anything wrong, being afraid that medicine might strike me. Medicine was there to protect the people from bad.

Since we do not have medicine as power now, we could use the culture and put offenders in training centres like this one, instead of putting them in jail where they are made worse, jail does not help them. They come back from jail, they get right back into the trouble again. These training centres should be used, they should be taught about our way of love, respect and love for one another, your wife, your children, your grandparents, those are the teachings. This training centre is set up to do that.

When people are put in jail, they are locked up, all they see are bars. As soon as they come out, they go back to drinking again. But if they are in a training centre, it would be a learning place. A treatment centre will go just so far, but when a client gets out they have no place to go and many go back to drinking. What they learn in a treatment centre could be continued in a training centre.

People need cultural training to learn about themselves, to feel good as Native people. The Elders that know themselves should be used, not the Elders that are White, those are apples, red on the outside and white on the inside. We do not want that. We want Native people who believe in themselves and know who they are. Maybe that can draw people in to come in.

The idea is that Elders can work in a training centre, a number of Elders can work along with facilitators. Children can be sent here too. It is good to have other resource people to come in from other places to work with the kids. People can come in at different times, training people how to live, the culture, what is love, respect, the teachings of love and respect. That is what I would like to see all across Canada.

There is a treatment centre on the reserve. I did not want White people to come in there, but now they have half and half [half White, half Native] people. I wanted to train the clients in the Native way, but the reason why White people are in there is because they have to learn our culture too, we have to share our culture, not to make Indians out of White men, they [White people] already did that to us, they tried to make us into White people, like apples. It does not work.

At the first of this interview, I talked about the four colours, the four races. That means that we have to share. In order to respect it, White people have to learn about our culture, they have to see that it is not satanic. We have to work together. They have to respect our culture, not to call us down and say we are worshipping the devil, they are wrong.

Concluding Thoughts

It is important to think of the things I talked about. Go somewhere to think, maybe go fasting for a couple days, take a holiday. A lot of these teachings are not written, based on the Sweat Lodge circle. Focus on the Sweat Lodge circle, treat people right, love and respect each other. It is important as well that we develop a good relationship with White people, we do not want to be off balance.

There are four peoples in this world – black, white, yellow, red. One Creator. All these people have their own way. Jesus was sent to the White people to help them. So did the Black people, the Creator sent them someone like Jesus but he was Black. You cannot follow two ways, you choose your way and follow it, you cannot follow two roads, when you come to a Y, you'll be stuck with nowhere to go.

This is my work, helping young people. Our young people are having a hard time, they are committing suicide, having problems with alcohol. They can get straightened out by learning of the old ways, our connection to the Creator. Our culture is all around, just look outside, it is there, in that tree, in that water. I always encourage young people to go to school, get a good education, but do not lose your culture, that is what makes you strong.

Mid-North Cultures

ELIZABETH PENASHUE (Innu)

Sheshashiet, Labrador

*'I really believe in the land and
I care about my people.'*

Elizabeth Penashue was born on 15 May 1944 in the bush at Waganogow,
near Churchill Falls, Labrador. She was interviewed by Emily Faries in the
fall of 1994 at her home in Sheshashiet, Labrador, near Goose Bay. Elizabeth had nine children and twenty-one grandchildren at the time of the
interview. She has lived most of her life on the land. The interview with
Emily took place in a tent, just outside of her home. During the interview
Elizabeth spoke in Innu, which was translated by her niece.

Elizabeth Penashue focused her interview on the land, sharing her
beliefs and some of her traditional skills. Elizabeth is an advocate for protecting the land and the ways of her people. She stood up for the Innu
Nation against low-flying jets at a nearby armed forces base, and spent
time in jail for her protest. She has also done presentations on this issue,
and has given talks on the traditional lifestyle of her people.

Life History

I was born in the country, in the bush, around Churchill Falls, Labrador. The name of the place where I was born was Waganogow. The name means 'round lake.' Where I was born, there was no one to deliver me so my father delivered me. He had to help my mother because there was no other woman around to help out. There were some White settlers near there who were hunting. They couldn't help my mother because they were men, so only my dad was involved in the childbirth.

I learned all I needed to know from my parents. I remember that my parents always lived in the country. That's why I'm encouraging my kids to come with me into the country, so they can learn that lifestyle. It was really good that my mother and father taught me how to live a traditional lifestyle. That is why I'm encouraging my kids to carry that on. I remember my mother and how she taught me how to survive in the country. I also watched my father teach the boys how to live in the country. I learned a lot of things in the country. Children in those days helped as soon as they were old enough to help. When I was old enough as a little girl my mother encouraged me to work, cleaning beaver and other animals. My mother would perform and the children would sit around and watch, so that they can learn.

I learned our role by watching my mother and father. I learned by our daily lifestyle, there were no other people around. There was no government saying that you cannot do this or that especially in regards to hunting. We were free, we knew how many animals to kill for food and clothing. We were told not to cut trees, not to waste, you only cut enough for shelter and firewood. We did not go around destroying. In the country there are brooks, waters, rivers, we never misused them. In the country there would be several families living in one place, and everything around the camp was clean.

We also respected animals. When a caribou was skinned, my father never left anything to waste, nothing was left lying around. Nowadays you see caribou skins lying around, it has to do with the younger generation not understanding the culture. Out on Churchill Road and up to Esker, there are always caribou heads and legs lying around. The older people, if they were alive today, they would be really be hurt and broken-hearted about what's happening today. It's White people and our young people who are doing this.

I remember seeing a lot of caribou killed in the country. My mother would clean the caribou and take all that she needed. Anything else would be put in the fire. My father would have a special place outside to put the caribou legs and bones. My father was a hard-working person, and my mother too. When they had to break camp to move on, they would have to build caches so the dogs could not get after the belongings. Any stuff we would leave behind would be put up on these high places, so it would there when we returned to the campsite.

There were a lot of animals my father hunted for fur, the hunting these days is only for caribou. In those days before, we hunted a lot of animals for fur and food. Today people only hunt caribou for food but before we ate muskrats, and beaver and geese, which we used for not only food but the feathers and fur as well. Native people used to eat mink and marten too. My mother always knew if the mink and marten were good for its pelt, but also for food. The animals would be cleaned and cooked on an open fire.

My mother, out of love and feelings for her grandchildren, would clean and prepare any animal that the grandchildren got. If they killed a squirrel, she would prepare it and skin it so that they would feel proud and useful and that their kill was appreciated. Respect to animals by using all parts of them was important. She never wanted to throw away anything that my brothers killed. She wanted to teach them that what they killed was to be respected and that it should be used. If my brother got a squirrel, my mother would encourage him, so that he'd keep learning how to hunt.

Traditional Values

We were taught a lot about living, we were happy out on the land. As soon as we'd reach the land where we'd be setting up, I was happy and excited to start work. We'd put up the tent, tea would be made. The grandchildren and all the children would be involved in helping. They had responsibilities as a group. The children were happier out on the land. When the hunters were out, those at the camp would prepare food for their return. Everyone had a role, everyone was important. Sharing, taking care of the land, respecting animals were the teachings that parents passed on to the children.

Children who are not taught these values are different from those who have been taught. Those who went to [residential] school are also different and have not been able to teach their children about survival and respect for Creation. I cannot speak or write English but I learned a lot about the land. It is very important that children go to school but also learn about the culture. Even though we have White teachers in school, we also have Innu teachers. But the White teachers are more powerful, kids are kept in school rather than going out in the country. The kids only go in the country for a while because the White system is more powerful. They need to be in the country more than two weeks in order to learn.

It would be good if there were all Innu teachers. The principal invites people to come into the school and if I went to tell her how I want my children to be educated she would not understand because she is White. She would not think that our culture is important. My older boys were taught in school, by the time they were five, they were being taught another way and now they have to learn their own.

My son got an education and works here for the Innu, he helps our people here. But that's not enough, he has lost some of his culture. I never heard my son saying that he'd like to be in the country. I know that his children will follow their dad and not continue the lifestyle and culture in the country.

My grandson wants to learn and wants to come with me out in the country. I teach my grandchildren as much as possible. My older grandson also comes with me and enjoys being out there, but I am still worried that my grandchildren will get an education and not continue practising our culture.

Traditional Birthing

My mother delivered a lot of babies when we lived out in the country. There were a lot of women who delivered babies. Many of the elderly women who delivered babies have died on. My grandmother delivered many babies. My mother learned how to deliver babies by watching many births. There would always be a younger woman sitting and watching an elderly woman perform her duties as midwife. There were always elderly women teaching young ones. When a younger woman delivered a baby, an elderly woman was always there in case there was an emergency. In time when there was no midwife around, the man would deliver the baby. My father delivered at least two babies.

I think most women would lie down on their backs. When my mother delivered my sister's baby, not far from here, she was lying down, but there were only a couple of people in the tent when a baby was born. All the children and men were not allowed to be present. If the birth was a breech, when the head is up, the midwives used to turn the baby around. They knew how to do that. Sometimes it takes a long time for the baby to be born, you have to get the stuff ready, it's natural medicine from the bush, they used to give that to the women to drink. They had their own medicine.

I remember my mother delivering a baby, and because there was no one to give the name in case the baby did not live, my father named the baby. They put water on the baby, they had certain words they used, it was like baptizing. It was a blessing for the child. Sometime when babies were born, they'd shake a bit, the Elder would know that this baby wanted to be named. Sometimes when they'd wake up screeching, it was a sign that they wanted to be named.

There were Christian names, but before they had different names. Today young parents name their children after TV names. They used to have beautiful names. They had names before like 'Arrow' in Innu. It's coming back slowly. My nephew named his baby Arrow like his grandfather. He was related on his father's side, so he named him after his ancestor.

Traditional Dwellings

In the old days they had large tents, like this one, they had two doorways and there would be many families in one dwelling. They would share the same dwelling. They used to use caribou hides to cover the dwelling before we got canvas. They would sew caribou skins together. People got along when they shared a dwelling. Everyone was happy, it was exciting. Probably three or four families would live together. They'd share everything with other families. If one man got a caribou, everyone would share the meat. Sometimes different men go different ways to go hunting. Some would get game, others did not, but for everyone there was food. If a man got an animal, it was his turn to share.

We used to have tents down by the shore here. My father used to set nets down there and my brother would clean the fish and cut it into pieces and it would be given out. As a little girl, it would be my job to take the food around in the village. They did everything in the dwelling where they lived, they dried meat in there too. They had fires in the tent and later on stoves for heating the tents. If you had a lot of children you always put the stove in the middle and another on the side to make sure that the tent was warm. Women helped each other because everyone was related even though they were not always related by blood. They lived together as relatives. Sometimes if a woman had just had a baby, another woman would take care of the woman who had just delivered.

Traditional Government

There was always one leader who would make decisions such as breaking camp. These leaders were knowledgeable. They know where the animals were. When a caribou was killed, the meat was dried so it wouldn't be so heavy to transport to the next campsite. People followed the animals, like caribou, partridge, and porcupine. They never stayed in one place long, so animals were not depleted.

A leader was chosen because of his knowledge and experience of the land. It was usually an elderly person who was a good hunter, the best one. This leader knew everything in the country, knew where the animals were.

My father was directed by an Elder who was the leader. He learned from that Elder. Everyone listened to the leader, there was no disagreement. Only when a person earned the leadership role, could they give direction. The leader had to know where they were going and know how to work hard in order to survive. The Hudson Bay post was where we got our staples and we had to repay with furs. We had to work hard to pay back what we owed to Hudson's Bay Company (HBC).

Decisions were made by men and women together. They'd discuss the problem or plan. Sometimes the men would be gone hunting seven to ten days and only women and children would be at the camp. The men would be gone out trapping. When all the men were gone, the elderly women would be the leaders, the ones who made decisions.

My father was a hard worker. We had to use toboggans. In the springtime we used canoes. Everything had to be carried even through portages. The only time we rested was when we slept. As soon as day broke, we had to start working again. Even the children had to work. This is where I learned how to work. Now I never sit idle. My father would sit in the evenings after the work was done, but he still had to talk to his family so he wasn't really resting. This is the time in the evening, he'd also meet with the other men to plan for the next day as to who was going to do what.

Elders

It depended on your experience and how you were respected. If you were honest, people would look up to you. Those people who had extensive knowledge of the land were also seen as Elders. The role of Elders is to pass on stories and values. That's how young people learned. They taught the younger people by telling stories, shared their experience, teaching respect for animals and everything on the land, also the importance of sharing.

If there were a lot of families, the Elder would say you always have to share even if it was just a little that you had. Young people were also taught to help one another. If they shared, it was believed that they would get animals in the future. They believed in the balance, if they did good for others, good things came back to them. After sharing, the men would go hunting again and they knew that because they had shared, the Creator would be generous with them by giving them animals on the next hunt.

Even though there was no priest around, we knew that the Creator was still here. We believed that if we are good to our neighbours, we feed them, then the Creator will be good to us. Praying was a part of our daily lives. In a big camp, all families would come together once in a while to pray together. But individual families prayed together every day. Children were raised this way and grew up knowing the connection to the Creator. My mother would teach us to pray, but these days it is not the same. The things I learned from my father and mother were important, such as respect of the water. We were also taught safety. If my father and brothers were gone, the girls and women did men's work as well. They kept the camp going.

As a little girl I helped my mother by getting wood and preparing it for the fire. My mother also taught us safety of handling an axe. I really enjoyed life on the land and listened to everything my mother said. I watched her and I learned. I knew how busy my mother was and we tried our best to help. She always praised us. Before we went to play, we knew we had to work, so we learned the meaning of responsibility at an early age. My father used to have a big toboggan and he rarely let us use it for sliding because he needed it for travel.

Heroes and Role Models

My Elders are my role models. They have a lot of knowledge and experience of life. It is too bad that they are not seen as important because of the changes. I look at my grandchildren and I am frightened because it is changing fast, our culture is in danger.

Traditional Healing

One time my father was very sick. My mother used two sticks and laid cloth and hide over them, that's how she got my father to sit up, he was weak. It was something like an elevated bed.

Sweat Lodges were used for healing. It was in the wintertime and my father had to Sweat inside the tent, we had to be careful not to get chilled. We used heated rocks to make a Sweat. It was built inside, a small one was built inside. My mother had arthritis in her knees and she'd put only her leg inside the Sweat. My father would breathe in the Sweat to help it going. They put the rocks right in a small hole in the earth and covered the area with hides and canvas. Sometimes a person's whole body would be in the Sweat if they were really sick. Sometimes they would just put their heads out for a while but stayed in the Sweat for a long time. They'd put water on the rocks to make steam. My father always had a Sweat inside the dwelling especially in the winter.

My Sweat Lodge is now for women, but men can come in. It's a praying Sweat. I have this tent right beside the Sweat for changing and also for resting after the Sweat. They have tea and sit around in here after the Sweat. People are encouraged not to go directly outside after the Sweat because they could catch a cold. Other people are starting to use Sweats for praying now. It's a praying Sweat and for sharing of burdens. It's good to use in dealing with our daily problems. Sometimes only women go into the Sweat. Women have special concerns and it is a time to share. They used to have Sweat Lodges here a long time ago and now it is coming back again.

Traditional Games and Toys

They had traditional games such as ball playing. There would be teams, this would occur when everyone got together in camps for the summer. The older people used to make their own checker games at times when they got together. Recreation was working and walking. Not much time to play.

The children would have toys such as wooden boats or dolls. For toys, we used to make things like toy boats out of wood and to use stones for pretend people. We played out real life, we would seat our 'mom and dad and children' in the canoes and we would role-play, talk the way our parents talk.

We also made our own dolls out of cloth or hide. She used to make a hammock for the doll, just like a real baby's. I talked to the doll too, just like a baby. They used to have cloth bags made of moss for babies, with lacing up the front. I have a granddaughter today, her dolls are sometimes one hundred dollars. It's a big change compared to what type of toys we had. My brother used to play with a squirrel and role-play, he would pretend he was skinning a caribou just like the way my father did. He'd even make a little bag where the meat would be kept. We imitated what our parents did, that was our play, it was our learning.

The games were made of caribou bones where you would try to catch certain holes. They would use the antler for a pointed stick and then catch it in certain holes. A beaver bone was also used for a game, they would predict how many beaver they'd get. We would talk to the bone, you got the dimple, it meant you would find beaver but not catch it, but if you got the big hole, that meant you would get beaver.

People would use a wishbone from birds and they would pull it to see who would be getting more birds. Children also played with string and made games out of them, they'd make designs. They made a string game with a wooden spool and it would make sound. The children would play with these.

Feasts and Celebrations

People had feasts after lots of caribou were killed. The whole camp would get together and feast. When a boy killed his first caribou, there was a lot of happiness in the village, and there would be a big feast. People would sit around and people would talk about the boy's accomplishment. The boys would get a lot of praise. They would get advice from everybody.

Marriages

Long ago, your parents decided who you would marry, but now it's different. People never separated or divorced. Parents did not look at how good-looking the people were, what mattered is how they worked. If they were good workers they would make good spouses. For the men, it depended on whether they were good hunters.

I remember this man and my older sister was inside, she was a good worker. The man asked if he could marry her. It all had to do with survival skills. Girls used to get married very young. This old woman told her story about how she got married so young that she was afraid of her new husband.

Traditional Music

They had hand drums, which were used by individuals. It was hung in the tent, you had to be very respectful to the drum. It had its special place. I remember the drum and I remember my mother singing in Innu, they would be praying songs. Drum was used for praying, it was spiritual. If a young boy went out hunting and didn't get anything, he would ask his Elder to sing on the drum for him so that he would get something off the land on his next hunt. Both men and women sang with the drum, although it was mainly men. Some of the older people still have the drum today.

Art

The only thing I remember is miniature paddles and shovels made for boys, these were made by the fathers. They would be replicas of the real tools. The caribou shoulder, there is a part there that used to make a little axe, these were used as little toys. On the partridge, the bag under its neck would be used as a toy for babies. It was used as a rattle. When a lot of partridges were killed, the girls wanted to help clean them, so they could get the bags.

Daily Routines

The first thing that I do is to make the fire and heat water for washing. I cook for my children and they eat. The kids are sent out to play. I get all the dishes and clean them. I clean up the blankets and clean the tent. If there has been caribou killed or any other animal, I clean the meat and prepare it for smoking or drying. I go out and get boughs for the floor.

Sometimes when it is really nice out, I go out and enjoy the weather. I take my kids out on a hike and we go out for partridge hunting. Sometimes I take food and we stop and make a fire and eat. Sometimes we go out and pick berries. Boughs on the floor are changed almost every two days in summers. In the winter, boughs are changed at least twice a week. Boughs don't dry up as fast in the winter.

Some days I just go paddling with my family, my husband and children. When the weather is bad, sewing is done, bread is made. When I go to the country, when I first get there, I set up camp, but we know that we have to move later. In the winter when boughs are put on the floor, they have to be changed regularly. In the spring we just pile the boughs on top of each other because as the snow goes down the boughs sink as well. When we are out in the bush, I also wash clothes and wash the children's hair. Clothes are hung right in the tent. There are certain days when it's good to make bread. Usually in the evenings we eat a big meal when the father comes back from hunting.

Grandchildren and children sometimes want attention and they still are put in a hammock because they want to be babied. I do this because I care about them so much, they want to be cuddled, rocked to sleep. When children go to sleep, you sing to them and they are held. They really like this and it is good for them. I also tell them stories about animals, stories are based on the natural environment, the traditional lifestyle.

There are certain things you have to do after the children are settled, one of them is melting bear fat. A woman has a lot of work to do at the camp, so sometimes I go out hunting with my husband, to get away. The older daughter is left in charge of the camp. The daughter is given instructions on care of the children especially with safety with fire, safety with cooking. Before I leave I have to really make sure all is in order. Instructions are left for cooking with the daughter.

The daughter is usually well trained and all that had to be done was completed and more. The daughter tries hard to do extra to please mother. There is a lot of respect between mother and daughter. They are always praised by the mother; the daughter always wanted to make her mother proud. If her mother was happy, that would make her happy. It was an honour to please the mother.

The men also had respect for women. The husband would help the woman. He would do some of her chores when she was tired. She felt cared for and really loved. He acknowledged and respected her for all the work she did.

Importance of Work

There was a lot of work to be done. You did a lot for your children and if they were happy, you would be happy. If other people around you are happy, you are happy. It's really different when we're here in the community. I remember when I was young I'd go berry picking with my mother. My mother always praised me and I felt like working harder. Everyone would pick a cup of berries and then they would pour it into a large pail, they worked together, when it was full, everyone was happy. They did things together.

Even though parents live here in the community now, they can still praise their children. It's good to praise a child because it makes a child feel good about themselves. It gives them self-confidence. They see themselves as being important. It is the same for boys and girls. If a man takes his boys hunting, for example, if he sees a partridge he'll let his son get it, so he'll have a chance. When they go fishing and the father knows there is a fish on the line, he'll let his son pull it out. He likes to see his son happy and he also praises him.

Traditional Clothing

I always remember cloth being around before clothes were made from caribou skins. I've heard older people talk about how they dressed. Rabbit skins were used to put around your feet, for the children, also around their hands. The parents would say, 'We're having a long trip today,' and the kids were happy to have warm rabbit skin socks and mitts. Moccasins were worn all the time. The folds of the caribou legs were used to go around our hands and feet also. People still cure their own hides. Even today we have our traditional shoes. Hats were also made out of fur. Sometimes today young people are shy to wear traditional clothing. They wear the clothing in the country though.

Ceremonies

They had the Shaking Tent, which was run by the shaman. It was used for praying and communication with the Spirit world. Sometimes I think about it and I know that God was important in our lives.

Traditional Burials

If somebody died in the country, the body would be washed. There would be a beautiful place to bury that person. They'd put a marker up, it was a cross. They would always remember where that person was buried. They would dig a hole, but later they'd bring the body to the country if they are not far. After a person dies, it is believed that the body stays in the ground but the Spirit goes to God. They believed that the Spirit lived on.

Traditional Beliefs and Christianity

The people believed in God even when no priests were around. They'd get together and pray together. Even the children were taught, the youngest child was always taught to pray. It was Native people that accepted the new religion because they already believed. As the new religion came to them, they just kept on learning about God. The two ways are related in that way, the holy water and all that, was just another step for them. The stories about Jesus were easily believed by the people.

Prophecies

A man who told such stories used the boughs of trees as an example. He said in all of Sheshashiet land, all the boughs will be changing, everything is going to change, nothing will be the way it is now. I think, he think, he meant that life would change. Before, long time ago, people lived off the land, using their hands to survive. But now there are different things that they get things like social services, welfare. A man would kill an animal for food or trade, they were self-sufficient, they didn't wait around for a cheque to come to buy food. Before they would do it themselves. They didn't go to social services to get something, they were independent. We can see and feel the difference now. Now we do not do things for ourselves, and I believe what the man with the prophecy said. They also followed the dreams of people.

Dreams

People relied on their dreams, they knew what their dreams meant. For example, my father dreamt that he was eating trees and the next morning he realized why he had dreamt that. He had been cutting trees for people across the river, White people, and they would give him money. He realized that he was eating what he had been cutting. People would tell their dreams to one certain person and that person would understand right away what other people's dreams meant. Dreams were used to tell people what to do, how to live.

A local woman, she is dead now, had a dream that she and her friend were on an island and this island was moving. Her dream meant that she would die soon, and she did. As the island was moving, it was getting closer to the end for her and that she was dying. Another time this woman also dreamt that she was riding in a car and she saw a pack of partridges. She was thinking, 'I should get these partridges.' She went to where they were and started picking them up one by one. The dream meant that because she has so many grandchildren and children, she felt that she should take the best care of them before she died. That is what that dream meant.

Time

They could tell time by the sun, by the shadows, by the sky. Through different seasons we pretty well lived off the land. With different weather, things changed. When it was hot, we would have to make fire outside so flies would not get into the food, we changed boughs on the floor more often in warm seasons, the way we cooked our food was different for different seasons. In winter we froze our food and kept it up on trees.

Language and Culture

Language and culture are related. If you know the language you understand the culture. Place names were in Innu, they described the places, rivers, lakes. Ownership of land was not known, there were no boundaries. Land was shared.

Economics

There were different kinds of fish like trout, salmon, and different kinds of fish and animals. Caribou was the big game. We also got other animals like black bear, and other animals. There were also birds like ducks. There were different kinds of ducks because they ate different kinds of foods. There was this one kind of duck that eats fish and therefore it tastes like fish. The others eat grass.

Preparing food involved smoking and drying. They would also pound the meat to make pemmican so that it would not spoil. In the summer food was dried and smoked. In the winter it could be frozen.

Transportation

They used toboggans and snowshoes. There were two kinds of sleds, one that had runners and one flat toboggan. They used dog teams as well. There were no planes or snowmobiles. My grandfather has six or seven dogs. The dogs were very respected, their food was cooked like for people. This would make them strong because they were needed, they helped so much. Before people would get a lot of exercise. Now they just jump on a snowmobile or in a car and go. No one walks anymore. Before people would move together, they would pull sleds. Kids would be praised for their work in pulling and paddling. Usually travel with another family in another boat. Everyone would try hard. Even the children had little paddles to use and they were always praised.

Traditional Medicines

There is still some medicine around that we use. When I go into the woods, I see medicines that my grandmother used to use. There is a certain kind of medicine made of tree gum, it is used for pain, sore throat, that kind of thing. They would put it on your chest and they would use a paper from a prayer book to stick it on, it could not just be any paper, it had to be like a sacred paper. For babies, they would burn the medicine a bit first before putting it on because it is too strong for a baby. You have to be very careful with the baby, if you can smell it on the baby's breath, you take it off because it now has worked.

Education

Education is good as long as you do not lose your culture. It is very important that your culture is not lost. Because the young people were born from their mother and their mother is linked to that culture, therefore that child should not lose that culture. A person can live in today's world and still have their culture. But sometimes there is too much White influence. There is too much technology. When small children watch TV, they grow up thinking like what they see, my grandson sees wrestling, kung fu, and guns and that is what he imitates. There is so much war on TV and it is not good. Guns for example, are used to get our food, but on TV they are used to kill people.

I do not know much about residential schools but I know people who were physically abused, but I don't know about sexual abuse, no one has talked about it. But my husband was physically abused in residential school. Today's schools should be focused more on our culture, it is very important that children be taught their own way. They should learn about White culture, but not only White culture, their own should be focused upon.

Traditional Justice

It is mainly the Elders who would deal with people who did something wrong. They would talk to them about their behaviour. In prison you are locked up, it just adds more anger and frustration. People should be taken into the bush, they could go hunting, survive off the land. They feel good out there, they will have time to think about how they are living, the things they did that hurt other people. When people are in prison, it does not help them understand. If a person was out in the bush, it would be different. When a person gets out of prison, they are full of anger.

Native and Non-Native People

It is better if Native people work with their own people. I do not think a White person can help a Native person, they are from a different culture. In regards to self-government, Native people should be working for themselves, to help each other. They understand each other, their culture.

The low-flying jets in this area frighten people and especially the children out on the land. Everything is disturbed because they are so loud. Usually parents take babies out on the land. If a person is not well with high blood pressure, there is a danger of a person having a heart attack. They also frighten the animals, so the animals are moving away from this area. I went out to the bombing range twice and when I saw the land, I thought of the animals. They survive on moss, roots, and food off the land. Trees are destroyed. Bombs are dropped out there. The animals are not healthy so our food is being contaminated. Animals are frightened and they are sometimes found dead. I think it is the jets which has caused this destruction. I believe the animals cannot stay in one place anymore. Long ago, they used to stay in certain areas, now they are scattered and people do not know their routes anymore.

Other Thoughts

There is something that I am concerned about, that is the young children. I really want my grandchildren to learn about life in the bush, but the White culture is so strong. In the community there is so much influence from the outside, children are steered away from their own culture. They are more influenced by White society. What my parents taught me about life on the land is very important. I used a lot of what I learned as a child out in the country. I can live out on the land because I learned as a child. I want young people to learn this as well, or else it will be lost.

I do not think White culture is important to me. I feel very happy and healthy out on the land, but here in this community there is nothing. When I was a young girl, I grew up in the country, on the land, it was very healthy for me. After we moved to the community, things started to go wrong. That is why I want the children to live in the country. I know what it is like out there. In the community the children are out late into the night, we don't know what they are doing. It is much better in the country, you always know where your children are at all times.

The problems we face today did not exist out on the land, such as sickness like cancer and diabetes. The older people would always know what to do if someone got sick with a cold, they used natural medicines. Lots of medicine comes from trees, and the young people were also taught which medicines to use.

Berries are also plentiful out on the land, that is good food. We get blueberries, but they do not grow like they used to. When I went out last year, I had to walk for a couple hours to get to the berries, whereas before, we did not have to go so far.

It is very important that a person takes care of themselves. The traditional medicines were more powerful and helped lots of people. There is a lot of medicine out there. There are still people, Elders, who know medicines.

The moss is being destroyed as well as trees and berries. We cannot stop the government from intruding on the land. They are changing the land and destroying it. There will be nothing left for the younger people. It will not be there anymore for them to live off the land. I get involved with protests and I will not stop. I really believe in the land and I care about my people. I will fight for my rights.

I am very angry at the government. The government only cares about money and does not care about the people who lived off this land for a long long time. When you get money it goes away, you spend it and it does not come back, but the land will always be there.

The Native people around James Bay and Labrador are just ignored by the government. The government acts like we are not even here. The land is very important to Native people, it is their culture.

I look at the young children. When he sees something he just plays with it because he is too young to understand. That is how I see the government, the government is playing with our land, playing with the lives of Native people.

The government is trying to take the land. Why were the Native people who live on this land never asked? We have always been here. The government does not own this land, no one can give that right to the government. No Native person has allowed the government to take the land. The government just takes what they want.

All the Native people across the land have never given away the land.

JAMES CARPENTER (Mushkegowuk Cree)

Attawapiskat, Ontario

'The Elders have waited for the young people to ask such things.'

James Carpenter was born in 1924 near Attawapiskat, in Northern Ontario. His traditional name is *Wawatay Eninew.* He now lives with his daughter and her family. Emily Faries interviewed James Carpenter in her home at Moose Factory. She described the interview as very rewarding, but also very tiring. James Carpenter spent five days with her, and she recorded more than ten audio cassettes of their discussion. The interview focused on James Carpenter's connection to the land, but he also discussed residential schools and Christianity in the North. Because of the length of the interview some of the material had to be edited, but it still contains many of James Carpenter's stories, and his images of life in the North.

Life History

First thing, I would like to say thank you once again for asking me to come to visit people here at Moose Factory. I am very pleased to be here. I didn't hesitate or wondered about your invitation to come for an interview. Now the question that you ask about my life, where I was born, I will tell you. I was born in Wetiko Creek or Nawahee(k). That is where I was born. My father went upstream when the land was almost frozen and the rivers were starting to freeze up. He went to the place called Land of the Fox, that is where my father spent his winter. Later he went to the settlement of Attawapiskat for the feast-day. He spent his feast-day there and the New Year. After feast-day, he left and went back to where he would come to kill rabbits and fish – the hunting grounds. There was hardly anything around as you see today. That is where we lived and when the time came, my father taught me everything, that is exactly how I learned. My father taught me to set rabbit snares.

I cannot say anything else different or about other people who lived before me. My father taught me how to set rabbit snares, set fish nets, trap, and even when the time came, how to hunt moose. That is what I did. I tried to go to school when they were gathering children in 1944, but some say it was 1942. But I had all I needed to learn, everything I was to learn, I learned, even how to make snowshoes. There were no chainsaws at that time and not even the handsaw, we just broke the wood with an axe. We carried the wood as there was no snow machines at that time. When you get wood you wear only snowshoes and carry them on your back. That's what we did. And that's how the place was where my father lived. Every winter that's what we did, you looked for a place where there are fish, where you are going to spend your winter, you look for that place. And when you know where there are fish and where you think you will survive through the winter, knowing what the animals are going to do. For two months, January and February, that's the way things were.

Later on, I became skilled at hunting from what my father taught me, by setting rabbit snares. I will tell you about the animals people lived on, for those young people who want to know, I will tell you about everything. Animals don't go far, everything hibernates during the month of January when people are burning wood. During the months of January and February the animals are not moving, not even at other places and that's when people were hungry. And those animals in the water, fish, and those who hibernate in the ground during this time, those we trap, like weasel, muskrat, beaver, they all stay in one place. These animals do not go far from their homes, they stay underground during the cold winter. Those big animals, moose, caribou, these animals don't get cold very easy. They don't get cold and don't hibernate. However, they seem to live in one way, they continue to live the same way. They live the same way as those animals that live underground. They have good hearing and you can't approach them close, they will run away as soon as they hear a noise.

Towards the end of February, those big animals started to change their living style, the wind is also starting to change. It is like the month of January when it is extremely cold and calm, we never stayed in settlement, not like what we're doing today staying in town. Everybody knows, those who lived during the same time as I did, that we never stayed in settlements. It was so quiet during the two months when we were out on the land. It was very quiet at that time, you were not bothered or harassed by the animals. You hear the spruce trees moving in the wind, and you hear the wind. You hear only things from the Creator. And you don't have to worry about locking your door while you sleep. It was so quiet, even though nobody stayed in settlements. That's the way we lived, that's the way everybody lived here around Attawapiskat, that's how I was raised. During the schooling I had, I didn't really learn.

I tried for two years at the school in Fort Albany. I learned what my parents taught me. At the school, I brought in wood, and washed dishes. I taught myself everything, not like the way the children are sitting holding pencils today, it is very difficult the way children are learning today. There was no hospital, there was no doctor, I didn't see a doctor. There was no detox centre. There was no jail. There was no policemen. I don't know what happened. That's how everything was when I lived during those days when there were no worries, just happiness. No sickness, you played, you feel healthy, you feel strong when you don't eat food from cans, tin food. You were very strong.

When the boat landed in Attawapiskat, the first product was ninety pounds of flour and sugar, even the sugar bags was pretty big. That's the way people's lives were before they ate the products such as today. We are poisoned now. Nowadays, I can't even break a grass, that is how weak I am. That is what I say about where I was raised, I can also tell you, in the month of June we arrived with our canoes and in August that's when the people leave the settlement again. When the people came to the settlement they gathered together, everybody that lived off the land came together. People found peace in the land, they were happy. It was quiet, that's the way we lived. You didn't hear what you hear today. Rarely you heard about trouble but sometimes you will hear of a person's gun had accidentally gone off or a person might have tipped over a canoe, that's all. There was hardly anything as sudden deaths.

There was medicine from the land. I can tell you exactly what the medicine is, the good medicine the people used. It was not like today, sometimes today a person gets the wrong medicine from the doctor or the medicine are leftover and the person takes it and later you hear they are dead. There was nothing like that. It was very quiet while I was growing up. That's the way we lived. It was quiet and so peaceful, a person didn't say, 'Don't kill more than five animals.' I never heard a person to say, 'Don't look at the sun,' if the sun wasn't supposed to be there, God would not have put it there. The time has arrived for suffering nowadays. This is what happened while I was growing up, the quiet times. That's what is still going on today for Elders like us. It's the only thing we learned, but we had poor English but we knew not to do wrong nor harm our fellow human beings. Of course, we learned so much about it and I don't have to rely on the priest nor for other people to tell me about the Bible. The people see how I live and the place where I live. I have lived believing in God for a long time. That's how we lived in the past, that's where we learned, we taught ourselves and those things that were written they are coming to be.

When we cook, somebody skins that rabbit and is taught by their mother. My mother told me and showed me how to skin a rabbit and I cleaned the rabbit and I would get a stick. Nobody will tell you to pay for that stick. There was no such thing as paying for that stick and today we pay for everything. Everything, food, trees, and water, is there for you before you are even born. Everything is provided for you just like right now, my host gives me a bed and brings me food, that's exactly what the Creator does for us, provides for us. You don't cut trees down for nothing and you use only what you need. That is what the Elders told the young people back in those days. Even the animals on earth, you take only the amount you need. Nobody came along to tell you not to cut the trees down or hunt a certain way, we knew how to live.

The same with the frog, you don't bother or tease the animal. It is a very dangerous thing to tease a frog. The frog seems humble when we look at him but 'He is used,' my father said. When I was young I used to tease a frog, my father was very angry with me. 'Don't tease that frog,' he said. When I was walking around along the stream, and while they were making a camp fire, they told me that the frog you tease is used by the Creator to make water clean and safe for us to drink. He is the one who helps you and makes the water clear. We still see it today, the frog makes the water clean and clear. The water now is cleaned by the frog when you go down to the river. No one destroyed the water in those days when I was young. I never saw anyone to make dams or close the rivers. The beavers were the only ones who had the right to dam the rivers so they can have a home and keep warm. Just like I have a house today, the Creator gave the beaver the right to build his own house. My father told me not to pull at the sticks of a beaver dam, because that's the beaver's life.

I am poor today, in a way of not knowing English. I did not get that kind of schooling. And even today, although I don't understand English the police haven't talked to me yet. The judge hasn't talked to me yet. Now where did I get it, the knowledge? I have not gone to the detox centre. Where did I get my way of life? From my father's teachings and advice, that's where I learned it from. And whenever I go, I feel peace and calm. I treat my fellow human beings and nature beings well. That is the way it was long time ago as I was growing up.

Now I am going to talk about something about how people lived. I used rabbit skins for my socks and I felt comfortable running around, when I played. That's what my life is about. There are many games, sliding, you pretend to be a wolf or whatever you want to do when you play. You are happy and have fun, and you are not bored. After playing all day, you pray before you go to sleep. When evening comes, people prayed, they gathered the children to go inside the *migwam* (home), although it looked so poor they prayed and gathered the children early. I will tell you exactly what the Elders said before the sun went down. We have already been sent in, they had willows sent in so that the Elders can feel powerful but not with the intent to hit the children just so that they will understand or listen. People misunderstood that the Elder used the willow to punish that way, but the Elders followed the good life. We behaved and listened well and we went to pray early in the evening.

Everybody was happy when they went upstream, and when they prayed in the evening, they prayed for help. There were no things that are going on today, there were hardly any news about what has happened two or three days ago when Peter Goodwin had suddenly died. Sudden deaths was never heard of. The things that are happening today, the life we have now, were unheard of. People had no worries nor had to think about what will happen to them in the future. The Native people relied and believed in the Creator, that's what gave them strength. Everybody that I came to live with in this life knew all these things, nobody had said that I will go to the hospital or I will get medicine. That did not exist. It just seems like yesterday that we saw these things.

I never seen people getting operations. I have never seen that kind of life and that was our life, nobody had given us operations. What is the cause? Who can understand? Can somebody explain what is the cause of it? Of course, there is a cause and I started to realize the cause when I was about fifty years old, and that is my life I am talking about. People would go away and are gone for about twelve months. That is where the Elders went and the women went someplace else. The men went out to get something to live on. They walked using snowshoes, they used dogs to pull the sleighs. That's the way we used to live while we were young. I can't particularly say what happened elsewhere but only what I witnessed through my own eyes. Nobody can talk about what they did not see. I am only talking about what I have seen or witnessed as what my life was like.

Today I am poor because I don't understand English. But I worked a little bit, I worked with the police for twelve months and while I was working there, I watched the prisoners. That's what I did for a job, but I don't have to talk about that. I just want to talk about life of long ago, the past.

There was a lot of happiness and compassion. People gathered together when the New Year approached. They gathered at the rivers and came downstream. They gathered together, played, danced, and whatever else there is to do to have a good time. They played and played, tug of war and all kinds of games. They watched each other and looked out for each other from starvation or sickness. That's the way people lived, those who I grew up with. I will tell you this other story of what we used a knife to kill a moose. Where did we get it from? If someone had no knife, he used a moose rib, scrape it down. You would use it as a knife when you eat. An Indian closes his eyes while he eats because the meat tastes so good and the only thing that is moving is your feet. You can make moose grease to eat. That's how it was when someone didn't have a knife.

What did the people do for matches if they got wet? They would put them on his chest if they were wet. They had no hip-waders, the hip-waders just came out recently. People wore moose hide moccasins. I used to run fast when I was young wearing moose hide moccasins during the summer days. The only bad thing about them was when you walked around on the hilly parts is that your feet felt like somebody was chewing on them, as they start to dry out. I would go muskrat trapping. I used to go with my father when he went trapping after the spring breakup.

Creation

It is good to want to know about that. But first thing about the Native people and our friends [White people] were different too. It is not necessary to talk about them, these are our friends, they are those who landed on the shore of our land, those who visited our land, on the land we were supposed to live on. The first person that was here was the Great Spirit. The Great Spirit wondered and said, 'I will create a human being to be like us.' That is what people inland are saying too. But I don't know what the strangers are saying, I cannot say. What I heard from other people is that the earth, land is round, in the centre there is a cross. Now if a person from out of this world comes to this world, I would call that person a stranger. And when that person is in the world, in that round world where the cross is, we are all one family. If I say this in the right way, there are no strangers, I will say that for sure, there are no strangers in this world. These people who are making marks and who are telling from the Bible, however it is possible to misunderstand how many suns will there be and that's the only way you will understand that there is a Great Spirit. Why is it that Indians suddenly die and why are there graveyards in every village? Yes, it shows that we don't own anything anymore, that we do not have control. When a person is ill and he thinks he is very sick, he sees a doctor. We believe that the Great Spirit made people and put them on the earth.

Some people find it hard to believe that it took six days for the Great Spirit to build this earth and on Sunday he was finished and that is why we have a rest on that day. That is what people talk about, I heard people talk about it even those who don't understand and those who never read the Bible or what had been written down.

We believe although that there is death, we believe also in living. We learn by the signs like the wood we see, a wood that is called a willow, you can cut it down, how does it look again when the summer begins? It continues to grow during the winter. That's what the Elders who understand are talking about. They are talking about life. Those Elders who are not public and do not share their speech are the ones who know everything and they tell about what life was like in the early days.

The very first time a human being was made. A man was made. A man was alone first for a long time. The Great Spirit had pity on him because he looked lonely. While the man slept, the Great Spirit took one of his ribs and then there was a woman. The Great Spirit gave him someone to care for him, to hold him and to comfort him. That's what it says and that's what happened.

The woman is very special and important. The Creator gave her a special gift, to give life. The Great Spirit gave the man and woman the children as gifts. They do not own them. There is also something else, that is being talked about how to live. It is important not to think that some people know nothing. It is very dangerous. A person who seems to know little can be knowledgeable in other areas more. It has already been planned by the Creator that each person has his or her purpose in this life. That's the way Indians have lived. We have had a rough time, lived poorly but the Great Spirit gave the people something powerful: courage. It is the greatest power and it continues.

Those people who took advantage of the Indian people and the resources will learn the hard way. They have gained a lot while the Indian people suffered. Those people who took control in 1905 [Treaty Nine was signed] will soon learn that the Indian will regain his pride. The Indian will start to look back on his past and learn his culture. He will improve his conditions and it will be better than what the White people 'gave' them. The Indian people will learn their traditional way of life again.

For example, an Indian is buried in the cemetery and the earth is used and the person turns to dust. A cross symbol made of ash is drawn on a person's forehead, to symbolize that Jesus was nailed on the cross and people turn to dust after they die.

When you enter the church it looks beautiful and you keep it that way. You treat those graves the same way, with deep respect. We believe that a person lives on, just like all things in nature. You cut grass, it grows again. When it rains and the sky clears and everything is beautiful, when you go along the river bank and see things that are growing, grass, flowers, the Creator is responsible for it. The Great Spirit has the power and strength. The Great Spirit gave the Indian pride in himself and he looks very poor at times but he will take control of his future and his world. It has been said that it will happen and that it's starting to show today.

In one of the towns, the land moved [earthquake] where these people who do not believe in the Creator live, and this will get worse, three times more than what has happened. There was going to be a great storm near Winnipeg but it happened in the east, as I heard on the radio. The passing of the storm left no electricity. We did not use electricity when I was young, we used the best thing, skunk oil for light. Fish liver oil was used in dark places such as a *migwam*, *askigan*, or in a wood or log house. There was no light switches in those days.

Where does the Indian come from? From the land, and he goes back to the land when he dies. That was the way he lived, the traditional way of life. That's why Indians get buried in the land. And when he dies, he will be in a better world. He will see the sun, and dangerous diseases and sicknesses will not be there.

How was it when we were young or children? There was hardly anyone who passed away early because diseases were never around. Unlike today, long ago the people lived a long and good life. The Great Spirit looked after the Indian people right. He shone the light on the people every day. He never passed judgment on them and he never asked for me to pay him and now I am eighty years old. He will never ask anyone to pay him because they have lived a long life. Let's look at the days, he has made everything beautiful. The Indian people lived in this land which God created. It is beautiful.

It is good that young people want to learn about their own ways. That is how we will have our future generations learn. It is slow but when a person watches for these things, he sees them. The mind is going to say many things and people are going to say many things. They are going to say them different. How does the sun look? You will never see the sun do us wrong. The sun will say, 'This is how you are.' The sun will look after you right.

I am going to tell a story. The people whose bodies have passed on or have been burnt have already been provided for. The Creator said, 'They won't lose one strand of hair on the last day.' For example, we don't see the flowers until after breakup and who looks after that, and where does the change of seasons come from every year? Why do new things in nature keep growing? That's why we should believe that the Creator has the power to create and provide. How long will the ice be gone, is it going to be summer forever? Is there going to be winter again, summer again? And we won't see new things in nature, the water that flows is not new. The people with their way of life and all creations are one. We are part of nature. When we hunt animals, they will always be provided. The sun will always provide for us. That is the way Indian people lived and worked in the past. It still shows today that Creator is looking after the Native people. We have always prayed and those who do not believe in God's presence will learn through earthquakes.

It seems only yesterday that the provincial judge came to this area. We never seen him when we were children. In those days, when Native people had problems, they would go see an Elder. The Elder's words were good and people listened and the Elder helped the people. Today things have changed. When Elders meet, they say, 'Let's give our respect to the young people now.' The Elder doesn't see himself as important anymore. The reason is he is going to the grave soon. In my early years, the Elders had talked about what was to happen in the future. Now today in 1994, those things are happening. My grandchildren will see things in the future that have not yet happened. And for those future generations, they will see three times as much harder times or dangerous times.

A long time ago people loved each other and it is still showing. We should not lose that, that's the way we lived in the past. Like the way I was treated here, they feed me and provide my air fare. The Great Spirit wants us to help each other. When I was young, my mother told me to behave myself. We are always told to live right and behave. In the middle of my childhood, people were in a sorry situation. One of the people [a priest] took a willow to the young people who did not behave. He cannot rule the way the Creator does because he lives on earth, he too is a human being. I seen the young people during my childhood, they behaved themselves. They went home when told to, before the sun went down. They get up early before sunrise and they pray. They pray for a new day and that it will go well. They thank the Creator for seeing another day. They forced us to get up right away in the mornings. They kept telling us to respect our fellow human beings as well as respect ourselves. My father, mother, grandmother taught me as I was growing up. That's what the Elders' teachings were, and somewhere along the way, something went wrong but there is hope. The young people today can fix the mistake that has happened in the past. A lot of the Elders had a hard time, like myself, that something went wrong, since a priest picked up the willow. This priest told me that when he was younger, a mother would pick up a willow. It was their way of disciplining their children. The Elders respected death because they knew they were going to die soon and that is what helped them live a good life. They learned discipline and good behaviour.

These friends of ours, the strangers [White people] who came here, they gave the book of law. I feel sorry for the one [priest] who picked up the willow because he cannot stand up and send my blessing to the Creator. He came to the Indian people as things were going good for them.

Native Culture

The Native people were given a life from the Creator and they had respect for it and for each other and they relied on their way of life. In their lives, the most important part was food, people would share their food, snowshoes, toboggan, and dogs. They shared all these things with each other. The dogs helped the Indian people and they respected the dog who was useful and important. He used to lead and always found the way on the road even not travelling on the same road for a long time. When he was hunting moose, the dog was able to hold the moose and corner it. The dog was also useful when hunting ducks, during the time when ducks were flightless, the dogs were used to catch the ducks. The dogs were also used to search out the ducks in the grass. Dogs were one of the things Native people used to hunt with and pull toboggans. The dogs were taught everything on their first time out. Such as today, the snowmobile and the boat are important to you. When you didn't have a toboggan, you would have to get one. You go to your friend to borrow these things. These things were considered important.

A long time ago, we used to have moccasins to run around in. There were axes, guns, and gunpowder, and people considered these important. When the toboggan broke, it was repaired and was still used. The same thing with bow and arrows, partridge, squirrel, and even skunk are hunted with a bow and arrow. The most important are those which helped Indian people to live. The land was also important and to have respect for it. There was also respect for the people and for each other. When people are short on something, people shared.

The Elders are seeing many changes today. Some of them don't really care for what is going on and they see the young people who are facing these changes. However, the Elders who have respect for the young people of today because they know that they will bring or continue our culture and pass it on. They will continue our life. The Elders' teachings and I have learned from what I have heard. I have seen the Elders use canes but they still got around. They were still active although they had the canes. Even the Elders were pulling the toboggans to get from place to place. They made camps and no one came to them to tell them to pay for the land. Everything was free, a free country. I never heard a person who had to pay for the land. You could use anything on the land and do anything you wanted. The Creator has given you these things to do. People thought the fish were important too because they provided food. Muskrat, mouse, birds, frogs and skunks, we respected all these animals. I am telling you what the Elders have said in the past, to have the respect for each other. Have respect for your mother and father. There are many things to have respect for on this land. Everything we needed was on the land.

The babies were taken care of by their mothers and they would be breast-fed. We respect the land that God gave us and we used the land as we were growing up. We were breast-fed from our mother's bosom. We did not grow up from the animal's milk. That's what the Creator gave us to grow, mother's milk. Everything that is on the land is important and only you can decide how much you want, how much wood you want to use or to make a paddle with. You don't have to take any more. We used the earth [moss] for the babies' diapers and for making *askigan* [dwelling]. There are different kinds of moss like caribous' food and the others that have no special use.

The Creator gave animals and humans special characteristics like the antlers on the caribou and moose. As each season changes the antlers change. The Native people were also given special characteristics to be different. Everything that we used was considered important. We used the moose antlers for our utensils such as spoons, knives. They were considered important.

Reaching Back into the Past

The young people should live in ways to help themselves. Suppose you go on a long snowmobile trip, when you go make sure you are prepared. Take the necessary items: matches, axes, gas, food staples or you will be in big trouble. These are important for your survival. You have to listen to your Elders and to what they are really saying to you. It is not hard to understand these things. A young person is considered capable of understanding what the Elder had told him. He will gain the knowledge to live and know what the Elder had told him as he gets older and soon when he becomes an Elder himself.

For those who don't listen are not left out by the Elders. They do not give up on them. We should help each other and to learn from each other. You, young people today, are going to be the ones who will teach the young ones. Nobody is considered better than the others, everyone is equal. Nobody should consider themselves too important. It is important to learn from our teachings.

I have seen a body that has burnt because of alcohol. I wonder how things would be if alcohol was not here. I have seen these accidents and trouble when people are involved with alcohol. My father has seen the effects of alcohol and told me not to touch the alcohol as long as I live. I have never touched it and all this time I have tried to be a good role model. Even when I go to town, I don't bother with alcohol.

Raising Children

Everybody never sat around, everybody helped with the chores, everybody helped with the child rearing, even the man helped deliver the babies. Everybody had a role to help in child rearing. The man had to get the moss and had to hang it to dry and to prepare for the baby to use. They took care of the babies very well. They never saw a child to be mistreated or for a child to be unhappy. The people took extreme care in bringing up a child. They helped each other in child rearing. These children were taken care of and grew up from mother's milk and later with wild food. The children were strong and healthy and big. The children were given gravy from fish and gravy from wild meat. There was never any milk.

The South people say that when a child turns sixteen, you don't have to take care of him anymore. That saying is not here. Once a person can take care of themselves, there is always someone there like their parents, grandparents, and other Elders to show them the way to live. When people use this way, it was good and life went well for everyone. People never stopped taking care of the younger people once they turned sixteen years old. There was no such thing in all of our land. Everyone took care of each other. This way the child rearing was very good. Everyone had to look after their children right. It was a peaceful and happy life. Everyone helped each other and if someone had trouble, they talked it out.

If a death occurred, everyone helped the family and gave them comfort. As I live now, these things are changing. I see it as strange to see these changes. The woman teaches her daughter how to sew moccasins. The man teaches his son what he has to know. The woman tells her daughter what will you do so that when she is gone, her daughter will know how to sew or make moccasins. It was important for the young girls or boys to listen and learn from their parents. By the age of about twenty-four for the woman and about twenty-five for the man, the parents' teachings have to be mastered if they are able to live on their own. The man has learned to make snowshoes and toboggans. The men also have been taught everything even how to sew moccasins. Even if a person is married, they don't stop teaching the person. The law that says a young person is on their own at the age of sixteen is the strangers' law, and is run by money not of the Creator. There are people who will talk about things that are not true, people should not listen to them.

The White man came to our territory and destroyed everything, just like a teepee standing and then the wind blows it down. How can we replace those things that have happened? We have to take the teepee down and rebuild a new teepee. We have to tear it down and rebuild. We can carry on our culture by turning to our Elders and that we should work together and that there is hope. We always ask for help, if turning over a canoe, you ask other people to help. What you are doing now is important by learning from Elders. It is starting to show that we are helping each other to rebuild that teepee, the three of us here. People used to say that we wish to gather the young people and now the Elders are going to the schools to see the young children. It is important for us to follow one way and to think in one way. This is the reason that a young person is special because they will carry on our traditions and our future. The Elder does not think highly of himself. Everyone is considered equal. The Elder gives his teachings to be carried on by the young people. We must put the Creator first so that he can help you and from there you help yourself. We have to help each other. You don't have to rely on the police all the time, you can rely on the traditional teachings. We try to help the person who doesn't know and try to show him the right way. If we don't listen to the teachings, it will take longer to rebuild. But I have hope that we will see better ways for our people.

Traditional Dwellings

The Native person made his bed and built a big fire, they slept on the ground and they didn't have blankets. Sometimes they would use evergreen or tamarack branches. That's what they would do if they were gone for a couple of nights. There are many kinds of trees that the Indian people used in different ways. When it is very cold, the person walks until he finds there is a lot of wood for fire and many trees. That is where he makes his shelter. *Askigan* [a dwelling made of moss] is what the Native person made for his dwelling. The person also made a spruce teepee. The Native person also made snowshoes. The top layer of the snow is used for shelter and the bottom layer is for making water. There are two types of snow, the snow that feels like sand and the snow that is hard and sticks together. We used the sticky snow for shelter. *Askigan*, spruce teepee, teepee made of small tree poles and black spruce shaped like a teepee, birch-bark teepee, there were different kinds. They used different spruce trees to make *migwams*.

In the spring season, the person can tear off the spruce coating of the tree using it as a covering. Using birch-bark, you can make a sweet drink. When one makes a *migwam* they use spruce trees, then spruce boughs. *Askigan* is different from what we just talked about. You can use mud or any kind of moss to make the *askigan*. When you don't have an axe there is wood that you can just push down. You will never lose the fire.

Traditional Self-Government

There is no leadership like today, but only in the families. The leaders were the man and the woman. When the people gathered together, there was no one leader. When it happened that certain skills are needed, different people would take over. Everyone was equal and treated one another with respect, and all were humble towards each other. Humility was important and the leader was humble towards his people. That was the only way leadership worked. If he was not humble it would not work for him to be leader. For those men and women, it was important to be humble to each other and they took turns being the leader.

The present government takes away your fish net, your gun, and your animals. These are the strangers, White man's government, and now it's showing that the government has no respect for the Native people and the White man thinks to be better than the Indian. Who knows what's going to happen? This leadership is not doing well and will ruin things. It is not going to go well for the government because of this mistreatment of Natives and their land and the things the Creator has given the Natives. Don't mistreat those White people who are mistreating you. Forgive them. Put everything towards the Creator first and he will deal with it. Our people who work for us, they pray first before their meetings. Those other people, they don't bother praying, they just start talking at their meetings. They don't talk to the Creator. The Elders have said to look up to the Creator first. If one does not look to the Creator first, they will suffer in their lives. This is where the suffering will come from. The Elders are preparing themselves to go away. Humility is important. The only way I see things is to help one another. If someone dies, we give each other comfort, we help each other.

Today we hear about self-government and it was there all the time. We hear also of starvation all the time, that's nothing new, the suffering is always there. When people go hunting there is about five or six people in one blind and if one Elder was there, he would divide the geese from the hunt. He would make the plans on how to hunt. The group would listen to this leader. Who would be the leader if the group went to the woods and who decided when not to overhunt the animals? The Native person looked after this and took charge. Nobody ever said not to overhunt the animals, the Creator always provided for the Natives. He hunted only as much as he needed. The only person that would limit the hunt is the MNR [Ministry of Natural Resources, *Amisk Okimaw*]. The animals always replenish themselves in those days even though there was no limits. The goose is now controlled by goose band necks and bands on the foot, but causes problems for him. There was one leader, an Elder, an old man, the goose boss, he never put goose bands on the geese. There was different management of resources in our traditional way.

When a young person is in trouble he goes to see an Elder, the Elders or people would tell the young people not to bother with the goose eggs or bird eggs. He would be told that they were destroying what was inside and that they should not bother with it.

Traditional Parenting

When the woman talks to the children, the man will stand back and not interfere. The man will help his partner when the young person is out of control. He will not say, 'Don't do that,' to his partner. If a child gets out of hand, he would be sent to the other tent and to see the Elder who he would listen to. The Elder will tell him how to live his life in the future. There were people such as this who counselled the children but there was no judge, only good talk, advice, and the teachings. That's how the Indian people lived as I grew up.

Treaties

This is what I think, if someone borrows money from you and he sounds sincere and genuine, you believe him. Time has passed on and you begin to wonder where is that money that he [the White man] promised. Now you have to remind that person that he has promised to give back. That is not nice that he has deceived you. He has that deceit in him, you don't have deceit in you. The paper that was used for that law [treaty] talks about the gifts that were promised. For example, I change my mind like the wind changes, East, North wind. I come to you and I don't have money. I sound sincere to borrow money from you and that I would pay you back when I get my cheque. When that time comes, I will say to you, the White man says this, 'As long as the sun shines and the grass grows and the river flows, I will look after you for your land.' I don't tell you that I will come to take your gun and food away from you. This person was pretty good at lying to you. You always think about what the person has told you, you still wait for that promise he gave you. You do and say a lot of things to remind this person of what he owes you. There are many things that happen while you wait.

The government is making a lot of money even though they say Canada is in a deficit. But the country is selling our resources and making a lot of money from our land. They never told the Native people that they would lock him up or that they would take his food away because of his land. I don't know where that promise went to – 'As long as the sun shines and the grass grows and the river flows, I will look after you for your land.'

Elders

As an Elder I have met many people and I tell them not to look up to me, I am a human being. Respect the Creator and look up to the Creator. That's how an Elder sees it. You will never hear an Elder say, 'Me, me, come talk to me.' An Elder recognizes humility and they must be humble themselves.

A person has many problems if he loses one of his children, they will know they have to go soon. Today, there are many young people who wander around at night. The Elder must step in to teach the young people. It is not right for the Elder to ignore the young people. There are Elders who say, 'I have lived my life and I don't have to say anything.' It is not right for an Elder to say that. It is just like a tree, there are a lot of branches, a lot of teachings, Elders' teachings. Why should he throw away a broken branch when he will start to get old? The Elder does not consider himself to be too important but the young people are important to teach. The young people should be around when he teaches and they should sit in a circle to hear him talk. The Elder should be surrounded by the young people. They have done this in places like Toronto, Winnipeg, Peterborough. We should have the young people sit in a circle like they have done in the past, to listen to the Elders. It is important to have translators and to keep it simple for the young people to understand.

Heroes and Role Models

We would go to see an old man or old woman and sit at the door of their tent. We had respect for them. We would drop off wood for them if they couldn't get it themselves. The Elder would say, 'You will have a long life.' Now where did he get this? I would understand and take the person's words as being right and if I misunderstood that Elder's word, I would not be able to live right. Should I blame him if things went wrong? No. I will blame myself because I didn't listen to the person. That's what we did when we were young, we would go see the Elder and he would talk to us and he would teach us many things. For example, we will see an Elder, he will tell us to live a good life, and he will try to show how to have a good life. He knows many things and he has an obligation to teach you. For example, to walk on ice, take a long pole, you might fall through the ice. In the spring, the Elder will tell you, 'You have to watch what you do, the ice melts from underneath and that you should be careful.' You watch for things to be careful, watch your teapot so it won't boil over. Those things are the same as everything in life.

Traditional Games and Celebrations

These are the games we played: your granny is calling you, hide and seek, sliding, *tabahon* [caribou bones from the spine tied together on a string], pretending to be a wolf, tag, tug of war, paddling, darken yourself with ashes, wrestling. Drumming was not part of the games, it is different. They are praying when they drum. High jump is another game. Before the sun set, they would sit the children inside, the parents used to tell the kids *Oojuskwacho* will hear you. If he was nearby you would not be able to stand his presence. You have fear and only a person who can stand or beat him is the one who is powerful in spiritual ways. For someone who doesn't know these things, that person would die of fright or death came for that person.

Your granny is calling you game, your *kojum* is going to get your children. Everyone is in a long line and the grandmother is after your children facing you. The line in a single line holding each other. Hide and seek, people hide from each other. Paddling, each person faces away from each other and to see who is stronger to paddle the canoe away. The canoes have to reach a certain point and retrieve something.

Celebrations, fun events. If you kill five geese, five fish, moose, or caribou, people celebrated, had fun, rejoiced because they have all this food because they will live a good life. They gathered together, to celebrate their happiness. They used a fiddle for a dance. They really enjoyed these events, dancing and a feast. They brought their food together. They stored their food before the cold came. They stored for Christmas and the New Year celebrations. Today, the birthday celebrations are done but not when I grew up.

In the summer, they gathered together at one river. When they saw each other, they played together and were happy to come together. They danced, the Elders had fun and played games. They made their own fiddles and violins, which were made from moose tendons and birch-bark wood for the body, they also used cedar wood. They looked like the ones we see today. They also made the drum, to pray and to drum.

Family Relationships

What age can a man take a woman and a woman take a man? Marriage is talked about when the time is right. Today, for now, and then what happened in the past. When a woman is ready, her parents will let her get married. She is taught everything before she is married, to sew, make moccasins, mitts, all the women teachings. When she passes, she can get married. Then she is let go. For the man, the same thing, he must know everything, how to make snowshoes, toboggan, cradleboard (*tikanigan*). He has to learn all these and to cut wood. The man must be ready before his parents let him to marry. The woman is told to find a man who is good at working, someone who can provide for himself and for a family. The same for the man, he must find a woman who knows all these things that a woman has to do. There is only one thing that exists, courtship. If a man does not like the woman he has to marry, she is told not to see him until he feels good about her. You won't have a good life if he does not feel good about you. He will soon leave you until he feels good about you.

Just like the wilderness, before you go into it, the people are prepared for marriage. They are told many things. The parents tell the young man or woman not to see the opposite, prospective partner or they will not go smoothly. They have to be satisfied with their partner to be before they are married. Sometimes they will change their minds if the couple does not suit each other as they might leave each other. The young man and woman have to feel positive towards each other in order for things to work out for them. They have to be happy with each other.

Sometimes a woman and man have a child but it is the man who takes the child. If a man or a woman had children without a partner, they lived through struggle, pain, and rough life. If they are left with the children, they will ask a single person to help them with their family. Back in those times, government did not help people. Those times were difficult. Helping is a strong and good value. The woman will have to find a man and it is the same with a man, he has to find a woman.

These people who are by themselves because of being without a partner, they will look at the person and if they are capable of supporting a family, the man or woman looking for someone who could help them raise their kids. Today people are watching out for alcohol and they check to see if the person has a drinking problem. This is what has changed. Look for someone who is spiritual or prays a lot. You will have a good life.

Daily Routines

Before retiring in the evening, a bush person makes wood chips for the morning fire and prays. He may put aside his axe. In the morning, he makes a fire, the children wake up and they pray before they eat. The man goes off in the bush to set snares, check his snares or trapping, checking the traps or go moose hunting. He will never sit around only on Sundays. On Saturday the person will prepare for Sunday. He will sit and pray and does not even get wood on Sunday. He has already brought the wood the day before. If he doesn't have a choice he will go out in the afternoon for his survival. That's what the life was like back then. Sometimes someone will go out on Sunday and maybe they will be successful in the evening. Today, Elders have wondered what has happened, things have changed because people go out hunting on Sundays. Even if someone did not have food that day, he still got prepared to have a good Sunday (looking good, combed hair). The Elders told people not to cut wood or play on Sunday. They couldn't refuse, they had to listen to the Elders. These were six days when the people really worked getting food for their children and getting wood also. Sometimes they walked all night to get the food back to the children.

Clothing

Our clothes were made of moose hide, caribou hide, otter skin, weasel pelt, rabbit skin. Those are the things we relied on for clothing. We had rabbit skin hats or rabbit skin parkas with hoods. Rabbit skin was the warmest for clothing. You can sleep anywhere with your rabbit skin parkas and just use spruce boughs for cover. For shoes which would not soak through, our moccasins were made from top of moose hide. The top layer of hide called *ootum isk* is smoked, turned over and over until it gets brown and then it is made into moccasins. Sealskin can also be used for waterproof moccasins, and mitts.

Traditional Ceremonies

We give thanks for peace, love, happiness. Native people also prayed in the wilderness. They read the Bible and everything, many things were talked about. At first, the Native people didn't believe it and soon after they started to recognize and understand that it was similar to what they already believed. He looked at life and death and he wondered about it at first before he saw it with his own eyes. There are two kinds of *Mundos* (Spirits) and one had wrong thoughts and one had good thoughts. They started to see what the Bible says and they started to believe. One example, I saw someone while I was lying on a bed at someone's house. He was afraid of his surroundings, why was he afraid? He does not believe in God, he did not believe or understand. It is important to believe and to show each other so that we can understand. I have seen some people who were cold in the wintertime, God showed them that he was real. Just like my father and mother. The same thing with God, he is teaching them, when winter comes he gives a little cold weather. The punishments I got from my parents were not the real thing but the real one was when God releases this cold weather. The earthquakes are the same message. They are not being punished but only being talked to or warned a little to show God's power. The White people had trouble getting their heat and light, and water lines were frozen. The Indian could live on the land, he could survive. I can't put the blame on God or anything if something was to happen to me. He used my father to teach me things.

The Natives had their own way of praying. The stranger did not understand it and he said wrong things about it. The stranger thought that the Indian was practising evil ways. Even today, the White man thinks that way. He talks about evil when he refers to the Native ways. The stranger has gone wrong because of his way of telling people that their way of praying is sinful. Now the stranger is starting to get into trouble. This Pipe, there is nothing wrong, that is just the way it is. The Pipe won't take you to hell, as they have said. There can't be blamed on the Pipe. There was ways to live, the Indian was given his way to live and the stranger fought very hard to have strength over the Indians.

The stranger was given his own way to pray. The stranger has learned by using telephone to talk to people in different places. The Indian had the Shaking Tent [Indian telescope] to communicate with each other. The stranger took these ideas from the Indians to make things easier for everyone. The Indians were given these things in the early times. There was no telephone or radio back in the early times but the Natives were able to communicate. The stranger had a low opinion of the Natives, by the way he looked at them and he was jealous of the Native people. And the Native person never did pay back any harm or revenge done to him. The stranger came to see the Natives, who ended up doing the evil and sinful things, it is the stranger who is doing these things. He has inter-fered with the Native way given by the Creator.

Long time ago, a Native would do something wrong and he would be asked to leave the village. The stranger should be the one leaving the place because he came to interfere, which was not his place to rule and have authority. It is showing that the stranger is doing a lot of things wrong and he should be the one to leave. White men are using what the Natives had been given, now he is saying to the Native, you are doing a sinful thing when they play the drum, use the Shaking Tent. The Natives have been told all the time that he has been doing something wrong, or sinful. Because the stranger wanted him to leave but the Native people didn't budge. The Native cannot leave the land the Creator has given him to live. But the stranger is not successful to move the Native people because his thoughts are not right or just. Because the Native person still prays when he uses the drum, it is the same thing to praise the Creator. Praying to the Creator, worshipping the Creator, the Natives have their own ways. There are two ways a Native can use his gift, one good, one bad, and the person has the choice in how he uses it. The Native was given those ways, a Shaking Tent is put up when you want to talk to another per-son but to find out how he is doing but it is not to be abused. If he's doing all right or if he is hungry or if he is rich with food, he will answer you back with his Shaking Tent and acknowledge you.

A place called Mamegu River, this is way past Weenusk and Attawa-piskat Lake, quite a distance they used the Shaking Tent to find out how they are doing. You could hear the person inside the Shaking Tent. The person who answers back is talking on from the top of the Shaking Tent. His brother-in-law would reply, 'I was just wondering how you are doing, if you are doing okay or if you have a lot of food or if you are hungry, that's what I want to find out from you.' The person in Attawapiskat would answer him back and tell him that he is doing fine, 'I have a lot of food and I am not hungry.' And that's when the Shaking Tent stopped. The Creator gave the Natives the Shaking Tent but not to be used in a bad way.

The Sweat Lodge was used for healing, the Shaking Tent was used for knowing the future or the *Oojuskechoo* and to see the future. Death came in different ways. The *packeshugun* would get people that drift around with the snow. The Elders, three generations ago, told their grandchil-dren not to walk around when it is snowing and blizzard. The *packeshugun* is the skeleton that tickles a person to death.

Grieving

When someone passes on, he or she is gone forever from this earth. We must love our fellow human being. We cry when our fellow human being passes on. It helps to share our sorrow with others. Those people who pass on, we will see them again. Before the burial, they pray for the one who has died. The tears we shed are there, to show us to use our tears. We use God for our comfort to see us through. We think of our loved ones and those who are grieving. We visit those people who are grieving, we give them comfort and to rely on God.

Territory

Long time ago, there were never people claiming land, they never said this is your land or this is not your land to each other. They never were told not to go to a certain place. God gave this land to the people. The Native people understood the Creator.

As the person is walking, he will see the animal in a trap and it is hung on a tree so it will not be taken away by animals. The same with the fox, if he is caught on the snare, the person will hang the fox on the tree for whoever the trap belonged to. The trails are many and lead to many traps, just like a tree with many branches. The government tells the Native people which river to use and he uses pen to draw out the map. The Native person was given the authority to lead his people in the Indian Act, and he became excited and thought he was the boss.

But this type of leadership was poor and they accepted the stranger's words and believed him. The Native people followed the stranger's words. Before this there was no doubts about each other. All this talk about this land, now look at this land today, Kash, Fort Albany, Attawapiskat, and Moosonee. You paid five dollars for the trapping ground licences. The only time the White men took the pelt was when you have paid five dollars. They said you have to pay for the licence and to sell your fur. And everything did not go well after that.

Wherever I go travelling, I see people from different reserves, Kash, Attawapiskat, and they like to talk to each other and later on love grows from there. That's how people fall in love and get married after. Creator never told the Native people not go to a certain place. The Native people took care of himself as this land was his home. He knew what to do to look after his fellow human being. There was never a person who said,

'This is my land.' People do not own land. The one who really owns the land will always be God. White man who started this trouble should have minded his own business, it is just like me being in this house. I don't own this house, I don't have the right to say this and how you should live, when you are a stranger. Native people now refer to each other from where they come from such as Attawapiskat person, Peetabecku person [Fort Albany], Kash person, Winisk person. There was no such thing back then.

The Native person hunted where he wanted. When you were successful in a hunt, you would go to the closest Native person, no matter how long you walked so you can be helped to get the food. At the *migwam*, the people inside will hear a noise and will say that a stranger has come to visit. This person can sense the stranger approaching. A woman can sense if a stranger is coming, she was given the gift, she feels it in her bosom. My mother told me this when I was young, the Elders and those who lived will tell you the same thing. That's the way people lived.

Prophecies

Before anyone can let go of a young person, he or she has to have knowledge, we have to give knowledge. It's like a woman can feel the sense in her bosom, if a stranger is approaching. That's one gift. This has been here from God. Then there is dreams. The Native person was given something else which were gifts. The Native ways and today's world is different. We were not given these ways to live. This gift was intelligence, to be successful. The Native people would have eventually lived a certain way if the White man had not come. The living would have improved. The White man messed up things for the Indian. The stranger came to upset the balance that was here.

Dreams were given to Native people. These dreams told the future if someone is going to die or if you will meet someone. It is referring to a spiritual presence. The animals foretell the future, God gave them this job. The crow will tell you when you get into trouble. The dog or whiskey-jack would come to you at night to tell you that someone is going to pass away or something will go wrong. One winter passes before the event you were told of will occur. The Native people were given everything to know about the future. If a person dies, that person would have known because it was given in dreams that he would leave. Animals are used by seeing them in unusual times and places to tell you of a certain event is going to happen like death. I heard that people who dream about a Canada goose crying means the dreamer will pass on and that would be the last time he would see the Canada goose. If a hunter wants to kill, the animal would be afraid of the person because the animal sees impending death on that person.

Stages of Life

From the time a baby is in the womb, he has so many days to live, it is already known how long he will live. The child is also told how to live. If the person doesn't listen to what he is told he will not have a good life. Your hair will not be white until you listen to what you have been told. We now see that is the truth. It is too bad that there is something that destroys us. Just like the pill I take is destroying me. The wrong kind of pill I took is destroying me. But it's there for reasons, the modern medicines. If the medicine is used the wrong way, it destroys.

There is medicine that is very powerful. There were many Elders, people who lived long ago, and the medicine was from the wilderness, the bush. It was everywhere. It is shameful that we threw this away, we have been the medicine. The medicine has been good for us. It's too bad that we denied the medicine. The wrong kind of medicine is powerful too and that what we took but now is destroying us. Only when a child listens to his Elders, he will live longer. If a young person takes the wrong medicine, he won't live a long time or live to see grey hair on his head. When you see Elders today, they never took medicine from the hospital. We had medicine for constipation. There was also medicine for sore throat. The Native people were very strong people. They never were tired and sat around. They could walk for long distances. When the old men met a long time ago, they smoked because they were happy to see each other once again. They didn't have any worries, they were so happy to see each other.

Time and Seasons

The Native people knew the seasons well and they knew when they would start and end. He used the appearance of the sky for weather. They also used the tides as a clock. When you want to go out to the Bay you want to know when the tide will come in. They used the tidewater as it would be hourly. They also used the sun to tell time. At certain times of the day they would do things by the light of day. How would one know what direction the wind will be? This knowledge is in the sky. The Native people were given signs by God. God has put those signs for the Native people. When you want to know how much snow there will be, you look at the stars. The star that points, the North Star, you use the star to see how much snow there will be. Birds that fly were also used, they tell us when it will be morning. Birds were used like the clock.

There is a Morning Star and there is a Male Star, such as the male and female. One is the leader and there are two *oogekituk*. That's how they knew the time, they also used these things in the sky to predict the amount of snow. An Elder would see these in the stars and then there would be a lot of snow. A long spring would be indicated by the male *oogekituk* and the star is far away, which shows that summer is a long way off. A young calf moose also will let you know when summer is going to be here. A weasel tells you that summer will not arrive soon. The rabbit also tell you that spring will take time and summer is a long way off. The appearance of these animals tells you that summer will be a long way off yet.

Native Languages

Everything should be respected and the languages should be respected too. They are based on self-respect of ourselves. Native people speak languages and we don't want to throw them away because they are from God. Ojibwe language, Muskeg language (*Mushegow ayumwin*), Anishinabe, and Ojibwe some. The Eskimo language also is different. The English language is also good. But when we had a meeting in Ottawa, the government said there would only be two languages and the Native language, Cree, would be disregarded. The official languages English and French were adopted, the Native people were angry. They realized then that they were being discriminated against. Native people were given their language, intelligence and ability from God. The government [Brian Mulroney] was in deep trouble with the Native people. The older people and Elders were also angry at the government. If Mulroney denies the languages of others then he does not accept God. The Native people will not throw away their language. There are still Native people who meet in Ottawa to have their languages retained or recognized.

Economics

The Native people caught fish by using a fish wire across a small creek. They closed it off. The fish knows when it will be cold so they travel downstream. The Native people built something when there were no nets. The Native people were given this knowledge on how to catch fish. In the evening, at night, the fish are going downstream, to go to the big river when they know it will be winter soon. The Creator has given the fish the knowledge how to live, that way he knows to live. We cannot see everything on this earth only what is on top of the earth. We cannot see what is underneath. That is how God had chosen it to be. God had given you a place to live, somewhere you will be healthy and to live. There is no other different place. The same with the fish. The fish was given to the Native people so he can live off them. They gathered food and prepared it in different ways. One is a rack above the ground, similar to a freezer during the winter time. They gathered goose, moose meat in September. If someone has food and those who don't, they will feel for those who don't have food. The food will not be wasted and it will be shared. There was no such thing as money. The people shared and the one who gives does not expect to be paid back. The people shared their food and that is how we lived when I was a child.

The fish was prepared in a dry crushed form *newayhigan* and dry meat was from the moose. A stick, usually tamarack, and a moose hide with the layer of coating (underneath the hair) is made into a bag, to store the food. The moose fat is put in with the dry moose meat and the dried crushed fish. This food is called *pemmican*, food that you can travel with and not worry about getting spoiled and is stored. They made a type of box, made out of branches or wood sticks, no nails, to store their food. The animals would not be able to get at it. The left-over wood was used for firewood. The Native people can build storage places for their food that even a mouse couldn't get at. You can also do the same for rabbits and you can store smoked geese, geese that is left in grease. You can also use the good head, wings, and feet. You can make gravy from these parts. Nothing was wasted, everything was used from the animal when animals were killed. There was a lot of food taken from these animals. From the moose stomach, you can make a bag, and store your food in there. The same with geese, the stomach [gizzard] is eaten first, it is good to give you strength. When you have a lot of food and have stored it, you have a lot of food when there are hardly any animals around. Any food you have left over, you give to the less fortunate. The people did not waste their food. They had feasts when the year ended and the New Year began. They danced while at these gatherings. There was peace, joyfulness, good fellowship and love.

Transportation

Today the transportation is expensive and money is needed. A long time ago, money was not needed, you decided when to leave, as long as you have snowshoes and dogs and a sled. You are responsible for those dogs. The transportation used today are nice but do not have Spirits. They are considered important and useful but you need money. If you use your legs you can decide when you want to go someplace. It is the same with the dogs, you put the harness on the dogs and the dogs are very fast and they travel far. In late winter when the snow is hard, the dogs can travel easier and faster. When you have six dogs it's pretty fast, just like a snow-mobile but with dogs you don't have to worry about falling through the ice. The dogs know where to run. When you use your legs you can travel far.

Relations with Other First Nations

There are other people called *powatuk*. This was true and an Elder had talked of this at Ghost River and at a place called Head River, *Moshowak*. This really happened, it is not a legend, this is a true story. People seen skulls and there were thousands of them showing out of the ground. There may have been more but some foxes took off with some. What had happened is the hair was taken from their heads. It was during the time my father was a young child. Who did they meet and killed them off? Fish River is the place, this side of *Winisk*, between *Moshowak*, there was a pow-erful medicine man, *Midwe* [*Mide*]. He was the one who killed them off and this is true. Women were not destroyed, women packed up and headed north. These people who did this were called *powatuk* and *wujusk osit* [muskrat foot, these *powatuk* are the ones who used the *Mide* powers in a bad way].

There were two men who came from this place where the people were being slaughtered and went to Hawley Lake to see *Mahegan*, a strong and powerful medicine man, to ask for help. *Mahegan* had two daughters at this place where the killing was going on. They made a bigger Shaking Tent and *Mahegan* asked for help to get these people who were responsi-ble. The Spirit of the turtle will help but the Thunder Spirit told the tur-tle 'No,' as he is a water being. The Thunder Spirit said if you hear me, half of them will be gone. *Mahegan* said he will leave three survivors. The battle was fought there, soon after the people left the area and scattered to different places. *Mahegan* went to Ghost River and asked who would come with him. Some people wanted to get off there and one old man said he wanted to continue travelling. *Moshowak* is a very nice place now, caribou use it as feeding ground. From Neyakowk and all the way to *Moshowak*, the land is very nice. This side of Fort Albany and to the north side of Moosonee, the land is good. These people who tried to destroy the Native people in this area were from the West.

Medicines

The Native people today regret that they threw the medicines away. But there is always one person who screws up everything, the stranger. Now the doctors want to study the medicines we have. The Native people did not need medicine when they went somewhere, like in the bush. The Native people will never run out of medicine because it is found everywhere. The medicine that is good for headache, cold sweat or if you are sick in your body is sand. The sand is put at your feet. The reason is that your blood will go towards your feet. It is dangerous to put it near your head. Native people knew about the sand as they were being taught but it stopped soon after the strangers arrived. They threw it away and followed the stranger.

Cedar is also medicine, you just chew it in your mouth if you have a cold, the leaves of the cedar tree, not the branch. The stone is also used, but not the black rock they crack and explode. The rock called *mutitin*, this rock is white. If you Sweat yourself with that rock you will feel better and strong. This rock travels around on the ice frozen, and the ice takes him away. The White people came to ask the Native people to show them the types of medicine that was used around this area. There are other kinds of medicine in willows. There are six types of willows. Our grandfathers used these medicines. Wherever you go and if you injure yourself, you just make the medicine right there.

The tree stumps that are grown over the moss are also medicine. The tree is boiled once and the water is thrown away. And then you boil the tree again and it is powerful medicine. You can also drink the water just like that, it is very good medicine.

Life in the Bush

It is good that you young people are coming to the Elders to find out about these things. The Elders have waited for the young people to ask such things. Even if the modern technology is important, it is still special to keep the bush life. When you use these modern technology, you are comfortable and life is easier. When you take these into the bush you have no fear to miss it the next day because there is no one around to take it. When a person is in the bush, there is no one to bother him. Maybe just a bear or a squirrel will bark or a whiskeyjack will laugh at you or the birds will whistle and you will feel like you want to dance. This is how it is in the bush, one feels content and relaxed, just enjoying life. You do everything, you set nets, set snares and you don't sit in your tent and sleep. You don't sleep very much but you are eager. Just like the beaver, he goes exploring his river. The Native person lives to paddle around in his canoe and look around. The Native person loves this lifestyle and he cannot settle on one thing, he has to explore at other activities.

The Native person feels happy when the river freezes up because the season has changed and he feels happy about doing different activities in the bush. Once the river is frozen, he is so happy that he probably wants to dance around on it. The Native people are very happy about the freeze-up. All I can say is that there is peace, freedom, calmness, and tranquillity in the bush.

Knowledge of Territory

I have never heard Native people to say they own the land. The land is for us to use and to live, this is where the food is, fish, rabbits, otter or any other animals for food. We know when freeze-up will happen. The Native person will know what he will need in order to hunt and fish. Wherever he meets another Native person on the land and if he has an abundance of fish, he will invite the person to fish there with him or he will tell another person you can trap with me where there are weasel, muskrat, and otter. That's what the Native person says to his fellow Natives. The Native person treats others with love. The Native person will not say to another Native person, 'Don't trap there.' He will never say to another person, 'That is my land.'

Before the mapping of this area and the boundaries were set, the Native people respected one another and their hunting grounds. It still goes on despite these limitations and boundaries. People took care of each other. If I see your trap with a fox, I would hang it on the tree for you so animals won't get at it. Before the metal traps were used, Native people used deadfall traps made of wood. The Native person had intelligence as he has survived for a long time. The Elders have taught how to make these deadfall traps, as I have seen. People would tell each other about where there were rabbits too and they would go there to hunt. Native people used to gather and sit and tell each other where there is food and where they were going to hunt.

The lifestyle that the Native people had is gone. The lifestyle of the bush is gone. If a person happens to find moose tracks and night is falling, he will wait until the next morning. He will then ask someone to help him track the moose and they will wait for the wind. The wind blows the trees and makes noise so the moose will not hear them. That is how it is done. If you wanted to make a map, you would draw on the snow or on the ashes of the fire. Why do I ask you to join me in this hunt? The reason is that I want you to live too. The earth is not here just for me. Just like the river that you see, it is not there for only me to drink from, it is for all the Native Nations. I won't tell another Native person, 'Don't get water from there.' That is not the Native law.

If I were to come to Moosonee Ministik from Attawapiskat and I didn't know where they get nets around here, I would ask you where I can get them. You would tell me where the nets are set and you also would tell me where the water does not flow swiftly. The information you tell is that you expect me to live too. I will live from the food you told me about.

The Native person did not stay in one place every winter. He had a different winter camp. The same thing is with spring camp. If breakup comes and the people are on low ground, I will help them to get to higher ground. The land we are on is the Native Land. The Natives have a name for it, it is called the Native Land. The land where the stranger came from is called something different too. If another group came here to take over this land, it would be better to send them back where they came from.

When the old men, the Elders, met along the river to talk, the MNR people told them to hang up [another's] trap if they see it on their trapping ground. The Elders laughed about it because that person is not being allowed to trap on his own land. The people are also not sharing if they do as MNR says.

Native people did not use compasses, he used his hands. He used the wind, in which direction would it blow in the morning. You walked along the bay and you go when it's a blizzard, you are able to go anyway. First you look at the way the snow lays, blown by the wind, how it looks when you walk. For example, if you want to go to Attawapiskat, I'll go towards the bay, the bush is too thick to walk in and the snow is too deep. If you walk along the bay, you also look at the creeks and how they lay from the west. The blown snow also shows which way the wind blows, usually from the north. The sun also gives direction when you look to where it rises. If it is a grey day, you use the snow to give the direction. If you use all these things to help you find your destination, you will not be lost.

At night time, you use Morning Star and North Star and which direction does the tree lean toward, which direction the branches are hanging. The tops of trees are leaning towards south because of the North Wind and the trees are leaning towards the east because of the West Wind. If a person uses all these he will not get lost. A Native person never got lost when he used all these things. That's what the Native people did when they walked around in the bush. A dog is much more better than a person for directions.

This land we are on right now is not very good. The land is much better farther up the rivers, where the reserve lands are not good for people to live along the bay. As you sometimes see, the houses are half in the water.

Education

In Fort Albany, the people wanted to find out what had happened in residential school. When a child was raised by his parents he did not see the punishment. The one who raised the children decides what punishment the child will get. The stranger, or priest, as he is called, because he came from a different place, believed in a different way. People did not know where this came from. Later in the seventies the Native people did not want to let their children go because they knew there was something wrong. They [priests] always told the Native people that they are doing bad things. Sometimes they are told this inside the church while they are in there. The Native person was also told, 'You are the one who is living in a sinful way.' Somebody else comes along who has more power. They told Natives if you don't let your children go to school, you will not receive money and you will not get Family Allowance. They will take the money and Family Allowance, that's what they said.

A lot of problems started from this place [residential school] where child abuse came from. I have seen it with my own eyes. They used sticks to punish children. I have seen the meanest person, the one who cannot hold back his temper, that is the one who broke the stick over the child's back, that is what I seen. How is he going to live right, if he looks back to being mistreated? It cannot leave him. Even though help comes from another place, it doesn't work. These people came and caused the suffering. That's how the residential school looked like. In the Native people's form of education, the Native person never went to a stranger's land to teach or educate other people's children. Wherever he may be is where he teaches the children, he also teaches a child without a mother or father or parents that passed away. The Native person will take the child as his own and will teach the child how to live. He also gives the child the supplies he needs, food, traps, snares, snowshoes, and toboggan. That is what the Native people did. Native people did not go out to teach someplace else and make the children suffer.

Today's schools are better but in the past they used it for the wrong reasons. The children were wounded. There was too much hitting, there was never forgiveness towards the child, although he was only a child. And a lot of children went through it. A child likes to play and sometimes he would get punished by the strangers. I have seen it with my own eyes one day, they were beating on a child. Now today, they are trying to look good, we will take it to court but they want to make it look good but I don't think it will work out. You cannot go back and fix it up. Many people are reminded by the pain or close to being killed. One cannot take away the pain he has suffered. Sometimes he takes his own life because of the suffering when he remembers. He thinks, 'I should not live because I was punished too many times, too much pain, too much suffering.' That's what I say about that school. School is still a good thing, but it was not necessary for the person who ran the school to overdo it. That's the way it should be, we should talk about the issues, talk about something that is not going well and to talk about them. Those children who went to school experienced a lot of suffering. This is how it looked. That's what I have seen with my own eyes while I was there.

The stranger's law was very powerful, but they broke the rules and they even called themselves a holy person. I am surprised about this person and still he did such things when he wounded his fellow human being and they still call themselves holy people. The reason I say this is Jesus never fought back to those who were killing him. This is the real holy man. He still had pity for them, he did not hit them, he did not break a stick although they nailed his hands and feet to the cross, he still had pity of them.

I wonder about the school the way it was in 1944 or 1942 during the time I am talking about. This is what they did long time ago. This is what school was like, it is too bad that this has happened. Even though a Native works on this, to try to make it better, there is something different being said. They want to take it to court. They look for the lawyer, the best ones, they said in Fort Albany. Jesus did not use a lawyer while he was being killed. He didn't look for one, as he knew he would be killed. And now it is showing this person is not really a holy person when he looks for a lawyer to help him. The best one to help him. The only thing they want from this person is to ask for forgiveness for these young people. Many young people do wrong things to themselves when they remember what has happened. When they were mistreated during 1942 and 1944. That's what I have seen and that's the way it worked. That's what I have seen where I go to church. It is a good thing that people want to know these things but there was too much suffering.

Warrior Traditions

The Shaking Tent was used to watch out for the people and to find out the whereabouts of people. There was fighting too, what I have already talked about of what happened at *Moshowak*. When there, thousands of people who were killed. That's where your grandfather met that person. He knew about him before that person arrived there. Just like what Alex Goodwin said. The person in the Shaking Tent looked ahead to see if a stranger is coming. He will tell you that one is coming. He also told where this person was. He also foretold you will be using a car and you will be getting on a train and you will be using an outboard motor on your boat. He also said that you will be getting on the plane and he had known all these things. It is very hard to believe it. These people were the ones who were watching out for the people.

Pretend we are making dough for bread and we don't put yeast, it will not rise. That's the way it looks, you have to search and to seek out the knowledge. It is rising. When a priest knows you are making a Shaking Tent he will tell you that you are doing a bad thing. But God has given you this gift so you will know what is going on around you. The Shaking Tent is not seen in an evil way. The same thing with the Shaking Tent, people think that it will kill them but it is not true, they are thinking wrong. Don't listen to the people who say that, the Shaking Tent will not kill us. You just want to rely on it. What does a White man do when somebody wants to kill him? He gathers up everyone but the Native people will not do that. The Native person will not get the White man if someone wants to kill him. The Native person will sit in the Shaking Tent, of course that is the father's son that is talking in the air who is protecting him. And what the White person will do is to gather up his bombs or he will use the place to drop off something. But the Native person will not do that.

What does the Native person do but what he has been given? He makes a little *migwam*. He tells when he wants to do that. It is very good that you want to know these things. Yes, there were people who did these things. When you are sleeping and you want to see that person or when you close your eyes. If you have gone to make this outside, if you don't eat for ten days, you don't drink for ten days, just when you are sleeping you will see the person who want to come and mock you. That's where you look at him from. That's where you watch him. You are not there where you are sleeping. Long time ago, the Native person never carried a gun, you will never see him carrying something. That didn't come from the Native way.

Traditional Justice

This is what happened. I never heard anyone say I will not judge my fellow Native person. The Native person has only God's ways that he will not bring any harm to his fellow Native person. Because it sounds scary when we judge one another. That is what the Native person has followed. Although, the Native person had to deal with his children, not his fellow Native person. If the child does not obey, there is a waiting period to see if he will do something wrong again. It is only then they will remind him again. That is not a judgment but only to remind the child, it is called reminding or recalling, if a child has done something wrong to a family. The man of that certain family will go to the child's father and remind him if the child has repeated his behaviour. He does not demand that he be paid a certain amount. I have not heard of anyone to say, 'Pay me and I forgive you.' That never existed when I grew up. People talked to one another when a child got into trouble. They go see the parents to remind them that their child is doing wrong. That was not court or judgment. I have never known for Native people to have courts.

The Native people call it or did talk until the person changed, *Wetamegwan* is telling or advising. That's what the Native people did and they treated each other well. When someone steals from another person, they would just ask for it back. But if the person does not give it back, he has to tell him. I will give it back at a certain time. He doesn't throw it in a disrespectful way or he will not tell that person this is 'what I will do if you don't pay me back.' Those Elders I talked about, they are dying, those who did not take their fellow Native persons to court. The Native people never had prisons, the only place a Native person had lived is in a tent and *migwam*. And whenever a Native person feels like going out he will just lift the flap of the tent and go.

Relations with Non-Native People and War

The first time the stranger came, we tried to live together and the Native people did not blame others for anything. Forgiveness should be accepted but it is hard to forget things. Those people who laid their lives on the line for World War One and World War Two. The people made the Remembrance Day so no one will forget about it. They put a cross for them. It will not stop. As long as the people were asked, if you wish to go, you were given these clothes so that you may be called a soldier.

The government had made a mistake about the war, the Native people should not have gone to war in another country. But if there was a war in Canada then they would have gone to that war. The families of the veterans should have benefits. Their fathers who put their lives on the line. That's how Native people have talked about the way the government is. No one cannot be the leader of this country Canada only the person who laid his life for Canada.

The government now wants to acknowledge the Native people's contribution, but this stranger can still do wrong behind the Native people. They can still do wrong but they cannot stand in the front line of the war in the future. The Native people did not wonder about it, they just left. Those people who went to war, this would be their resting place. Those who left and did not come back, of course, they will not come back again. That's the way it was. The Native people have said that for this sort of thing not to happen again. Make sure we don't let the government do this again. The Native people used their arms to paddle up the river in Kash and Attawapiskat, to go to the war and that is going upstream. I went to Calstock to see where my father had left to go to war. The train came to Pagwa to pick up my father to go to war. The Native people walked in these shoes, which were red and hard.

There is a monument near the Pagwa River to show where the Native people travelled to go to war the first time in 1914. He didn't only love himself but he loved his fellow human beings, that is why he went to war and to look to the future. They gave up their lives for us. The Native people who went to war did not go for the White men but went for us the Native people. They wanted to show their love for us, those who went to the Second World War. The special thing they have done will not be forgotten. Just like what Jesus did, that's what these people did for us. The Native people talked about going to war for their children and their future. It is being said that the next war will be three times as bad. Now the government came to Attawapiskat and gave people uniforms. They gave me a uniform and I told him I can't fight in the war, I am too old. He said, 'This is a token.' He asked me, 'Do I have anything to say?' And I said, 'Yes,' and he didn't like my response. Because I told him in the First World War, they gave people uniforms and were told that they would have cows, farms, and nice houses. When the Native people heard this, he didn't have second thoughts. This is what the Native people did.

I talked to the leader about this and when we were having a meeting with the Canadian Rangers, the leader asked, 'Are there any questions?' Right away I remembered what my father had told me about his experiences. When a Native veteran dies, the things he had talked about will still continue on. I have never seen my father bring anything back or get those things that he was promised. When my father came back, he walked from Cochrane to Moosonee and towards the Bay to Attawapiskat to get back home. He was just pulling his blanket and they said he is a soldier.

A government military person came to recruit the Native people. What he has said is still going and his lies are still here. When the government came up to Attawapiskat, the children of the veterans talked to them and reminded them of what had happened. This is why it is dangerous to do something wrong to a person.

We have to keep our promises. You have to have meetings and here to help yourselves and others, not only yourself, to improve the lives of everyone. I expect you to gather together. Money is not always needed to have life. It is easy to gather together young people, to tell the younger children and to talk about schools too. It is important. That is why people put children in schools so that they will have a good education to feel good about themselves and to get good jobs. A child, young people, leaders, tell your Elders that you want to have a gathering. We have heard of other places that have gatherings of young people.

It is good to fight for your young people just like your grandfathers have done, so that things will go right. The Elder should not say I have done my job by raising my children, it is not necessary for me to talk anymore. This Elder has many children and great-grandchildren to talk for. The young people need to take the Elder's place later on and to talk about these things, the troubles, the hard times, and the deaths and suicides. It is hard for the young people and for them to take their own lives. Why does he do it? He is frustrated and feels sad and does not care anymore. We have to remind the children that we love them. It is better for him to wait until the day comes for him to die because they put their mother, father, grandfather, grandmother and cousins through heartbreak when one takes their own life.

And that's what I ask you to do is to sit in a circle and tell the leaders that they are helping young people a lot when you talk for those who have taken their own lives. That's what I expect for you people to do. They have done this in Attawapiskat, Fort Albany, don't be afraid, don't be afraid of anyone. A person will be happy to talk about these things instead of their child taking their own life. This is what we have to fight against in the future. This is what we have to remember and be thankful for when we sit together one day. This is why it is written on paper because I don't hold a pen, I cannot say exactly what I want to say. It is a lot easier to print on paper and to read it and for another person to ask me what did you talk about at the meeting?

There are many questions and you just pick up a paper and this person listens to you and what you have talked about and that's where he believes it from. And if a person didn't see what has happened in the meeting, he will ask where is your paper. For this meeting we are having, it's important to remember those who have lived before us. That is how it is done when they talk about something that is powerful. It is important to rely on God because we cannot make it on our own. My grandchildren, I will tell you, when you go to every meeting, it is important to pray even if you are alone wherever you may be. God said, 'I will be there.' That's what God told us. I hope that you will have a good life and things will go well and God will be with you. We have to take care of each other because life on earth is short and we should shake one another's hands when we meet because we don't know what lies ahead of us. No one knows what the future holds, until we see it ourselves. We are now finished with this gathering, we are remembering those who passed on and we will say a prayer and we will get up so that we pray to see this gathering again. We love one another as in one family, as there is no other divisions in this life. Let us now get up and pray.

Inuit Cultures

RACHAEL UYARASUK   (Inuit)

Igloolik, Nunavut

'Life today is what I find strange.'

Rachael Uyarasuk was born in 1914 near Clyde River in the Eastern Arctic. Her traditional name is *Pitaluk*, and she has ten children and many grandchildren and great-grandchildren. Emily Faries spent four days interviewing Rachael at her home. Emily found the Arctic barren and harsh, even in the summer. She joked and said it 'seemed like nothing but rock, water, and icebergs.' But Rachael's home was very comfortable and the interview went well. Rachael spoke in Inuktituk, which was translated by her son. Rachael focused the interview on traditional Inuit culture, and what the Arctic used to be like when she was young.

Creation Stories

I have heard it like this. It is said that those two people, the first people, one was a man and the other was a woman. The man, it is said, was named *Aakulagjug* and the woman was *Umarniqtu*. It is said that these were the first people. This is how I heard it.

Traditions

Before the White people came, people helped one another in order to go hunting and get food. The only food was animals. We didn't know of White man's food. We helped each other with our catches, the skins for clothes, the meat and fat. When we saw that someone was running out of something, we would share. The family could go to a land where there was more food and share. We would have food together. No one would have to buy. Back then, before we were in contact with White people, what I found to be most useful was, when I had many children, before we got store-bought clothes and when our children had to have clothes and boots and our husbands and men who were not our husbands but our relatives who always went hunting, needed clothes that were warm. These were my hardships. Our children too, we would have to look after them and we'd have to make the clothes. Our husbands would help us. They would soften caribou skins for us. Our husbands would be our helpers and we would help each other. That's how we were husband and wife before we get store-bought items. This is how we survived, it made us try and catch up. We didn't want people getting cold. For those who go away and hunt and our children, we had to make sure they had clothes. That is what we really used.

Young people are beginning to forget because they now have so many things to do. They now go to school and are learning the ways of the White people. They now have so much more to do than when we were young. Some of them are forgetting their language. But because now there are many things, trying to use our past today looks difficult. When there weren't too many influences and we were living only our way it wasn't as hard. There are many more things that have to be done today than at that time. Now that men have more to do than just hunting and we women have let go of the things we had to do and those were our hardships then, but now we make warm clothes only for those that go out camping and hunting, but for these children that don't go hunting, we buy them store-bought clothes.

Traditional Birthing

Our Elders, our *sakiks*, and our mothers, these older people would be our helpers when we first had to give birth. They would instruct us. Here in the house, sod house or *igluvigaq* (igloo) or tent, we would give birth as taught by our Elders and following their instructions. When we give birth, when we have our first child, we need their help. In the following pregnancies, we were able to give birth alone. It was probably not only me. That's what we used to do. I had to give birth by myself with no helper even though there were people at our camp.

I never lived where there were lots of people so once my husband would help me. I gave birth once when we were alone and when he was away and there was no one else, I gave birth. Another time although people were at our camp and he was away, I gave birth alone. Some of them could give birth standing up on the knees and some who could lie down like this and give birth. We had different ways of giving birth.

Dwellings

In the spring we would live in a tent. We would live with the older people, our own parents, in one tent. The younger people and the people who went with the hunters would come home to this tent. We would try to get animals in different places by going away from our camp on dog team and we would return home to the tent of our parents or parents-in-law. That's what we did. The older people here on the land would just be waiting but they would also hunt seals from the sea with their kayaks. However, the young people would be hunting for clothes, for caribou skins, all summer walking around on the land. Sometimes there would be few caribou and they would have to walk far away looking for them. As we walked on the land looking for caribou, we would use a sealskin tent to dwell in. We would be up on the land all summer. When the snow started to come we would return to our relatives that we had left along the beach. When we arrived home to our relatives we would start preparing a sod house. Again this would be a place where we met. In the winter, we lived in sod houses. That's how we were.

Traditional Government

There were many adults, many parents, that is how we lived. These older people would attempt to have meetings with their grown sons because they wanted them to help one another. That's how they would have a camp. They would also have younger people, their relatives or children, as their helpers. That's how they were controlled by their father and mother. The people who went out hunting would return with meat, then the father would divide the meat. They would eat with the fellow camp dwellers. The father would decide where the hunters would go hunting for the day. Before going hunting in the morning they would first check with their father and when they returned they would go see their father. When they got older and got their own house after sticking together, but then our younger siblings would be living with the older people. We, the older people, would have our own place and our husbands would go see their fathers, if they were planning to go hunting, and when they returned they would go see their fathers. So they would find out what their fathers wanted them to do. That is the new way it was, their fathers and older people controlled them. When there was someone who did not agree with something, when they did something different even by their children, all these adults would discuss together how to deal with their children or younger siblings when they weren't listened to. The adults together would discuss and try to fix things up, not only men but women were involved. We, the women, were often instructed by older people such as our mothers or mothers-in-law not to tell stories to our husbands about things that were sad and not right in the life. That is what we heard from others such as parents-in-law. When a woman tells too quickly she was said to break her husband, because he loves her so much. Even the younger siblings, older ones and the men would start separating, it was said to happen because of his wife. Because of this we were warned not to tell our husbands these stories. We believed this. Some people believed it and made an attempt to follow it, we did try to follow it.

Elders

When we were young girls, the older people would tell us not to listen to them as they talked among themselves. They did not tell us some stories. I think they didn't want us to think like adults or to know of adult doings. I don't know what their reasoning was. We were told of the things we had to do well. We were told to help Elders, to love them, to go to Elders with problems because they wanted us to be good people. We were told to obey and listen to adults and we were told to love orphans. We were told not to fight, not to lie, and not to steal. This is what we were told.

We were all different. We all have different lives. There are the *tatitujut,* 'the slow people,' the people who slowly plan to do things or slowly get around to doing something after they've been asked to do it. Then there are those who quickly complete a task that has been assigned to them. These people were respected while others were seen to have room for improvement. That's how we were. We weren't like that deliberately. It is just human nature that makes us like that. There were us, the people who complete tasks slowly even though we tried hard, making things slowly, and then there were those who complete it very quickly. And people would say to us *Uarajaralungasil,* meaning 'you are so slow again.'

If a young person has something that is bothering them and wants to talk to an older person about it, that is all right. In fact it is welcomed if a young person has something to talk about. However it is seen by older people to be unfit if an Elder approaches a young person who has been doing something wrong to talk to him about it and the young person starts arguing. We were told not to argue or talk back to our Elders. The old people who could no longer hunt or who had a harder time doing certain things did not forget incidents as quickly, so we were told not to talk back or against these older people.

Heroes and Role Models

A friend of mine, about the same age as me, is my role model. She didn't get scared too quickly, and she didn't get intimidated quickly. I looked up to these traits. For me, I got scared quite quickly and intimidated. That's the way I am. Once in a while when I heard of something scary I would start looking up to my friend even though she was just the same age as me because she would not get scared. Because she was not scared I would try my best not to be scared and if she was not intimidated I'd try my best not to be intimidated. That's what I did.

Recreation

These are the things we used to play, dog team race, igloo-building race, and ball. We used to play these, and at night we'd play wolf, *uatanianaqtu,* and juggling in the spring. These things are what we played and used during our leisure time. And in the spring we would have a pretend tent and just outside it a sod house and we would fix the bedding. We used to enjoy playing like this. We would celebrate by getting together, by dancing. People would come to celebrate. It was a happy time when children were born. There would be games. When there was a birthday there would be running races, or playing ball, or they would get together and eat because they were so happy. That's what we did.

Family Relationships

In-laws and *nukaungurit,* brother and sister. When the brother gets a wife, now she is the *ukuaq* of the sister. We were told to be friends with our *ukuaq*, sister-in-law or daughter-in-law. If we had something we had to share it. We didn't buy and sell things. If she had less, we gave her some and then when we had less she gave us some. That's how we were. We didn't buy and sell, we didn't sell. We were told to be like this by our mother-in-law and also we were told to treat our mother-in-law like our mother. We think of and treat our *ukuaqs* as our own children. We love them like our own children or maybe even more. As mothers-in-law we tend to be like this. Like a mother, that's how they are and if they were male they would be like a father. It was law we had. And we didn't want to refer to our daughters-in-law by their name because we loved them so much. When we were together we didn't call each other by name because we loved each other. Like that, we had a law. And our children, my *saki-ataa*, brother-in-law; *nukaunguta*, sister, and mine, because we wanted them to be friends we'd try not to be overprotective of some only. We'd love them all. That was our law so we'd try to be like that.

There's always been adoption even when there were no bottles. When babies got hungry, we would feed them meat, broken up like banana, broth, and water. That's how we would be brought up. Some women who could not have children but wanted children would adopt. Lately I have heard that some people have too many children now and they give them up because they do not want them. Usually babies were given to relatives because the mother sort of didn't want to give it up totally, so that baby is kept in the family. Sometimes prior arrangements for adoption would be made during the pregnancy. Sometimes the mothers would change their mind when the baby was born. This has happened.

Roles of Men and Women

Women were in charge of the house. They'd have *qamaqs*, sod houses, tents, and igloos. They'd work on trying to keep the house warm. They'd work on clothes for their children, their husband, and themselves. We just had handmade clothes out of caribou skin, sealskin, things that are alive, we didn't have cloth. We'd have sinew from caribou and whales.

Men went hunting and looked after their dogs and their harnesses. They'd make rope and harnesses from bearded sealskin. They'd make rope from sealskin. They too would use only things that had been alive. They'd use polar bear skins as a cover, like a tarpaulin, or for the lowest part of bedding.

Women would learn to do what their mothers did by imitating them.

We'd see what our mothers made and by copying we'd be able to sew and cut patterns like our mother. We would work with *quliqs* (seal-oil lamps), because this is how we kept warm. We would pound the fat for the lamp, we would fetch ice and fill pots with snow for water. Also men would go out with their fathers and learn to hunt, how to get ready, how to take care of dogs. And this way they would learn the ways of their fathers. We would copy our parents and try to do things. If we made a mistake they would correct us and we'd do it again. We learned this way although we didn't think we were learning.

Marriages

Sometimes marriages would be arranged by their mothers. Also when they were children, parents would see a particular person that they would want as an *ukuaq*. This person would have a son and they would arrange it. Eventually the children would get together when they grew up. Some would be like this, others would go right up and ask. Also if a camp went away and they were too far from the wife-to-be or husband-to-be they would then marry someone else. That was how it was. A man who knew who he wanted to marry would get his mother to ask for him. The mothers would talk and if the answer was no, then nothing would happen. If they said yes then they would get together. It was never that a man and woman would get together and then the parents would find out later. They would always tell their parents first who they wanted to be with before they could, if the parents agreed. If the parents did not agree, although he wanted to, he would not get his way. If the parents decided and they agreed then even if the daughter didn't want to marry she would have to, because the parents have decided. That's how they did it.

Tricksters

That is what we call *arqsiq*, that which makes us laugh. Relatives would *arqsiq* together. There would be two groups. One group who did not want to laugh and the other group who tried to make them laugh in many different ways. If one person from the first group began laughing they would all switch roles and the second group would try not to laugh. That's what they did. Even adults would play this and enjoy it. There wouldn't be just one person. People when they didn't have much to do would play *arqsiq*. I like laughing, myself I enjoy laughing. We don't worry when we're doing this, when we play this game, *arqsiq*.

Music

Those people in our past used to *maksai*, which refers to going outside with your child and singing to them. We would sing to them and stay outside with them even at night as long as there was a moon. After being outside, when the child was brought in he would be more settled and happy. When they are tired of being inside, babies start getting fussy. We would go outside with our children and take them out on trips because they get tired of staying inside. When they got tired of being inside we would take them outside and sing to them songs that we would make up. However, in my generation, we started singing hymns to our children.

I grew up without drumming. Only after I moved here to the Amitturmiut region when I was an adult did I start hearing about drumming and singing. When I was living with my parents they didn't want me involved with this. Apparently the shamans used to drum. My parents had become Christians and they didn't want to use shamanism so they didn't use this singing and drumming. I was told not to do it, so I grew up never knowing about it. Here and there I would look for something to see and if I wanted to sing I would sing. I would walk up there looking for something to see, wanting to see live animals as I sing. That's what I do.

Daily Routines

Out on the land we, the girls, were told to get out quickly when we woke up. In the morning we would wake up, put our clothes on and go outside to pee, and we would stay outside. When we got outside we would try to predict what the weather was like, that's what we were told to do. When someone was going away hunting we would wake up early and help get ready. The boys who were going away would help and they would be told to go out early. If they were sleeping they would be waked up so that they could go.

If we do not have a sickness we do not just sit around. I don't think there is or used to be anyone who didn't do anything. When you have the ability and are not sick you don't just want to sit around. You always feel [you want] to do something. It is better than staying still. By keeping busy you do not sit and get bored. When you do not keep active, you begin to be lazy and because you have so much time with nothing to do, you begin to think too much and you probably get sad. Also, you start to get tired easily. There are some people older than I am in my community. Although they are old they are younger than me. A lot of people get rides to get around the community. I always refuse rides and I walk. Now those people who get rides seem to get tired much faster and I think it is because they do not walk. It seems that way.

Traditional Clothing

Before we had cloth, the clothing we had was caribou skin and in the summer we started wearing sealskin clothes. In the summer we used caribou skin clothing that was not new and those that were getting thin because it was getting too warm. They would have pullover coats in the summer made out of old thinned caribou skin. Men would have sealskin boots. Sealskin clothes were good in bad weather. That's how we were in the summer. But when winter was coming we would then try to get warmer clothing. We would try to get new thick caribou skins and use them. The clothes we had during the summer, we would just forget about them, because they'd be no longer good.

Spirituality

For burials, you would roll up the body in old caribou-skin bedding and place it on top of rocks. You didn't weigh it down with rocks, you just placed the rocks on them. I have heard of people seeing people who have been dead, but probably only through a shaman. It used to be said that when people were looking for caribou up on the land that sometimes they would see dead people. That's what I have heard. But I don't hear that anymore.

Children were named after dead relatives. If they knew of a relative that was dead, they would name the newborn child that person's name. I didn't know what to call my children so my mother in-law would tell me what she thought the name should be and then that was their name. We would name them after a dead relative because we wanted our relative to continue on, so we would use their name so that we can continue caring for them. If the baby has a characteristic or way of doing something which is the same as the relative he is named after, you start to love him even more or to spoil him because he reminds you of your old relative.

When a child is adopted, for example. My parents told me I was adopted and although I never saw my real parents until I was older, they would talk about my real parents and brothers and sister and I knew about them. I knew about them but I did not miss them. I did not want to return to my real family. I wanted to stay with those who raised me.

Traditional Beliefs and Christianity

Back then they had shamans and believed in shamanism. They tried to follow this. Today we have been told about Jesus and God and Christianity and I believe this to be true. I don't see them as being the same. The people that believed in shamanism, it seems to me, believed in the outside and they could see dead people. That's how I see them to be. Now with Christianity, we have to think of our Spirit, our Saviour Jesus and God our Creator. I believe in this more. It is said that before Christianity people would pray and ask for help and guidance through the help of shamans and from the first man, *Aakulagjug*, and first woman, *Umarniqtu.*

Values

We were relatives, our parents, their children and grandchildren. We would live with our relatives. People would visit each other only in the winter when the ice froze and they would use dog teams. This is when they would hear from each other. Sometimes there would be some people who didn't have enough food or lacked something. When this happened they would get additional people in their camp. Sometimes it got quite crowded but not like today, where everyone is together. This was in order to help one another, hunt together.

   We would live life forgetting things that were no longer needed except incidents that were scary or amazing. There are those others that don't forget anything and remember everything. That's how we are. We start to believe things unquestionably. I've also heard it like this. I'm not a liar. I don't lie when I say things. Even when a person lies I start believing. I've also heard it like this. Because one is not a liar he is a believer, however if you're not a liar you do not believe. Even if he's told the truth he will not believe it. That's because he's a liar.

Prophecies

How I seem to remember it is that people started talking about what would happen in the future and they knew that things would change after having had contact with White people. Before that, I don't think I really heard about it. They just talk about the weather and wonder if it was going to be bad or good weather.

Time and Seasons

The body gets used to waking up at a certain time. It continues to wake up at this time for quite a while. This would give us an idea of what time it was. Also, for example, a person goes away hunting and every night he makes an *igluvigaq* to sleep in. One night he makes it much later and falls asleep later. Logically it would seem that they would sleep in but they do not. He would wake up to urinate. People have to urinate and this would help to tell the time even though there were no clocks. Also sometimes we would make a little hole in the igloo wall to look outside and to check the weather. Mainly it was whenever we woke up that helped us know what time of the day it was.

People tried to prepare a place for themselves before it became too cold or it became spring. They prepared a dwelling and they would try to collect food during the summer by burying the meat in caches. If a person goes hunting on the land, even if it is far from our land, and he catches many animals, he would not just leave the meat, he would cache it because when the time came when there was not much meat available, he would remember the meat he had previously left. He would go looking for it by dog team and if it had not been eaten it could once again be used. People would try to have these caches fixed well.

If it was bad weather during the summer then in the fall it would have to be good weather. That is how people would try to know it. In the spring, if it was bad weather then it would be good weather during the summer. That is how people would know. Also in this month if it is this type of weather then in the coming month it would change. It is also in this month that animals move to this particular area. That is what they said because they wanted to know for their hunting.

Language and Land

We can understand better only if we can understand what they are saying. If we are trying to talk with somebody with a different language or dialect we cannot understand some things. Even Inuit people do not all have the same dialects. When we first hear a dialect we do not understand each other for a little while even though we are both Inuit. Some lands are named after people. The ones I know of have the names of Inuit. Sometimes I've heard this. In Pond Inlet there used to be a woman named *Uyarsiaq* and now there is some lands called *Uyarsiaq*.

We used to call the land we were camping on 'our land.' Even if we had lived there a long time, when we moved to a different camp we would then start calling that our land. That is how we were. If we moved to a different camp we would not only start calling the land our land but we would also attempt to talk the dialect of that camp. The people of the camp were Inuit but I cannot learn the language of the White people.

Caribou was our main food. Rabbits, ptarmigan, these are our food from the land. In the summer we would dry the meat. When meat is dry it doesn't spoil so fast. Also we would cache the meat. Although it would go a bit bad it would still be food. That is how we were. In the winter the meat could be frozen, then it wouldn't spoil. If we thought the meat was too spoiled we fed it to our dogs and tried to eat the better meat. That is what we did. We had meat along with our dogs. We tried to give them the bad parts. The meat we didn't want as our food became dog food.

Transportation

There used to be kayaks, which were used for hunting. When we wanted to move our camp, we women would cross the land with the dogs, who would be carrying packs. The men would go on kayaks, which also carried some belongings. Also there was an *umiaq*, a 'boat' that was covered with sealskins. It was used to carry belongings. It could carry a lot. When we wanted to move we'd fill it up and we the women would walk overland. That is how we moved. We would carry with the dogs. These sleds are called *qamutiks*, and they are pulled by dogs. Nowadays we use snow-mobiles.

Today, I like the fact that modern machines get you to a far-off place faster. The only thing is that they break down. Before we had this modern transportation we were able to get to distant places although we had to set up camp. We would go slowly by dog team and we would often walk or go through deep snow but we would slowly get closer. Eventually we would arrive at our destination, even if it was far. As long as we had dog food, our dogs would continue as far as we were going. When we stopped the women would continue to walk towards our destination while trying to keep warm.

Dreams

Some people believe in what they have dreamed. Certain dreams told of the future catch of a certain type of animal, rarely caught. When you hear a ringing in your ear, something happy will soon come your way. They probably did the same things with dreams. I have never known of anyone who could interpret dreams. I have heard that sometimes you can dream that a relative will soon die in another camp. If you dream something to do with death, you get a warning that you will soon hear from a relative. Some people think they will hear of a death through their dreams.

Traditional Medicines

I know a few medicines for cuts and scabs, and also I know of some types of bandages. When there is a big cut that will not stop bleeding we crush rabbit manure and stick it on the cut to stop the bleeding. Also *puya*, old fat when it becomes sticky, is a good bandage. Seal's *sunga*, which are located in the liver, would also be used to cover a scab. These are the medicines I know of for problems with the skin. People who had colds or sore throat would swallow seal flippers. Constipated people would boil *qunguli* and then eat it and drink the water. These are the few remedies I know.

Because I did not live with many people I never heard of people dying for a very long time. Only when I was an adult did I know of dead people. I did know that when people got the cold or got sick that it seemed that everyone got it together. Here in my camp no one ever died as I was growing up. I did not think adults could cry because I never saw any of them cry. I thought that when you became an adult you no longer had the ability to cry. I started to be aware of that at the time when we had Christianity, so then I knew that we would pray for people. They would try and help sickness by praying. I have heard that before my time, the shaman would try and help. Through the shaman they would try to find the cause. Apparently they would try to get them to say, if he did not say they could die, but if he did say there would be a way of ending it. That is how they would end it. I have just heard this.

Life on the Land

It is enjoyable to go out on the land away from the settlement. Staying here in the settlement can cause loss of energy, you feel tired and lazy but by going away you get more energy and start feeling happier. I think that is what happens. By looking at and examining the different surroundings in the other location you start feeling happier. I've noticed this to be true.

There are many *inukshuks* up on the land, not only along the coast. It is clear that these areas did have people. There are also markers, although not close together, for dog teams that would cross across the mainland. There are many of these *inukshuks* up there on the land, not close to the sea. There are even some old remains of sod houses. Before there were rifles, *inukshuks* were built along the edge of the river where the caribou herds cross. This was done in order to use them as camouflages or decoys, hoping the caribou would be steered towards the hunter.

Education

I do not remember anyone being taught formally. By following and copying the tasks of the mother, we would be learning. This is how we learned what has to be done with the dwelling, clothing, and seal-oil lamp. We would watch how our mother did things and learn from this. Boys too, would go out hunting with their fathers and by observing they would be learning. Although we were not learning with a teacher, like today's schools, we were able to learn.

Residential Schools

Now, after hearing about some things that happened at these places, in retrospect I can see that they did have bad effects. These people have to talk about it and let it out, then they should be happier. They should tell what is on their mind, don't keep talking about it, just tell it to someone who won't talk too much, one who will listen. Tell what is bothering you about the wrong things and bad things that happened to you and then by letting go you will be more able to be happy. First you must tell about it.

In today's schools it is thought that Inuit culture and language should be taught with the help of older people. They were going to try to set it up like that, but I don't know if it is implemented or not. I think it is good that Inuit culture and language are included in education. It was going to be arranged so that older people could get together and direct what should be taught to the youngsters. The Elders should also be involved by telling them stories and talking to children about how to live a good life.

Traditional Justice

Before there were courts, the older people would talk to their youngsters. If the children did not listen, the Elders would get together with other Elders and try to solve the problem by talking to the youngster. There would be two Elders at first, and if nothing happened more would join in to talk to them. If the youngsters listened, that was the end. Today, Elders, a male and female, should sit with the judge. After judging, the Elders also talk to the person to try to make them understand. I think this would be good.

If one person saw that someone was not behaving they would advise that person. However, if nothing changed, the older people would get together and talk to the person in the hopes of change. Some would listen to what was said, while others were harder to persuade. That is apparently how they were. That is how they were.

Our traditional justice system could be used to help. It could be used to help judges, through the Inuit way. I believe this to be a good way. However, it is not possible alone. It has to be that a group of older people get together and help. I'm thinking about it like this. By putting together the Inuit system and the system of the courts, I think it could help without putting young people in prison. This system would be well understood and obeyed. When a person does not want to listen and obey, then it will not work.

Non-Native People

We are now all trying to follow White people. We hear that a White person is doing something, then we want to change and be like White people, following their ways, but we are not able to. That's how we are sometimes. However, White people can help us with material objects and with health care and medicine. Inuit and non-Inuit could live together harmoniously if they have an understanding of each other's lifestyles and if they are willing to help each other.

Concluding Words

Before the White people came, we did not have many things to see or experience. Older people told us things to do and things we should not do. Some of us wanted to follow this and some of them didn't want to. However, all direction came from the Elders. Now that there are many things to see, you talk to a young person or advise them, but if they are doing something they enjoy or have a friend, it seems like they cannot hear. I have sometimes asked, 'Can you hear me?' But they reply that they can hear. They do not listen as much today as they used to. I think they listen a bit more if there is a discussion, like sitting where there is more than the talker and listener. Because there are now so many things that are distracting and things to see and experience they often do not want to listen.

When they get a mind of their own, then they will start realizing what to do and what not to do. As young people, when we are enjoying something we just think of that for a while or if we see some friends having a good time, we want to be a part of it. That is how we have become. All of us have been young before and we've all been like this. Back then we got scared a bit quicker and we had fewer people around. That's how we are. The people who want to listen when they are told will not forget. They can start realizing their way of living. Sometimes we get defeated by having fun and doing things we know we should not. That is how I see it to be.

Life today is what I find strange. It was said that we were changing and I used to wonder what this meant and how we were changing. We have changed since back then. We are no longer scared of death. As I grew up I was controlled and guided by my older relatives and parents. I was not left aside. If we were like this now, it would be better. We are just disintegrating because we are outside. Our young people of today have a different life now than when we were young. They now sleep over with friends even though we parents do not want this to happen. There are times now when we do not know where they are, even though this is not the way it should be. When young people do not have someone to guide them, they start approaching bad things because they have their own minds. The parents are not listened to. Even though we continue to talk, they just don't want to listen. They just want to do what they want to. It is hard to know where they are and they tend to be quiet. No wonder we are now different. If we listened more to our parents, even though there are teachers, we would probably stop hearing so many bad stories. I've heard some things that have shocked me and I start worrying that my little ones may be a part of this. I too do not want them to do bad things.

PAULOOSIE ANGMARLIK (Inuit)

Pangnirtung, Baffin Island

'I never say what I have heard, I only tell what I have experienced, because I do not want to lie.'

Pauloosie Angmarlik was born in Kekerton in the eastern Arctic, on 1 October 1911. He was raised on the land and learned the traditional ways of the Inuit from birth. In his early adult life, Pauloosie moved to Illungajuq, where he met his wife, who was from Tuvarjuaq. He moved his family back to Kekerton, where he raised his children. He had five children, three of whom have died. He had approximately nine grandchildren by 1994, the time of this interview. Pauloosie received no formal schooling, but learned all about the land and survival skills as practised by the past generations of his people. He now lives in Pangnirtung on Baffin Island.

This interview has been translated from the original Inuktitut to English.

Life History

I was born in Kekerton. I was raised there. That is where I grew up. Later I moved to Illungajuq. That is where I learned how to hunt and I met a wife at a very young age, and she was from around Tuvarjuaq. I was taken there and brought the family back to Kekerton. I did not have actual teachers that time. The women and men had always had different roles. We did not know at that time but we were being taught by our parents. We did not have houses as we have today. To get any kind of education, the boys followed the hunters on a hunt. Looking back now, I realize that we were being taught.

Creation Stories

To the question of the creation story, I cannot answer it fully. Our ancestors were the ones that gave us our lives, they were ones that gave us our culture and laws. We, the present Elders, have this as we were the ones that were close to that generation. Whatever was to be followed, we followed. Nowadays it is totally different. The Elders of those days lived the way our ancestors lived and experienced. We followed it and were advised on what to do. There is no Inuk who can say this is how we were created, so we cannot answer it fully.

Traditions

The most important aspects of our traditional lives, as I see it, is that there were not too many bad influences like we have today. Our ancestors, adoptive parents, and parents advised us of what we should do in order to live a good life. Thinking back, and I have a lot of time to think these days, we had a very good life compared to what the young people are used to now. We are just following the law that the non-Natives have introduced to us. I know I am not the only one who feels this way. Other Elders feel the same way. The natural law cannot be grabbed, I know this for sure. The younger kids or babies learned from the parents, and when they are at that age they do not see a lot of influences. I believe we should start gearing to those youngsters for them to learn the natural law. If they are taught from an early age I believe that they will be more than eager to learn what we the Elders know. The young people have grown up and have adjusted to what the non-Natives have brought. I believe that most of them will not want to follow the Inuit law. We have to start with the youngsters. The young people have adjusted to the non-Native culture and values. If the youngsters are taught at an early age, they will learn more and know that the Inuit have their own laws too. They can be taught that a criminal activity is not the way to go.

Traditional Birthing

I have seen one child born. That was the only time I was part of a birthing process. My wife was in labour, that was when my son, Seemee, to his mother, was born. I helped deliver that child. As I stated earlier, I lived in Illungajuq. I was usually asked to go where there was a woman in labour and I performed a prayer. That was the only way I took part in a delivery. But as I said earlier I only experienced one time where I helped deliver my son.

Traditional Dwellings

Family members were a household. I have a daughter, for instance, so I live in the same house with her and her family. Even if a son had a wife or a daughter had a husband he or she usually stayed in their parents' household. The type of house we had was a sod house. There is an example at the visitors' centre [in Pangnirtung]. During the spring we went out hunting. When we went out hunting, we used sealskin tents as those were the only ones available. Sod houses were used during the winter. The feathers were used to keep the house warm. The igloo could be used for hunters, and families. The inside was kept warm by having the sealskins on the walls. There was not anything to cover the igloo walls.

Traditional Government

I have been around when the non-Natives were already up here. The other two older people, Etooangat and Kudloo, were born when the non-Natives were already around. We all remember when they were here. We did not really know the non-Natives' ways. The Inuit at that time did not really know the lifestyles of the non-Natives. The real leader that I was aware of while I was growing up was my stepfather, Angmarlik. He was the leader for the Kekerton area. Even when Pangnirtung had non-Natives, they followed what Angmarlik advised them to. The Hudson's Bay Company manager at that time respected what Angmarlik had to say and followed his advice. Angmarlik knew practically everything. The men had their own roles as the women did. They had separate leaders as they had separate roles. People were aware of what their tasks were. Angmarlik's wife, Aasivak, who was my stepmother, was his helper. They seem to be the leaders at that time. I was not aware of who was another leader.

The people that raised me were my heroes, as they raised me well. Maybe I was too young at that time in order to see if there were great leaders but the two people who raised me were my heroes. I listened to what they told me. Everybody worked together that time. I am not aware of who may have been the greatest.

Traditional Games

We played games outdoors. The indoor games were string games and *inugaq*, which are small seal bones, and we would pretend to hunt animals. There was a focus on role playing, imitating adults and their tasks. We used our language to pretend that we were out hunting somewhere. That was our main game for the boys. The girls played their own games too. They played together. The boys and the girls played together too, pretending to be a family. We pretended to be a certain family when we played together.

One of the outdoor games was where we used an ice chunk as a *qamutik*, which is a sled, or frozen ice. We made sure it was smooth and we used it as a sled to go sliding. The sleds were not available at that time so we had to use our imagination. We pretended to have our own dog team. We used seal bones as dogs and that was one dog team. We enjoyed these types of games because it was part of our culture. Nowadays, it is not used anymore. People can learn this game very easily and bring it back to our culture. It can be learned in a short time.

Family Relationships

Maybe certain families did not cooperate with one another if they did not get along. Traditionally, families worked together, supporting each other. If a certain family was in need of something, that family was given what they did not have. Sharing was a very important task in our lives. Helping one another was of importance. From what I know, children, aunts, and uncles, cousins were relatives. For instance, we are related to the Kooneeliusies. Nothing major has changed in the family relationships. We have always cared for one another. Another example is if I did not care for my children, Seemee and Mary, we would be a dysfunctional family as we would not be helping one another. We have to care for one another as a family.

I can only say that the children have learned from their parents about going out on the land in order to learn skills of survival. We have gone hunting when we were quite young, in order to have the proper skills when we reach adulthood. It was always obvious when one did not take part in hunting activities, one did not know some of the skills needed on a hunting trip. When one is taught at a very young age, one can grasp certain skills. Girls were also taught at a young age to sew dolls, *kamiiks* (sealskin boots), mitts, and clothing. They probably did not realize that they were being taught how to sew, how to design.

Traditional Marriages

Marriages were arranged. Marriages were different during my time. They were arranged by the parents. A young man would not even choose a girl but all the marriages were arranged. A young girl would be crying, saying she did not want to get married. Even in this manner, the parents would let her be as she would adjust to the relationship. I do not remember seeing young boys crying when they were told they have marry. We had no choice but to listen to our parents. In my case, I went very far to marry. I never thought of marriage at that time because I was too young. A year later I took my wife and her family to where my parents lived as we never experienced hunger in our area. They lived in their area before I was brought to where my parents were. I was taken to their camp to meet my future wife.

Maybe there were separations in the past, but I have never known a divorce. When one was asked to marry by the parents, she or he had no choice but to follow their parents' advice. In those days, arranged marriages worked out very well as the couple adjusted to each other. They would start loving each other. A couple like any other couple might argue with each other but would forgive each other and everything was back to normal. These days there are no arranged marriages. Young people don't even ask permission from the parents if they can have so and so for a partner. The couples nowadays get together by going for walks and that is how they can get close. The couples these days break up more than they used to.

Traditional View of Sex

Sex can be interpreted in a bad way, but while I was growing up I did not hear of negative attitude towards sex. We did not have a judge at that time, so therefore people were not taken to courts for having sex. I have thought of the term sexual assault in Inuktitut, there was no term for sexual assault. When I meet with the judge again I will ask how the interpretation came to be. The interpretation did not come from the Inuit, it came from the non-Natives, the justice system.

Tricksters

I have heard of tricksters and clowns. The clowns like to make people laugh. Humour makes people feel good. Humour does not cause harm against one another. It is to make people laugh and enjoy themselves.

Traditional Music

In this area we did not grow up with musical instruments. We did not use any type of music like Igloolik people and the western Arctic people. Other Elders, like Etooangat and Kudloo, would answer the same thing. I don't remember many carvers in those days but carving was always used where I had lived before in Kekerton. When I was a child I noticed a man who could barely walk whose name was Iasa. He was a real carver. He was not able to hunt so therefore carving was his specialty. People have said that he had hunted too but I did not see him going out hunting. When whaling was a big part in our days, he used go up to the hills to use his binoculars to look for whales.

Daily Routines

When we woke up, well, we did not use any machines those days so we were able to help out by getting the dog team ready for our fathers. This was learning experience but I did not realize it at that time. It was the same thing too when the hunters got back from their hunting trip. We would free the dogs. When we did not follow our fathers on a hunting trip we would have outdoor games, that was our main thing to do. Working is different today as we cannot buy goods without the money. Employees earn their money by working and I think it is very positive. I think it is positive if one of my relatives has a job. I will just encourage people to work. It is not a bad thing. The development of a person is very positive as he or she is helping out the household by buying food.

Traditional Clothing

The types of clothing we wore were all skins. We did not have any materials like we have today. When the new types of clothing were introduced, we would wear them during spring and summer seasons. These types of clothing that we started wearing were not waterproof, so we used the sealskin clothing instead when it rained. Sealskins were mainly used during spring and summer seasons. The caribou skin clothing was for the winter months. Our *kamiiks* (boots) without fur were for the summer months. The *kamiiks* with fur were for the winter seasons.

Spirituality

Spirituality is for the good of the people. For example, if either one of us were not spiritual we would not get along together at all. We would not be able to communicate with one another in an effective way as we would try and destroy each other through our words. We are ruled by our Spirits. If the spiritual part of our beings were not present in us, I think we would be at war most of the time like the non-Natives. The spiritual part helps us in being good people.

There may have been shamans. I have heard of them. I cannot really answer any questions regarding that as I did not know a shaman. There was an individual, Uqaittuq, he was a shaman for this area.

Traditional Burials

The burial practices were handled like today but it seemed less of an event. People that were grieving for their children, partners, and relatives were well cared for. The people made sure that there were people at their home so that they were not alone. This has been practised ever since I can remember. When their grieving has lessened, that is when the people gradually stop going to their homes. Support to grieving families does not instantly stop, this has not changed at all how the grieving is practised in our society. Christian teachings are of great importance, they work well for the people and someday there will be a great day when someone high up comes down.

Names

The names that we have reflected on how people knew you, or your char-

acter. We did not have clans. We were given Christian names and if someone passed away a newborn would be named after that individual.

Teaching in our language is positive and this can be used to teach our
law. That is how it can be understood. If we try to learn our law to the best
of our ability it can be done. The names were acquired any way they
wanted them to. My stepfather, Angmarlik, was named after the current.
It means that the sea ice is circling in one area and the whitecaps are supposedly to erupt. That is how he told me. I think he was named by a shaman. His name was named after a strong current.

We acquired names anyhow, and there are names that are called *inukshuks*. These are people named after the marker *inukshuk*. People were
named after the land and the sea, but starting from a generation ago, we
were given Christian names, so my name Pauloosie is a Christian name
but Angmarlik refers to the sea. When we were given last names here in
Pangnirtung I got my stepfather's name as a last name. I was only known
as Pauloosie before. Those people named Aqsauik got that last name
through their ancestor, Aqsauik. Toqamanuk and Jonasmarkik, they got
their names through their ancestors.

Predicting the Weather

I will not answer the question fully regarding of people telling the future,
but we have always been interested in our weather and predicted how the
weather will be the next day. Maybe there were prophecies but I don't
know of any. I know though that when the full moon is around the corner, people with sicknesses tend to get worse during this time, even the
sea. I know though that, well, I have been operated on before, and when
the scar gets itchy I know that bad weather is just around the corner. That
is the only way to predict weather. We don't analyse it but we know it. I
will give myself as an example. While I was growing up I had to respect my
Elders and learn their teachings. While one was growing up, one was
taught well about how to survive, to be independent when one got older.
When we were born, our people already had clocks. All the Inuit did not
own clocks at that time.

We know of all the different seasons because of the weather. During
spring we had bad weather, our ancestors would say that we did not have a
good spring. Thinking back, we went off to a trip for a while and we left
during the summer, midsummer, and we were heading into autumn. We
had excellent weather when we were out on the land. We cannot control
the weather. We knew when the season would be changing by feeling it

before the technological weather updates became available. We viewed the weather and that is how we can predict the weather. We do not have a full understanding of it but we have an idea how it is going to be. When the sun is covered by clouds, although it is visible, if there is a circle of clouds or it seems distant we know that bad weather will hit not too long from now. Clocks were already around.

I always mention Etooangat and Kudloo because they are the only two people that are older than me. We have talked among us that we should be reaching back to the past and hang on to some of our culture before it is too late. The natural law has been damaged by people who are younger than us, maybe around the late 1960s. We reached 1965 and we still had a hold of it. I left Pangnirtung in 1964 to go to Broughton Island, and it seemed as if our law was not being followed around 1967. The Anglican bishop asked me to go to Broughton Island to be a minister because they did not have one. Our natural law was still being practised. When jobs were created the Sabbath day was not being followed and it seemed as if it was broken.

Language and Culture

Our language and culture are related. It seems as if we have lost some of our values because of the non-Native culture. The non-Native culture has always had its laws written, but the Inuit have kept their laws memorized. The non-Natives' law seemed to be changed, be amended, but the Inuit law has always been straightforward. Our youngsters who are still at home should be the targets for passing on our law, as they still have no knowledge of the non-Natives' law. Some of the young people will not want to follow our laws because they have grown up thinking and believing that the non-Natives' law is what we should all follow. Our babies, youngsters, will be a good age to start passing on our law.

The Inuit ownership of the land was never mentioned but people used to say where they lived and came from. Like for instance, we still say that, these days, people say they own land. It was never mentioned before during my time.

Transportation

We know of *umiaq*, well, they are referred to as boats being made by Inuit. There is an example at the Angmarlik Centre, where a boat was made by the Inuit. I had wanted to ask Angmarlik if he was named when a boat was going through rough waters. We were born when the boats that were made by non-Natives were already up here. The dog teams were used during the winter months. Those people who did not have dog teams walked a great deal. Those people without dog teams were helped out to go out on a hunt.

The modern technology has changed drastically. A couple of days ago, we were on a trip. The trip would have taken days and days to get there without an outboard motor. We would have travelled rowing, sailing, for several days, but due to modern technology our trip was made possible in less than a day. They are so fast. There are advantages and disadvantages to the modern technology. I cannot really say anything negative on the outboard motors, but the snowmobiles have caused many deaths compared to the past when we relied on the dog teams for transportation. It is still possible to travel by dog teams and it is the case for the snowmobiles. I can use myself as an example. When I lived in Igloolik before we moved here to Pangnirtung, I used to travel to Neptun by myself to hunt caribou and foxes. I used to be gone for approximately two to three weeks by myself to get food for our camp. I would be alone with my dogs. I am not the only one who was able to do this but I just used myself as an example from my experience. I never say what I have heard, I only tell what I have experienced, because I do not want to lie. I did not hunt for my family only. I hunted for the people at the camp. I thought of them and tried to get enough for everybody. Our camp was the size of Pangnirtung. I wanted the people to enjoy the food. Today it is completely different from what I grew up with. Today people in the community would get along way better if they did not steal someone else's property, for instance, gas. It would be a better community if this criminal act was not a part of our lives. This has somehow destroyed the sense of a community. I have not seen people not getting along so badly. I have heard of people hating each other and the shamans trying to get back at each other, but I do not have a full understanding of it. The shamans would try to outdo each other. That is what I have heard of.

Dreams

The role of dreams in people's lives. I am a hunter. I used to go out caribou hunting with a helper, and one time, I do not know why, I dreamed a certain dream that referred to the non-Natives while I was out caribou hunting. I dreamed of a non-Native that I knew I was going to see sometime following that day. If I did not have a dream like that I would not have seen any. I remember I dreamed of a huge police officer and that day I caught a male caribou with lots of fat. That was my interpretation. If I had a dream of female non-Natives with children, I probably would have seen caribou like that. That is how I interpret my dreams. Dreams are a special part of our lives. I believe in my dreams as they become so real.

Another dream I had before I was moved up to Broughton Island by the archbishop was that I dreamed of my mother while she was still alive. She was in my dream where Jesus was. I had stated that he was near Clyde River, which was when I was going to be sent up to Broughton Island on an Anglican mission. I cannot forget that dream. I do not know if all the dreams were all interpreted, but because I was a hunter, people used to ask me if I dreamed of non-Natives. If people knew that I had a dream of non-Natives, the other hunters would expect to see caribou that day. That's how it was.

Traditional Medicines

I do not know what type of traditional medicines were available. I had not experienced them. From the knowledge that I have, the mushrooms that grew up here were used for cuts as bandages. They would have to be dried first and cut up into small pieces. We did not have bandages at that time, so we used those instead. If someone made one, we would use them as needed. I know traditional medicines were used but I didn't use them so I cannot really say much about this topic. I also have not heard of medicines being used in foods. If someone was seriously ill, people would delay their trips for days to be around that person. This has always been the case since I can remember. The person who was sick would have people around to help. If the weather was good, a hunt would be made to have meat ready for the people.

Life on the Land

Going out on the land is of major importance to a person. When we went on a trip recently, we were all happy and it was probably because we were tired of being in one community. But after that trip, my legs were getting tired. It was not from walking a long distance, it was probably from the boat ride back. I heard that another Elder, Etooangat, was not feeling well, but I have not heard anything. It is a wonderful feeling being out on the land. It is very soothing for the mind to get away for a while.

Maps

Even if we had not seen a certain land, for example in Kekerton, if our destination was Gloolik, we would be told what type of land we would have to look for in order to find it. That is how we learned to recognize, which was by word of mouth. It used to be clear. We used to go caribou hunting too with directions from people who had been there before, even if it was quite distant. *Inukshuks* were used as markers, *inukshuks* with holes directed straight ahead, even if there was a hole in the middle, but at the top of the *inukshuks* there would be a slim rock to indicate to the right. That is how we knew even before we had maps. For instance, there are trails of *inukshuks* where people should go. If I were near Cumberland Sound, I would follow the direction, or the direction would be word of mouth. I would be told to look for a flat area of land around Cumberland Sound. I would go straight to that area as I would have reached my destination. People always knew where Inuit lived. The land was divided in a sense as people lived in different areas.

The sod houses that we had are indicators of where we used to live; for instance, the areas are Nunataa, Quajamaq, Illungajuq, Sauniqturaarjut. I do not know if there are certain areas of land in Iqalulik for sod houses for markers. Our ancestors are the ones who stayed at these camps. Certain areas were dangerous and people avoided them, and they were told to watch and not be there if it was dangerous. If the pathway was good, people used it.

Education

We were taught by our ancestors, not in a school system, about hunting, survival skills, and so on. The school children are taken out in good weather only. From my experience, the school children should go on outings even if it is not good [weather] so they will learn skills that they need when bad weather hits. They should be taught how to make an igloo if it is really windy out or in a blizzard. That would enable a person to learn the skills in bad weather. One can never know what will happen out on the land, that would make it necessary to construct an igloo if one was not able to get home. What I had just said would be an ideal situation. I have not brought this up yet, but I have been meaning to. If the kids are taught how to survive in bad weather, it would mean building an igloo. I do not have a real knowledge of residential schools, so I cannot get into that topic. As I have said our ancestors were straightforward. I use that as a guideline, follow what is told to you. Our influences these days or trying to have a hold of it has helped. If an Inuk did not know some of what makes our culture, one can learn then. The individual who took us on our trip recently stated that he was learning new things from us about our culture. I know certain people that do not have a whole knowledge of our culture. If people want to reach into the past they can learn from us. I do not think a person can have a hold of Inuk and non-Native cultures at one time. The two cultures are not related at all. There are probably certain ways that are similar and one can try to make them work together. There is usually a stumbling block between the two cultures. If the Inuk had their laws written, the non-Natives would not seem to have so much power over our laws. If our laws were written I think some people would follow our laws if the laws of the Inuit and non-Natives were put together. I think that would be an ideal situation, even though the non-Native laws are completely different.

Traditional Justice

I believe there are alternatives to prison. If people followed the Inuit laws people would not be sent out to prison at all. The people would be brought together to talk and advise, not lecture, and bring everything out in the open. After discussions, forgiving would be a major role. People are now being sent off to prison for minor offences. If we followed the Inuit law that would not be the case at all. That individual would even probably be whispered to while getting advice. People who are sent to jail are sent out right away. If someone tried finding out why that occurrence happened, it would be useful and from that point whatever needed to be corrected would be done by word of mouth. There are usually two people involved when someone is taken to court especially for sexual assault offences. I think it would be even better if they were brought together at the same time. This would enable them to tell the truth. These days whatever is said is not always true when the complainant tells one story and the accused tells another version. The case these days is that they are giving statements while the other does not know the details, which may be false. The police complainants usually give false information to the courts. This in turn can allow false information to be judged.

Bringing the opposing individuals together would be better to fix whatever has happened. Everything should not be given to the courts. When there are delays for court days, one can get carried away and there have been suicides that could have been prevented. If the Inuit law were enforced I don't think there would be suicides, because I know that a person can get a lot in one's mind if there are delays.

Working with Non-Native People

The Inuit and non-Natives can work together if the two cultures do not keep attacking each other by making the Inuit culture less than what it is. If they are not getting along in the working environment, one can quit their job if the other culture is trying to be better. The non-Native law is so different from ours. The non-Natives try to rule over the Inuit. There may be educated and able Inuit out there, but the non-Natives try to step over the Inuit who have the ability to work. I think that Inuit should be given priority.

Inuit Law

I have a lot of time to think these days. The Inuit laws and non-Native laws are very different but what I often think is that the Inuit should go back to their law and the non-Native back to theirs. Then we could lead a better life following our own laws. The non-Natives could follow theirs. I think that would be better. I will bring this up the next time I have a meeting with the judge. What would be the case if a non-Native broke the Inuit law up here, the non-Natives would take care of it. As an example, we could have an Inuk police officer and the non-Natives their own officer. The Inuk officer would be able to handle cases, and if there was a serious offence, that can be turned over to the non-Natives to deal with. For those Inuk who do not follow the Inuk law, they should just follow the non-Native law. The young people have adjusted to the non-Native law so I think they would be more tuned to the non-Native law. The youngsters should be taught to follow Inuk law at an early age. This is my thought. I have not discussed it with another Elder.

Plains Cultures

EVA MCKAY (Dakota Sioux)

Dakota Tipi, Manitoba

'If they read what you are writing, this is the teachings, this is some of the teachings that we want them to read about.'

Eva McKay was interviewed by Emily Faries in the fall of 1994 at Dakota Tipi near Portage La Prairie, Manitoba. Eva McKay is a Dakota Sioux. Her name, *Ptetawotewastewin*, means 'good foods of the buffalo cow.' Emily described her interview with Eva McKay as busy and hectic. There were many distractions and people would just drop by and listen, but the interview went very well. Emily considered Eva McKay a 'real grandmother,' and she felt very comfortable in her home, and in the community. Eva McKay has twelve children, and almost fifty great-grandchildren.

In her interview Eva McKay discussed her residential school experience, and stressed the importance of talking about those times as a form of healing. She also stressed the importance of relearning the Native languages. Her life history emphasized her Sioux heritage, and she told a wonderful traditional Sioux creation story. Eva McKay runs a Sweat Lodge. She has received medals and honours from the YWCA and the

Canadian government. She created Dakota-Ojibway Family Services, and works for the Parole Board and the National Native Women's Association.

Life History

I was born near the town of Portage La Prairie in a little village, a Sioux village. Then I went to Portage residential school in 1927 and stayed there for ten years. That school is now Yellowquill College, outside of Portage. That is where I went to school.

It does not matter what we are going to do or what we say, the time that we spent in residential school always comes up. For example, we had an Elders' meeting yesterday and that came up again. Residential school did a lot, whether it was for good or whether it was for bad, we certainly survived, because the residential school in the name of education was more of missionary work. The thousands of us who went to residential schools came out very confused. To me that was the beginning of the destruction of Indian families, and today in this generation we still see the young people suffering from that, seeing them in the penitentiaries, or seeing them in the women's jails. That is what happened.

When we look at the child and family services, we see what it has done to our children and grandchildren. White people become their foster parents and then they were adopted, and I believe that story is heard right across Canada. But one good thing is that at least we are doing something that we had wanted to do, or never had a chance to do. The Dakota-Ojibway Tribal Council has this family services program, which came about ten years ago. I can say that I am the mother to that program. There's a fifteen-minute National Film Board documentary called *Taking Care of Our Own*. That is what we are doing with the child and family services program. So at least we have our own foster parents, and we ourselves were foster parents, because we kept teenagers after raising a big family. When your heart is out there to do something for your people, you have to volunteer your time to do it.

At the residential school, we were being taught something that was not right. The missionaries, the reverend was the principal, calling us pagans. He says, 'Come over, my God is better than your God.' That's what I heard, but when I came to understand what he was saying, I'll say our God is better than yours. So our God that we knew is coming out today, all over Indian country; what the missionaries had did not work for us.

One night, a few nights ago, we said God must be a Dakota because he gave us a language that we are to use, but we have forgotten and this is what the government wanted, us to forget our language, not to use it. But we survived. A lot of us kept our language, but it is the young people that do not have it. That means they are losing everything. Now that we are coming back, what we have to share with young people is our knowledge, our experience, and how we survived. We survived through a lot, a lot of things, from the time we went to residential school. My husband also went to residential school. So it is a long story, but we have to tell about it. Probably people reading this have more questions in order for them to really understand why we were stealing.

Even stealing is something we did not do at that time. Instead of stealing we would ask for it, and then the White people said we were begging. So we learned to steal because we were hungry. The things that we went through, the physical abuse, the verbal abuse, the sexual abuse were there. We had to close our minds to what was going on, thinking this is the way, this is the way, and it wasn't.

In residential school, we were not allowed to talk our language and we learned from books about ourselves, and young children believed what they were saying about us. An Indian reading about herself or himself, from material which was written by a White person. Kids thought that this might be true, maybe my grandparents are heathens. We believed it. So we came out having different ideas and a different outlook on what we were about.

So I was glad to have the opportunity to work with Sioux Valley, after moving from Portage. I came here in 1934. Up to that time we had the Indian Agent – he was the policeman, he was the inspector, he was everything. This doctor used to come from the town of Griswold and he would do the dental work, he would pull teeth out without any anaesthetic, no wonder even today people are scared to go to dentists. So this is one of the things that happened to us, it was the starting of fear of dentists, it still exists in the old people.

Experience of residential schools of not being able to talk your language. I did a lot of work for the school that is now here, we talked about how it was in school back then, and how we want the school to be today, where parents would be involved, parents can make decisions on behalf of the child. We looked at local control of education, and that is what we worked on. So now we have our own school. Even though our school is in isolation, we still have the provincial curriculum here and our kids are doing well, when they get to grades 9 and 10, they go to Brandon.

I grew up in a Sioux village which is Dakota Tipi today. That is the name of the village now. We moved three to five miles west from that area to the present location of Dakota Tipi. So we have a different language and we have maintained our culture. Even though it had to be done under the table, we hung on to it. Today Sioux Valley thrives on its own culture, the traditional ways. Our young people see what we are doing, without having to sit them down and say 'Listen.' They let us see what we are doing.

We have twelve children. I spent my time with my family, my children. When I was fifty I had my first job outside the home, with the Manitoba Indian Brotherhood. I told them I have no skills, I cannot accept my job. Dave Courchene, Sr, said, 'That is why we want you to come.' I asked, 'What can I do?' He said, 'For being a mother, having a family, we want you for that.' Since then, I have worked out of the home, I have helped Native people, it didn't matter which tribe, I went across Canada. I spent a lot of time with the women, we formed the National Native Women's Association in Manitoba in 1969. We organized and formed our own Native Women's Association and that is what we did, and other provinces followed.

Women like myself, the old people, had a lot to do in putting these women's groups together, Canada's association. Some of the women did not talk English so we had to be interpreters. There was no money. The Secretary of State gave us enough money to travel and for our room and board, that was all we got, no honorarium or anything like that. But our work came from the heart. I see some of my old friends now, some are older than me. I still see them once in a while. I think we did a lot. I see that we have had to come a long way, but the one thing that stands out most is that being brought up in the residential school, that was the beginning of the break-up of families.

We had a reunion about three weeks ago in Brandon, the Brandon residential school. There were some Elders from Saskatchewan that came, they came to see the school. We went to visit the cemetery above the school. They brought food and had a feast there, and we talked about what happened in this school. This school that stands there like a skeleton. People from Carry-the-Kettle reserve had been there. When we visited there, it was a spooky place, it felt like you could find somebody dead in there, because of all the memories that they have of abuse. It came to them. They had a flashback, because they were back at that school. It was scary, it was scary for me too, because of the things that happened to us in a school such as that one. We felt different, we felt very different. Even today we still feel those flashbacks and what that school, what people in that school did to us. Even though it was a long time ago, it does not go away. It has affected our young people today. But what kept my family together is I still have the language, my family knew the language, and because I was brought up in a traditional Indian way, that I teach my family here. I believe that is how we survived. So that is the residential school, we can go on and on talking about it. It has affected every Indian person in today's world.

Creation Stories

Yes, yes, yes. Not necessarily how we got here. Our ancestors say we were always here, this is where we always were. There are two big islands, one is North America, the other is the one across the big waters, the ocean. The Dakota people have a story, there was a camp of Dakota people, they had leaders, today they are called Chiefs, but they were called the Headmen, meaning they were the ones who were heading, keeping, taking care of, protecting their people, which is the band.

This Chief called a meeting and talked to the people. He said, 'I want ten of you to go out and travel to see how big this land is. You will have to travel until you come to the end of this land.' So those ten volunteers, they got ready for that trip. They had extra moccasins, extra dried meat, they travelled all summer, they walked, they walked. They were travelling west, they had scouts that would go in front of this group, and one day they said they could see far off and that they could see hills. As they came closer they were not just hills but they were mountains. So one of the scouts went up while they camped. They watched him running back down, criss-crossing. They knew he had something to tell them, that something was happening. They waited for him, when he got to them, he said, 'You will have to come with me, there is somebody on the other side of this place.' They said, 'It cannot be because we are the only people that live around here, there is nobody else that can be there.' The scout said, 'This man saw me and looked at me and said do not be afraid.' This person talked Sioux, of course I am talking about Sioux people. So they all went up and he motioned to them to come down and when they went down, they saw a big cloud of dust or smoke, they could not see, there were animals walking around. When they got to the spot, it was another Indian man standing there, and he started talking in Dakota to them and he said, 'Look at me and I will show you some things.' He took the dust from the ground and he blew it, that is what caused a big cloud and something was moving as they peered up, and those were horses. This man showed them other things. He said, 'This here is for sickness,' and he showed them different plants. 'This is what you will use for medicine, this Sweetgrass is what you need to use.' He took them to smell it.

They told the man why they were travelling, but he told them, 'You cannot go any farther now. Look at this water. You will never cross that water, so go home, go back to where you came from but take these horses. If you sit on the back of this horse, it will take you home. This horse will drink water and will eat grass, so go home now because you will never cross this water. This is the end of this land.' He told them a lot of things, mostly about medicines. He said, 'I am going to cross this water and I will come back someday if they do not kill me.' These men had been gone for a long time, when they got these horses, a strange animal to them, but they were told they could sit on their backs and take them home, which they did.

Coming back, they noticed that when this horse lowered its head it wanted to eat. They would stop and it would eat the grass. It was a strange animal but it took them home. After being away so long, the camp was still there. When they were nearing the camp, the people could see a big cloud coming and something moving in there. The people were scared, they did not know what it was. The men told the Chief at a meeting that they had seen somebody over there at the end of the land, that this man had told them to come back home as they could not cross that water. 'This man said he would tell us more when he comes back, when we fill the pipe up, we are to use this grass here, Sweetgrass, and when we pray this is how we are to do it, so that the Great Spirit will hear us.'

So this is a story that has been passed on and told many times. I know my dad told me the story many times. So part of the story was that they were given horses, but this experience of having met this stranger who talked the language and said that he was going to cross this big water, that part never left us, people continued to talk about it. It was years after, when they heard about the Bible and heard about how Jesus was born and how he was killed, that they say maybe that was Jesus that we saw because he had said that if they do not kill him that he would return to tell us more. That is the big question with Sioux people, was it really Jesus that we saw, because he said he was going to cross the big water. He did not come back, as he said they must have killed him.

So we say the world should not blame the Native people for the crucifixion of Christ. We had nothing to do with it. Leave us out of that. They have tried to blame all of us for that, but no, we did not take part in this crucifixion. So that is what the residential school taught and the other is what our people believed. I have had a lot of time to think about this. I am a traditional woman. This is how I live. I do not know how many more days I will be here, but I have lived a lot, experienced a lot, and you honour me by coming here because I have been saying that I have got to write some things about my culture, a Dakota dictionary, even though there are dictionaries around, there are some things that are missing. I do not know if I will have time to do it, but I will see.

I have a cousin and his wife who are over ninety years old here in Sioux Valley. They went to Portage residential school. They have lots to tell too, but they are just quiet, they do not want to come out, but someone has to talk about it.

Legends are in the form of animals or birds because we understand all Creation to be of one. We are divided into groups, when a man has two legs and walks, another being has four legs and walks, another being has only wings to fly, another being is used to water. We know them as humans. Even the horses and dogs out here are seen the same way. We have stories and that is part of our life. Without them we cannot say I am one, we have to include them. We also have to include the trees out there. I cannot say I am one without that tree. Everything that has life is Creation. Creation is what the Creator made and we have not seen it all and will never know it all, but being power, he made everything. That is where we say we are equal, that is why we are Anishnabek, the Dakota people, we are different from all other peoples of the world, because we were taught in a sacred way without the Bible. This is how you do it. This is what you do. When the Creator said that, he showed us through our visions. It is White people who make their own laws, we live naturally, we are a natural people.

Culture is a way of life. Every person and individual of the world has a culture. So our culture is how I live, what I believe in. The culture is how I am supposed to live. To me, the most important thing in my culture is my family. Then in my culture I have to live the way it is supposed to be, as a woman, as a mother, as a grandmother today. That is my culture. My grandmother at a very early age taught me things and it stayed in. Once you tell a child something, that is why they say, 'Listen when people are talking.' The Elders said that in a meeting yesterday. If young people want to learn about culture, they have to listen. We are not going to have classes to say this is what culture is. You just listen to people talking. Culture is every person in its own way.

The culture is respect, respect of everything that moves and has life.

And those are the lessons of life. We can talk about the black bear and what it means to us, because in my culture we say that the bear is a being with four legs and it walks and it eats and it sees. That bear is part of my culture. Even the thunder is part of my culture because I believe in those things, and I could go on and on.

The past can help us today. There has to be a big revival. To gather all the nations, even getting together in a community. Use the Elders. We have life experience and we have knowledge.

When they learn their culture and language, then they are a whole person now. Indian people who lose their culture and language, they are not Indian, they have no identity. Identity means my culture, my language, my traditional ways, that is what it is.

Traditional Birthing

There were midwives, women who helped other women at birthing time. Women had the responsibility – if I can help you at that time, I will do it. We were not chosen, we were supposed to be there for everyone. We learned by watching. It is the responsibility of the mothers to teach their daughters. I have seven daughters and I have taught them everything now that I know, so my girls are like traditional women now.

My boys, I have five of them, being a twin, and being the keeper of a Lodge, I teach my sons today, my grandsons about the Sweats. I have a Sweat Lodge down here. The biggest mistake that has happened is women going into Sweats. That is the biggest sin we can commit is to have a woman go into a Sweat. It is not our place. Women did not have Sweats. I see a lot of women today going into Sweats and that does not help. If it is a feeling of feeling good, they should go on to a sauna. That Sweat is a sacred place where only men can go. Women have another way of cleaning themselves. That is through the teachings of Elderly women, it is what you should do at that time of the month, you do not have to go in a Sweat. Our monthly periods clean us and we are whole again. We are purified when we have our monthly periods, that is the spiritual part of it. On the physical part, cleaning ourselves is using the sage. For the men, they have nothing to purify themselves, so they have to go into Sweats. We have more power, that we have power that we can kill the power of a pipe in there. When we go in there as women that have monthly periods, that is the biggest mistake Indian people are doing today, even White women are doing that. These White people do not know anything about the Sweats, but I have seen them go in.

Men were not involved in childbirth, but if a man was out on the trapping line with his family alone, he could help his wife, but no other man could do that, just the husband. That happens on the trapline or if they are travelling and there is nobody around. At that time every woman knew what to do about birthing because they all had experience and were already taught.

Traditional Self-Government

A leader was chosen as a role model, by what he did. First they would look at a man who took care of his wife and his family, they would look at a man who provides for their needs, in his family first. Outside his family, he was a person who was there for everyone that would come to him for help. He would help them out. In those days a man became a leader by his role, by what he was in his own family, because families were so important. They did everything to keep themselves from starving. There was so much food at that time, there was no such thing as begging. There was so much animal food and fish food and berry food, which was all theirs. That is how they survived and later on they had gardens.

They governed themselves the way they governed their own families. Self-government was in the form of a family, looking after his own and extending it to other families in the community.

A woman has a very important role in the family. That was to be the mother and grandmother, because women were stronger than men, they took on very difficult roles which the man could not. The man was just the provider; the woman kept the fire going, women bore babies, raised babies, and were teachers. They played a very important role in the family.

Women took part in decision-making traditionally, they were accepted. Today you hardly see any females in these First Nations organizations. Women always seem to be in the background. I guess it's all right because women have the responsibility to see what was not right, who was not right. They made decisions, being the mother of all children, which includes men. They had that very important role, which people do not seem to understand today, women have a very important role as keepers of the fire.

Treaties

I guess the Ojibwes and Crees signed treaties, but not the Dakota people.

It was mentioned last night in a self-government meeting that we did not sign any treaties. In Southern Manitoba we have four Dakota reserves and four Ojibwe reserves, which make up the Dakota-Ojibway Tribal Council. These Ojibwes have their own treaties and we do not, and yet we live adjacent to each other.

Elders

Today this word Elder has come out so much and now they are saying that a man who is in his fifties is an Elder. That is not so. Old people in age and life experience are the Elders. I have a son who is fifty and they are trying to make him an Elder. My husband and I said, 'We are still alive, how can our son become an Elder?' [Laughs.] The number of years that they have lived, they have life experience of everything. Some bad experience, some good, but they have lived a number of years and they have seen life, so that is an Elder. I do not believe in an Elder who is fifty and has not lived a life yet. I would like to mention this here, because there is confusion as to who is an Elder.

To be an Elder, you have to suffer a lot. We suffered a lot up to today. The Elders who are around seventy, eighty, ninety years old have suffered a lot. These young Elders have not seen life, they do not have the life experience. Some of us are not the way we used to be physically. If they could understand how we feel they would not want to be an Elder.

For approaching an Elder it depends on what kind of help they are asking for. Is it spiritual help, or is it healing, or do they want to visit? You have come here to visit, you wanted to ask me something. For spiritual help, like asking for a name, they would bring Tobacco. It is so important for everyone who is an Aboriginal person to have a name, an Indian name. One of our stories is how can we be recognized by the Creator if you do not have a name? Because he is a Dakota.

Role models of Elders are Elders who tell life stories in a way that teaches others. For me to be a role model, I have to tell my life story, for them to understand me. We also have to look at Elders as role models when they share with other people the things they have learned, and enjoyed. That I feel is very important, because without the role models of Elders, how can our young people survive? I survived, so I have to tell my experience of how I survived. Some of our Elders did not survive.

Some Elders today do not care, maybe because of frustrations of what residential school did to them, it has affected them so they are not taking the role of an Elder. For instance the Elders who are walking down the street staggering or those who left their wives and families, like those who spent time in jail. For these people, something went wrong, this is what happened to them, and we cannot blame them for that, because we all have that feeling of being a special person – that is when we say we are very special because I have a name that will give me life, that is my Indian name. That is what is missing with some people.

For some young people, even though they have lost the language, they still come and ask for an Indian name. It is very hard for me to say this is your name and they cannot say it. So language is so important in today's world. For myself, for Elders, we have our language, so we can talk openly and freely. It is the young people who are going through such a hard time because they do not have the language.

Epidemics

About 1918–20, we had an influenza epidemic and it killed a lot of people. Then we had a tuberculosis epidemic. There is a sanatorium in Brandon. A lot of Native people died and there were quite a number of people from up north that are buried here in our cemetery. They could not send them home, this was in the 1940s.

Traditional Games

They call it the moccasin game, that was the Dakota people's traditional game. It was mainly for men. Of course we had our traditional Powwow, which is a gathering. It was like a celebration and feasts were held, all gatherings have feasts. Moccasin games involve four squares of material and they would hide a bead under one, and the other team would try to find out where the bead was. The two teams would sit facing each other.

Other tribes had hand games of their own, children did not have toys, they would play in the bush, using their imagination. They had fun rolling down a hill, climbing up a tree, wading in water, whatever. They did not need toys and that was clean fun. Now this TV is destroying all the young people's mentality, their minds are being killed by this TV. That is why we have these gangs here. That is why it is getting so bad, gangs are being formed because of the influence of TV. We didn't have that. A girl's role in life was known before, but now she does not know. She does not see that on TV. A lot of young mothers who are teenagers do not know how to look after their children.

Traditional Roles

The role of women was taught to us at an early age. I was seven when I went to school. As soon as a child could speak and understand, they were already taught. They were already taught what they were to do when they grow up. I was told that when I grew up I was going to be a mother. I was about five years old, I heard it and that was it. It was years later that I remembered and I knew what my job was in life. It was to look after my children, which I did. I raised twelve of them. I listened to my grandmother's words.

I learned everything that a woman should know, cooking, sewing, everything, at an early age. Before I was seven I had a trunk. I had beads, ribbons, thread in there, I started learning. I did not spend that much time with my mother, I stayed with my grandmother in Portage. When I turned seven I was put in school. I lost track of my mother and my grandmother for ten years. When I came out of school after ten years I lived with my mother for seven months and then she died. I do not have many memories of my mother at all, and that happened to a lot of us. Some of the girls lost their mothers while they were at the school. Isn't that sad? But it was my grandmother who taught me everything.

Marriages were arranged traditionally. It was the parents who would choose who their daughters would marry. They would get in touch with the boy's parents. Women were quite young at marriage, fifteen or sixteen. They got married at an early age because that was their way of life. The girl was to settle down with a husband and to have a family. That was their role. It was the only role that they had.

Homosexuality

Yes, they had people who were homosexuals. They were special in the way that they seemed to have more skills than a single man or a single woman. He doesn't harm nobody, he has skills like a woman and he would also have the skills of a man. He is two persons, this is when people would say they have more power than a single person. They were treated with respect. There are some here like that today. They could be a niece or a nephew, so what, they were born that way and we cannot do anything about it.

Art

Art of the Sioux people was mostly in beading and quill work. For the men, carving was their art, not big ones, but small carvings made of forms by using a knife. Everything in art meant something. Gifted women could just lay out the design. One of my daughters has that gift, she is gifted in designs and colours. Seven girls of mine can all bead, but one is especially gifted. I have one son who is a member of the Eagle Society. He has an Indian name of the eagle.

Everyone is gifted, it is just that young people today have to find out what their gift is. Some young people are gifted with special things, and because they do not understand what it is and they do not go to an Elder for advice, they drown themselves in alcohol and drugs. Everyone is gifted. Long time ago the grandfathers and grandmothers and mothers would watch their children as they grew, to see if they were gifted in any way. When they found out what their gift was, they started preening that child for that role. That was part of child rearing, they spent a lot of time with the child. That does not happen today, children are left on their own.

In general, I do not have any children living with me anymore, they have all left. But they are like birds, they come back to the nest again. So my husband and I are the only ones here. I get up in the morning and I do not have to make a big meal anymore. I just use a little pint saucepan to cook the porridge, and the toast, and maybe tea. I take care of my husband, he is not well. I am tired but I still want to help. I have had to cancel some other things like a meeting with National Parole Board, because I am not feeling well myself. Praying, of course, is a part of life. I do that every day. I pray not only for myself, but for all the Aboriginal people. We need help from the Creator. I ask the Creator to listen to voices coming to Him asking for help.

Work is important. Elders tell us every day of our lives we have to move, we cannot lie down and sleep because when you lie down during the day, you are sick and cannot do your work. As long as we are well, we have to be up and around; and I think that is what keeps us going. As long as you can walk, you can do something. The physical part is very important.

Ceremonies

Dakota people are a very cultured people. In spite of what has happened we still maintained the basic spiritual activities that we had, like the Sweats for men, ceremonies where names are given, going to the cemetery to feed our relatives, that is a big celebration. We have about seven cemeteries here, we have the Catholic and Anglican, but we have family plots as well. We have summer feasts. We have kept that all these years. We have also kept our Powwows. The women here are noted for their costumes. All my girls dance, they have loads of costumes. All my boys, except one, dance, but he is a singer. Did you ever hear of the Elk Whistle Singers? They are my family. Gordon is my son-in-law and my grandsons are in there. They sing in big Powwows, but they are also my singers at my ceremonies.

The Sundance is giving of oneself to the Creator. It is a time for prayers, for forgiveness, for repentance, and giving of yourself to the Creator. That is basically what it is. People dance for three or four days. The Ojibwe Elders said that the Sundance belonged to the Sioux people in the beginning, that was our ceremony. The Ojibwes liked what they saw, so they took our ceremony too, but they use their own language, the ceremony was shared.

The Ojibwes and Crees say that they never had the drum, it was the Sioux people that had the drum. So we shared that drum with them. The headdress belongs to the Dakota people. A man cannot wear that war bonnet unless he has earned it. Today just anybody wears it. But that war bonnet is ours, the Sundance is ours, the drum is ours, the war bonnet is ours. A man has to earn the right to wear it. That man has to be a spiritual person, a role model. People who wear that war bonnet while drinking are not doing it right.

Burials

Long ago Dakota people put dead people on rafts, or stands. Later they were buried without a coffin. They were rolled in blankets and buried like that. Later on they used the box, the coffin. Their bodies were buried, but their spirits live on until the day the world ends, and then we will all be there. That is why it is so important to be identified with a name, there must be millions of Emilys, millions of Evas, but when he calls out Emily, we will not know who he is calling. But if you have an Indian name, he will call you by that name. So we believe that the spirits of our loved ones are here until that day, they are just gone physically, but they are still around. We will all be together one day. There is a road leading to that place and that is a sacred road of life that we travel on, and if we do what we are supposed to do we will meet our relatives in spirit.

Traditional spirituality and Christianity are related in some ways. For example, we know that we cannot kill another person, we know that we cannot steal, we just have to ask, but that is not begging, we have to honour our parents and listen to them. Native people have been saying these things without referring to the Bible. Are we always acknowledging God as our father? Or we acknowledge Him as a grandfather, and we feel close to Him in that way than just God. And that's the difference again, we are much closer to the Creator than the White people, because He has created for us to live, and we are all related, even the dog out here. After we pray, we say, 'To all my relatives' in our language, in Dakota, when we end our prayers. It also means the spirit relatives too, everything that God has made, I am addressing them too.

We have clans by name, like I have the name of a buffalo, for those who have names referring to buffalo are like a family. The Indian names are their clans. For example, eagle names are in one group. They are not born into clans, but their names will tell which clan they belong to. Also each family is a clan on its own. My own family is one clan.

Prophecies

I hears lots and lots of stories. Keep that fire burning – if you do not keep your fire burning you will be looking at another man's fire – the smoke coming out of his camp, his chimney – meaning that you have to make sure that there is enough wood to cook food for you and your family. If you do not gather that wood or bring in the meat, your family is going to starve. Keep that fire going, we all have to have fire. People have to see smoke coming out of your family, like this house.

Another story is about two brothers, they will be sitting on each side of the fire and one day these brothers are going to become in-laws because his daughter is going to marry his son, and that is what is happening now, intermarriage, and that is not good for the child. Same blood, that is not good.

I heard prophecies that told of what would happen and it is happening today, like today, there is no respect among the Native people, there is so much in-fighting, it is not supposed to be that way. Today the young generation want to become medicine men, they want to become Elders, so are fighting among each other. That was prophesied. There was a Medicine Woman, a healer, who said that one day someone would even say that, he is God's son, meaning Jesus, somebody will say that, and that is when the world will end.

The White Calf prophecy belongs to us, the Dakota. It is a sacred story, about this White Calf Woman who brought the Pipe long ago. She brought it to a camp and she told them, 'This Pipe is what you will use, this is what you will do, so that you could have a good life. But in order to use this Pipe and live a good life, you have to go to the Sweat, the men, not the women.' The woman was the carrier of that Pipe. That was the message that she brought. This is where Elderly people like myself remember that she brought the Pipe to the men, to find a spiritual way of life by going into Sweats.

We were at a Powwow when it was announced that there was a white buffalo calf born, by that we knew the fate of the Dakota people, here it is again. At the time when the White Calf Woman brought the Pipe, she brought the teaching to the men. Since then everything has been mixed up, there has not been a white buffalo calf since then. This is a reminder that something is happening. That white calf should have come just once but it came a second time because people have lost their way of life, it had to come back. It is like when Jesus will come to earth for Christians, it is the same with the white calf for us.

Life Stages

Different people go through different stages. When I was born I was a twin, but my brother died at birth, so I carry with me the responsibilities my brother would have had. I carry the burden, maybe that is why I have this Sweat Lodge, why I have a drum, that belonged to my brother, but I keep it. So since birth I carry the responsibility of my brother.

Very early I was taught to be a woman, at four years old. With that, I went to this hill and had a vision, and that is where I got my name. So I went through different stages of life myself. I have had many visions, my first vision was at four years old when I got my name. I was born an adult. I am an adult by birth. I am an Elder by birth. When they saw that I was different from the village children, the Elders came and they took me and they taught me things I was to know as a woman healer. I am supposed to be one, but that residential school of ten years took away all that. This is what happened to our people. But I have to live today in two cultures to do the work I am doing. Today I am the way you see me, but if I am going out I dress differently. So that is how we have live today.

They lived by the sun here. When the sun is up, we are supposed to be up with the sun. We knew what we had to do for that sunrise, we knew what we had to do when the sun was way up here, and what to do when it was going down. All these three stages of the sun's position have their own story that takes in the cycle of life. Early, it is just like life, we are born, and we die when the sun goes down, and this is middle ages here.

At nighttime is the stage near death. We shouldn't fear nighttime because nighttime is when the sacred beings are out. They call them ghosts. That is why children were not allowed to walk around at night. Today they walk all night, getting into trouble. Instead of staying home to rest at night, they stay up and sleep all day, as if they were sick and dying. It is sad to say but that is what is happening. There is something wrong.

Weather

There are many ways of saying what the weather is going to be like. Even when the sun comes up, it's going to be windy when that sun comes up so red. It is going to be windy tomorrow because that sun going down is just red. It is going to be a storm if the wind is from the east. When the sun is far south, we know it is going to be very dry, we have to do what we have to do before it gets too hot. We always have to prepare for these seasons. That is one of the things we have lost today. We do not even care if it rains or it snows, we take it for granted. Our people had reasons on what they had to do, because it could mean life or death. You are supposed to plant your corn on time so your children will have something to eat in the Winter. Now we do not do that.

Language and Culture

How can young people learn when they do not have their language? I know in this Sweat that I have here, I have had a Native person come in there who did not have his language, so he must have prayed in English, that is not the language he was to use, he should have used his mother's language. Language is so important. When an Elder speaks, he talks his language. How can the young people understand what he is saying? How can young people find spirituality in the form of a ceremony if an Elder prays in his language, and if they do not know the language? They are not hearing anything. It is going to be a challenge for young people because they need to learn the language. They have to try to gain what they have lost, and that's the language. Without the language we have lost everything. You have no identity, you are an Indian, but what tribe if you do not have that language.

Places had Sioux names, they described the place. Just the Elders know them now, but not the young people. English names are used, but a few, like Waskago, are in the Dakota language, meaning white snow, wise snow. Young people should try to learn the Indian names of places.

Traditional Foods

Traditional foods was deer, muskrat, ducks, wild rabbits, after the buffalo was gone. About one hundred years ago all the buffalo were killed off. I never saw wild buffalo, but I have seen them fenced in. So it has been a hundred years now, without buffalo. That is when these other animals came in, like muskrats. There are not too many fish because you see the Assiniboine River, it's just a small river, there is not too much fish in there. We dried food to preserve it. We got berries, saskatoons, choke cherries, cranberries, pinch cherries, and all that. We had them here. They were dried, too, even the meat, pemmican.

Transportation

Traditional transportation was mainly walking. Then the horses came, there were more and more horses. Before that they used dogs sometimes, but there were not many. It was mostly horses leading when people moved around. Modern transportation can be good and it can be bad. It all depends on how you use it. Some people fly to Powwows, so that is good. With cars, sometimes we get overweight because we do not get exercise, especially with diabetes we need to walk.

Relations with First Nations

I know the Dakota people were fierce people and they didn't get along with the Ojibwes and the Crees. They were always enemies attacking each other. Even that exists today yet. You know, I know we see it. It is what we were discussing yesterday, too. They made Chiefs, but the descendants of those Chiefs that made peace, these young people today who are the leaders don't take too much of the Dakota people.

Dreams

Dreams were the only way of communicating with other beings, even to know what to do. Elders at that time had dreams and they were instructed to do what they were supposed to do. That is where these dreams and visions came in. They gave them direction on what to do and how to do it. Dreams could be interpreted by Elders. This is where experience comes in. If they have life experience, they are much aware of the spiritual life of the people. So when dreams come, they are able to interpret what that dream is saying to that person. Because nothing is even written down like that. Sometimes young people want to know everything all at once, but it takes a lifetime to know these traditions, culture, or a certain ceremony they have to do, it takes a long time to understand.

Traditional Medicines

There is not as much traditional medicine around. The Elders took them with them, because nobody asked for them. People were learning of the English culture and they forgot to ask. Very few people know about it. There are very few medicines, too, a lot has been lost. Certain people were born with the knowledge and gift for healing. Nobody can be a medicine man today unless they are directed from the traditional Indian way. That is what the confusion is about today. We have so many young people who are doing Sweats, and they do so many and then they say, 'I am a medicine man now.' They do not know that it takes a lifetime, a lot of suffering to become one. They have been appointed right from birth. There are very few left, like in Sioux Valley we had those people but they are all gone now, so what has happened is young people are saying, 'I want to be a medicine man.' So they go into the Sweat, but that is not the way it is done.

Living off the Land

There is nothing that can be done for people to say I live off the land in this area. There are lots of farms here, no one can trap and hunt for livelihood, so we are in a tight spot here. There is nothing much left. We cannot live off the land anymore. The generation today has lost their culture, so they are suffering. You see them in jails, they are people without a culture, they have nothing. They get into alcohol and drugs, they end up in penitentiaries. They are lost. A lot of them have come from broken homes, gone through foster care, so they have nothing. Those raised by White foster parents have lost everything.

Residential Schools

My generation did not lose the language, even though we were punished for speaking it. We still kept it. What I find today is lot of my grandchildren are not full-blooded Sioux, they are Ojibwe, Cree, or Métis. It is hard to teach grandchildren if they are Cree or Ojibwe, because they have to know the culture of two tribes. In those ten years of residential school, I lost ten years of teachings, but I did not lose parenting skills that my grandmother taught me. I had that, but today, if we had not taught the daughters the parenting skills, those grandchildren would have nothing. We should teach our children the things they need to know. Now my daughters are teaching their daughters, so I am happy that my family are aware that they have to have their culture and traditional ways, and they have good jobs too. They went to school from home, it was better for them, they did not lose anything.

We have to heal ourselves by talking about it, the residential schools. We cannot keep it within ourselves because we have done that for so many years. To heal ourselves we have to let it out, tell about it. But we are beginning to tell about life in residential school. To heal the hurts, we have to go to our traditional ways to be healed. This is where I find in ceremonies here, young girls who have been raped or suffered incest have come here. This is the first step of healing, there is nothing shameful when that happens. We have to let people know you were hurt in that way.

So it is a time for healing. We can talk about residential school and cry about it. Yes, we have suffered from residential school, but we are survivors. I heal myself by talking about it, and in my own way, I forgive those teachers who did wrong. You also know that you are not alone, there are others who were hurt. Some were only three years old when they were taken into residential school and they were there for a long time until they were eighteen years old. By returning to culture, it helps people heal.

Warrior Societies

Warriors are men who are there to protect, to look after people. In ceremonies we had men who looked after things on the outside where the ceremony was taking place. For example, if a group of people were camped somewhere, young men were chosen to look after the place. It was the men who protected and took care of people, they are protectors. They were not there to fight, but if they had to they would fight, but they were there mainly to protect the people.

Traditional Justice

People were shamed in public, in front of the whole village. They would say, 'This man did this and he is not a man if he is going to give a good licking to his wife, or if he steals. He is not a man if he lets his wife bring in the wood.' That was justice, that was something done in families. But if it came to crimes like murder, this man would be released from the camp, he had to go away. If his family wished, they could go with him, and that was the punishment they gave. He was never to come back, until such time that it was decided that he can come back and that is how a killer was punished.

I think that traditional forms of justice would work today. For example, young people from up North who were sniffing and were sent to a Healing Lodge in Alberta, Poundmaker, those were children who need the Indian way of counselling. These young people need spiritual counselling, they need to have an Elder to pray for them, that is what they need. Because that healing takes quite a long time to get, that child healed, to get to the bottom of why they are sniffing, there are deeper reasons for their behaviour. We have to look after our own. Taking care of our own, that is what we say because we understand, we know what they need.

What I have seen is men just sitting in jails. They should be out. This is where a council of Elders could be there to talk to them. Because whatever they have done, they have families, whatever he has done, he was angry. To get even with his parents or something, he did this, he has to understand why he did it. I would feel justified to know that we can help them. They spend so many years in jail, they come out and they go back in again, it does not help them. We had nothing to do with them when they come out. We should be given a chance to look after our own inmates when they come out, to make sure they get the traditional teachings and spiritual guidance, which involves ceremonial gatherings where the Pipe and Sweetgrass are used. This will help this person. To release his anger, we have to talk to him in a nice way. That is what I believe, what inmates need is guidance from Elders.

The Pipe is a connection between people and the Creator. The smoke is the connection. It is like taking the Bible to the altar, that Pipe has an altar too. Sweetgrass is used for purification. Catholics burn incense and use holy water, they have a reason for using that. It is the same with us, we have a reason to use Sweetgrass and our medicines, which are holy water. Sage is women's medicine for cleaning themselves after each month. You can burn it in the house to purify the house.

Non-Native People

White people like what we have. A lot of them come to ceremonies even though they do not know what they mean, but they are doing it. If they wish to learn, if they like what we have, why not share it with them? As long as we qualified people I would like to see our own people working for us, but first we want them to have their education. Education is important for Native people because we are living in a White man's world now. Whatever a young person does with education, they should reinforce their education by following their cultural values and traditional ways to help them. They should know who they are, by the names they have.

Some Thoughts for Young People

If they read what you are writing this is the teachings, this is some of the teachings that we want them to read about. A lot of people think they can't take it, the teachings, because they have nothing, so they take to drugs and alcohol and commit suicide, because they know they do not belong anywhere.

WILF TOOTOOSIS (Saulteau)

Poundmaker First Nation, Saskatchewan

'It is there, it never left us. We left it, it never stopped, but we left it. And this was one of the predictions, that our traditions will come back someday.'

Wilf Tootoosis was born on 14 April 1930 at Poundmaker First Nation in western Saskatchewan. Emily Faries originally called for John Tootoosis, but they replied, 'Not on this earth.' She interviewed Wilf Tootoosis in the summer of 1994 and spent three days in the community. The weather was mild, and most of the interview took place outside.

Wilf Tootoosis has six children and eighteen grandchildren. He has written *The Cree Life of Allen Sapp* and *The History of the 1885 Rebellion in Duck Lake*. He worked ten years for the Saskatchewan Transportation Company and four years for the Saskatchewan tourist industry, among many other jobs detailed in his life history.

Wilf Tootoosis' incredible sense of humour can be appreciated in his life history. But he weaves his humour through complex stories and traumatic events. He has many important things to say. In this interview he provides valuable teachings and shares many Plains Cree traditions with the readers.

Life History

I was born on Poundmaker reserve. My grandfather had a ranch, two ranches on the reserve here, and everything disappeared during the thirties because of drought; horses, sheep, all the fowl used to be around. It was very tough for all of us. I was born in 1930, April 14th. I was born premature. I think I was born two months early. My grandfather held me on his hand and you can still feel his fingers about my head, here. I had a deformed head, he just pushed it down with his hands soon after I was born, it sharpened up. When I was an adolescent, kids used to call me pointed head. I get a kick out of that now. That's one of the things that always comes to mind before entering a stage or Powwow. We always called each other nicknames. I'd get over to the microphone and I'd often wonder who would be next to come and call me that. My granddad, his name was John Tootoosis, too. John B. Tootoosis the first and I was raised with the grandmother, and then I must've been five and my other, maternal grandfather came after me from Thunderchild. That's where my mother was from, Susan Angus, and my other grandfather was also a Band Councillor, he was one of the first Band Councillors from Thunderchild. That was soon after they moved. Their reservations were here in Delmoss, about fifteen miles from here, and they traded, they moved up north. So I spent a lot of time in north country.

One thing I didn't like up north was going on the water. I got sick. I don't know if that's what they call seasickness or what it is. Because he [grandfather] always insisted that if something happened we were going to swim, and I couldn't swim. I got sick. He wanted me to go with him, get his nets, get the fish in his nets. And I hated to turn him down and I got sick in the middle of Turtle Lake. I don't know if that's what they call seasickness. I don't know, it was something quite wrong with my stomach. I didn't throw up or nothing at all, but I just kept staring at the boat. He'd keep asking me why I kept looking down. I'd say, 'Oh, it's those little fishes.' I'd lie, I didn't want him to know I'd got sick and I thought maybe I'd get over it.

And travelling through the wagon trails in the bush, I didn't see anything but sky. I guess when you're a Plains Indian you stay in the plains. I still get that way. I don't feel comfortable in a closed-in area, in the pine trees, spruce trees. I am used to being able to see far. I was talking to one of the teachers yesterday, he came to visit me, interested in Indian art. He told me he'd get that way too. I guess that depends on where you were raised. It must be, but once you hit the open and drive along the lake, I'm okay. I was invited to a youth workshop in Turtle Lake. It's about four hundred miles north – miles and miles of nothing to see but the sky and trees. I become irritable but outside of that, I like going up north. I do enjoy it. I really love it up there. I spent a lot of time in Thunderchild, in fact I went to day school there for a couple of years. A woman there with an English accent was a schoolteacher in a log house. It was like a one-room school.

A few of them are still alive that I went to school with in Thunderchild as a young kid. My granddad had a bunch of cattle there, too. We'd go up north to Turtle Lake there hunting, during hunting season we lived in Turtle Lake till the snow came, then we would come home. We always had a couple, two, three milk cows, we had our own cream, made our own, my grandma made her own milk.

And my grandmother was a translator. At her age she was the only one who spoke English. Her dad was a Chief down by here, there used to be another reserve and she was one of the first students at a school in Battleford, in one of the first schools. She was one of them in there, that's how come she spoke English. Any kid that ran away from the school would get their braids cut off and head shaved. I used to laugh when she told me that, she'd look funny without her hair on her, always had long braids. I asked her what she did when she was a kid and how come she spoke English and how to speak Saulteau. My father was Saulteau, my mother was Saulteau. I spoke a little and understood Saulteau, I still do. If I stayed with Saulteau people, I'd pick it up again. They spoke Saulteau to me, as well as Cree and English.

Residential School

I believe I went there when I was nine years old, 1939, residential school in Delmoss. That was a rough place, rough, tough experiences of my life, as a child and an adolescent, coming in there. My dad kept coming there and complaining about the children's handling in schools. Kids were coming out of there after four or five years, not being able to read, speak English. The nuns spoke French. We spoke Cree. The only time they spoke English was when they spoke to us. A lot of kids didn't understand a word. Teachers had a French accent. I can hear it from anybody that comes in here, and they say a few words in English, I'll know he's been in a residential school, from Catholic or the Anglican, two different accents in English.

The ones that went to Catholic, they all have accents in French. I really get a kick out of them, they don't seem to notice. Instead of 'there,' they say 'dere.' 'Yah, I gotta be dere.' I spoke that way too. Oh, goodness, when I left Saskatchewan in 1948, I moved out of Saskatchewan when I was sixteen, I was on my own since I was fourteen, I worked around, where I could get away from my mother. I could have been out working when I was fourteen, quite easily doing chores on the farm, but she didn't want me to leave. I always kept in mind, 'One of these days, if I could get away from my old man, I am gone!' So I left Saskatchewan in 1948, I couldn't cross the border before that, you had to be eighteen to cross, or you had to have a note from your parents. So that's how I got away, mingling and mixing up with the American Indians, they even picked up on my accent. They, too, tried to correct me. 'Don't say "I," say "Ah." When somebody talks to me, say "Ah."' I don't know where I picked that up, I believe it's an English accent.

I had quite a rough experience in school. I'd get picked on. The nuns and the priests spoke against my dad's movement, everywhere, in church, in the classroom. And when somebody did something wrong they ganged up and blamed me for it. Anybody would smash up a window, I'd get blamed for it and then I would go and get strapped, for things I didn't do. They could have had my dad shot if they had a chance to. I had rough experiences, I was sent upstairs to put on a nightgown, they put me on a stage, and put that nightgown over my head, and stripped me naked. Right on the stage. I always say that this is where I started my stage work in acting. Yes, naked, and got strapped ten times on the rear end. A lot of times for things I didn't do.

I only know one kid who went through that. It's another man, much older than I am, he's still alive, a very quiet person, very quiet. He left Saskatchewan here some time in the fifties, he never came back to Thunderchild. I attended two of his brothers' funerals, he wasn't there. He came for his mother's funeral and went right back again. I wanted to interview the man. I watched him get a hundred lashes from the Catholic priest, naked on a bed. I was wondering if he wanted to talk about it, to have it publicized. He's in Alberta somewhere, somewhere in Alberta, I keep asking about him. I want to talk to him and do research also about residential schools, to find out stories by interviewing a few of them, doing the research.

I got there when I was nine years old, 1939. I left when I was fourteen. I couldn't read or write. I could read a newspaper to know what it was talking about, but I couldn't pronounce all the words. I'd always have a pocket dictionary, I still do. I still do. I have about five different dictionaries. Yeah, five of them, one I paid $85.00 for it, and this is where I picked it up. How many things, wrong things across the U.S. border? I hear it every day in Canada. The hitchhiking, and I did a lot of hitchhiking, I saved my money and sent some home. And I'd always have a pocket dictionary with me. I only have about a grade-two education, grade-two level. I just taught myself.

I have done a lot of travelling all my life. This is between here, Poundmaker, Thunderchild, and sometimes my granddad would come down with the caboose – this is a little trailer on a sleigh – and go back up north, sit there a while. Back in the forties when they were setting up the World War, some of my uncles were in Germany, 1942, 1943, somewhere in there. I travelled with my parents from Poundmaker, travelled all the way up north to every reserve, organizing conferences. By horse. I didn't see anyone travel by car. And sometimes a circle of tents, a hundred, seventy-five, eighty tents around where they'd have conferences, Treaty Six conferences, all the way up to Cold Lake, Alberta and Lake Chippewyan. They got together to talk about different things, education was one of them. They wanted better education, they wanted to have their own education and better conditions on Indian communities.

I liked travelling, I still do. In 1948, I left on a two-week pass from my dad, which I stretched for two and a half years before I came back. But I didn't want to leave. They came here on Poundmaker asking who wanted to go to work in the sugar bush. I finally persuaded my dad to let me go. Sugar bush work was in Montana. He [my dad] would get up sometimes four or five o'clock in the morning, writing letters to Chiefs, every day. I'd ask him the day before, he wouldn't answer. I woke up, he was still writing, four-thirty in the morning. I was living in a log house. I asked him again, 'Can I go to work? I'll be back for haying season in July.' I had to have his signature on that paper, please, so finally, he looked angry, signed a signature. I said, 'Okay, I'll be back in two weeks, three weeks.' Which I didn't. Two months went by, I never came back. I had good jobs, that's why I didn't want to come back.

I had seniority in the sugar factory. I didn't like sugaring work. I hated garden work. So I worked in a sugar factory and they wanted to ship me out. I was underweight, under age, they didn't believe I was eighteen. I weighed 135 pounds. I said, 'Give me a chance, put me to work, give me a chance. I can't pull it, okay, ship me out.' So they did, they put me on for one month. Put me on a tough place. I worked in a vibrator and it's all paper bags, it's that peeling, sugar beet peeling. They feed sheep and cattle with that, mixed with molasses. We had to wear masks and had to fold the paper bag just smoothly so it would go through the next man with the sewing machine. Everything done by hand. A pipe would come down, and this man would guess, it was about 150 pounds, and he would guess, then bring it down to me.

Then there were other guys that had dollies and they'd push them to the boxcars. And there would be two guys in the boxcars stashing those. A lot of people worked in there. This was my job and it was tough. I had a lot of help, the man next to me was Joe Standingrock from Rockyboy, Montana. He'd stand next to a man with grey hair, oh, he was cranky. Just a little kink in there and he would kick the bag over. Oh, boy, that pile, it was shovelled by hand, and I would go by coffee break. I'd get the place clean and when the supervisor came down he would be satisfied. I didn't complain, I didn't complain about this old man. And there was nothing I could do, he had more seniority than me. I didn't want to complain, he was ready to retire anytime. So finally time came up on the bus, foreman came up, and said, 'Supervisor coming to see you tomorrow. What do you want to do?' 'I want to stay,' I said. 'I'm not going to leave Montana, I'm going to stay, to heck with a ticket, I don't want it. I'll go work on the ranch. If they don't want me here, I'll go find me another job. I'll go work on a ranch.'

He said, 'I'd like to keep you, but it's up to him. You are doing okay, it's just that you are underweight.' 'I'm not underweight! I'll bet you five bucks, I'll lift this fifty pounds with my teeth.' 'Hey, don't do that. You can't do it.' 'Here's five bucks, throw yours on the floor.' Took five dollars, a lot of silver dollars back then. I threw silver on the floor, and then picked it up with my teeth. He said, 'I don't know how you do it.' I said, 'It's no problem, I'll pick up a hundred pounds with my teeth.' Throw another five. 'Okay, here's another five.' But there's a trick to it. If I bend down, I can't lift it, there's a trick to it. You bite that thing real hard and then put one foot forward, kind of slide it up and once it reach your chest, straighten out. There's a trick to it. An old man showed me how. Boy, oh boy, he just shook his head and walked away.

I didn't finish my coffee and sandwich when the supervisor came up. He said, 'You can lift fifty pounds with your teeth?' I said, 'No problem, five bucks, I'll do it.' I made another ten bucks. Ten bucks was big money back then, I was eating in a restaurant, it was 85 cents for a full-course meal. A glass of beer was ten cents. And I was under age to drink beer, I was always on the Mexican side, dressed like a Mexican. And here they were yapping away in Spanish. When they laughed, I laughed too. I didn't understand a doggone word. But that fooled them, fooled the bartender there and the cops too. They thought I was a Mexican. So I stayed right through. He said, 'That's good, because everybody wants to leave and we're gonna be done maybe a week before Christmas.' We shut her down. He says, 'No, right through.' We'd scrub floors. 'That's it, we got to clean up everything. Health Department are coming in.' I said, 'Okay,' and I stayed right up to the end, nine guys left. I lived on UIC for a while and worked in restaurants, five dollars a day, washing dishes. Oh, boy, big money.

Then this old couple sent for me and I went to Rockyboy with old Joe, Joe Standingrock, and worked with him, adopted by the family. They kept telling me our great-great-grandfather came from Canada. Little Bear. I didn't know who Little Bear was. It was years after I found out it was Big Bear's son, Eyemesees. I've done most of his story, that's when he took off, took off to the U.S. border, and Big Bear got arrested. Followed us to Frog Lake and on to Montana. Oh, I moved back and forth. When the Korean War broke out, a whole bunch of my buddies joined the American army. They had to join or get drafted and up to this day I've never asked anyone. I'm pretty sure some of them played Canadian. You're a Canadian, they don't draft you. At least they weren't supposed to but they tried, they tried. I joined up, I joined up when my friends joined up. For two years I was rejected because I was considered alien. I said, 'I'm not alien, those are the stomping grounds of my forefathers.'

My great-grandfather and my grandfather, maternal grandfather, my mom's parents, her dad came from Montana. They had the opportunity to stay in the States if they wanted to. My granddad wanted to stay, my great-grandfather said, 'No, when I die I wanted to be buried in North country.' He said, 'My father is buried in Duck Lake, he was shot in the 1885 Rebellion.' So my grandfather told me that in those days we didn't argue with Elders. We moved, we moved and that's it. So I left all my friends and came to Canada. And I have a lot of relatives in South Dakota, North Dakota, and Montana, on the Poundmaker side. You see, Poundmaker's father was a Sioux Indian, Assiniboine. Back then they only went by Sioux, by the name of Skunkskin. So when they hear my name, their Nepowwow Rodeo gathering maybe, they come find me. 'So Tootoosis, we heard your name over the mike.' I say, 'Yeah, that's who I am.' 'Who's your dad? And who's your granddad? And who's your great-granddad? My forefathers used to tell me who my relatives were. Someday maybe they'll come looking for you and find you somewhere.' So, wind up shaking hands and we're brothers, it's my great-great-grandfather, too, they knew. So a lot of relatives are around there. A lot of them have a little

Powwow, some in Morley, Alberta, who made it. They go by the name Tooyoungman, they're from the Poundmaker family, the Sioux.

Poundmaker was under Red Pheasant, south of Battleford, and as a young man he was adopted by Chief Crowfoot. A lot of White people convinced me that a lot of our people are part Blackfoot, Chief Crowfoot's son. No, that's not his son. The information I received is that he never had any sons. But he had a lot of adopted children, it is a Native tradition. When you don't have kids, you raise somebody else's, which is still practised up to this day. Now I don't really know, I don't have any evidence, whether they had children or not. But when he saw Poundmaker as a young kid, a young man, I don't know how old he was, he just lost a son that looked just like that boy over there, what's his name. He said, 'I'd like to adopt him.' And Chief Poundmaker was raised by his grandma and my granddad, too. They were raised by their grandmother. So the messenger went to the grandmother at Chief Crowfoot Lake to adopt her grandson. She was very happy, quite agreeable to it. So he was adopted by Chief Crowfoot. That would be somewhere before 1885.

I don't believe Poundmaker took part in the Cutknife Massacre. I never heard his name at Cutknife Massacre. He may have been a young man by then, that happened somewhere in 1860 or 1865. They had rifles, they had binoculars or telescope, the one you stretch out, metal or bronze, whatever it was. When Cutknife was first noticed he had one on top the hill over there, he had a telescope, looking around for the camp. And when one of the scouts approached, two scouts approached, he never noticed. He had a telescope looking around.

This morning looked real beautiful. But I was too tired, after dancing around for three days to get up. You get up on top the hill before four-thirty in the morning. There's fog all around, all around the Cutknife Creek, it stays there, looks like a silver ribbon. And out there by the lake, Adams Lake, summer resorts over there, fog. So that time of the morning, he had to be looking for smoke going straight up from the camps. He had a telescope with him.

Cutknife was a Sarcee, a famous warrior, very popular with the Sioux, Blackfoot, and outsmarted other tribes, stealing horses. Not stealing, I don't like that word, use what RCMP used, confiscating. RCMP take something from Indian it's confiscating. When Indian takes it, it's stealing. I joke a lot with RCMP. I worked in court, I had a lot of fun with them. Sometimes, they won't appreciate my jokes, they won't laugh. They sure don't see things the same way. But after three, four years, we get along fine. I do the same to judges, many times at coffee breaks, they'd say, 'No, no, don't call me Your Honour, Wilf, I'm Joe or I'm Lloyd.'

So he [Cutknife] came on foot and that's where he must have seen that hill, two high hills here, high points, cutting that hill there. I'm still trying to find what it was called before they called it Cutknife Hill. Before they called it Cutknife Lookout and Little Pine Reserve is Blue Hill. White people called it Blue Hill, before that name, Indians called it After the Buttocks of Elk, because the white part of the elk and white-tailed deer. Sometimes they still come up there. It looks like the back.

Waskachoos, that's the original name of the hill. So he may have gone down there first, I'm not sure, then he came here, looking for the camps, he knew this, one of the oldest, I often wondered why Chief Poundmaker selected this place. He didn't agree to stay at Red Pheasant and his followers were willing to come with him if he took another reserve. He needed twenty families, twenty families of the Aboriginal Band members of the reserve. So he decided with Indian Affairs and took this. So Cutknife noticed that this was camping area, between here and the Battleford and Battleroad we called in Cree. That's where it ends, the Saskatchewan River. That's one of the things I haven't done yet I wanted to do, is make an Indian map and tell the history.

We know Battleford as *Sagatowash* and today a lot of Indians don't know Battleford as *Sagatowash* and today a lot of Indians don't know, young people, don't know what that means [*Doeseebee sagatowick*]. It enters Saskatchewan River, Battleriver Delta. Got its name from way back. When Chiefs, when the Sarcee, Cutknife, found out the original name was Brokenknife but the White people changed it to Cutknife, named the town after it. It's Brokenknife. He was out there, sitting there with this telescope, was spotted. You see, every morning scouts went around on horseback, way before sunrise, looking for intruders, game buffalo, whatever. Early in the morning, they noticed some tracks, people walking, so they went up that hill and just below they hill they saw some smoke where they were barbecuing meat. And here was this man lying down with his telescope looking around.

So one of the scouts told his partner, said, 'You wait here, I'm gonna go. I'm going to ask his name, if he moves, we'll kill him. In case, just in case, if he beats me to it, if he's quicker than I am on a draw, head for the camp. Go tell them, there are intruders up here at this high point, this hill.' Says, 'Okay, he'll go. I'll be ready to shoot too.' So they sneaked up to him lying down, pulled the trigger. 'Who are you?' Cutknife rolled down the hill. He fired and he missed it. So this misfired. 'Head for the camp. Go tell them there's intruders here, I'll keep him around here. Go and circle, on foot, there's no horses down below.' So the other guy heads for the forest, to a camp, there's the Saskatchewan River up there, springs and cold water comes, even now, July. The water comes right out, the cleanest water in the country. Oh, it's ice cold. Oh boy, oh boy, it's beautiful. There's a camp around there, at that time. So this other scout heads out, the one that stayed kept riding around in circles, hollering at these warriors. He didn't know who they were.

'This way, this way, come this way, follow me, the kids are over here, the children are over here.' This is the way they spoke to each other. The children are over here. They didn't say men, they didn't call themselves men, *Odeh, odeh, je ge washishuk*. And they always have intruders from other tribes, they had translators that understand Cree. How this came about is, most of the tribes that I know didn't kill children or women. When there was anybody killed, if there were any children up there in the camp, they didn't leave them, and they didn't dare take them back, they'd likely get shot. They just picked them up and raised them and use them as translators. Because they would've already known how to speak their language. They learned both languages.

A lot of times they had a woman here, Blackfoot, Sioux, other language. So they kept running after this man on horseback. Oh maybe, a couple of miles from Cutknife Hill. The people came on horseback, some on foot, knives and whatever they had. When these intruders from Brokenknife saw them coming down the hill there, they start making what they call potholes into the ground. They knew they were going to be surrounded, too late to run. They were coming on horseback. So while they were digging, before the Cree people arrived, one sneaked away and went under overhanging willows, hid under there. I can't remember the name of this plant, it stands about three feet high, it's got a hole in between. In Cree we call it *Ooskadash*. Sometimes we hear it at night, it's got a hole in it, I don't know, when the wind or the breeze hits it, it whistles.

He took one of those, cut it and stayed under water, he was breathing through this. This is the story I heard. When everything was quiet, in the middle of the night some time, he took a run and headed home to tell his people there was a massacre, and everybody got killed. When these people were coming down, running down that hill, they knew that these intruders were surrounded. They saw someone going around on horseback. They'd go up on a hill, turn a horse real fast in circles, that means they'd spot an enemy. This man was up on a hill and spin a horse, fast circles, and run downhill with his horse again. When they saw that, they came running. And one woman was in the running, a young woman. I think she had one child, came crying, crying and saying, 'This is the man they heard was Cutknife, Brokenknife, this was the man who killed my husband. Any man who kills Cutknife can have me for a wife. I want to wipe my tears with his scalp.' So the message went right back to these people. These intruders, digging holes, stay under there. Their intention was, I'm pretty sure, to sneak out at night. And Cutknife was good at it. Oh, I don't know how, but he sneaked away, never got caught. He was a good man. But this time he was surrounded in the daylight. So the message went to the warriors, anybody who kills Cutknife, cut his hair and give it to the woman, they knew that woman was single. Only had one child.

So the orders they received for the warriors was to jump him in daylight. Dark, he'll be gone, he's a hard man to catch. You might catch his men, but once it gets dark, he's gone, so we're gonna jump in those holes, which they did. So this one warrior, who maybe got his second or third wife through killing, he had one of the fastest horses, took off, heading for those potholes, and firing their guns. He jumped off his horse and went for Cutknife, a big tall man, had his knife and they were wrestling. Some young punk from the back cut his scalp and took off with it. This young punk never had taken part in the tribe or the skirmish of battle, took it to this woman. So that's where he [Cutknife] was massacred, the bones are buried there somewhere in that area. I haven't bothered to look for them. The Elders told me about it, and I think I can find the bones. Very likely, just south of here. Not too long ago they found dinosaur bones in South Dakota. There's an area there where they found lots of dinosaur bones. So the bones are likely there, still preserved likely, but they usually take knives. Other objects would likely still be buried in there. Since then, anywhere around 1865, this area been known as Cutknife territory, it was named after some settlers came in and named it. They named it Cutknife, but later found out the real name was Brokenknife, it's the correct translation.

When I came home from college I was appointed to the Saskatchewan Tourist Association, the Board of Directors. After three months, I was appointed to the Advisory Board. So I went to work and people both Indian and White came to me, to correct the name. I said no. Leave it that way. And Chief Poundmaker is not the right translation. I said, leave it that way.

I prefer to keep it that way for spiritual reasons. So we were informed not to name Elders after they're gone. Just say so and so's father, so and so's great-grandfather. But they used the name, and abused it, a lot of artists. I wish they'd stop them. I hear of a painting of who's supposed to be Chief Poundmaker and it's not him.

An Indian artist, doing the work, same with Big Bear, they are both buried here. That is the argument that Indian people are having now. One Elder before he died, took me to Little Pine and said, 'This is where Chief Big Bear is buried.' And a clergy, an Indian clergy, Reverend Adam Cunningham, came to me after I finished my prayer, before you do the final announcing, and he said, 'I want to show you something.' I said, 'Okay.' So he did his final prayers, he said, 'You got time?' I said, 'Yeah, continue to call the drums now.' Prayer songs for the drums. So I call my brothers over to sing. I went to him, I said, 'What is it, Reverend?' Keywhwahoma said, 'Let's go over here, Chief Big Bear's grave.' 'Yes, I heard that before, an Elder from Poundmaker told me.' A lot of people say he's buried on Poundmaker reserve. I knew Big Bear came to Little Pine then. And so did his son, according to records. His son, Horsechild, that was his son, that was the youngest son he had. When Horsechild married he moved to Poundmaker under the name of Timmy Jobimmee. They say a lot of people in the 1800s, 1905, way back, didn't use their grandfather's name, or great-grandfather's name. They changed it, because a lot of times the clergy, Indian Affairs, mistreated those that were involved in the rebellion. They were punished, see, this is why Big Bear has no reserve, he's accepted treaty, but he has no reserve in Saskatchewan. Lucky Man, same thing. Lucky Man got a reserve, what is it, about four or five years ago, they moved in. He took part in the 1885 rebellion.

They weren't treated right. The families were also mistreated, and those families that were dedicated to the Indian way, Indian Spiritual ways, the traditional way. Ooh, you go to church more times, you have a better degree than grade five, grade two, because Indian Affairs and the Catholic Church and Anglican Church administered Indian education until 1948. Then Indian Affairs took over after a whole bunch of Chiefs went to Ottawa. My late dad was one of them, Andrew Paul and a whole bunch of buddies went with him. Andrew Paul, Jimmy Gladstone. I used to know them all. They raised heck with the churches, the way they handled Indian education and gradually changes started taking place. Day schools were back on, some of them were log houses, but at least the kids were staying home now.

A lot of changes took place. That was in 1948. We have a lot of graveyards around here. Oh, way back, way back, this is one of the things I plan to do, it's a difficult task but I'm going to do it one of these days. Right by the graveyard there's a location you could see the little mark about the, maybe smaller than this room here, council chambers, maybe smaller, that was the first day school here in Poundmaker. Just one room and one teacher lived here. My dad went there, one of the first, smallest boy that went there. And the same thing has happened today. Today, I work with the young offenders. I guess it's the same thing, it's always been that way. One time, the biggest boy, old Bill Weany, tired of school, nice day out, go play, go down the creek and swim. He told the boys, 'Come on,' then I said, 'Let's go, everybody run out in different directions. He may catch on, we'll go down the river and swim, it's too hot to stay in the room.' So after recess they went back in and sat, and then he hollered, '*Egwah.*' They all jumped out, one of them got caught and they went swimming.

Yeah, my dad attended that and then he went to residential school. My mother's dad, Joe Angus, he was in residential for about a year and didn't attend any classes at all. He'd work in the barn, in the field, labour. But he had a farm, he always had cattle. He didn't know how to speak English, couldn't read, and my great-grandfather didn't like that. They moved to Saskatchewan about 1905 when the Indian Affairs asked where they wanted to stay, south of the U.S. border or north. They had a choice. What do you want to be, an American or a Canadian? He chose Canada, because his dad is buried in Duck Lake, killed in 1885. And his grandfather is likely buried in Northern Quebec, Wapiska.

Very likely, yes, yes, his granddad is buried over there. That's something I have to work on and find out. He was a high official. That I have to find out yet. I often wondered why they gave my uncle the name Angus. Louie Angus, you see they accepted treaty in Duck Lake and then he moved away from there. And he was, cutting a long story short here, I gotta do more research on it. Always lived with the Métis in Montana, Métis, like when he lived in Montana, he lived with the Sanrines family, always with those families. They're still there, they're still in Thunderchild. LaFramboise are still down in Montana and there's some in Saskatchewan, I heard there's some in Calgary. Iooskun was the old man.

A lot of places are named after what happened there. Incidents that occurred and Indians called it. There's one place where it may have happened, a battle. There's one I've been wanting to go to, Indian people still living there today who know that area. I want to see it. I want to see it. It would be a real good historic site. For tourism and so on, creating a town for Native people. *Gun-ee-tung-ga-keesh-go-ba-toh.* In English, a sudden, it would be something they weren't prepared for, never noticed, a sudden attack. In spite of that, they didn't fight. Back then when there was such an incident, I declare that happened, they didn't fight, they shook hands. It's a high-point hill and they came, the Blackfoot from the south side and the Crees from the north. And they wanted some of that hill. They wanted to go up and see, to look around.

It was a lookout. So they went up that hill with their horses, and it was almost the same. Some of their horses fell down, right back down again. Went down. And the regulations there that they practised, if they wanted to use Indian law, they'd tie their horses, leave their weapons behind, and walk up that hill and shake hands. They didn't fight. Any incident that ever happened, they noticed each other, this is what they'd do. So they took off their weapons, tied their horses, and walked up the hill, and about the same time Blackfoot people came up too, all shook hands, smiling. They outsmarted out each other. Something that very seldom happened. Same times. 'Cause a lot of times they'd get a mission, intruders come in. At that particular time the head Chief, head warriors from both tribes, didn't notice a thing. They'd come up that hill, lookout, to look out for each other, and 'bang,' right back down that hill again before anybody fired a shot. They were both surprised. I have to go see that place yet, and those were the regulations they lived by. Anything that happened, they shook hands, made peace and went home. No fighting.

From the time I was eighteen, I spent a lot of time down in the States and did a lot of hitchhiking, more hitchhiking than bus or Great Northern Railroad. I'd hitchhike and at night I'd take the bus, different locations, reservations, tourist sights my great-grandfathers talked about. Places where they'd been, of course they travelled by horseback. There are different tribes over there, the Sioux, Assiniboine, and the Cheyenne, and the Crow. They get along fine with different tribes over there. I made a lot of friends. Another historic site, to me anyway, is Great Falls. I always hear about *Nebeedahbukwe*, Great Falls, Montana. It's a huge spring coming out of the ground entering the Missouri River. I got a job there, I worked for three years. After two and a half years I was next man from the foreman. Then the Korean War broke out. Then I went right down the bottom in seniority, right back down where I started. Because what happened was reserve army were called back upon to go for service, so they quit working, back in the army. Others past eighteen were drafted, or they had to join up. So the whole plant had to be remodelled, automation moved in. A place where I worked with ten to twelve men, there was only one man working. So way down the bottom. So I continued working until one night a man walked in in civilian clothes, with a suit and tie. Says, 'Who are you?' I say, 'I'm Wilf Tootoosis.' 'Where you from?' 'Originally from Canada,' I says, 'the province of Saskatchewan.' 'How long you been in Montana?' I says, '1948.' 'Are you an American citizen?' I says, 'No. I'm not a citizen, sir.' 'You're being drafted.' I says, 'Sorry, buddy, I'm not a citizen of Canada, I'm a treaty Indian.' He says, 'Okay, sign your name here, you're being drafted.' I says, 'Sorry, buddy, I'm not signing anything. I'm not signing anything. Two years ago, 1949, I signed up in the American army and I was rejected 'cause I was an alien. I'm not from the United States and my forefathers came from Montana.' So I says, 'I'm not going.' I says, 'I think I'll go in the Canadian army. A whole bunch of boys from Poundmaker joined up that time, were all Canadian, about eight of them.' So I thought maybe, what I had in mind was two years in the American army and two years in the Canadian army. So none of it worked out. So he said, 'Okay, sir, if you don't sign your name you'll be deported tomorrow.' 'Okay, fine, good vacation. I'll draw my social security.' So I walked out, four nights he came and said, 'Sign your name, here's your ticket to Fort Walsh, basic training.' 'Nope, I won't sign anything.' So they finally let me alone.

They wouldn't bother me. I continued working so in 1955 I came back to Canada, 1954, I came back and joined the Canadian army and I was rejected, for lack of education. I only had a grade two education. I said, 'Look, I was rejected from the U.S. army, U.S. air force.' They couldn't believe me. They took me to a depot, two weeks, so finally I decided to come home. Boy, I made my mom happy, 'cause she cried when I left. She was happy when I came back. I stayed in Canada for a while, then in 1955, I went back to Montana, then to Idaho working there for a while. Then I went to Washington, and came back to Montana, back in to harvesting, a combine operator. A good job, I got to work in eight different states. Some place in Censes, some kind of a seed, they combine out there in February. So this guy asked me, 'You have a visa?' I say, 'I don't need a visa, phone immigration, anywhere you want.' I say, 'I'd like to live here,' and they liked that.

I told him what happened to me in the army, with the army, he lost men that were drafted or had to go back in the army. So I had a good job. He said, 'Okay you start here in a month's time.' Yes, 'cause I already had another job, combining. So one day on a Friday it rained, I stayed in and the boss comes in. He says, 'Wilf, you need a haircut.' I didn't wear braids back then. 'Need a haircut.' I said, 'I don't want to go to town, I don't want to go anywhere. I want to stay here until you're done for this combining, trucking and that's going to be it. Then I'll move on to Omaha,' I think it was, a combine job, I'm going farther south. And then start from the south again next spring. They do Montana, then they do Alberta. Custom combine, Saskatchewan. This is what I had in mind, but I told him 'I'm not leaving till you're done.' 'No, no, you can stay here, but you need a haircut pretty bad.' So I said, 'Okay.' I went to town, had a haircut, went to a bar and started drinking beer. They had a shooting range and I got into that. The loser pays a beer. There was a gypsy guy there with us and one White guy.

So we had enough beer, went for dinner. He says, 'Hey, I just got my new truck, want to go for a ride, Wilf?' A brand-new 1956 truck. They come out early over there, September. This was September 9th I'm talking about. I said, 'Okay, let's go for a ride.' Went up to Blacktop, oh boy, beautiful ride, smooth. Then we came back. Well, 'What do you want to do now?' I say, 'I don't know.' 'There's a rodeo practice up here on a Blackfoot reservation, let's go there and ride.' 'Okay, let's go there.' That's where I make the mistake. He was driving too fast with his new truck. We went on a turn, hit the gravel on a turn and we skidded over. Last thing I remember was a telephone pole coming right at me. That's it, 'crash.' I woke up, it was dark when I woke up. He was standing outside. Says, 'Wilf, are you okay?' I say, 'I don't know.' I had cowboy boots on. I said, 'One of my boots just turned red with blood, maybe I broke my leg.' Says, 'Can you move?' 'I can try.' I couldn't open my door, smashed in. So I grabbed the steering wheel and tried to move out, one of my bones came right out the elbow, about three inches. That's where the blood was coming from. 'Oh boy,' I said, 'I bust my arm, my legs feel okay.' I was way, way up in a ranch country. 'Can you walk, take you to the hospital. I've been trying to flag somebody, nobody's going by.' I says, 'I can try.' Soon as I hit the dirt standing up I blacked out.

I hit the dirt. I went down. I was completely out. So I guess from there on he went cross-country, ranch country, pasture. For twenty miles, he walked twenty miles to get to the Blacktop, state highway, then hitchhiked from there. So I don't remember but I walked a half a mile without knowing anything. I was lying on the road, a rancher come by with his wagon and picked me up. He almost passed me, he thought I was dead. Lost a lot of blood but he backed up and checked my pulse. So he lifted me up and put me in his station wagon and took me to Serf. Anytime we went up a hill, I went down again. I came to, and he said, 'Hey, don't move, you're in hell of a shape and I don't want you dead in my car.' I couldn't talk my mouth was so dry, I never had my mouth so damn dry, ever. Must have lost all the blood and oxygen, whatever. I remember again, lifting me up into a sheriff's wagon, a red light going on and got rushed to the hospital, took me in, then the nuns came out. Doctor wasn't around, it was Saturday night.

So finally the doctor came out, says, 'Put your name on here, I want to cut your arm off, have to amputate your arm.' I said, 'No, I don't want to live without an arm, I'm not signing anything.' He said, 'You're in a heck of a shape, you might not make it till morning, lost too much blood.' 'No,' I says, 'I'm gonna live.' I knew it. There's a nun standing there shaking her head, says, 'Look, you talking to one of those Plains Cree Indians, gonna die in that chair, so do something, doctor, please.' Says, 'Okay, take him to operating room.' Took some x-rays, gave me some needles, I don't remember a thing. I had an operation. I didn't wake up for four days after. Out. Finally came to, I was half-blind, I could see the door, that's it. Heard people going by. I just laid there, feeding me with the intravenous. My arm was hung up like that, straight out. I was out for four days, they came to me, talked to me. I tried to talk back, they were working on me. So I busted my right arm in seven places, the chip of bones coming out up here. Well, the doctor saved my life, Dr Hamilton. He gave me my arm back, they kept me there for three days. Indian Affairs wouldn't pay for it.

I had my card number and everything. They phoned Canada and everything. A couple of months later they found out Canada wasn't gonna pay anything. It's not too much, I owed $1,500.00. I said, 'Look, if they don't pay it comes out of my social security. That's the deal.' They said, 'Okay. Fine.' So I phoned home and got my brother to finish my job for me. He just got out of the Canadian army that time. He was out of the Canadian army, he came there, worked, but he got another job. He's out there now, Sweetgrass Ranch, goes back and forth all the time, doing that for the last twenty years. Since he got out of the army, so my dad phoned, said, 'Look, I'm going to find you the best doctor, come home. It won't cost you anything.' I said, 'No, I'm coming by insurance, I'm okay, I'll go home.'

So I came home to Battleford. One day, a doctor comes out, says, 'So where you want to go? There's a doctor waiting for you in Winnipeg, one in Edmonton, Dr Gray. They're the best doctors, bone specialists, you can find.' Oh, I says, 'Ship me out to Edmonton, by plane.' Gee, I felt good, felt like a free man for a change. I thought I'd sneak away, which I did. I landed at the airport, I didn't go to the terminal, I ran outside all the way around. My hand was still in a cast, I jumped in a taxi, head for the bus depot. I knew there would be some Indians around there. Oh, crazy, a driver looked for me, paged, checked out the airport, looked for my name. I landed, that's it. But the driver knew right away, I guess, to head for the bus depot. I was a free man there, oh, about fifteen minutes. It wasn't a half hour I was talking to some Indians from up north, Hobbema, visiting a while.

Seen another guy, I don't know, he says, 'You're Wilf Tootoosis.' I say, 'Yeah, who are you?' 'Breeland, I work for taxi-hospital, we have a bed for you, if you don't take it tonight, we have to ship you back home. It's going to be occupied before midnight. A bunch of Eskimos.' Oh, he just gave me a line, 'there's a bunch of Eskimos coming in from Frobisher Bay, they are going to take up all the room and you are going to have to go back to Battleford, wait for another month. Come on.' So I didn't want to lose my bed so I went back. Heck, about a couple of days later I discovered about ten beds were vacant. So I stayed there almost a year. Went upgraded, took classes, and I came back to Saskatchewan, went upgrading. It was about 1959 when I came back to Saskatchewan.

I was in the hospital for about eight months, in the hospital, but they needed my bed, my room, they had a place, an apartment in town where they kept other patients, what they called the trustees. Well, I was a trustee before I could go on out. I was able to walk, my arm was in a cast, and I worked in a handicraft shop, the Fisher Therapy. I worked there. When they needed supplies, I'd get on a street car and go. I knew where to find what they needed. I'd go buy it, they'd give me the money after I get back, leather, leather crafts, tools. They had files for the Eskimos doing soapstone carving. Oh, I had a lot of fun with Eskimos, they couldn't talk English. One word they'd understand is poker. Ah, poker, every night. One time a matron comes in. 'See you guys are gambling. Gambling's not allowed here.' She was a real mean matron, took the cards away. So next day there's one guy there, he played poker with us every day. You know that guy was a cop. I didn't know. Yeah, he was a Cree. There was a hideout there, and he was trying to stop a fight and somebody hit him with a stick below the knee and bust his bone. I didn't know he was a cop.

So we went to this guy. 'Let's play poker,' he says. 'We can't, not supposed to.' 'You let me handle that, I'm a trustee.' 'How in the heck are you going to swing this one?' 'Ah, don't worry about it, don't worry about it. We're gonna play, we're gonna play it. Next time I'll be going to town, two days at a time and I'll get chips, poker chips. You're better acquainted with the Northwest Territories than Eskimos, you handle the bank. You give me ten bucks for the chips, put the money, hide it someplace, where the orderly or nuns or the staff won't find it.'

'Yeah, just for fun.' 'Hey,' he says, 'good idea, do that, come on, Wilf, and here's five bucks for the chips.' They were like seven dollars, real expensive chips. Here, we got together again, playing poker. The same nurse came up. 'I thought I stopped you guys from playing poker, no gambling.' 'No, no, no, we're not gambling, just for fun with chips, no money.' Nurse shook her head. 'Mr Tootoosis, I sometimes wonder whether to believe you or not.' But we never got caught. Eskimos, they didn't speak English, but just that one word, 'poka, poka.' And they did beautiful work, handicraft work. Every time I go out, I'd sell some for them, leatherwork, wallets, beautiful handicraft work they'd done in there. I'd sell that and then they wanted my bed and find a place here in town. With other patients we did homework.

I was upgrading, came back, went to Regina, and one day Indian Affairs called me. 'Hey, you've been selected to go to Nova Scotia, University.' 'I'm not done yet.' They never said anything about it. There's one selected every year, St Francis Xavier University, Extension Department, the Cody International Institute. I said, 'I'm not going to turn that down, I'll go.' 'Everything is going to be paid for, you can take your whole family if you like.' 'Okay, I'm taking all my kids with me.' So we did.

Eighty-five countries were represented, different states, Latin America, Guatemala, Brazil, met one from Mexico, Ecuador, two from the Philippines, all over Asia. It was quite an experience to hear those people there, their economic conditions. It was a social leadership course. They have a summer course through July and August, again from different countries. Starting with self-help projects and on and on. I like community development, I'd worked on before. Like I said, tourist promotion was my favourite, I'd worked on long before going to college. I worked on, done research on it, and got information from both sides, United States and Canada. So it was easier for me to get on it, and then when I came home I was appointed by our MLA to the Saskatchewan Tourist Association Board of Directors.

I was on there for quite a while. And then about a year I was on the Advisory Board. And then a couple of months later, I was appointed to Saskatchewan Transportation Company (STC). I was there for ten years. I was doing research. I'm on the board, so before I even talked to him, after we left the city, he looked back at me. He said, 'You're that Indian on the Board of Directors.' I said, 'Yeah.' 'Where are you from?' I said, 'Poundmaker.' 'What do you talk?' 'Northern Plains Cree.' 'Oh,' he says, 'my mother's Indian, Northern Quebec. I speak Cree too and French.' A couple of White women sitting next to that, boy, they looked and were staring at each other and turning around at the other people, so we had one in there. A driver that nobody knew about. He never told anyone that his mother is a Cree. A French half-breed for a father. But now, we have them now.

I think I saw one STC bus driver appeared to be a Vietnamese, or he had Oriental features. He wasn't Indian. So I'm still doing a lot of projects, tourist promotions. Powwow's one of them. I started back in 1960. Come very emotional hearing American Indians sing Indian songs I never heard before. Nothing at all, you know. I says, 'One day, some of these days, when I go back home we're going to have a Master's,' which I did. Out of that group we had one, maybe two or three became Indian actors, my brother Gordon, Bob Whelane, and there's another from Toronto, he's an actor. He's from the director, more than out of that troupe of Poundmaker Dancers, we have one Miss Indian World. We have one here, the first one in Canada, is from here, from our troupe of dancers. She's now a schoolteacher.

I started dancing in 1948. Going to these Powwows. It was really nothing. I went to Browning, Montana, Blackfoot reservation over there. A buddy of mine I met in the rodeo. His mother came from Rocky Brothers, half Cree and half Blackfoot. So I made friends with them. There's twelve different groups playing hand game, gambling. And over there there's only one drum, only Elders singing. Elders, real old people, singing a Powwow song and only one dancer. That was the Powwow in 1948. Then again in 1949, there wasn't much of a rodeo, a lot of drinking, hand game. In 1951 they had four hundred dancers, some from different tribes, some from Canada. And it picked up from there. After that there was seven, eight, nine hundred dancers, oh, boy. Looked beautiful.

So I always had in mind to start up a troupe here. If I ever decided to come home. Finally, after I got smashed up I couldn't go back to my work. It didn't matter if I had seniority. I could've stayed up there, lived on security. Oh, now I had to do some work, I don't want it. I'll get it now, I get my social security and my insurance. I'm getting it now. Came home in 1959, I only had about three horses. I had a thoroughbred, when I left I had a thoroughbred, I bought it after a horse race. He had a broken leg, they were going to shoot him. So I went up and asked, 'Mr Murphy, what do you want for this horse?' 'Oh, this horse is no damn good, want to shoot it.' 'I want to buy it.' 'It's no good, okay, how much money do you have?' 'Fourteen dollars.' 'Okay, you bring it in and you can shoot it on the reserve.' So I walked all the way, thirteen miles, with this horse, brought it home. He didn't have a broken leg. But boy, I got bawled out by my uncle. 'What the hell you gonna do with this crippled horse?' I wanted it for mare, you know, so he went out there in the bush and got some medicine and put it on the horse. Three months later the horse was running. Oh, a beautiful mare.

And then he had a Clyde horse, big horses, and my mare, instead of taking it to a race horse, big horses and my mare, horse, a great big horse. A year after, it had a colt. I rode the horse when he was two years old, bucked me off, then I left. When I came home the horse was six or seven years old. Broken in, I rode it, got bucked off, still have an aching back from it. Bucked me off, I took a somersault in the air and bang, hit me on my back with his head. I took another somersault. But I hung on to the rope, I hung on to the rope and just about to TKO there. So I stopped him, I said, 'Give me a hand.' 'No, I seen this horse, but take it home.' I said, 'Nope, hold it for me, I'm going to get on.' So I did, he didn't buck again. I got home, put it in the barn, hooked him up on the sleigh. He was a real good horse. Towards the spring my uncle came up, said people having a rodeo up north of here in Coshin, a summer resort. 'They want some bucking horses,' he said. 'Do you have any? Fifty dollars a day, hey,' he says. 'Take my black.' I said, 'Okay, you take your black and I'll take my pinto over there.' So we did. After the rodeo, the contractor was going to pick up a bottle of beer, and he picked up a wrong bottle, drank gopher poison. Dropped dead. So we lost our horse. We couldn't claim again. Next thing we hear they were bucking in Calgary. And then in Oregon and Madison Square Gardens. War Paint, that was my uncle's horse and mine's name was Midnight. Fifty bucks we lost, and they became the two world's champion bucking horses. Mine's buried somewhere in Wyoming.

They have world champion bucking horses, cowboys get together and buy some acreage where they bury these. I was going to get into that, but Elders told me it was too mean to horses. When you race bucking horses, that's cruelty. So I quit, I still had two horses left, no three, I didn't know exactly how many I had. Anyway, one old man came to me and said, 'I hear you have a grey horse.' I said, 'Yup,' and he said, 'Give me that grey horse and I'll give you a two-year-old heifer.' Good, that's how I started my ranch, one little heifer back in 1959. I wound up with about thirty to thirty-five. What I used to do is go to people I know, White people I used to work for. Go out there and borrow fifty to a hundred dollars, whatever I needed. 'If I can't pay you come get my calf.' So they'd give me the money. They'd always ask me if they were branded. Indian cattle were always branded with an 'I.D.' for the Indian Department. And if they were branded you needed the permit to sell. So I never branded mine, I always told them, I know which ones were mine, we'd go up there loaded in a wagon or truck. They'd lend me money, I'd never have to sell any. I wound up with just a half one, with thirty head. I took sick. I sold everything, paid my bills. In case I died. I was really sick but here I am. Starting at the bottom again.

Before I started with the Justice Department, I worked for Social Services, Welfare, assistant administrator when they first started giving the welfare administration to Indian people. That was back in '67, '68, no, no, no, in the 70s, that's when I took sick. Wound up in a wheelchair again. In 1979 I started walking around, I had a job with the provincial government. But my dad didn't want me working for provincial government, federal government, or Indian Affairs. I had a job, this came to my mind later, the Indian Affairs trained me to work for them. All the training, eh, I used to get mad, couldn't work, my dad didn't want me to work for Indian Affairs. Today I'm happy, I'm happy I didn't work for the Indian Affairs, or the government, or the Federation of Saskatchewan Indians. I'm sure happy, but it was something I didn't know then.

So I had a job, community development officer, with the provincial government, to work on reserves. They told me to come back in two months' time. During that duration there was an advertisement to apply for a court worker. I thought I'd try just to see, a stepping-stone of the other job I really wanted. I was accepted, started work, boy I hated that job. I've never in my life hated such work, the way the RCMP looked at me. And the police stations, the judge looked at me, prosecutor, boy, what a heck of a.

After a few months, after having coffee with the judge, hey, this was just a normal guy, so was the prosecutor. Just another human being. RCMP take off their uniforms and just ordinary guys. Once I became acquainted, I liked it, after three months' probation. They asked me if I wanted to stay. 'Okay, I'll stay on for another six months.' There was one election in that duration, another provincial government came in. The job I had applied for was out of the question now. So I stayed on, I worked there five years in courts, and then the program was terminated, no more money. But they were still using me. RCMP would walk in here and say, 'Wilf, I need you in court in two weeks' time.' 'No, I'm no longer on staff.' 'Okay, Wilf, we'll give you a subpoena,' and if I fail to appear for a subpoena it's going cost me two hundred. Two- hundred-dollar fine, without a good excuse, sick or had to attend funeral or wake, but outside of that I have to go, these kids, early released. That's what my daughter does here. When she's not acting on *North of 60*. He keeps a couple of boys, too. But I don't, my house isn't finished.

I didn't know where I was going to go. I had a notion to go back to Germany. Yuh, I had a job over there in Germany. In 19–what-the-heck when

I came home from Nova Scotia, I got a call from my brother-in-law in Ottawa. He worked for Secretary of State, Kenny Goodwill and Jean Goodwill. 'Hey, you want to go to Europe?' 'What the hell you got over there, Sioux Indians?' 'No,' he says, 'I'm serious. There's a guy here looking for a troupe of dancers.' It was to Holland first. Holland, Neimyer Tobacco Company, you know that pipe tobacco Sail, that's the company that was celebrating its 175th Jubilee. For that they wanted Indians because they have tobacco plants and tobacco from Ontario. They came there – who was it had a trip there that time? He's a Mohawk Indian, Gruelouie, Gruee, had a troupe, but they weren't satisfied with Gruelouie.

So they phoned Ottawa and said, 'Which troupes were at Expo?' 'Oh! The Northern Plains Dancers. Sioux, Cree, Blackfoot, Saulteaux. Five different tribes began.' So they phoned my brother-in-law, he started making calls to see who was interested in going. Some guys didn't want to go. I said, 'I'm going. Put me down, put me down for Holland. I'll go out there and get me a pair of wooden moccasins from Holland.' So we flew down. That was the first long trip for me. A bunch of guys there, it was during the Brantford Powwow. I was announcing for the Brantford Powwow. I went to Smitty to get another emcee for the last day, I'm getting off. So, everybody's sitting around at the airport. We expected to be called. We sat there right through and the airplane took off. Somebody says, 'Hey, what's happening here, we were supposed to have been gone an hour ago?' Somebody walked to the ticket man. 'Your plane is gone.' So we grabbed the next one.

That was in 1968, we went to Holland. Expo was the big one for us and then Holland. We had to go to Leduc Airport, that's Saskatoon. Anyhow, I wanted to go back to Toronto but they said your tickets say Leduc Airport. So I drove to Edmonton in fourteen hours from Leduc to Amsterdam. Quite a trip. Then they came up, they wanted to see Indian people dressed in Native costumes when we landed.

So they came over and asked me if I'd be interested and I said, 'Okay, I volunteer.' So here I was, putting on my feathers, 35,000 feet up in the air. Landed. Great big sign at the terminal at the airport. 'Dancee' big sign. How they got that nobody knows, I don't know. 'Dancee, pitowow, Dancee, pitowow,' big sign it said. I had a great time in Holland. We had a special visit for the Prince Nemeyer, the flying deathron, what they called him. He gave us each a silver spoon. A silver spoon from him, I still have it back home. And I have a silver, a silver tray with my name engraved on it, from the Saskatchewan Transportation Company, that's a silver tray, too. After ten years' service they give you a tray. One guy who came here to visit from Arizona said, 'Hey Wilf, what is that?' 'Oh, that's a silver tray, and that's a silver spoon.' 'Let's take 'em to Albuquerque, and the Indians will melt them and make rings.' They used to do that with silver dollars. Yes, now it's, oh, I don't know what, nickel, more nickel than anything else in the silver dollar in Montana anyway. They were a lot heavier years ago.

So, after coming home from Holland, I started getting calls. I been to every major city, most of them at certain times. Let's see where was the next one, oh yeah, Saskatoon Pioneer, and then Winnipeg River Exhibition, I went there for a week with the Reverend Adam Cunningham. That's when I met Reg Little and the Morley Singers and a whole bunch of others. And then the following year was Klondike, Edmonton, at the official opening, they wanted me there. Sure, who all's coming on, oh! Jack Benny, okay, fine. I never met Jack, Jack Benny, who else, Nancy Greene, good. So I went out there and had a great time.

I went to church and the priest started talking about my dad. 'John D. Tootoosis works for the devil. John is fighting the church, he wants schools to close down, he doesn't want the church to come on the reserve. He works for the devil.' I could feel the sweat pouring into my eyes and all over my neck, just broke up into a sweat. Oh, they did everything to fight him, they couldn't stop him, too many people on his side. Yeah, the ordinary people, they wanted better education, better housing, sanitation, you name it. No, they couldn't stop him, he kept going. About seven or eight years later, maybe two or three people went to church, that's about it. Yap! They weren't interested in it anymore. I guess they weren't going there. Get favouritism from Indian Affairs, and the churches, but ah, could affect the Indian that bad. Some of them did, I suppose. And the ones, the reservations, who gave up the Indian way are having the tougher time today, because they didn't keep that connection, it's gone, it's gone. Now they come to us, to go help them out, they don't know, they're lost. Some of them are worse that way, too modern, which is really bad. And I know Indians and half-breeds who never gave up the Indian way, off reserve. It's amazing how they kept up. They talk about their grandmothers living away from the Indian Society because of alcohol. They didn't want to live away out in the bush, so they stayed there, got Indian medicine, herbs.

Creation Stories

I have questioned some of the people here, but I think it's a bit late, the ones that knew have passed on and it's confidential. It's something that cannot be written, this information, the first ones who were here. I checked with the archives and they don't have it and the other universities wanted it. I heard of some existence of people coming to this country, and it was confidential. Not too many knew the story, and those that did didn't talk about it, only in ceremonies. Outside of that, I read a lot about the White man's research, but so far they don't know how people crossed and if they crossed.

So there was a lot of travelling around, the people travelled a lot, there was a lot of intermarriage with people from other areas. Here in Poundmaker reserve, we are a mixture of Plains Cree, Sioux, Chippewa, and Saulteau. Those ones born here are considered Northern Plains Cree, but if you check the history of five or six generations the grandmother could be a Sioux or the granddad or great-granddad a Sioux, or maybe a great-grandmother a Saulteau, Chippewa, Cree.

Health and Values

Important values are health and to maintain health. It's very important for a Native person to try and practise the rituals of our ancient forefathers. Some people say you can't live a hundred years back, two hundred years back. I say we can with modern technology, you can drive a car and still pray the Indian way and use Indian medicine without going through any operations. I got a phone call from Edmonton for one of the women for a contract when I took sick. I didn't want an operation for kidney stones. They said, 'Do you know of any medicine that can cure AIDS?' I said, 'Not yet but do you think it's possible?' Nothing is impossible with Indian prayers. You start thinking negative and nothing is possible.

There's Indian medicine that came about in later years for tuberculosis, which they didn't have before. Just like arthritis, cancer, they said people are coming from Manitoba here were invited to go there, I think it was two invitations. Youth Camp that I have to attend and chair the meeting. And translate for the Elders and youth coming in from the city, they don't understand Cree or Ojibwe. So I'll be doing in English, and then I want to visit those people there. There's one Indian there, I know is dying of cancer, bedridden, he's walking around today. Those are the things I'm talking about, when I say health, you can take a pill but I've never been cured by a pill, but it may help. A lot of White doctors have helped me. I went through a lot of operations when I got smashed up, truck accident, getting bucked off a horse, smashed up, they helped me. I'm not calling it down, you know. If I go to Europe I have hospitalization plus insurance, I'm covered over there. Anywhere I go, I pay that first, make sure I stay healthy, 'cause without health you can't live right, can't think right. When you're sick, you can't concentrate on anything at all.

That is tradition and culture for me, the values are more important, what the Elders teach, and I can't go by a Navajo, I can't go by other tribes. It's not for us, we're Cree. Believing is the word. Believing, don't bother giving Tobacco, Pipe, or print to an Elder if you don't believe, it's not going to work. You can fool a human being, but not the Spirit. You can fool a human being easy, very easy to fool a human being, and a lot of times you can't fool the Elders. Not the ones I work with anyway, you can't fool them.

Traditional Birthing

I was born in the traditional way, with midwives, no doctor, nothing from the pharmacy, no drugs, just Indian medicine, Indian prayer, that's how come I'm alive today. Now whether these people were chosen or just born to be for that purpose, it's sometimes what I wonder about.

A woman may have no children but she never missed or lost one child in midwifery. That's what she practised and she was really good at it. She had adoptions, but she never had any children. And she's always well prepared, they seem to know that someone is going to come that will need help during the night, that's when they start praying, then somebody arrives there, telling them 'My wife is sick, gonna have a baby,' away they go, they all got together, they helped each other, and there was always one head one, telling them what to do, the young ones would follow.

I've never heard of a man being involved in midwifery. Outside of the prayers, they got involved in prayers, asking for prayers, 'I'm expecting a child,' that was their part. They went to an Elder, that's what they're going to do, if the child lives, there would be a big feast, ceremonies or take part in Sundance or Giveaways or Powwow. If this child sees the next Powwow, the parents give away. They come with two or three hundred dollars in blankets, for just that one child, it's a celebration. It's like a big birthday party for the kid. Even if it's not their birthday, that's the pledge they made.

Traditional Dwellings

For a teepee, the Cree start with three poles, and if you look at them they look like that, like they're twisted, if they're tied correctly, they look like they are overlapping, twist clockwise. When you pull the rope tight, that's how they go. I saw that some of them were different for the leaders, medicine men, when they travelled not all of them travelled with teepee poles, except here north they had to go chop them first, so you don't make a fancy lodge, just go fishing up north, hunting. But here, the Headman, they travelled with the poles, the poles were tied together and the horse dragged them.

Some teepees are small, some are big. The biggest teepee I've ever seen belonged to one of the Elders, Albert Lightning, who travelled quite extensively. It took a ladder to tie the sticks that hold the teepee together. They used to make teepees like that for Headmen. They used to use them to hold meetings, there would be a circle of teepees. On the west side they would be like that in the middle, those were the Headmen, the warriors, the White people call the warriors, I call the defenders. They didn't look for war. That's when they had to fight to protect the women and the children, that's when the fight started. Buffalo hides were used to cover teepees because buffalo were there year round, but there were birch-bark teepees further north where they have more birch.

Traditional Self-Government

A little better than a hundred years ago, they still practised it, but not anymore. The behaviour of a child was very closely attended, and they, the Elders, talked about him. They would say, 'Remember that old man, he was their father and he was a good leader, and his kids seem to be that way, they are not like the rest. This child likes to command the group, if this child is raised the proper way he'll make a good leader, a good warrior.' They knew right away, how they behaved as children and then from there on, how dedicated they were with the tribe or camp. If they wanted to take advantage of the people or other tribes, Elders didn't appreciate that, it all depended on how they acted. If they were out on a raid, risked their lives for the community, they were the ones that became leaders. They were watched as they grew up.

If they got out of hand, disturbing other tribes, they didn't make good leaders. Those that wanted to live in peace and were good hunters were the ones selected to be leaders. Then again, there was a circle, where they lived, sometimes with two or three wives, now should this one notice to get out of hand – it was like a board of directors, they got together in one of the teepees and spoke to him. 'You are doing this, you're not supposed to do! You're taking good things for yourself instead of sharing with others! That's no good, don't do that. Should you continue you'll have to move back from the circle!' So if he still gets out of hand and doesn't do things right, they immediately call him in. So they get together and say, 'Okay, you have to move back, we have to select another one. You could injure women and children if something happens, storm, fire, disturbed or skirmish from other tribes, you're going to make a mistake, something is going to happen, you need to straighten up your head, you are not thinking right, somebody is going to get hurt, should you go as a Headman. Women are going to get injured. You are not living right or thinking right, move back.' So that was it, Elders talked about the Headmen, could be the man over here, this is what he did, this is the way his mother was, they start looking at the characteristics and behaviours of the parents, how his father behaved, how his maternal grandfather, paternal grandfather spoke, this is what he did for the band or tribe. He made good, that man has good answers, very clean, lived clean, he's healthy, he'll risk his life any time for women and children. He's not going to run away, because they always had people run away.

But White people call them warriors, and savages. No, no, they weren't savages. The United States President, Truman, was a savage, when he ordered the A-bomb. For me, that's a savage, killed people, poisoned things but again they defend the country. But if Indians did that a long time ago, killed a whole bunch of people, like Brokenknife massacre, they were doing that as defenders. They were defending the women and children and Elders, because he was coming in there to take horses, women, property, whatever they had that they could take and leave. That's why they got together, they did it not for the fun of killing, they were not savages, they were defending their families, children, women, and old people. So this is how the leaders were selected. They weren't there because their dad was a Chief, they weren't there because they were wealthier than the Indian people. The greediest person, nowadays, becomes the Chief, because people expect something. In the old way, the most dedicated people of the Cree Nation were selected to be leaders.

When you're attacked, you can't go to your woman to defend you, you risk your life to defend the woman and the Elders and the children. According to information I received many Native people left Canada with a woman leader. Many of the ceremonies down south, women take part in them. In Cree tradition, men handle everything. The women cook, but in the ceremonies, men handle everything.

According to information I received, when these Cheyenne people left, they had a woman leader, because when they reached the South Saskatchewan River it was already frozen. And this woman had a hatchet, she'd go into the river and chop a hole in the ice to see if it was safe to go across the ice to the other side. It was only when she said, 'It's safe to cross,' did they cross the river. They had to get to the other side for some reason. That story was from a ninety-five-year-old, that's about ten years ago. Some tribes may have had women leaders, because I see pictures, old pictures, two, three hundred years old, with a woman holding a Pipe. And now some women are starting to practise that, the Cree. But years ago I never heard of it. Women were not involved in any decisions but they may have been with the medicine. They had women like midwives and they all had their own medicine.

Treaties

The Indians never sold any land. Land was never sold, and Indians never asked for a treaty, the treaty was offered or they had the opportunity to live with the White people, I mean the Métis. Chief Poundmaker selected to live on reserves for the children and women for the future. It wasn't for themselves, it was for the children to have a place, they knew a lot of Europeans were going to come and keep coming and this land was going to get crowded. There was going to be no land for Indians unless they had money to buy it, they'd have to pay for it through taxes.

So they accepted the treaty, for the future of the women and children, to have a home, a home base. Then the Indian Act came in and they had to get a permit to leave the reserve. That was to discourage the assembly of our people. So they don't get into contact with other Chiefs and people. They [the government] were afraid of the Indians. They knew they might start shooting again. The guns were all removed from Poundmaker, except one, one Indian went out into the bush and hid a gun, and everybody used that in the winter. They took all the horses away. So that's the Indians' self-government, the other one they have today is the Indian Act. Indian Act, self-government, is what they're talking about now, where the Chiefs are the bosses not the community, that's happening now, on Poundmaker. Prior to that, the whole community had a say, why they don't like it, others talked why they like it, why they won't accept it, and then had a vote, and it was rejected or approved. But what's happening now is the Chiefs have all the say of the Indian Act, not the band, not the community, no more, just Chiefs. So this is my reason, I don't accept or approve the land entitlement, all the people over sixty, my age, received two thousand dollars from that money, but I didn't take it. I preferred to stay with the Chief Poundmaker's Treaty. They had a land claim here in Saskatchewan and they will be receiving money over the next ten years or so, to buy land. No, I have reasons to believe that, that is not part of the old treaty. It is not!

There were different interpretations of the treaty. On Poundmaker, they believed they were agreeing to live together, share land with the Europeans coming in, sharing land. We can't sell the land where we pick up our medicine, our herbs, we can't sell it. We can't sell the stone, it's sacred, and other objects. We can't sell them. They rejected the treaty and left Regina and came to Battleford. But here the Elders have said way back then, no, we can't sell the land. The land Mother Earth is our provider, we sell that then we sell our game, the animals, medicine, the lakes, the fish, the water, that's selling, but when you share you keep your animals, the game, fish, lakes. The lakes are still ours, we can fish any time of the year, in spite of it. Of course, the government is still after us, for fishing. So, those are the Indian interpretations of the treaty. They didn't sell land. They agreed to share.

The Elders

There are several ways of approaching an Elder, different tribes have different ways of doing it. Now an Elder is just another human being. They have good Elders and some of them were bad. But there were always good Elders. I always say there is a enormous amount of respect with these Elders. They do not get behind a mike and preach, they won't do that, they won't even pray over the mike, they'll put the mike away and then pray.

To approach an Elder, Sweetgrass and something else. It would be up to the Elder to pass on the information to you. This is the difference. If he says this isn't the way I was told to do – you know the look – he's not going to say you are rejected. You still have a chance to correct yourself. They know who should have this information, once it's obtained from an Elder, they seem to choose. There are some things passed on orally only, sacred.

A lot of times this certain work we are doing as volunteer work, sometimes they give me money, as a gift, but sometimes I just pass it on to someone older than me, sometimes I get for a meal or gas. Sometimes they come up and tell me about Indian medicine. One time this Elder died about four-thirty in the morning. The times changed like after dark, and when it is night time at midnight, again there is a Pipe ceremony the time change or the song. The Sioux Indians they sing every four hours, the drumming, the time changes after midnight and in around four o'clock or around some planet that comes up star, time change.

The Elders are the keepers of our faith, religion, medicine, and the old traditional ways. They are the peoples and medicines passed on to them and seems there is no end to it. I don't think there ever was. I know the people are discouraged when these Elders die, but they have passed it on. People have it somewhere, but they don't go around announcing it.

Again, going back to the Elders, they have this information of who were the heroes and who were the bad, who were the bad ones. The people sought the information and they can tell which is the bad way, which is the good way. Why was this Elder or man considered bad? What did he do? If he was bad at killing, killing is bad. It's always been bad. For one defending themselves, it's different, but this is where the White man got the idea they're savages, they're killers. But it was in self-defence. When they weren't attacked, they didn't kill. The Elders discouraged killing. A lot of the history is sacred. The most important history of the Cree Nation is sacred and it is not passed on to the general public, other than talking about the country.

Time

Times of the sun eclipse, that's how they kept track of time. Incidents like that would happen, they go where it happens. If there was a tornado that went by. This is how they told of events. They also went by incidents that happened like battles. Stories of dinosaurs have been passed on. This Elder did not have the whole story of it, but it was about an animal who polluted and killed other animals because of its natural gases. And they had one exactly like that in Asia in White man's research. But there was such a dinosaur that they spoke of, that caused pollution.

There was a dinosaur they just dug out of here, just south of here in Unity [Saskatchewan]. The Indian name of that area is the Big Snake Holes. There are holes of different sizes and big snakes around that area.

One Elder once told me that White people had the same power as the Native people years and years ago but they lost it, it was taken away from them and that's what is going to happen to the Indian people if they don't live right. There will be no more faith healing of the sick people if we don't live right. We are going to lose it like others have already lost it.

Traditional Games

One little game that children played was like a plant, it's about over a foot high and there's a little ball at the end, a little rattle, and it gets hard and you open it, there's seeds in there. When it got hard, really hard before it broke off, children would pick it up and they would match. The one who gets knocked off is the loser. That was one game the children played in the prairie. The other one is the stick game, the hand game. One is marked and the other one is not marked and they guess. Out West, we used to play it when I came home in 1959. I knew a few songs, I went back to Elders, my dad used to like that game. I picked up those songs, we started singing them. We used to play Friday night, Saturday night, sometimes all night. And betting, they had no money so they used a box of .22 shells, anything at all they would come in there, you see they only used horses. The women used to come places to sing, they knew the songs, they would hit the pole while the game was going on. We had lot of different songs. That was a game, an ancient gambling game. And sometimes it got so bad you'd lose everything, and they couldn't believe they could lose, a good hand game.

You could see once you started playing with the other person, or even them hiding them in the back, or they'd have a coat or blanket, you try to guess which way he's going to hold it, left or right. Sometimes you can tell how they come out, one hand comes out this way, the other one upright. And they try to fool, and you can tell which, they hold the one that's marked. And once you study the person, you can tell. Because they're trying to fool you but they can't. The easiest way is the eye, or a twitch or the way they move their head. They always move it some way or other.

Well, we have horse racing now. It seems to fade away at times. Like it faded away for a while when Indians were allowed to drink, because they would come to sports day and be drunk. People get disappointed and discouraged. They sell their horses, but I was back on again. I have two thoroughbreds and I don't know if they are any good because they are three years old.

The old people I can remember, fifty years ago in Turtle Lake and Thunderchild, they played dice. But that's not an ancient game. How they played, I don't know but they bet. My grandmother is really into it.

Family Relationships

I found out that the relationships, maybe not all of it was the same, where the son-in-law didn't speak to the mother-in-law, or the father-in-law didn't speak to the daughter-in-law. That's exactly the same form of conducting a relationship here. Some of them still practise it, and then maternal cousin like my mother's brother's daughter, that one I can tease or kick or throw water in her face, which we still practise. That's the ancient tradition, and you didn't walk in front of the Elders or somebody grabbed you. Don't do that, ehhh! That's an old woman, you don't walk in front of an old woman, you walk around. And if Elders are talking you don't talk, you keep quiet, sit down and keep quiet or leave, go and play. You don't ask for things while Elders are talking. Those are very strict and second cousins and first cousins say it in White man's way, you didn't marry those. Natives tend to discourage anybody who marries a cousin, they call them 'beaver,' because beavers will mate with their cousins.

They are very strict in respect to the Elders. So it was, I used to tell the Justice Department, we are a Nation and we live in our own way, we don't need police or a judge, the Elders are the judges, and the advisers. Grandmother is the adviser for every young girl, young woman. If she don't listen to that Elder, she is going to get out of hand and going to get in trouble. Not only with the Indian people, but with the law. Same with a young man, they don't listen. They're going to get in trouble, then they aren't going to live right. This is the role of the Elders, In parenting, the parent, usually the father, went to an Elder, a very old man, and asked the Elder to talk to his son. I want to raise him the proper way.

Traditional Marriages

It was the parents who decided. If the son wanted a wife, he's to tell the father, there's a joke about that too. There was this very nervous young man, eyeing this young girl, and they would look at each other. He went to his dad, they had lots of horses, seventeen head of horses. It was lots back then. He went to his dad, 'Dad, we have lots of horses now.' 'Son, we don't marry horses, we'll get you a woman.' 'Get your best horse and go get Tobacco, Sweetgrass and go get that old man to do the talking for us.' It wasn't purchasing, it was an act of honour, for what the mother has done to raise the child, the grandmother and all the whole family. You would say, 'Here is a horse, my son would like to have a wife.' Other parents gave their daughter away. 'Here is a fine man, good-hearted, very dedicated to the community, risked his life, good hunter, I want you to marry him.' So they gave the daughter away, whether he had another wife or not. The amazing thing is, how the wives got along, they were in the same home.

As time went on, if they could not get along, they broke up. She then went with another man, or another woman or two wives, that's the old way they used to live, before the White invasion. But they all still maintained their duties, they never deserted the children, children were never deserted. There was always some relative to take care of the children if the father left, still fed them. Because when someone killed a buffalo, people were called to go there and help themselves, to cut any meat they wanted, dry meat, any kind. Hardly ever anyone would go hungry.

I went to this Elder to pass on songs to me. I had been wanting to do that, been waiting for you to ask. So I went there and gave him Tobacco and started singing. Then he said, 'This is a very sacred song. It's my mother's song. You see when a song is passed on to a woman she has to get a man to sing it for her in a Sundance ceremony. That's her song. This is sacred to me, "my mother's song," it was passed on to my mother when she was about twelve years old.' Now this man was about ninety-one. It was a medicine song, a healing song. He told me the story of where the song came from.

Tricksters

Tricksters and clowns were a form of entertaining. They were very useful at a wake, when people were crying. They'd come and tell stories. There was one at Little Pine, and he passed away three or four years ago. Oh, he was good, he really drew a crowd, telling stories, humorous stories, how he played tricks on others or funny things that had occurred, what happened with them when technology first came in, like when they first saw knives. He always talked about something funny a person did.

They were always playing tricks on each other, like to create a funny story, something to laugh about. At a wake the tricksters would be there telling stories, keeping everybody awake, laughing. This old man that passed away three or four years ago, I knew the stories he used to tell, they were long stories, some of them are a half an hour, some two hours. But he only picked the humorous part of the story, something to laugh about. So he'd sit there and tell short stories, only the funny part, where people played tricks on each other, played tricks on each other. I wish I'd had the tape recorder there to pick up the stories that this old man had.

Music

What we call music, what we still do is singing songs. A lot of people say it's a chant. It's not a chant. That's the old music. The other is a sacred, you don't play it, just blow into it, you don't play different tunes, it just comes out that way. Every eagle whistle is different in the Sundance, every one sounds different and it sounds beautiful from a distance. But that's for ceremonies, the sacred whistle. The other instrument we play, in the spring – you cut about two or three inches of white poplar bark, two pieces about the same size of bark. And in between the two pieces of bark you put a leaf, in between, and you blow into that, you play some tunes. Any other kind strictly for entertainment, I can't discuss those that were sacred for ceremonies.

Art

I suppose it could be called art, considered art, but it's, again, non-commercial, it was something they didn't sell, it was passed on. A design on a teepee or a horse is a very sacred thing, you just don't choose the design, or your own bird or the colour of the teepee, it's something that gets passed on to you and you get an artist to do it. A lot of art on horse designs, you can see pictures of it way back, what they considered a war pony. They had those artistic designs on the rump, hip, forehead, and around the eyes. Those are sacred things, you just didn't go out there just for the sake of entertainment, no. They had people who were allowed and passed on to them to do these, but it includes Native prayers, and you just don't go and fool around with a teepee.

Daily Routines

Routines were prayers and that would be it. The Sweat ceremony, some claim they have to do it once a week, somebody else may say different. When they say once a week, this is the way it was passed on to them. Some might say no, that's too often. But this is the way they are passed on from the Elders, but the routine is that they have to perform their rituals as they were told by the Elders.

At gatherings, it is part of the prayer, people work all day, all night, and nobody gets paid. If you help somebody out you get something out of it. When the reserve had eight hundred head of cattle all the young people worked, nobody got paid.

Clothing

The clothing of the Northern Plains was mostly of buffalo hides, deer hides, and the same with moccasins. Indians tanned buffalo hides before White people came, using certain dry wood, no steel, no metal, just wood and bone, they took all the hair off by hand. I know that this is the way it was done years ago, rawhide. And there was no thread, they made strings with rawhide, ropes, other ropes with rawhide, the back of the animal, those are the thread. Most of the people around here smoked and tanned hide. This certain type of clothing that they wore was made of fur. In the Plains here it gets cold, it is colder here than a hundred miles north, because in the North they have pine and spruce trees that provide shelter. But here in the prairie the winds hit you right directly, it is all wide open.

With clothing again, almost every tribe had their own design in moccasins, almost every tribe was different because they all live in different environments, they are all different, not the same at all. The Northern Cree were different from the Southern Cree, they were different. The long journeys, the three or four pairs of moccasins were made, make sure that they don't go barefooted, and in the winter time, they always had a headdress here, fur usually, fur headdresses in cold weather, cold days. But they told me the warmest blanket is the buffalo robe, lying on them, one on bottom, one on top, fifty-below blizzard, they still sleep nice and warm. The other blanket they made here was the rabbit. I watched them do it, they made ropes or strings cut in circles and outside a teepee or lodge house it's seen from a distance, from a long ways. They keep them hanging outside for a long time, I don't know why, just so the loose hair would come off, I guess. Just hanging there, then they would, what they did fifty years ago, how they'd make it, before I left the reserve, one of these old gunny sacks, with holes in them, that's where they go and weave it into their strips. And then sew it together later, that's supposed to be almost as warm as a buffalo robe. But that one, I think the cold wind may blow, that may take the breeze right through it, whereas the buffalo robe will not. Those are the types of blankets they have, and other headdresses, for ceremonial purposes. There's one here, here at the museum, I have the story about that one. Used in 1885, that one is skinned owl, skinned owl headdress, that's only for war, for attacks, the last time it was used was in 1885.

Traditional Spirituality

For that you'll have to give me a smoke. Yes, like I said, it's difficult to explain, I don't know if any are now practised the proper way or not. That's not up to me to say. A lot of them say the Sundances, that's not how they used to do it years ago, but it's impossible to go to a Sundance with a buffalo robe anymore. We still have those and other ceremonies. So the Sundance would be for thanksgiving, a time for prayers. A time for praying and for people who are sick. They'd pray and say, 'If I make it through winter or summer, I'm going to fast, if I get my health back,' or they'd say, 'I'm going to take part,' depending on their health conditions, what they can do, stay there for a while, or go fast, dancing, whatever they can. It's just to do that.

There are other ceremonies also still practised. But according to other stories, some of them are still very strict, some places they are not. Some of the places, if you are drunk, somebody takes you far away and drops you off. They will do that, or some places they will allow somebody to come in.

Burials

They had four poles, put into the ground, and the body was wrapped in rawhide and laced with rawhide, real tight and put on a rack on the stakes. The last one here on the Sweetgrass reserve, he asked to have his body treated that way, he didn't want his body going under the ground, but he was the last one. Then they practised with the clergy, priests, and buried bodies. But this one particular man wanted it with the four stakes so they did it that way. And it was fifteen years ago, when I was interviewing this Elder, he told me five years ago he still used to go up there where this man was put on that rack, four poles, and could still see the human bones on the ground. The RCMP and Indian agent came down, and told the people to bury all the bodies. I've seen Indian art paintings around here, a lot of the American Indians treated their dead that way, on four poles and put them up in rawhide. That was before they did it in the modern way.

There is no hell for Native people, that is what one Elder told me. She looked at me seriously, she said, 'That's for White man not Indian.' They lived for the hereafter, this don't mean nothing, we're only here for a little while. Material things didn't mean a darn thing to them, food they'd prefer to share it, than keeping everything for themselves, everything, clothing. If someone admired something you had, you gave them.

Traditional Beliefs and Christianity

A lot of the Elders I work with today believe in Christianity, but they don't belong to any congregation, or any church. They believe in Christ, but then they say they cannot work for money, in the Indian way you don't need money, you just go there and pray. You do need money when you need to buy things like Tobacco, but you don't charge money for your services. If somebody wants to donate something for a giveaway, gifts, those are acceptable, in fact it's bad to turn it down, it makes people feel bad when they give you something and they know you don't want it.

We were talking about this before, and there's an Elder living in poverty, and maybe part of his beliefs is to give everything away, what's to do. And I know some, as long as they eat today, they're happy, or a little bit of Tobacco. Twenty-five years ago everybody worked, forty years ago there was no such thing as a pension, everybody took care of their own Elders, everybody did. The were happy and they were a lot healthier. They Elders today have gone through this rough life and different diet, the change, they don't eat as much meat as they used to and fish, not anymore, it has been rough.

Clans

I've heard of those, but from different tribes, those that belonged to Wolf Clan, Bear Clan. Around here I've never heard of such clans. There may have been a couple hundred years ago, different groups. The Crees are the largest tribe in Canada, the Cree Nation, right from the mountains clear to the East coast. I may be wrong, but it seems like other tribes that couldn't get along with the Cree, they left and went south. I have yet to find a Cheyenne to tell me why they left, beautiful country up there, lots of game, lots of fish, why did they go south? It's pretty country here than where they went to. I know because I know they had buffalo there but still this beautiful clean country, beautiful lakes, fish, why did they leave those waterfalls to go south? The Dene couldn't get along with the traditions of the Head Chief, they didn't want to duel or fight, so they left. They took themselves until they came to the place he had dreamed about, and they are now called Navajo. It's the same culture, the same language.

Prophecies

Earlier, when I spoke about people moving from Saskatchewan, you see a woman led the caravan and she predicted it was going to happen, they had to leave, and described what the country looked like. They didn't want to go too close to the Sioux. This is what she described and predicted and they'd be safe there.

One Elder once told me, he says, 'You go to the White man's church, they talk about their prophets, they talk about Jewish prophets, and many of them can't get along with Jewish people, they still go by Jewish prophets in the White man's church.' Why should the Creator leave us without prophets? Every Nation, every country, they had prophets too. The story was told to me about a group of people who left Manitoba, when this Elder had predicted they leave or they were going to starve. And he described what the area looked like in B.C. He said there's a lake near those mountains. There were prophecies made that Elders had predicted and are happening today. But usually they don't talk too much about it, just with Indian people themselves.

Important stages. Honouring a person, this took place if they earned it. Many times they were given a prayer song, you earned this. And they would explain, this Elder he did this, his medicine song, use it. I've heard it with Indian veterans, before leaving they went to an Elder, 'Look, pray for me, I'm going to war and I want to come back,' and they were offered prayers, when they were in distress or difficulty, they used the prayer.

Traditionally, they were honoured when they returned from a battle, highly honoured. If there was a woman they admired, they said, 'This is my wife.' The parents didn't say anything, he earned it. Back then they took good care of each other. You're not a man if you beat up a woman. They knew they would be well taken care of. They were honoured if they did something great for their own kind. And many times, when they made an attempt to do something, they were gifted by the Elders, something to use in the battle.

Those were the different stages where people were honoured for doing something for their nation, tribe or band or for the people. And there are special songs for them, they sang them when they saw them coming. We still use them in Grand Entries, and Honour Song, and giveaway, flag songs, to us in the Powwow, equivalent to 'Oh Canada,' as a national anthem.

Predicting Weather

We still say, how many winters had he lived? Weather was predicted by the animals. The birds would sing a song before it rained and they would fly around, make noises, before it rained. I asked one Elder, he said, 'Get the pegs ready for the tent, it's going to be windy, it's going to rain.' It was a nice hot day like this, no dark clouds. I said, 'Yes,' and I asked, 'How do we tell? No clouds.' He said, 'Listen, that's the only way you'll ever learn anything, listen and look around.' And this bird started making noise.

I heard on the radio there was going to be an eclipse but it was cloudy, it was in the winter. There was snow on the ground. So after I had dinner I went into the barn to throw some bales to the cows. They all had their heads stretched out, really stretched out like that! All of them, looking up! That was when there was an eclipse. I couldn't explain. And then I heard a mockingbird. We don't hear mockingbirds when there's snow. They go south. Maybe the mockingbird came north because of that eclipse change. The change in the weather or wherever the change takes place in the duration of an eclipse. It's still a kind of change. Before the Poundmaker tornado, a hummingbird flew inside the house. I didn't know what it meant until after the tornado, when these things happened, and then I knew. They know a whole lot more than human beings about the weather – the beaver, muskrats, birds. The weather was predicted by the way the beaver made their dams. A lot of times they predicted tornadoes and cyclones. Here we have four seasons. We have the summer, then the fall, the winter, and the spring. So, these seasons are like the cycles of time.

Time was kept track of by the first alarm from the birds, the change of time from night to daylight. They were the ones, they were, that were the alarm. They knew whether it was cloudy or not. You looked outside, it was dark, but you knew it was going to be daylight pretty soon because the birds knew that first. If it wasn't cloudy they could tell by the stars what time of the night it was, and the planets. They knew what time it would be daylight. And they knew what time it would be noon. By the shadows in the evenings. Again, they went by the animals if there was going to be a change in the weather or if they were going to have an early spring. Around here they said, 'When the horse is starting to shed the winter hair it will be an early spring.'

Language and Culture

I often think of questioning the Elders about this language. How the Cree words are used differently in the North. Different in the East. It's Cree, it's a Cree word. The people are Cree, you can understand it. But the words are used differently, because the culture and the environment are different. The Northern Cree here in Saskatchewan, they travel by boat. Southern Cree or Northern Plains with horses and on foot. Like from here to the Sioux country or to the Bear Paw Mountains they used to run.

And on hot days they would sleep. They only run at night because it was cool. Everything was quiet and they didn't frighten the animals at night if it was quiet. They were on foot or they were on horseback.

Traditional Names

Indian names are a very sacred, spiritual thing. They never talked about it. I didn't know my father's real name until about three years before he died. He told me his real name. It's confidential and so were the old people years ago. Their real names weren't used, only in ceremonies. Each Elder had a nickname, that's what we go by today. The people are named after the nicknames because they didn't want to use the real name of the Elders at the time of treaty. Places around here also had Indian names, every place did.

Ownership of Land

Land was shared. And this is what it says in Treaty Six. Treaty Six, the reserve is under a common ownership by the Aboriginal band members. Then when my grandfather started farming, the people, a lot of them, farmed. They didn't want to get paid for it. It's still the same way. If the people in Poundmaker got together today and voted, they could put the people in the council before sunset was out. That's the band custom! That is the band custom! The bosses, the rulers are the band, not the Chief and Council. Whereas in a two-year term, the Indian Act Chiefs are Chiefs and the band cannot overrule the Chiefs, until the two-year term is over. And the band custom, that's the old Indian way. If a leader gave you here in a paper, like in that circle. If they didn't behave they had to move out because they would misdirect the people. Same way.

Today, in the band custom, it's the same way. They have four Chiefs or five Chiefs. The band says, 'Look, this is what they are doing, this isn't right.' We elect a new Council and then they vote on it. If the majority says yes, new councillor out. Then others are elected. If one here is okay, that guy is okay, they can re-elect this guy. He works hard for the community, he's an honest man. We've done it before in Poundmaker. Or they say, 'We want a new Council.' They don't like the way of it. Then we have a meeting. The leader, the band councillor or the Chief, would say, 'Okay, I resign. I resign, you people elect somebody else.' So, this is the way. There's farmland on Poundmaker, one guy has got 500 acres, 300 acres, 100 acres. They don't own it. It's owned by the band and are common owners of Treaty Six, but the people approve it. Let him farm there, he's got his own little pasture. Fine. Let him have his own, put his horse in there or whatever. They can assemble tomorrow and call for a meeting and they can break that up by a vote.

That's the ownership of the territory. They had other ways. I can't say it's a map, like there is a lake here, eh. Over there on the southeast lake, and it would be along the bushes, some hills over here. This is Blackfoot country, this is Cree country. Over here in the south, which is now South Dakota and North Dakota, that's Sioux country. But nobody really owns land. This teaching is passed on from the Elders. There is only one owner and he is not a human being. He is the one who owns the land and we are here to live together and share the land.

Traditional Food

The food preparation was berries mixed with the meat, pemmican. So this is how they preserved the meat for the winter, pemmican and dried meat or fish. Dry it in the sun and smoke it and then put it in the bags. One Elder told us not too long ago, he told me one moose, if it was well cut up and dried, would give you one bag of dry meat. One bag, that's how small it gets. Then you pound it and make pemmican. This is how they preserved and put it underground, they came back to it if they couldn't find food in the winter time, any game – elk, moose, deer. With logs they would make a bear trap and they would explain how the bear got in there and got trapped in the logs.

A long time ago, say maybe two or three hundred years ago, there was dry meat, the pemmican, different kinds, they shared food. There is one story, it was more or less to give an example to the next generation. They couldn't find any game at all and one Elder went out and he says, 'I'm going to get food for the women and children,' and he came back with one little bird and fed about fifty people. How he did it nobody ever knew about it, but this is what he did. And people can start running from here and go south and there are shrubs, the plants, the little nuts they can eat, they are real nourishing and have a lot of nourishment. They look for that little shrub and it tastes really good. And the other is like a carrot, it's white, that grows in the prairie, but it's edible only for a little while and it turns into like wood, it hardens up. Oh, it is good in the spring, it looks like a carrot but it is white. It's the same size as a carrot, that's what it looks like. Those are the foods they used, but they preserved the food, dried meat, fish, buffalo, and other animals.

Transportation

The horse would drag the teepee poles because in the prairie there they can't cut poles every day when they move camp. When a camp was no longer used, they would move. And the buffalo were about forty or fifty miles away, they would move camp. And this how they moved these tee-pee poles, put them on a horse.

Modern transportation made a difference because they could visit relatives two hundred miles north, west, and east with the vehicles within in a week. Whereas when they used horses or went on foot it took almost a whole summer. A lot of times they would pick a runner who was a good and strong runner, healthy, to run down east, south, or west and see and ask around which relatives are alive because here they had to prepare food for the winter. They couldn't leave on horseback and wagons. They started on horseback and running, sometimes they ran and went to visit out there and when they approached the camps, they sat on a hill until somebody came after them. And they asked about the relative, the name, and asked about relatives and who was there. And they would stay there for a while, seeing all the relatives and the people they asked about. There was nothing written, memorized everything, the names of the relatives and they asked about this person, this is his name and this is his wife's name, 'Are they here? Their relatives want to know how they are.' So they'd say, 'Yes, that's their lodge over there, that's their residence, that's where they live.' Or they would say, 'He died and he is no longer with us, passed away.' And then after the visit, they would run back, come home.

After that they had wagons, it was about ten days or twelve days from the Battleford area to Rocky Bow with a wagon. The same with Hobbema, a wagon and down East too. Two of my great-grandfathers came from down East, Red River, and it's in Winnipeg. Around the Regina area, east of Regina, I have relatives over there. One time my grandfather came to visit here from over there. My great-grandfather's brother came by freight train. Got on a freight train and came over to visit, stayed quite a while and then went back home. And now I can hit the road and before mid-night I would be in Montana. If I can get across the border, visit a while, come back, the next day with a car or truck.

Relations with Other First Nations

When people talk about free trade here, well, that is nothing new to the

Indian people. We had that a long time before the White invasion. Horses, they go out there and trade something with other nations, and we still do it that way. The other thing that is considered sacred by the Elders is that we don't accept money. They would say, 'Give me something for trade, trade something from Canada.' We still do it that way, in the same way.

I remember my grandfather in relation to other First Nations. They lived in Montana prior to 1905. This must have been in 1899, 1901, somewhere around there. They used to go on horseback to visit the Crow, right across the mountains and back again.

One time they were going south, they got on a top point of a mountain-side and looked out over there, there was something out there glittering. 'Oh, that's the Crow Indians dancing.' Checked his horse and took off full speed. They got there and there was a circle of wagons. 'Oh, there's Crow Indians having a round dance.' They got off and took the saddle off and turn the horses loose, take a rest. In the evening they were asked to come in, and so they sat down there by the wagons. His cousins knew what was going to happen, my granddad didn't, but they were always teasing each other, were talking about trickery, this was one of them. They were doing it for a laugh, they were doing it to create a story when they get back. Somebody gets bored they would tell them this story and make him laugh. Indian medicine, laughter. So they didn't tell anything to my granddad, they sat there and then the Crow Indians were talking, they didn't understand a word, all they knew it was a round dance. They would go and dance around in a circle when they start drumming. So the drummers got in a circle, the middle of the circle, and started singing. Here comes about a six-foot, maybe more, Crow Indian woman, this was her traditional way of welcoming visitors and she was wealthy with a lot of horses. She was a wealthy woman but my granddad didn't know this, his cousins knew what was going to happen. He was a stranger, his cousins weren't, they had been there before and they went through the same experience.

Here comes this great big tall Crow Indian woman. Nobody said anything. I guess my granddad told me he started to sweat and get very uncomfortable. This woman was coming directly at him, so he pulled his hat down and looked at the ground. This tall woman just grabbed him by the hand, by the arm, and he tried to pull away, couldn't do anything. She was a very strong woman eh, and put her arm around like that and started dancing. Just the two of them, oh my goodness, the Crow round dance, everyone clapping, everybody. He got so embarrassed, he left there and crawled out, got on his horse, and came back. Waited in the mountains for this cousin. So I guess this Crow Indian woman came back with two new saddles, three new blankets, and a rifle and a whole bunch of stuff for him. So after it was over, it got dark, they left and brought the saddles home and the gifts back home. They came back and this was the trick they played on him, just for laughs.

Another time his cousins had rounded up their horses and said, 'Hey Joe, Ashtum Joe, pick one. These were quiet, well broke, you can have one.' Put a saddle on it, he got bucked off, the horse wasn't trained right. Something to laugh about, but they gave him the horse. So they trained that horse and rode it around, rode it around there. They got along fine with the Sioux, Groveon, and the Chippewa Cree, but they never went on the Blackfoot side. They never went over there, they went to the Crow, they got along fine with the Crow. Traded and had good times together. But there is always one or two that got out of hand, which caused these battles, and then they would kill each other defending themselves. Somebody would go out there and steal a horse, same as with the Blackfoot people, the same way, and then the Elders would go, one would go and make peace and it would be all right for a while until someone got out of hand again.

Healers

They were able to heal over prayer. They had healing powers, and I heard the Sioux Indians say the same thing then. The ones who were half man or half woman or a woman acting like a man, dressed like a man, or a male who is very feminine, they had healing powers, very respectable, but now it seems like everything has gone haywire somewhere.

Life on the Land

This is what I am trying to consider with all the technology and chemicals they put into the ground. It is not healthy, it's not. And the same way, I know White people – there is one who came to visit a reserve and stayed with us for a few days. And he couldn't get along with his brother. He refused to feed any kind of chemical to the cattle. He never buys any meat to this day, in the store. You can't tell whether those cattle were fed with chemicals. What he does is raise his own beef and eats it, the same thing with chickens, he's quite a guy. He's always with Indian people, always with Indian people, studying the Indian way and he's doing good. But anything that might cause pollution or contamination with technology influences, he really speaks out.

Many Indian people, the Plains Indians when this was predicted again by Elders, they moved up north, right from this area. And we up North Saskatchewan and some of the more Northern Alberta, they don't like that, you know. They want to go where there is clean water and clean air. Here it is not clean air. You don't know what kind of chemical blows into this town from these sprays these farmers are using. And now some of them are using airplanes, they spray the crops, there is something wrong somewhere. There is a place where I worked in Great Falls, Montana, for about three years, I think two and a half years, it's a smelter, there is a big smokestack. Oh goodness, I don't know how many hundreds of people were employed in there. I was one of them in there, and there was a big smokestack going up in the air and that was supposed to take care of everything in at that time.

Now this was in the fifties, but later, even when I left, when I left in '54 after I got smashed up, I read in the papers the farmers were complaining about the smoke. From that smokestack and that smelter, this smoke didn't go up, it landed on all the ranches in and around that area, east of Great Falls, when there is a west wind you know, grass doesn't grow. Polluted the area. Now just recently, I have postcards of the place, it's not there anymore, they shut the plant. Oh my goodness, we had everything in there, we had our own parking lot, we had our own nightclub and the people belonged to the union. Oh yeah, we had our own big dancing area, but they closed it down because of what was happening to the area. Now we don't know what we take today when we eat a slice of bread, how much chemical goes in it.

I have to have meat, wild meat, oh goodness, I have it all the time. If I have to go stay up north, I'm going to go stay up north so I can get wild meat. I can't hunt around here but I don't believe anyone knows how much technology has contaminated the earth. They put chemicals in there to kill weeds and now I don't know how much of that goes in the stomach. How much of it goes in the cattle and then we eat that. It takes a while before the technology, scientific studies to discover these things. A lot of drugs are now banned because they were harmful. They were causing a lot of harm to people and sometimes it's too late for some of the other people. You know their health is ruined, we don't know. A lot of times the people up in the bush, up north, are better off than we are. They have more game, the fish, beautiful fishing country. It's difficult for some people who can't leave. They can leave the reserve, it's just they are not interested in leaving and going some place else to hunt and fish.

Education

I was talking to an Elder, they were the first ones in the Battleford area to go to residential school. The people who would be eighty or ninety today. This Elder told me, he says some of them were damaged for life. Now they could never think right, others came out of it well enough to get out and work and take care of their families. Others were so badly damaged like they came out dizzy, they didn't know, they couldn't decide which way to go, with the Catholic priest or the Indian way. Others said this church is no good, it's no good for us Indians, we don't want it. But again they experienced more difficulty in every-day life from Indian Affairs and Indian agents and the churches, who were in full charge of the Indian education at that time. Others were real strong, fighting people and spoke against these residential schools. Government is supposed to give us education, provide education to the Indian people, so we want schools in Indian communities on Indian reserves and not administered by the churches, Anglican church and the Catholic church. So the healing that is necessary is to work on those people even today, a lot of them became alcoholics.

They are damaged, they hide everything, they won't talk about it. The ones that open up, now, they are the ones that we can help, help themselves. It's to help themselves, we can't do anything if they don't help themselves. The same with alcoholics and drug addicts, help your-selves, try and do something for yourself. We can't hold you by the hand and pull you away from the bar. No, you got brains in your head, smart enough, intelligent to say no, stay away. And they start talking about rough experiences and so do I. I also got rough treatment in resi-dential school. I was lashed while all the other children watched. Today they [the clergy] say they are sorry, well, let us try to help these people who were damaged, came out of there damaged and have a negative attitude, to White society, to the church. When a priest starts abusing children, sexually abusing children, women, no, that's not a priest, that's not their traditional practises. They are there for free board and room, which they get from the tax dollars for the past two or three hundred years. They have done more damage than good to the Indian nations. There is too much information hidden, they are too secretive about it.

We can hang on to our culture, but today this culture sometimes is a different thing. Like this Elder was talking about in Little Pine Powwow, when he said now it is commercial. A lot of those sacred things are being purchased with money, that shouldn't be. Hanging on in a real way is a very difficult thing now. Today an Indian lives in a world where money talks. When money talks you don't listen when it comes to the Indian way. You go there where there is a ceremony, we're supposed to, and we're also expected to go there and volunteer our labour, to help them out, work all day, all night, whatever, until it is over. Nobody gets paid. Now a lot of the young people today can't understand that, those kinds of healing no longer exist, it's for people, before White people came here. It's only the White doctor who can, well that's entirely their own opinion, nobody is going to change, they can only change themselves. But you can still live in today's world with ancient beliefs and be whatever technician one wants to be, teacher, lawyer, but the more money they make it is easier for them to get out of hand. And a good time, you can still have a good time as a volunteer worker, in fact have a better time, a real good time, everybody jokes right through the day while doing volunteer work for Native people. And still send your kids to university. It's very important and there are people who are doing it.

Warriors

Now in the traditions, warriors are highly respected people. The defenders is what they are. Everyone had respect for them as they defended the community. But they were called warriors, they were called warriors because they raided the White people. When they first moved in, the settlers were causing a lot of damage, they were breaking up land, they killed off the buffalo, and these people were defending their Indian way. This was their way of life and their food was being damaged, medicine being ploughed underground. White people started cutting all the bushes down and then they got angry. They were defending, not merely wanting to kill someone, and when they got shot at, this is when they shot back. And if they did they did as a defender of the nation they belonged to, and community people looked up to them. Special songs were made for them, they received special treatment because these are the people who provided, defended our freedom. Nobody is going to raid this community, because these people are going to risk their lives to defend our children. Our children are going to be safe, so they respected them. They made and gave them beautiful clothing or a beautiful horse, the best horses in the community. Those were the warrior traditions or the defenders of the community.

Traditional Forms of Justice

Forms of justice, I'm not saying it will never work, but it will take a while because the Indian society has already been misinformed, and if they lie in the White man's court before a judge representing the Crown or Queen, they have a chance to lie, they'll lie. When they know there is no way of providing evidence. I don't lie in court, I'm commissioned to take oath and I am not going to lie for anybody, I have a job to do, seeking justice.

You know, there is a requirement for you to be punished for the wrong-doings, for what you are accused of, if it is true. You will have to go along with that. But if they have a chance to lie, they will lie and get away and laugh about it later and I hear about it there. They come to me and say, 'Hey, Wilf,' usually when they are half cut or high on something, 'you said you don't lie in court. You know at the time when you appeared for that guy.' I said, 'Yeah.' 'Well, you know you lied.' I said, 'Okay, I lied, he lied, that's why I lied.' And not only me, so did the lawyer. There are people who worked very hard all their lives to raise their children properly. Then they get with the wrong kind of company in there. Next thing you know they're involved in criminal activities, because of drugs and alcohol. So a lot of young people told me, 'It's none of your business if I go to jail, it's me who goes to jail not you.' But it affects the whole nation, the whole reservation, of what happens. If we have more young people in jail, the news goes right across Canada, which is bad. You need help so you can correct yourself. You need help if you don't want to spend your life in a penitentiary. This is where you going if you don't change.

But if justice is administered the old Indian way, it is the best thing that ever will happen to them, the best thing that ever will happen for the Indian and for tax-payers. Today I think it's close to a thousand dollars for a court date that RCMP, judge, lawyers, paralegal aid, secretaries, it is about a thousand dollars. I checked this about four years ago, that time it was eight hundred in Saskatchewan. It's different every province, a little more in Alberta, the expenses a little more in Alberta. When a young offender goes to jail the government spends tax-payers' dollars, a hundred dollars per kid. That doesn't include transportation. They fly up north to pick up young offenders.

When you start to estimate cost, it's what they spent in that institution, staff, food, and the cost of the keep of the building, power, water, heat. It's over a hundred dollars a day, same with the penitentiary, same thing, it was seventy-five dollars four years ago last time I checked. But I want to know other figures now, I want figures on justice department. How much it cost for one inmate in a penitentiary, and the youth centre and correctional centre. What does it cost to keep kids there? What I would personally like to see in regards to justice is have those institutions by Indians. I would like to visit them before I give an example in Manitoba; Arizona; Denver, Colorado; or South Dakota. I would like to visit those first. They're more effective to correct the youth because they're trained to respect themselves. Respect the Indian way and then from there on respect their neighbour, other people. Without that respect they're going to commit a crime, they are going to commit a crime and revenge. With respect, they will avoid the revenge. They have to understand the duties of the RCMP and the law. The law is written to protect society. The law is not written to offend citizens of this country, it is there to defend, and that's what it is there for, but it is very important how it is administered. Years ago the judges only gave jail sentences when the Indian appeared. You'd go there, sleep in white sheets, three square meals a day. Prior to that, my father's age, they were embarrassed. It was the biggest insult to spend one night in jail. One uncle came out of the army an alcoholic. One day I asked him how come he quit drinking. He said, 'The dirtiest thing that could ever happen to me in my whole life, I spent one night in jail. I spent one night in jail because of drunkenness, the dirtiest feeling I ever had.'

Now they go to the correctional centre, they go to jail, they come laughing about it. 'Oh! heck, I can do that standing on my head, that's okay, I'll go to school in jail, I'll finish school in jail, I won't able to go the bar.' This is it, they talk about it like it's a part of life, part of their life that they lead on the street. Where years ago, it was a terrible insult when they went to jail. They didn't want their brothers to know, they didn't want their grandfathers to know that they'd been in jail because the Elders would be insulted. So this first has to be worked on those children. Self-respect! And they cannot be expected to respect other people until they have some respect of the old Indian way. This don't mean they have to go back to the buffalo days or dinosaur. You could live in the city, work every day then come home to your community and go for the healing from the Elders, Indian prayers. It is there, it never left us. We left it, it never stopped, but we left it. And this was one of the predictions, that our traditions will come back someday.

Dene Cultures

MARTHA RABESCA (Slavey)

Fort Good Hope, Northwest Territories

'Our culture will not die because our culture is nature through God, that's the way it's always going to be. It will never die.'

Martha Rabesca was born in 1911 near Colville Lake in the Northwest Territories. She was interviewed by Emily Faries at her home in Fort Good Hope in the summer of 1994. During the interview Martha spoke Slavey, which was translated into English. Martha has nine children and more than twenty-five great-grandchildren. She was very busy, but considered the interview very important. Martha discussed living on the land, and the importance of language and culture. She told some incredible traditional stories, and also shared her traditional teachings, and some of her experiences living on the land.

Life History

A long time ago, when our Elders talked to us, they continually were telling us to do something and we always had to listen to them. I was born in Colville Lake, my mom was from Colville Lake, and my dad was from this area. In the summertime they would go fishing here, go out to the fish lakes. My mom is from Colville Lake. She likes to go back to my people in Colville Lake at certain times of the year. That's where I was born and raised up in the bush. Long time ago, that's where everybody was raised, up in the bush.

A long time ago, there was no settlement, there were just three cabins down in the valley here and on top of the hill there were a couple of cabins, there were no settlement. All this here was just straight bush. There were no settlements in those days. We travelled a lot in this area, but most of the time we spent on the fish lake called Rolly Lake, and that's where my dad spent most of the time. I have three older brothers, one older sister, and one younger sister. My youngest sister is the one that died at a young age. The rest of my brothers and my sisters are all older. All their children were all grown up when they passed on.

I was the one that my parents really needed so they didn't want to let me go, so I didn't have a chance to go to school. But my older brothers, they all went to school, they were gone for five years to Fort Providence to residential school.

The Origin of the Tribes

My parents knew all the legends, stories, so they always told me. So I'm quite familiar with those stories. On how the world came to be, they don't talk about it. They never did talk about it. Long time ago, nobody was educated and they very seldom saw the White people, European people, or anybody. It was just themselves or what they told was never made known.

The stories I heard from my Elders were that Dene people turned themselves into different types of animals. They had the power to turn into a human being or an animal. A long time ago, before there were different tribes, it started with just like a log that rolls and rolls, when they put that log into the fire. That's how it originated. Then from there the crow came into being. That's how the different tribes started, a long time ago when a human being with a special power turned themselves into animals. While you're in the form of the animal you're not allowed to go in its presence or go close to it or get in contact with it. But it did so happen that there was a human being that saw this animal and killed it with a bow and arrow. He tried to kill it and shot at it. He hit the animal and the animal yelled out, 'Oww,' and then it was a human.

Then that is when everything started happening. At that time is when the log that kept rolling went into the fire, it is the one log that they have to keep pushing so it burns. You keep pushing the log so there's no end to the fire. It just keeps burning. There was a time when the people started freezing, it was cold there, they were freezing to death. Then they told the crow and the crow said, 'What is wrong with this wood?' And the crow started tearing the wood and piling the wood on top of the one wood that was burning, making it bigger and bigger. And that's how people discovered fire, to keep the heat and to keep them warm.

The crow was known to lie, to steal, it was always being dishonest. The crow has all negative characters. But people were grateful to it because it helped the people a lot, they learned from the crow. The wolverine is special. People suffered long time ago and the beaver was known to be a real rodent. It was feared because it had such dangerous teeth and its tail that it uses for its defence. The beaver ran into one person, a human being that was knowledgeable with the animals and smarter than the beaver, and it was known that this person knocked a beaver right on the mouth and the teeth were real dangerous because it used to kill people with them. But then this one guy knocked the beaver's teeth out and as a result he's got only two front teeth today. This person's name was *Adabeken*. He was the special person that the legend was built on.

Adabeken, after he performed his battle with the beaver, he took off from here and he didn't go too far and he ran into a lynx and this lynx was huge. It was so huge it was the size of two lynx together. It was going around in a circle because he was proud of his long tail. So this *Adabeken* was trying to outsmart the lynx. He yelled at the lynx and told him, 'I'm blind, I can't see. Can you show me the way around because I can't see?' While he was saying this, he was kneeling on a log. Then he told the lynx, 'I can't see. Could you put your tail on this log so I could feel it?' So the lynx turned around and put his tail on the log for him so he could feel it. So the lynx put his tail on the log and *Adabeken* was feeling the tail. In those days they used to carry a little hatchet like a small little axe. *Adabeken* had one. As soon as he was pretending to feel his tail, all this time he was able to see. He took out his little hatchet and he grabbed the tail and chopped it off, cut it right short on the log and the lynx just yelled out crying and took off. That's why today the lynx has a short tail. That's the story of why the lynx has a short tail.

Adabeken is the one that got rid of the bad things in this world. It was known that he got rid of the giants. He even chased the giants away. The beaver was a giant, the one beaver that they knocked out his teeth and he had his two front teeth left. It was a giant beaver and the animals were huge through the legends. The giants were eating up people and just making people suffer, that is why *Adabeken* chased them away. He really helped people. He was said to have married a giant's daughter. He and this giant's daughter, after they were together for so long, they got into a disagreement. *Adabeken*'s wife went down this way and he went south.

After that *Adabeken* corrected all the wrongs and got rid of the evil and the bad. I guess the people were wondering who was going to be their leader, and of course, the crow right away said, 'I will be your leader.' But the people told him, 'No, we don't want you as our leader. You're too bad, you lie, you cheat, and you wouldn't make a good leader.' Even though they really relied upon the crow, he did a lot of good for the people, but still he was known to lie too much and to cheat.

So I guess that is when they accepted a higher power, God, because there was nobody that they could turn to. That is how the different tribes started, after the incident of the acceptance of God. Everybody went down to the burying lands and that's where they gathered. The children were playing and they did something to a young owl and that's when all the trouble started. They started a war over that, and that's when the people from Sahtu region, they were the Caribou and then they went towards that way. One tribe were the Dogs. Inuit people were the Beaver and the small children. There was just old people who were useless and weak, that's us in this area. So everybody wanted to run away from us. We were left in this area. That's what happened, why there are now different tribes.

Importance of Culture

Today, it has really changed, it's not like long time ago when we had to listen to our Elders in order to make a living for ourselves. In order to make a good living we had to listen to our Elders. We listened to them, they talked to us, they told us what to do and we did it. But today the young people, even some of the older ones, they don't listen to the Elders. Sometimes the Elders try to talk to them and but it seems like they don't listen.

Traditional Birthing

When a woman is in labour, they put a stick across so that they could put the woman over and then that's the way they delivered the baby. The woman would just hang on to the stick and do what she has to do and the baby is born. A long time ago as they're walking, while travelling, the woman goes in labour they just prepare the woman for delivery and when the woman has the baby they just continue to travel.

Only women helped one another. Whoever was there would help that woman who was having the baby. Men didn't even consider watching. Once the child was born and as the months rolled as the child grew older, the men taught him the different skills to survive out on the land, to hunt, and fish. Girls would learn how to work on the hides.

Traditional Dwellings

The dwelling houses a long time ago were in outdoor camps. They started with a moose hide or whatever hide to make a shelter. Then they started afterwards with teepees. That is all that was used for dwelling places. Many families lived in the dwelling, they got along good. It was good because in those days there was no alcohol and everybody supported one other and worked together and then in the evening time everyone would sit around and tell stories. There was no problem that time.

Elders

The Elders were the ones that taught how a community should be run. They were the ones that made the decisions on how to make a good living and how people should be getting along together and just everybody to live in harmony. And they were the ones that taught their sons, their children, how to live a good life.

When you see an Elder sometimes a gift is given. If a person approaches the Elders they are always ready to give good advice and the person is always ready to listen so that the individual will benefit from the advice from the Elders.

In the Bush: Games and Feasts

A lot of times that I have repeated this. In order for our young people to be raised up in a good way, always teach and encourage the youth. When fall time comes go out on the land and start teaching the young people different survival skills that are needed. It is a good life out in the bush. They could stay there as long as possible to learn everything there. It is important to go to school now so they could learn the traditional and the modern ways.

A long time ago, people were out on the land all winter long and they came in about springtime. At this time of the year, everybody was happy to be together again. There was so much joy, everybody was hugging one another and everybody was happy to see one another. There were always ball games when everybody joined in the game.

Then in between, there was stick gambling going on with the men of the settlement, and on top of that, there were drum dances going on, tea dance, until the wee hours of the morning. Those days playing ball was not like how they play ball now. You never heard swearing words, in those days the people didn't know how to swear. They never got angry, they were just living in harmony, but now alcohol seems to take the fun out of everything. It just causes trouble. But a long time ago everybody had a good time.

There used to be feasts held whenever a young man killed his first animal or his first wild animal. They had a big celebration for that.

They had a bone from animal bones, the leg, the feet part of it. There's a little bone there and they made a hole in it. One end has a bigger hole than the other and they put a string through it and there's little things at the end and they do this to it and they play like that. It was a string that they used. It's a bone and has a string at the end of it. It was like a plaything. They played games with it and there were certain ways you go to win, there were little holes at the end of the things that catch on when you're going like this, then you lose. It had a pointed end.

Weapon of Protection

I heard stories told of where they were working on a flat rock. It was around, and they worked at it until it got round, and then after it got round they chipped all the ends out. Right in the middle, there was a pointed object and that's what they wore on themselves so when they got attacked, whoever attacked them, they would deliberately make sure that they got hit right here. That sharp object was used like a weapon. It protected them.

Daily Routines

Long time ago, they used to get us up real early, right at the break of dawn. They did that to make us energetic and make us smart and knowledgeable of survival. All day long, they were doing chores, setting wood, and we never stopped. We had to work to survive. When our dad would go to the fish net, we had to go there to assist them. We had to haul brush for the flooring in our tents. We did a lot of work. After you got a little older, they started teaching you to tan hides. Now that I think of it I don't know how I did it, all that hard work.

We were continually sewing and sewing. There was no end. Not once did they ever have any pity on us, they never felt sorry for us that we work too hard. They just kept us working and working and the Elders said, 'If anybody tells their child they're working too hard and start feeling sorry for them,' they always said, 'your child would grow up to be useless.' They wouldn't have any ambition in life.

Traditional Clothing

We only used hides, tanned hides. All the people wore hide clothes. That's the way it was, everything made out of hide. Even their shoes. Everything was made out of wildlife, marten, rats. Clothes were made for children with rabbit skin. People wore rabbit skin parkas, rabbit skin pants, rabbit skin hats, it was all made from rabbit skin.

The way they used the rabbit skin is by cutting it into spirals, and when it's long, they use it that way, then they put it on a spool, a stick spool that they keep stretching and fixing as they go along and when it's ready to use then they braid it up to make the clothing. They even made blankets, they work at it a different way, they make sure that it's on a high place and all wind up [in the wind] and make sure that it's dried. But with clothes they use it damp and then it dries on you, but for the blanket they dry then they make a blanket. You'll never get cold when you sleep in that. They also used hides for blankets, warm blankets. They scraped all the hide and then they put two hides together.

Traditional Burials

Some of the people used to dream that this person was in a different place. Whoever had a dream about where this person was going, that's the only way it was known. Sometimes they bury people, [sometimes] they make like a stage and then they put up there and that's the way they put the person to rest.

Long time ago, people hardly died. They lived to be really old. When they get tired of living they swallow something in their throat here, and it gets stuck and they just drop. My dad used to say that long time ago, people never did die of sickness or anything. There was no sickness, they just died of old age. When my dad heard that Europeans are coming in, my dad used to say, 'Now all the different kinds of sickness are going to come in, and people are going to be dying from all kinds of diseases.' That's what I used to hear my dad say.

A long time ago, when the people were living good lives with no diseases, no sickness, they were so old that something started growing out of them just like little growths, that's how old they were. But after the White people came, people just started dying with all kinds of sickness. My mom used to tell me that the people from long time ago lived to be so old. Just like a little plant that would grow on them, it's soft and it's round. That's what you see on the ground sometimes [referring to mushrooms], and it grows, it won't grow on the soft spot on your skin. It grows on your cheekbone or under your nose and right here. My mom used to say that it really looked nice on a person when those things started growing. It looked really cute because it's round and white around and it's red inside, the middle, it was a sign of old age. That's how old they got to be. A long time ago, that is how it was, there was no sickness, everybody lived to a ripe old age. We didn't know anything about sickness. So that's the way it was.

Traditional Beliefs and Christianity

Long time ago, there was no religious group that came around like a priest. There were no missionaries, people were just by themselves and there was praying. There was an old shaman around a long time ago. While he was doing his ritual, he was fasting and he had a vision of angels, a lot of them. In that way our Elders said there was something that was more powerful than people.

When missionaries first came, because of the strong belief in a higher power, they believed in the priest so everybody turned to the priest and that's where they got their present religion. A long time ago they were really always praying because they had strong faith in God. They were always praying to him, for whatever they needed. Their faith was strong but nowadays even that is dying away. People hardly pray anymore.

A long time ago, we were just taught to always respect one another, to be good to one another, and that if you're this way today, in the future everything will work out good for you. Even today it is still like that. We still go by our upbringing where we know that whatever happens in the future depends on how we live in the present.

Stages of Life

There was something similar to that where you were brought up. Even a long time ago, when a woman or a young girl goes through the woman stage, when she first gets her period, they put them way out alone in a camp because they're not allowed to touch the ground. So they build a platform high in that open camp for her and that's where she stays. Then they make a pole that is real sharp, they make it sharp at the end, so there it's standing and they hold that stick. If they fall asleep, their head would fall down and the sharp end would poke their head. They wake up, then they have to start working again right away. She's to stay on that platform because it goes against nature if she's on the ground and starts sitting in the ground. They say that she wouldn't feel energetic, she'll be lazy, and she wouldn't have any energy if she does that.

They want that young girl to grow up with a high self-esteem, not to get offended so easily in the future and to handle things in a real positive way, not to be negative all the time. They don't have to do that all the time, it's just for that once when they first start their womanhood, and then after that they live normally. It's just for that first time in their life when they go into their womanhood that they have to abide by all these rules the Elders give them.

Seasons and Weather

Through the summer months into the fall time, everybody always prepared for the winter. They made all the winter clothes because they knew it's a long cold winter. They have to prepare for the winter, so that all winter long, they have warm clothing with hides. And then getting close to spring when it is warming up, they get rid of their winter clothes and then start preparing for spring and the summer.

They were able to predict the weather by the moon and the sky and the clouds, by these things they were able to predict what kind of weather it was going to be. Mostly by looking at the sky or the sun.

Native Language and Culture

They needed one another, long time ago, that's the way it was. But it is still like that today, but there are too many changes now. Our culture will not die because our culture is nature through God, that's the way it's always going to be. It will never die.

Traditional Names

It depended on the family, their outlook on life. It depended on how they were when their young ones were born. They named them as to circumstances that they were born under. Long time ago there was this woman in town here, her name is *Louatin*, the old lady across here, her name is *Louatin*, but her grandmother was called *Abetelin*, and she was called that because there was a big family, they were always given away. Then her grandmother was born and was poor and had no clothes. So somebody else took her grandmother and raised her, so that's why they called her *Abetelin*, which means naked. So that's why she was named that.

There was another person in town that is still alive today. Her husband's mom called her *Coeyga*, that means from under the fire. What happened, there were some people out on the land travelling when this baby was born. I guess when they made a campfire, everybody was ready to travel again. They put out the campfire and underneath the ashes it was still warm there. They put the baby there and they left. As they were travelling one woman found out that they left that baby in the fireplace. So she went back and the baby was still alive because it was kept warm from the embers of the ashes and she took it and she brought it up. That is why he was named *Coeyga*, in the fire like.

Every place that they travelled had a name. So they did have different names. A long time ago, our traditional Elders were the ones that named these different places and it stayed. Some of them are still named that today.

The Land

Long time ago, we didn't know anything about owning land. The land belonged to all of us, so we all shared it. All we know is that the Creator put this land for us to use it and that is the only thing we know, is that it belonged to us.

The only thing that people lived on was wildlife and they killed that with bow and arrows. Long time ago people made their living by wildlife. They made nets out of the hides, they cut them thin. Sometimes with strong thongs they built nets out of it for beaver and that was how they trapped their beaver. They caught all kinds of different wildlife from all the thongs and the sinew, which were made into nets. My dad taught me all different kinds of survival skills that our people needed to survive out on the land. So that's how they did all their hunting and how they survive on the land for their food.

Transportation

Before all the modern things came to be, people used to travel on their own. They made sleds out of the caribou legs and moose legs, sleds were made the height of the legs. They just sewed them together and made sleds out of them and used that for pulling. They made it into a sled and they used that for travelling. They had snowshoes around here and afterward they had dog teams.

It [the modern things] really changed us and it's not positive change, it's negative. Now the snowmobiles are here, nobody is making sleds, dog harnesses. Long time ago that was part of our culture to make things. Now they don't require snowshoes, they don't net snowshoes with *babish*, and that's why since those changes, it has not been a very good thing.

Traditional Medicines

I know of certain tree barks that when a person is really injured, they use a bark of a certain tree and that is the strongest healer for certain kinds of injuries. Nowadays, there are all kinds of sickness, but long time ago there was no sickness. Only our Elders used to catch a cold, there was no sickness that time. If people had stomach aches then they used to boil this willow, there's a willow root, a black thing in there that they used to boil and they drank the juice from that, and then it would just clean out a person's system like the stomach. But now different kinds of diseases are around.

Sometimes there would be a person that is very sick and they would go to this individual that knows and is gifted with some kind of medicine. They would go to this person and this person would fast and do some chanting and then the sick person would be healed. I know my dad was a kind of a shaman that had powers. I heard of incidents where he healed people and he had special powers. When a person was sick he could heal them, and he did a lot of other things. It continued on into our generation. Some of my brothers were gifted in that area. They had special powers but they never let it be known, they just kept it to themselves. And I'm the only one left out of the whole family and I feel that I have that power but I never let it be known. I just keep it to myself.

My dad was not originally from here. My grandfather was from the

Dogrib tribe and then he came here and married here and my dad was born. Then my grandmother was lonely so she asked to move back to her people so they moved back over there. That's where there were some more kids born and raised over there but her dad was here. After that her grandfather wanted to come back to his people this way, so he came back here after his wife died over there. Then he got married to an old woman here. My grandmother was from the Dogrib tribe. My dad was a Dogrib.

In this community here, it's Slavey, Hareskin Slavey, here in Good Hope. Fort Norman and Fort Franklin are different. They have a differ-ent dialect but we could understand them. There are Hareskin, there is the Mountain Indian, there's the Colville Lake Indian, in our language we called them *Newgoda*, meaning 'from the other end.' So there are dif-ferent dialects. The whole Sahtu has different dialects. You probably know about this old woman that people go to for healing, spiritual and physical healing. There's an old woman that people go to, my dad used to talk about it. That's why the whole community at this time is chipping in and making donations of cash so they could bring Alfred, who is my sick son, over there. That place is called Snowdrift. That's where this woman lives.

My dad knew the place over there. Through my dad, I have family ties in Fort Rae. People travelled on the Dehcho [Mackenzie River]. They made connections to other places. Not only on the Dehcho, even on the land, people did a lot of travelling on the land. And when they ran into other people from other places they gathered together where people got to know one another. Nacacho Hill is named after this guy *Nacacho*, and he's the one who was kind of like a peacemaker in the region. He was try-ing get the people to start working together and that's why they named that Nacacho after him. So this way our people were able to mix together, to meet with one another.

There was a lot of conflict, lots of wars and everything with the Chippe-was and the Crees. I heard that this *Nacacho* is from around that region and the Dogrib area. He's the one that really put unity into people's minds and to have all the Aboriginal people united. He is in the legends, in the stories that people tell. There were stories about him, that he was active in the war with the Chippewas and the Crees.

Education

I really believe it's a good idea to work both ways out on the land and in town here. This way our children need to be out on the land to learn things and start feeling good about themselves because there are so many changes now, but maybe eventually we might have to survive back out on the land again. In order to prepare we need to educate our young ones about the survival skills of the land. Even now it is good to have the young ones on the land so we could teach them this is how you do this and make them feel good about themselves.

I really believe in the healing and because of the residential schools there has been a lot of damage done, but now people who were damaged are starting to think about their life. I really think they could help themselves by coming to us Elders. They should tell them about what is bothering them and the Elders could tell them a lot to make them start thinking good about themselves.

There was a lot of damage done in the residential schools. When the children came back, we were still traditional. There was no modern living. The people from those schools did come back and they would go back to the land. The Elders re-educated them back into our way of living. For them it was not too bad. However there are those went through school and didn't bring up their children right. There is so much abuse nowadays, but going back to the land helps.

Traditional Justice

I think that today when people do something wrong, I really think that if they go and send those kind of people out to the land, to live out on the land, it would do more good than damage. It would be better than sending them to jail. Alcohol is the reason for a lot of this trouble. It has created the biggest problem in all areas of life. A long time ago we didn't depend on alcohol. Everybody was happy to see one another, everybody got along.

In the springtime everybody gets together in town, they have a big feast and they sit around and one person tells a story and everybody sits around listening, even the children. We enjoyed life because there was no alcohol. Today because of alcohol it is becoming a big problem in town here.

Relations between Native and Non-Native People

White people will always be there, but I strongly believe that Aboriginal people in the communities will go our way. We should get our Elders involved and start working with ourselves, then we control our lives our way, not by the government or the White man's way. We always depend on the White people when we want things. We don't want it like that anymore. We want to be able to control our own lives. If we continue to go the White people's way there is going to be continuous alcohol abuse, child abuse, our children will continue to get into trouble. But if we go the Dene way and live our own way, things will start happening for the good of the Native peoples.

Conclusion

Our children are the way they are today because of the way we raise up our children. It's partly our fault. Because I lost my husband, I always have to struggle by myself. I raised all my children and I struggled a lot. When my children came back from residential school, I was always giving them advice on lessons of life. I always told them you need to do this to survive. Now Gene has his own house, and he is building another house. He knows how because I taught him.

He knows how to work on snowshoes. He knows the survival skills that are needed out on the land, because I taught him that. His other brother, the one that I got here now that stays with me after he got out of school, he was in different areas of work out of this community in the south. Finally, after so many years of different types of training skills, he finally came back to the community. Because he learned the White way, he earns his own money. At the same time it is very important not to lose your identity, culture, and values.

Give your children good teachings and values to learn. Nowadays with our young people, I don't know what kind of upbringing we are imposing on our new generation now. A long time ago our Elders always told us as young children go help that individual, go cut wood, go carry water, and we used to be able to do that for our old people. But now they see us, they see us Elders, they don't even acknowledge us. If they are taught right and wrong our young people will be okay. It's just that we need to set examples for our young people, then they would be okay.

GEORGE BLONDIN (Slavey/Dogrib)

Rae Edzo, Northwest Territories

'As an Indian I love my Indian culture. I still am in love with the land, I am still in love with my history.'

George Blondin was born on 14 May 1922, at Great Bear Lake in the Northwest Territories. He was raised on the land and knows the traditional ways of his people. George spent four years in residential school, which he describes as 'a very sad story to talk about' because of the degradation of Native children and their dignity. He raised seven children and, in 1994, had ten grandchildren. George has encouraged his own children to get a good education so that they can help their people, and today he can see the results in their different fields of work.

His involvement with politics and the rights of the Dene people spans more than twenty years. He is pleased that the government is beginning to recognize Dene rights and that the church is acknowledging the damage it inflicted on Native people. In the 1980s he was awarded a certificate of Recognition of Past Service by the NWT government for his efforts as Chief in his community for several years.

George Blondin has written the book *When the World Was New*, a collection of old stories and legends of his people. He now lives in Rae Edzo in the Northwest Territories.

Opening Remarks

I would like to talk the way I am talking now to have more understood. So it is the way, like I said, it is the conflict between two nations that don't understand each other. The lifestyle is completely different. Everybody is having troubles, the government and everyone is having troubles to deal with the Indian people. I guess now the Indians are trying to get educated and look into their rights and the constitution and they are getting educated so they look into back where all the mistakes are. The government realized, through the renewal of Canada and the constitution two years ago, that that opened up the whole of Canada, that the Canadian government has done real damage to Aboriginal people.

So they changed their attitude. Instead of going the way they were they changed their attitude, and are trying to correct the mistakes that were made a long time ago by the missionaries or by the early government and by the system they imposed upon them. Now they are trying to change things. They are trying to get all the leaders involved in areas such as park management, law, and administration, and all kinds of things that are being imposed upon the education. They are trying to get many laws and probably from now on they will try to change their policy and have some of the culture mixed up with the general system, whatever it is. Is it education and law? Or anything.

We appreciate very much that happening with the government, but it is so hard. Even if the government wanted to mix the people it is still hard mixing the people. We have been separated for so damn long that it is so hard for us to go to the White people and say we are equal now. We can't say that, we have been separated for so long. The only way that is the best thing to work out is our treaty and the treaty make us separate and trying to work out something better. Self-government especially. The land claim and we have a chance and the government only agree because they talk to each other and give a chance to the Indian people so that they have their own affairs, their own self-government. They can run their own community, take over education, take over medical, take over police, take over the church, stuff like that, whatever they can handle, and so we are happy that there is a chance that we can run our own affairs. But then, like I said, we had a hard time up until now, everything is lack. Lack of education, lack of skill, lack of this, and lack of that. We're not trained to run our own affairs such as take over housing, take over church, take over police, stuff like that. Welfare and stuff like that.

So we are lack of stuff again, plus that when they posed the education they already had the treaty. The Indian Act says the treaty extinguished all your rights. The government make it clear to all White Canadians that we have no rights at all, so whatever they say is supposed to be right. Whether the education they imposed upon you is supposed to be right, but later on it wasn't right because they extinguished all of our rights. What about our culture, our own teaching system that we teach our children for thousands of years so they survive with good people. They extinguish everything and replace it with their own system of education from the outside world, and this got our children all mixed up. They don't listen to their dad, don't listen to their mom, lots of crime, alcohol, and because we lost all of our teachers, the Elders don't call no more. The Elders they were our government, they were our teachers, and the movement extinguished all of what they were doing.

Right up to the Elders here they were sitting over there and not saying a word and just watching their children go to jail and nothing to say, even parents, mother and dad are the same way too. So children I would say just raise themselves by their own. Some of the smart ones, the lucky ones and smart ones use the education the right way and with stubborn willpower they elevate themselves by themselves without help from their parents or Elders and they get jobs and try to make good living, but very few of them, and say ten per cent maybe. Ninety per cent of the people, just the way I explained; no skill, nobody to lead them. What I said, they come out of school and they go out on the road and that is it. There is nobody to steer them, nothing from the parents, nothing from the Elders, and everything looks like it is based on what they read from education. This is the kind of problem I want to explain. I think you understood everything so I think you could start asking something and maybe I could answer the best I could.

Life History

I was born in 1922. I have a Bear Lake map over there. That's where I come from. You see way out there, that caribou. There is a big lake out there called Horton Lake, right on the barren land, and that's where I was born in 1922. That's where, when I was a baby in that area all around the Bear Lake area, that's where my parents came from, and that's where they raised me. From there in 1928, I think it was 1928, I was only six years old, somehow the priest talked my dad in that I should go to school, I should talk English. The school was in Fort Providence, and they got me a ride there, and they just took me from my parents and put me in school. This is a very sad story to talk about. It's because I already talked about, they imposed things from the outside world upon people and there is no difference with the church. The church also did that, and with the government. And I think the church had more power than the government that time to deal with the Indian. Maybe later on I will talk about spiritual issues because it has a lot to do with the movement of Indians. Like tomorrow they are going to St Anne's Lake in Edmonton, the whole flock is going up by bus. Spending their last money. This is the kind of people, their attitude is very religious, spiritual issue is very important to them.

Anyway they shipped me to Fort Providence and I was only six years old. And I didn't know how to say yes or no. The sisters there, the nuns that work, are very rough on children. They told me, 'You can't talk Indian no more, Indian is not a language. You either got to talk French or English. That is the language. Indian it come from the devil.' And what are you going to do? You don't want to talk English so you don't talk. You just say yes or no, and the same-age children as you are don't talk. We learn that way, and the country was so poor, we didn't have no schoolbook, they teach us from the blackboard. We eat, it was terrible. We eat fish for breakfast, fish for dinner, fish. It's a tough life and you are only a kid and you don't know anything better. We think that was the best I guess. You went to school then and they teach you, and everything was geared in their own way. Their own way, what they want to. They're trying to convert the whole Indian people in the North here so they use their children that go to school like that to convert. They use that in school. Instead of learning you to go upgrading they don't do that. All they talk about is heaven and hell. You sin and you bum forever and ever and you got to go to Communion every day and the type of these kind of things that I went through four years in school in Fort Providence. I went back to my parents sometime in 1932 I think.

I went through over to Burley because it was the gold rush there. Some prospectors found pitchblende, which produced the atomic bomb. That is the first kind of uranium in Canada. That was the first find there and very strong, very pure like, and a lot of White people went down there to get rich and my parents were living there. I came back to them and I didn't know how to talk Indian anymore. In the first place they called it

Eldorado, and then later on the company changed it, and during the Second World War the government took the mine over to make atomic bombs. In the last state the mine belonged to the crown so they could work faster to take ore out and make atomic bombs. Then later on another different company took over again. That would be Olacinder. A lot of minerals down there.

So I had to change again. When I came home my mother said, 'Don't talk English. It's no good,' [laughs]. So poor me I have to change all the time. Inside of one year I did not know how to talk English again. I just talk Slavey Indian. According to what my dad said I would go in the bush all the time and I learned how to hunt, fish, and my mother learned me and they told me, and at that time the Elders were still storytellers and they had lots to teach yet, at that time.

I remember my mother pulled me to gatherings every day, talk over here and talk over there. My mother pulled me there. 'Listen to those Elders, listen, you might live good.' Every day you are supposed to listen to them talk. They talk about how you should live a good life and how you should not interfere and make somebody mad. They talk like the Bible. Love your neighbour, love them very much. Don't make somebody feel bad with your actions or with your words, or try to be very polite as possible with your Elders, with everybody, and you will live longer and a more happy life. And if you do that, so all the children, in the book I write [*When the World Was New*], the people of that period are all polite. Maybe later on I will say why they are that way. They have a completely different system. I stayed in the bush with them, and finally I came here somewhere around twenty-five years old and my dad and my mom and my grandfather decided I should get married. Not the girl that I wanted, 'Not that girl, you are supposed to marry that one.' It was arranged for you and so I got married.

Life, in my life was pretty rough, and later on I start to work for the Canol Project during the Second World War, 1942, when the Canol pipeline came through. And the American army came down to the country here to build the pipeline to Whitehorse and I had my dog team with me and a couple of us guided the pipe crew to go to Whitehorse to find ways, and there I started talking English again. I talk to White people and right away it comes back to me, and then I start to self-learn everything, read newspapers, write a little bit, and it's amazing how a guy could do. In general for government I am grade three, but I might be professional, I don't know [laughs]. Grade three I started learning all this time, a long time I read *Time* magazine. I can hardly know what they mean. They use big words. Right now when I read it becomes clear to me that I understand everything. Maybe self-learning done that. I'm upgrading myself by myself.

So I got married. In Indian custom you are under your dad all the time. I was married. I had five kids. I still listen to my dad, he give me orders to do that, there is no such thing like, 'Okay, I am old enough, I am on my own, I don't have to listen to you. I go on my way.' The Indian they don't say that, because they been taught that way since they were small. So I have five kids, I was taking orders from my dad. What happened to me that changed my mind was that when I have five all girls and then I had a boy and somehow he got sick. We come from around 1910, around that period up to 1940 maybe. It was terrible country down here with people bringing disease from the outside world such as measles, TB [tuberculosis]. TB was the worst one, and no doctors, and people just die and die. You know in my family there was sixteen children, fifteen died, and I am the only one survived and I am the oldest one. That's how bad it was. Everybody. Half of their family lost by TB. Terrible. There was no doctors, there was no hospitals, and things were like that and, anyway, it caught up to me.

Probably I was carrying TB. I didn't know. Anyway my boy died in Port Radium. I really felt bad. I only had that boy and the rest were girls, and I never went no place for a week and I ask my wife that I think about it. I thought about it, talk about White people. The White people they live good. They live beside doctor, beside the good school, they work every day and they make some money, and put money away. Well, you have a strong will-power, maybe you could do that. Maybe I could do that. If I do that, that means that I have to throw away all my culture, away in order to do that. Like my grandfather and my dad, they teach me how to survive in the bush. Hunt moose, trap, fish, history, all that. I have to throw it away in order to do that. So my wife said, 'You're my husband. If you want to go someplace I will go with you.'

Her too, she never went to school. She come from Fort Franklin. She doesn't know nothing about school, so I approached my dad and told him how I feel. That I should look for a big school, a big town, and go there. He was mad. He was real mad. He yelled, shouting at me. He told me I was crazy. I told him things would change down there, he didn't believe it. 'How can things change?' he said. He never went to school, he never went nowhere else. He didn't even go to Slave Lake here. I said to my dad, 'You are wrong. Things will change and people will need money. People will need education. My kids they never went to school. They are too small to go to school now but later on they will have to.' Boy, he was mad. So I said I was going to go home, but I would come back tomorrow night again.

So I went home and I talked with my wife again. I couldn't change my mind because of him, because of my dad. I thought I lost all my sisters and brothers and I don't intend my children to die, all of them to die in the bush. I don't intend, if I have to suffer, if I have to transfer to White people's world, I will do it for the sake of my children. And I come from way, Bear Lake where there was no school, no nothing, and it's six hundred miles from there to here, travelling by dog team.

And I went to my dad and I told him again. He was mad. Finally I got the courage. But Indians, they don't talk back to their parents. But that's the only first time I talked to my dad. I tell him, 'Look, Dad, it's very tough. I love my boy, and if I stayed close to a doctor from the beginning my boy would be still alive. I am sure of it, and I don't intend to lose any more children. I think I am my own boss now. For a long time I stay with you and I take your orders, but no more of that. I will go on my own. And look, Dad,' I said, 'I blame you. I lost fifteen children, I lost fifteen brothers and sisters because of you. They are buried in the bush all along Bear Lake. It's all your fault and I don't want you to talk to me roughly again because I am going away.' And I stopped talking. 'My boy,' he said, 'maybe you are right, maybe you should do what you want, but don't forget us. Go if you want to.'

So I gave away all my traps, my guns, everything what I had. They can have everything. All I need is my dog team and my blankets, a small tent. I load my children and I go to Yellowknife. Six hundred miles from there to here in February. In the cold I arrive in Yellowknife around 1950. Oh tough. Tough for an Indian that don't know anything. I come from the bush, I don't even know how to work for White people. I never worked for anybody yet. To work in the city, I know nothing about that because I come from the bush.

And I look for a job, I look, and finally I got the job in the mine, $1.49 an hour. And I have six children to feed. I managed, but in a small shack and the toughest time in my life was Yellowknife. I tried to live like a White guy but I couldn't do it. I had to buy everything from a store every day because I had to work every day. I had to pay for food. I have to pay tax on the house. I had to learn how to get credit from the store so that I could buy stuff and try to manage. The worst part was I didn't know the value of money. Indians are all like that. They don't know how to handle money. Money it is just like paper. To the White people it is just like God, but to the Indians, right here there are people like that. Money it don't mean anything to them, it is just like paper.

But when they run out of it they feel bad, but when they have it it was the same as me there. A tough time, boy, I am telling you. I can hardly make pay cheque from payday to payday. But I made sure all my children went to school. And they all are educated. I got my boy sitting over there at the house, he is master negotiator for Dogrib Nation to the federal government. He went to the University of Alberta, the University of Vancouver, and my other boy went to the University of Alberta, the University of Lethbridge, they just came back, they are very educated. So my children are like that. I have another boy went to university in England, and Montreal, and talk French, and I got no problem with my children. Sometimes I sit down here and I feel like I did the right thing. But lots of Indians are against me. They told me you throw your children to the White people, and you are poor now. I sit here alone, and they are too busy to come and see me. And they tell me that, but in my heart I think I did the right thing. And at least they can make a good living for themselves because of education, a university degree and all that.

And then after I lived in Yellowknife my wife died of cancer. I felt so lonesome I had to quit the mines, and I worked there eleven years. I went back to Franklin and I went trapping for seven more years down there in my country, and at that time the Indians are starting, around 1973, they are starting to get a bit smart, and they are starting to investigate their old treaty of 1921, and they find that there was everything wrong with it. The government imposed a lot, misleading the people, and the Indian Act extinguished their rights, and all the land title, and all that. It was written by the Indian Affairs and it wasn't agreeable in the general treaty. They took the government to court and the court decided that these Indians should have another land claim, another land claim, a new one, so the court decided that this should go, so that is why we are the only treaty Indian in Canada, that we have treaty, but we could also start a land claim for ourselves, and renew that treaty of 1921. Extinguish that or use it and mix it up with your general modern land claim, and try to have a complete agreement of what we want from the government.

Twenty years I been involved with politics, the rights of the Dene people. Talk about their rights and go to these meetings. It's amazing that the whole country, because of the change, the government want to deal with Indian a little bit better. They realize that there were a lot of mistakes because they imposed on them and even the mission, even the Pope came here and said that we made a great mistake and we are sorry we treated the Indians like that. So they give a chance to hear the drum in the church, use the culture in the church, and we will say nothing and the priest will treat us much better now, and the government too, some of the government realized that there was a lot of money for that big land and they try to square things with us today because we yap and yap and twenty years I have been talking. And help the Chief and when, I been a Chief, and when I wasn't trying, they elected me Chief. So I been a Chief for two years in Fort Franklin. But I had no kids there, my kids were in Yellowknife working here and there. I moved back with them here, but when I went to Franklin my children are in Yellowknife and here so I'm staying in the old folks' home here to be close to them. And I get involved with all their meetings and all that, but my boys say, 'Don't do that. Take a rest. Take it easy. We will do the work. You have a rest,' but I don't know how to rest, I keep going and walking.

So in the meantime I wrote a book, *When the World Was New.* I wrote that when I was travelling in Fort Franklin. I carry this in my bag and when I sleep, travelling alone late at night I take my pencil out and try to talk about legends. What did my grandfather say? What did my dad say? What did my mother say anyway about the stories? I lost half of all that history and legends anyway, but the main one I captured. So in the bush there, fifty below zero maybe and my hands stick out and I reach down and just keep writing [laughs]. And that's how I wrote the book.

Now I want to write a second one. This time I know a little bit better, according to my grade three, just grade three I guess, but I am much smarter now. So I went to Fort Smith, Resolution, I went back to Franklin again to pick up some more legend stories and put them all together. And that's what I did for the past two years. I got a grant from the government. Me and my boys are going to help me and look for a publisher and we are going to Toronto next month to the university over there to retype. It's typed already. The way I write it's terrible. My boy says you can't read your writing, the language is bad. So retype it in better language. So they retype in better language. All the words my boy typed for a month. The whole manuscript.

So with this kind of movement I went through a pretty rough life. As an Indian I love my, the way, my Indian culture. I still am in love with the land, I am still in love with my history, and the way they teach, and I knew that there were good Elders that teach good. That's what kept Indians in the line, there were no police, no force, but there were very good people, and they were in line. And it surprised me at this time with all the TV, books, teaching, school, priest talk, police, yet crime is steady going up.

Every week they have a big court case and it's all like that. Why is it that Indians .have run their own affairs pretty good? Why at this moment in time are things like that? We have the education. We have big good schools here, yet it's not any better, I cannot see it in a better situation the way things are going. So this is possibly my life story.

Creation Stories

I agree with the scientists. But I still believe that storytellers of the Aboriginal people come from a long ways. Further back than any scientist. The scientist uses special knowledge, special action like reading marks on the earth, rocks. That they read and they got the evidence how old things are and they go back and stuff like that, but before I say that, I want you to understand the general attitude of the Dene, how they tell stories.

One of the things in the area of storytelling is a strong culture in the Dene Nation. Anybody that becomes Elder, their responsibility is to tell story. Not only the stories to teach all the young people of how to live a good life, and you have to say that every day. Elders give advice to parents to talk to their children as soon as they start to talk, as soon as babies start to talk, their mother is supposed to talk to them, 'Your grandfather said that you are supposed to live like that.' If it's a girl you talk to her as a girl. If it is a boy you talk to him as a boy, and they grow with it. As they grow they grow with it and it becomes part of their mind and they will never forget it as long as they live because they hear that every day when they were small, and they still remember and they have to live like that. The very strong culture that is embedded in the people. That's why they were good.

One of the things, it's so complicated to understand, that is why I had a problem to publish *When the World Was New*, because I don't know the whole world, it's not only North American Indian that have medicine power. The medicine power is something invisible, yet has existed. All the Indians have used that power and they really live according to that power, and that is where they made laws and that is where the teaching come from. That is where great medicine people made laws across the Nation. That comes from medicine power. There the people have power and I have tried to in these legends that I am writing in the second book, I have a hell of a time because I have to do lots of definitions. I wrote a three whole page definition of medicine power right at the start, but the medicine power is so great, so complicated, when you write stories about the person that did that there is a need to define his or her medicine power again, so at the beginning of a story I have to explain what kind of power that he was using when he did this and did that. So one definition is not enough to explain, because medicine power is a Spirit, is a power of Spirit, invisible, capable of interfering with space, sun, moon, on earth, insects, all animals on earth. People have medicine power. Some of them lots, some of them just one, some of them hundreds and hundreds. Some of them got too much medicine, some of them none. So people live like that so their law come from that. So you were talking about the beginning.

My grandmother was a great storyteller. She said, 'In the beginning,' she said, 'in the beginning there was no people, there was no person, no woman or man on this earth.' According to the storyteller. In the beginning there was all the animals. There was fish and there was animals. But in the long run, somehow, the movement took place from animal. Then our form started to change as a person. Medicine power. All animals had medicine power as well. Animal, moose, caribou, bear, they all had medicine power. So when man, when man became human they, they transform from animal and they still had medicine power from this animal. So it was no problem for them to talk to animals. That's why we are saying that human beings, because we are coming from animals, our medicine power come from animals. And medicine people, not ordinary person, but people that have medicine could talk to crow, could talk to raven, could talk to wolf, could talk to caribou, thousands of miles away, just like a telephone. Could talk to fish, could talk to chickens. So they have no problem with communication with animals. They talk just like we are talking here.

When human beings developed at the start, a lot of problems, because we are half animal and we don't think straight. We are probably smarter than animals because we are starting to be human beings, and we have a lot of problems for a long period, probably two, three hundred years, maybe five hundred years. So with medicine power strong, some of these people are very strong. Some of them were just like God. There was this young man named *Yamoria*, he came into the country, he realized that, tried to separate the human beings, separate it from animals so that they could be human beings on their own. So he did that, he had a lot of power.

His definition, which means 'person went around the earth,' that's what the name is because maybe that's what he did. And he had such strong medicine power that he could control people's minds. Suppose he come to Fort Rae and he want to have a meeting with the council, and he don't have to shout to people. He will make everybody think his way. Controlling the mind. So everybody will have to rush down there without being told and listen to him. That's the kind of person he was and he went all over the world, not the world, but part of the country that he was. And he tell people, 'I come here, a special person that comes here to help you people. You are human being, you are not animal. You are by yourself, and you are much smarter than all animals so you have to come together somehow and try to develop leadership.' He didn't say government, but he said leadership. 'Group together and have a leadership and your medicine power will still be with you, and if you have a problem right now, say it and I will try to help.' Some people start to have lots of problems. They have dinosaurs, they have flying bats, big bats, bigger than this house that just pick up people and eat them, pick up people and take off flying all over, dinosaur all over the country. And you can't kill it with bow and arrow. So this person said, 'I will get rid of all this animals.' They don't like it the Indians. They are too big, they can't eat it, they can't kill it, they kill the Indians instead. So he transferred special disease to these dinosaurs and made them all die across the country, and he did the same with big bats too. It's no good for people. And he did that and everywhere that he is travelling, people tell him their problems and he straighten out everything, and there were a lot of bad medicine men too, and then there are strong medicine people and not all of them were good, some of them were wicked, some of them had too much power, and were just killing people and forced people, people were scared of them. They confront them, some of them, and they just kill them.

And he told other people that medicine power is to help people not to fight people or not give hurt. It's been given to you by the Creator to help. To survive, to help each other, to give food. To get caribou to come to you with your medicine power, moose, fish, and all. You use medicine power to kill it, and feed all the poor, and treat the sickness. Treat the sick people and govern people by yourself and use that law, and use that medicine power too.

So these kinds of things were like that so, and he's the guy that made the law, and he made the law for the people, and he said, 'I will make a law and you will have to use it and all parents are responsible to teach their children as soon as they start to talk.' I have written here somewhere in the house. One of the first ones is about sharing. Sharing is a big umbrella law. That sharing is about the branch that you have to look after the sick people, have to look after the Elders, look after the widows, and you have to, if you kill moose or caribou, you have to share with all the people, and help each other and all that. Love each other and all that sharing and other law says love each other, don't hurt nobody and have laws for girls. All together there is about ten. He's the one that made that law and my mother used to teach me about that. '*Yamoria* said that, and you better be good if you want to live long. You live according to the law.' I didn't know what he was talking about, but now I know. When I was small I didn't know. When I went to school they all mixed me up, but I tried to write a book and tried to make people remember that their system was really good. So one of the things that I wanted to say is the creation of people. That's how they talk about it. They didn't say that they came across the ice bridge like the White people say. They didn't say that. They said they were transferred from the animals to human beings. So according to the scientists' report dinosaur was here 63,000 years ago. Here was all ice, they say. The storyteller talk about dinosaur just like it was today. And yet they were talking about the creation of human beings transformed from animals.

So if the human beings exist when the dinosaur was here they are talking 63,000 years ago. And we go by information from storytelling from year to year and day to day up. So the beginning, the beginning of the creation of human beings, it could be another thousand years somewhere around when the dinosaur was here. So it's a good chance to say the Aboriginal people come from storyteller, that they have a history for 100,000 years, and a very very good one, very dear to all Indian people, and it really worked good their storytelling, because nobody interfered with that. And when an Elder talks everybody is supposed to listen and they go day to day. Every day Elders die but there is a new one coming up, and every group of people travel all over. Elders were with them and their storytelling group, for thousands of years it's been going on. It's a sad thing to talk about. These kinds of good things from the Elders were extinguished, came to a complete stop around 1940, when they brought in the department of education and started to build schools. A very strong power, education.

They imposed, children started talking English, not listen to their mother and dad anymore, and they're thinking of school, what they learn and read, and not listening to their mom and dad anymore. Not paying attention to their grandfather anymore, to the Elders, no one listens to them, nobody pays attention to them. So they don't talk anymore. They did a complete stop. Their mother and dad too. Their culture of teaching their own children came to a complete stop too. What happens today, children on their own, raise themselves I would say. I have a hell of a time to get stories from these people. Elders, they have been not telling stories for a long time. I been lucky enough to have ten. I visit them and I keep on trying to get stories from them. Oh, there were good storytellers, but they all died out. And new kind of people, they don't know how. That is why. So you got a little bit of information of creation of human beings, that's how they tell it. It's a bit different from the White people, but not quite different.

I read *Life* magazine one time a long time ago that shows in a great picture a monkey that, first it was fish, the fish jumped on the earth and started walking and eating leaves and became animal, a land animal. Animal changed all the time and cross-breed, and pretty soon you have monkey, and as they grow, thousands of years, millions of years maybe, it change, it change, and it looks like men. And finally it developed into human beings, and *Life* magazine said that's where we come from and the Indians here say we come from animal and maybe they are saying the same thing, we don't know. We could be talking about the same thing.

But the church have their own history. God made somebody with one rib and so on. But that's just how the Indians have their own belief. That's how they say. So they knew, they knew about the creation of human beings because they used medicine power, and medicine power is something very powerful, that which is beyond human beings is a power, and they knew the earth was round. The Indian knew the earth was round, the Indian knew the earth was turning because they had medicine power for that and certain people had medicine power for that and that person could talk to the public, that this is the kind of earth we are living on. But the rest of local people, they don't pay attention. They think this guy is crazy. They think the earth was flat.

He is crazy, and he try to explain, but people don't pay attention because nobody wants to learn in these days. They believe in what they see and they are happy about it. So this is the kind of issues that I try to do my best on the creation of human beings and this second book. And I try to write a lot about what I am talking about now in there, maybe a couple pages, I try to write about the education system they teach, really effective, and really make good citizens. Because of the extinguishment of all this culture people think at this moment, maybe the school thinks this way, I don't know, we use our own system, it is the best, forget about Indian culture. But lately all the schools across the country are trying to pick up some of the good things for the Aboriginal people, and they are trying to do that. That's one of the reasons I really pay attention to the education of today, and see if some of the professors or leaders of education could pick up good things out of Indian legend. That's not the first time I talk like that. I did a lot of work on trying to write curriculum. And I help lots. So this is a pretty close idea of the beginning of human beings.

Importance of Culture

Yes, because you are Indian, you are an Aboriginal person. I am one Aboriginal person. It doesn't matter if I went to school or was educated very high, it doesn't matter. My heart, my love, is in the Aboriginal people. My ancestor, where I come from, my grandfather, I used to sleep with. The reason I sleep with him when I was a baby, all Indians crave to have medicine power. One aspect of the culture is when a married couple have a baby, a boy or a girl it doesn't matter, and they push this baby to sleep with its grandfather and grandmother, in between them, small baby. In order to inherit medicine power. In order the possibility the grandfather will have an idea that his grandson is a medicine man and they are very happy about that. They crave for medicine power. For that reason, my dad and mom have pushed me, I have two medicine grandfathers. They lived long, they lived up to ninety because they were strong men. And I slept with both of them but I didn't inherit no medicine power.

Medicine power is supposed to be, to go to only good people. I think in person, and my grandfather explained to my dad he can't be a medicine man because he is too haywire, he is not a good thinking man. 'Forget about George having medicine power. But raise him good he might be a good citizen.' For these kinds of actions they did to their grandson, as small children you become very in love with your own people. They did this for the good of you. They teach about the land, they teach about Mother Earth, and you fall in love with your Mother Earth, you fall in love with the things that Mother Earth provides, animals, fish, plants, and all that. You spend a lot of life on that. I spent a lot of life on that. I really cannot change at this time, even though I work for White people for forty years and live in Yellowknife without going back in the bush. Yet I have never forgotten my own people, and their culture. The way they teach. I have never forgotten my language, and I have never forgotten my culture because it was embedded in my body since I was a baby, and I have never forgotten. Never change. I have talked to my children the modern way instead. Well, they went to university so they learned the modern way, but for me, leave me alone because I am going to be that way until I die.

Because that is the way I am supposed to be. My grandfather says, 'You are Indian, you are supposed to be that way.'

So I believe in all, what mostly what they say. So at this time I compare with all my writing books and thinking about the movement of Aboriginal people in my area. The extinguishment of all their rights and culture and language, and loss of all their land, and their loss, their attitude and thinking that Aboriginal people, their own people is right. Other children don't think that way, they think that modern people are right, that's why we are going to make money. So there is this great conflict in the public of Dene people down here. There still is. They are negotiating a land claim in Fort Rae. Most young people are thinking in the modern way, and negotiators, the leaders negotiate trying to make an agreement with the federal government. With the large piece of land they want to hold.

So children of the future might come back and use that land, and use some of their culture to trap and hunt and think of that. Looking for job too is one way, but it's almost impossible to have a job for everybody. So it's a very great conflict. It is a sad thing that all your culture is going away. It is understandable, I don't think you are too smart. You got to be smart to know why things go on like that. Any person can figure out why is that. It's a general movement. It's the way things are. Well, I would say okay. I will just talk about Paul Grey.

People there, that I knew when I came here, the first time I came here around 1940, 1938, I think I came here. I came here with a dog team to visit. At this time there was just the Hudson's Bay and the priests and a few Métis had a house, a log house here, and the rest of the place was just tents. They had tents all over. There was no food, there were no doctors, there were just priests and Hudson's Bay. And they live off the land. They were happy, they got tea dance, hand games, dried meat. They weren't rich, but you know, they live off the land. And they are using their law, as I was explaining, they use their traditional law to be good. So it's later on when they put up schools that things started to extinguish all their language and listening to their laws, their laws, their Elders' teaching, their parents' teaching. And later on, because education forced them to stay in communities, because all children had to go to school. So the government had to develop welfare so that they could live in town.

So with this kind of movement power, it pushed people around. Soon, they don't want to trap no more. They don't want to hunt no more. They are using the welfare to feed their children, to feed themselves. And some of them they don't go in the bush now for years because of that. So I would say, with that kind of movement, power, that pushed people around. You don't talk about, but I sit down here and recognize what power does. You don't talk about it, but it pushed people around. It pushed people to eat. For example, they were eating fish and moose and caribou, no more of that. Instead of that they get chicken shipped in and pork chops and all good stuff from Alberta shipped in and they eat that. They are not eating muskrat and beaver and caribou. They are not eating that no more. They get me into a habit to eat that, so the children don't like to eat wild meat no more. Instead of that they like to eat all the fancy food from the store. Ready-cooked chicken and stuff like that.

You can understand what I am saying. This power changed people to be that way, so at the same time it extinguished your culture. So it's not the government saying you can't do this, it's the movement and the power, the way you eat, the way you live, the power change you to live in a house instead of in a tent. Don't live in the bush. You come to live like that, therefore you don't need your culture. Just live the way you are and welfare will look after you, and if the kids commit crimes the police will take them away, well, that's their own fault, and all kinds of things like that. So the movement becomes a system. A long time ago they used to live in the bush and dry meat. This has been extinguished by this power and movement. You understand what I am saying? It becomes like that.

Therefore today life becomes that way, not on its own course, but on the power of the movement. The people live on welfare, some pay rent, some got no money to pay. Court every week, they have no money to pay court, they take them away. And if they got money, if the Elder got a pension, the children take the pension away because they share everything. They give all their money to their daughter or son. Babies cry for money all the time, so pension will last for two days and then it's gone. Then you wait until next month, but kids come every day for money. It's like that. So we feel sorry that we lost our culture and the most important one, but what can we do, the power of movement is so strong, and it becomes part of daily life, and at the same time it robs you of your important culture.

It would be good for people to write down culture in education in the system, that you say you pick up everything from the Elders. Trying to get the system, that Dene teaching would be involved somehow in the system. One of the general things is that they should have some kind of action in school. Possibly they should give five minutes to a good speaker, to an Elder. If they give five minutes, it's not much. Ten would be a lot better, a half an hour would be a lot better, but the department of education does not want to spend money on an Elder. An Elder can go to a big room in the school where all the kids come. Spend five minutes so the Elder can talk about the culture. He can say love each other, because love each other means you would work together and do no harm together. The children or the teacher would help the Elder, and tell the children to pay attention to this Elder and don't say a word. If it's too long, five minutes would be the best and children will concentrate for five minutes every day, but they don't have that. I know the children in school, they just go to their own class and yell. To me they are not using Indian culture. They use the system in the education. The system that they are supposed to run the school. Well, maybe it's good, that's how all go through education, but we are losing our culture and that's what my concern is.

Using Traditional Culture Today

I really believe that we have a system somehow to get across to our children. Our system, before the White man came, it was a storytelling system. This telling, the Elders have that, and all parents attend that kind of gathering all day and the Elders will tell the parents, 'Teach your baby when your baby starts to talk. Teach him about *Yamoria* law, how to be good citizens. How you can love each other and work together. Good, no violence, no fighting, love each other that way you will do good.' The danger in their time was medicine power. That is why *Yamoria* made that law. You can't tell a guy has medicine power. It is a spirit. You can't tell by just looking, you wouldn't know because it is invisible. But the person that holds medicine, he is going to look on ordinary people, like me and you. Maybe I got a temper, maybe I got a real temper, and I don't know what people are saying. If I am capable to kill somebody with my medicine power nobody will know anyway. I could use that power to kill that person and nobody would know. I would not be punished. Nobody would know. For that reason *Yamoria* made that law. People get mouthy and go out, especially strangers, and laugh at somebody. That kind of attitude disturbs medicine power. Bad-tempered medicine man. And in the history a lot of people lost their life, because of that. A lot of bad wicked medicine people killed a lot of people just because they didn't like people, just because somebody made a joke about them. They didn't get punished, but they killed a lot of people.

In order to live good with that kind of life, *Yamoria* made law that you should love each other and *Yamoria* told the parents that they should teach their children very very good when they are small, not to be mouthy, not to hurt nobody, love each other, and help each other, and share everything that you got. That way you could live a long life. Sometimes people lost their lives when they were young because their parents didn't teach them. For that reason I think I told lots of ways how can we transfer some of our culture at this time when everything is extinguished. All medicine power of Dene people is extinguished forever, it's gone. There was some medicine power in 1925, but when the flu epidemic came around 1926 [1928] it wipe out all the Indians, it wipe out all medicine people, and it's completely gone after 1926 [1928]. After 1926 [1928] there is hardly any medicine people. Today I can safely say there is nothing left. I live here two years, I hear people say if you get sick visit some medicine man over there to be cured or to look into the sickness. So there could be some odd one or two here and there, not worth to talk about, not like long time ago there was lots of medicine power, but not now.

So I am locked in the way that quality of lifestyle of the present people, and the modern education, how they use the system. How do we transfer some of the culture, the good culture from the past? If you could manage there are plenty of people to talk about that. Some of the laws are very good. You could still use it today, such as be polite to each other, don't steal, don't make people feel bad. I think if we could capture what the church talk about, it's so hard in the area of how people become this way. I mean the young people of today, how they become that, maybe the White people are like that, but I always think about the area of Indians, maybe it is because the education is not completely a strong system that deals with people. I think the children that are learning are not like White children. They are half brain-washed, half coming from their mom and dad who never went to school, they will probably talk about their culture, talk Indian, and then they go to school and then they talk English. There they learn different types of systems, like the law and all that.

There is two types of things small children are caught in between. They grow, they are not completely one person thinking the same. Maybe the department of education has something good to learn them, but one person looks like two kinds of person, that kind of thing. I've been doing a lot of thinking on education, sometimes I write my views of the North. I used to write on the *Native Press*, but they went bankrupt. Two papers went bankrupt.

Traditional Birthing

They had their own way. They learned how to be midwives, they were very important. When I lived in Franklin in 1975, when I was a Chief, a government official came down there, they wanted to give a medal to a boy who saved someone's life who had fallen through the ice. So these government officials people were there for a couple hours. I come home, I told my friend, I said, 'This really make me think,' I said. 'I come from great history. I have seen lots of people who deserve thousands of medals who have done good things for people.' One is my mother-in-law, she was a midwife, very well-known, no matter what it was she was there all the time to help. I would like to write about her. I went travelling to communities and met lots of people who said they were delivered by my mother-in-law, 390 in total. So my daughter and I wrote about her grandmother, my mother-in-law. It was talked about all over, next spring the government and a group of women came to see her. She was recognized, presented with papers and medals, and it was good.

She had learned about midwifery. Women were always told not to sleep, to walk around when they were pregnant. When women delivered babies, they did not lie down like they do in hospitals, they used a special kind of wood, a log, they would lean on. Today there are no more midwives. They've got nursing stations in every community. No one is in the bush so all babies are born in nursing stations. They are forced to live in communities, so the way of life has changed.

Men, however, taught the children. When babies are small, mothers are a bit weak, so the men would do all the work like cooking, gathering of diaper moss. In the wintertime the moss is hard to find, you look at the lay of the land and you know it's in the valley. Men would go in the bush to get this, they would thaw it dry and clean it. Babies would be fed broth, moose or fish, besides mother's milk. When babies start to talk, men, mostly men are responsible for the teachings. My mom and my dad used to say I have to teach you children every day. They get tired of it, but you have to change every day. My oldest daughter that lives in Yellowknife, 'Sometimes I don't like you,' she said, 'you talk too much, you said something yesterday, tomorrow you have to say it again, tomorrow you have to say it again, I have to listen to you all the time' [laughs]. So that is why the teaching system, even though they repeat it over so they will not forget. Just because I said it yesterday doesn't mean I have to say it again today, it's not like that you keep on going.

Traditional Dwellings

I just talk about my own. Mostly tent but sometimes cabins because their system of life they have to travel a lot because if they stay in one place too long they clean out the land of wildlife. But people have cabins, sometimes there is a good fish lake out there. Sometimes a family would establish themselves there and build a cabin. But travellers mostly had tents. In the tent their floor is brush and they change it every second day, close to the stove the heat is, they dry up faster and they will replace this part with new brush. They used canvas tents, they got a big wood stove, they made duck-feather blankets, they don't have to have a fire going all night, but they have to restart the fire. They had to make a hole in the ice to get water, but most of the time they used snow, not the top layer but underneath. The best water is snow water, good for tea. Even here people go way out for snow, it is better than water from the tap.

Traditional Self-Government

Like I said already, all their life was based on medicine power, and it is really something that they look at it as a power that everybody is supposed to use, and they really respect that power. I have done quite a bit of definition of why they are doing this. That's all they had in the area of depending on somebody. They look at medicine power as someone with the power to govern you, and look upon you and save you, because they have that power. The system of acquiring leadership is not the same as anything you see today. All they decide is a group of people, they are always travelling. Each group would have a leader, that decision would be made by most Elders of that group. They decide, 'This guy will lead us, he will be the leader for this winter.'

When I interviewed Elders, lots of lots of Elders, in order to write a definition of medicine power, some of the Elders were saying, 'Some of this power is spiritual, it is holy, it comes from the Creator.' That is why they believed in the Creator before the White man came. They have a special way that these medicine people receive holy medicine power. Some of them acquire holy songs, develop holy songs, and the people start to learn from these special people. It spread throughout the public and other groups of people would start singing them.

Sometimes these prophets would sing without a drum, they would concentrate on their prayers to the Creator. The tea dance would usually start off with a prayer song. The drummers would slowly start to hit their drums, then everybody would get up, concentrating on their own problems, like their family, wife, children, they pray for love. As this prayer song goes on, the drummers would sing a special prayer song. A speaker of the drum would tell the people, after the song is done, about the prayer to the Creator. Another song sometimes would be sung by the drummers, people would be standing up concentrating on their prayers. That's the culture, I really believe hard in that.

We were very disturbed by the treatment of the church, the early missionaries. They would tell us our culture is a devil culture and that we were singing to the devil. They even got a law to stop us, but lots of Indians did not quit, their belief was too strong. Sometimes they would tell us in church not to sing those songs anymore, they would tell us in public to tell the people. Some of the early priests had a bad temper and they would yell at the people. They would say there is only one culture and that is our way. But that is not true. Even though people were told, they still continued to sing because their belief was so strong. They see something that the priest does not see, they see something good in that.

This gathering that people are going to in Edmonton tomorrow. Almost all of Fort Rae is going, they believe in their hearts so strongly, I am going to write a story about that, because we are poor people that something good will come to us. The Indians never forgot their own spirituality. Some have acquired this special power through medicine power, they see something holy coming about. That is why they establish these songs. For example, one old man was a Chief of a mountain Indian tribe before going to the Yukon. He was a leader, a lot of medicine power, he owned quite a bit. So maybe five or six years before he died, he told the people, 'I have somebody to give me songs for all the people, to practise as a prayer song. It has been given to me by a high power, the Creator possibly. I cannot say I see something, but I hear a voice telling me these are the songs for you. The song that I will sing, it is coming from this high power. I hear them singing so I take my drum and start singing. I don't practise, I don't have to practise, it is made especially for me so that everyone will acquire it.' And he said, 'It is a miracle what power this land has to acquire this kind of song.'

He comes from Fort Norman [Tilita], his name is Andrew, that's why there is lots of Andrews in Fort Norman. The year that he acquired these songs he came with about 53 prayer songs. Not one of these songs nobody was heard say he practised, he made these songs, nobody said that. All of a sudden he said, 'I am ordered to sing a song right now.' They beat the drum for him. He had two daughters, and four boys, and they all own the drum. They come to aid their dad. 'I sing one song and you guys have to follow to sing it.' So he takes the drum and he sings the song. A brand-new song that people never heard in this country. Now he

said, 'You guys follow me with this song.' So his mother, two girls, four
boys, they follow their dad, they're singing. Here is a brand-new song.
They did this all winter with 53 new songs. A special man did that. It is
incredible how that person did that. People from all over began to sing
these new songs, it attracted everybody. All kinds of people came to hear
these special songs, from other places like Good Hope, all over. This is
an example of how the prayer songs came to be in the North. These
prayer songs were sung before White people come. Even today the people sing these songs.

All tea dances started with a prayer song. Around the middle of the
dance, they would have another prayer song where people would concentrate on their prayers. A tea dance is a prayer dance, it is a bit faster, so
people will dance, they follow in one circle, one row. Sometimes they
make two or three rings if there are lots of people. People are happy at
these tea dances. When drummers get tired, they change drummers.

To choose leaders of the group, they do not go through voting. The
people who pick the leader is usually a medicine man. A medicine man is
important to the people because he has power. People fear the person so
they have to listen to him. Sometimes great people had so much power
that they could kill a whole flock of people without even touching them.
There were people like that. That was why they would pick out people
with power so that people would respect them. There are stories of leaders who were able to feed everybody. Some were able to call for caribou
using this power. They also had power to protect their people from other
people.

These leaders would have meetings every day. When people committed
crimes, they would confront those people who did wrong, fear was how
leaders controlled crime. They had the power, people feared them, leaders were usually medicine men. There was usually one medicine man who
had more power than others. He would be the top person, which we
could say is the government. For example, the Dogrib Nation has a
school named Edzo. Edzo was a leader, such leaders were legends,
nobody could kill them, they were so powerful. Edzo was the one who
made peace with the Chipewyan all by himself. He only had his brother-
in-law and a small child, there were three of them, facing thousands of
Chipewyan. He was not afraid because he had medicine power, even if
the thousands attacked him. He might kill the thousand men, the
Chipewyan leaders knew that, and they feared him. So when he talked
about peace, everybody listened to him, he achieved peace with Chipewyan and since then there has been no war.

There is a saying in the Beaver tribe, when the first priests arrived there in the mountains, the Rocky Mountains. The priests were talking about Jesus. One old man approached the priest and asked what he was talking about when he talked about this person who did miracles and created the world, and that we had someone living among us, he is the one that did miracles for us, he made a law by which to live by, respect Mother Earth and respect everything Creator has made. He made songs for us to pray and we sang and that is why we are good people. He was talking about *Yamoria*. The legend of *Yamoria* is all over the country.

There is a legend of giant beavers that *Yamoria* chased out. He chased them into this lake and into a channel, they were tired. What happened is the giant beavers were eating birch, they were making so much noise in the channel, the people did not know what it was, so they got scared and ran into the bush [laughs]. *Yamoria* chased them into Slave Lake and down the Mackenzie River. So that is how he got rid of the giant beavers. *Yamoria* is a person with great power.

That is generally how they governed themselves, with people with medicine power. It was mostly men who were leaders, but some women had medicine power too. One story is about a medicine power woman. There was a hunter who went hunting by himself, he was a young man, on the edge of the barren land. He saw something coming. At first, he thought it was a caribou and when he got closer it was a woman. He hid and watched her. She was carrying a big bag. He wondered what she was doing all alone out here. He thought of himself as a strong man, so he approached this woman and asked her what she was doing there. She said, 'I am ordered to this area to help people, that's why I am walking around.' The man was not thinking straight, as she was a beautiful woman, he tried to play with the woman. The woman said, 'Do not touch me, don't do such things because I am not allowed to do that.' But the man didn't listen, he kept bothering her.

Then she went right into the earth and disappeared and she was gone, the big bag that she was carrying broke open, there was all kinds of metal in there, they melted to just like water. The man got scared, he never saw anything like that, he was excited and told the people what happened. The old people told him that he should not have tried to get after this woman, that he could die. A whole crew of people went there where this had happened, it was now rock. People chipped at the hardened metal and took some, copper, iron. They made knives and arrowheads out of this. It was a powerful woman, but it did not work out. Perhaps if the man would have left her alone, she would have come out to the people to help. It was not only men who had power, but there are stories of how women stopped wars.

Treaties

The Aboriginal people lived off the land, with completely different attitudes from the White people. I have went to great length in discovering, I am trying to find out what happened when the first White people got here in this area. In general they came from the south. They brought articles to trade with Indians. The Indians did not know the value of things. Indians did not know what trading was. If someone needed something that they had, they would just give it for nothing, they would share it and they would practise learning how to make things. There was no selling or trading.

When Europeans came they had articles like matches, knives, guns, things that the Indians never saw before. They looked at White people as powerful people, they never looked at it as if the Europeans were robbing them, even though they were giving lots of fur for only one gun. They did not know the value of money, they were simple people. The Europeans took advantage of them, the Hudson Bay Company traders were acting like the government, as well as the priests. They wanted to control the Indian people. The priests too took advantage of them because they were poor. They would give the priest their furs. The Indians looked at these people as ones who wanted things, so they gave them.

The Indians never fought over their land, the White people just came in and took over. Trading took place, pretty soon they had a railroad, steamboat, more people came. Up to 1921, Indians had tents, blankets. The first indication was in Norman Wells, when oil was discovered. Some people from Alberta said there was oil there. It was decided then to sign a treaty with the Indians. The Indians did not know what a treaty was. The White people said it was an agreement. 'You will get five dollars, you can hunt wherever you want, we are not after the land, we will give you five dollars to show we are generous and we are friends. If there is a war we will not use you in the war, if you are sick we will help you, if you need things we will give you what you need, but we have to make laws.' So in general that is what the Indians say.

When the treaty was signed, for the first time, they elected Chief and Council the White man way. No one said anything about the land. The Indians did not know that the government was claiming it. The Indians did not know how to read and write. The treaty said that all their rights and also the land was going to the government. They made all the leaders sign the treaty. They signed with a cross because they could not write. It was a hypocritical paper. They took everything, the land, all for five dollars. It was a big lie. The Indians thought they were being paid just to live together. They did not find out until later, in the 1960s when some of our people became educated. They started looking into the treaty, the more they studied it, the more crooked it became. The lawyers looked at it. Some of the crosses were forged, some of those people were not even there at the treaty signing. There had been a lot of crooked work on the part of the government.

The young people said, 'Maybe we will take the government to court, maybe we will try a new agreement.' One judge, Morrow, really helped the people. He travelled to all the communities, they said land or extinguishment was never discussed in the treaty. Some took the government to court. He said these people need a new agreement, a renewed treaty, that is what we call the land claims. We are talking about how to deal with the government. They talked about compensation. The longer it takes the harder the government is to deal with. It is now twenty-one years and no claim has been settled. Some people got tired, they broke away and acquired their own land claim in one year, not a good one because the government forced them.

The Dogrib put in a claim and took a strong stand, it does not matter how long it takes. They are also going to entrench self-government into the claim. The government does not want to listen. They would rather see the Indians extinguish everything. It is stealing.

Elders

Elders from the beginning have been seen as their own government along with teachings. Everything was based on Elders' teachings, they were very valued in Native culture. This has been going on for thousands and thousands of years. When the dinosaurs were here, there were lots and lots of people here. The scientists say it was 63,000 years ago, the Indian people talk about it like it was not long ago. Stories were information of the past. So Elders were important, they knew the stories.

So Elders were seen as good people, they would sit every day. They had gatherings all the time. All the people had responsibility to attend these meetings. Most of the talk was on medicine power, so people respected them. They were taught to be good to each other and children were discouraged from going out at night because Spirits are out at night. This is one law we should be following, there are some children running around at night. Elders are those who can pass on knowledge, now there are not very many Elders left. It seems like they are not needed anymore, the power of White society has changed all that.

Heroes and Role Models

Today role models are those Native people who have made something of themselves. They get an education and get a good job. My son is one example. He went to university and now holds a good job, has a vehicle, has a house, money in the bank, works and helps his people. Long ago when Elders were still important, they were the role models, but today it is different.

Traditional Games

Young people were encouraged to move around, not sleep all day. They walked, went swimming, which was important because those skills are survival skills. For example, if they tip over in a boat, they will know how to save themselves. Hand games are the thing that has been kept alive. Sometimes there are thirty people to a team, they guess who has the stick, they drum and sing at the same time. It is lots of noise and lots of fun. Celebrations long ago were held mainly in the summer gatherings. They had feasts, dances, laughing, everyone was happy.

Marriages

Marriages were arranged. Elders and parents decided who their children would marry. People got married at about sixteen years of age. People did not separate or divorce, no one went against what had been set out. Sex was not talked about, it was sacred. There were no teenage pregnancies, single mothers. People did not get involved with sex until they were married. Now that we do not have medicine power, it is out of control.

Daily Routines

One of the things I really watch is the Dipper, the stars. If you see that right above you, if it turned to the north, that is when you would get up. They could tell time by the stars.

Rarely did Indians get lost in the bush, they had a sense of direction. They used all kinds of things, the position of the sun. If the clouds were thick and there is no landmark, they would put a stick in the ground and they could tell where the sun is. They used mostly the sun for direction. Like in Great Bear Lake, there is no land or no sun to follow, and you cannot see, they would use snowdrifts for direction. Snowdrifts are used because the wind blows in a certain way all winter and snowdrifts are always in one direction. When you travel, you travel on an angle, you use the snowdrifts for direction. That is another good compass.

Importance of Work

Indians are good at that. A long time ago they never got paid to work. My dad always got me to work and he said when you work all the time you are healthy. The girls are the same way, they cut wood (we did not have power saws), dogs to feed, dry fish, there was lots to do, sometimes they worked late into the night. Then you have to get up early in the morning. They would listen to what the Elders say. Today people sleep until late in the day, it is a shame. I get up at five or six in the morning, that is the way we were raised. Now young people sleep longer, Elders think maybe education has something to do with it. But they need people to tell them what to do, like long time ago.

Clothing

There was a lot of suffering to go to the barren lands from here, about eighty miles. The caribou migrate to barren lands. They go back and forth. The people would try to get them. The best time is August and September when new hair grows on their fur, it is short and strong. They made clothes out of the hide. They would make dresses, jackets, and shoes. They also used fur, mink, marten, beaver, we used everything. They used sinew and sharp objects to sew it together, they made moccasins. They even made rabbit skin suits, braided rabbit skin like a rope. It looked good, my father had a rabbit skin suit, it was warm. They used caribou hide to cover the tents, they would leave the hair on for extra warmth. They had no problems.

Good hunters needed good strong clothes. They also made clothes for old people. Some are not good hunters and their clothes get worn and they get cold because they cannot get new hides.

Traditional Spirituality

Medicine power is something that you cannot talk about, because these days people might not believe you. I will tell you a short story about medicine power. These people were coming from this mountain river, those rivers have lots of rapids and canyons and rocks all over. Long time ago there were mountain Indians travelling together, one family in each canoe. They would float down the river, sometimes they would have to paddle. The water was low so the rapids were wicked. These people were loaded down in boats, dogs could not run along the shore because there was no shore, just canyons. One canoe got stuck on top of this big rock, the canoe turned around, people yelled and were scared, no one could do anything. There was lots of medicine power at that time. There was one old man that had power for rocks and he would talk about it and people knew about him. One Elder yelled at him and said, 'You have bragged about having medicine power over rock, it would be a shame to have your nephews and nieces die because of this rock. Do something.' The medicine man yelled, it was so loud the rock broke up. His power was so strong that he was able to break up the rock. These kinds of stories might not be believed by some people, that is why we have problems trying to write about our stories.

Prophecies

As I said Native people already had spirituality, they prayed to the Creator, they recognized creation, they prayed for Mother Earth. In our area people travelled all the time, communication was poor. Here they talk Dogrib and then there is Slavey and then there is Chipewyan. They stayed in their own area, each was a bit different from each other. Some were more powerful. They all prayed and recognized the Earth as our Mother. They say Creator, not God. Long time ago we did not know God but we believed in the Creator. The Creator can override everything, all people and all medicine power. It is not new to Native people when priests talked of miracles or talked of stories from the Bible. They already believed in these kinds of things. Native people had their own prophets.

Ayah died in 1941, he was a prophet. After he died, some Elders claimed to be prophets, they say they saw them in visions. One young man claimed that he saw a person in his vision who had been sent to talk to him and that he would return when he was ready to preach to people, he was too young at that time. He said, 'I will be back if you deserve to preach to people.' This person waited forty years, waiting for this man to return. He lived a good life in the meantime, waiting for the return of this man. He helped people as much as possible.

One night the same person came to see him in his vision and told him that he was a good person and he was told what and how to preach and talk to people. He became a greatly respected prophet. Lots of people came to see him. He knew lots of things, he predicted lots, he predicted all this change that we are going through today. He predicted, it did not really happen yet, that disasters would hit Mother Earth, people would starve. There would be lack of rain, it would get too hot and dry and it would be hard to grow food. Starvation would hit the south first. The people in the north would last longer because of the cold and snow, but people have to be spiritual, they have to pray to the Creator all the time. There will be a time when people from the south will come up north to look for food. This is what he predicted.

It bothers me because I hear about news around the world. There are lots of things happening to Mother Earth, lots of disasters. It is predicted that there will be eleven billion people by the year 2000 and they will need food. Is this where starvation will happen? It makes me think of Ayah and what he predicted, maybe that is what he was talking about. Ayah is buried in Fort Franklin [Deline], that is where he was from. People visit his grave. He is not the only prophet, there are some in other places. Ayah was an Indian prophet, he could not read or write. The church had nothing to do with him. He had to wait forty years to do that.

Burials

I always talk about medicine power because so much has happened from it. Medicine people in early days were spiritual people. There were some who had special power for ghosts, for Spirits. So when they were asked to help a sick person these medicine people would make medicine and some of them were more powerful. They say that all individuals have a Spirit, that is part of our body, they say without it we cannot live, the church calls it soul. The first thing a medicine man does is to check to see if the Spirit is still attached to the sick person. If it goes away, leaves the body, you get sick, sometimes they have to search for it, find it and bring it back and the person gets better. If the Spirit does not come back, they die. Today people do not believe this, they do not believe in Spirits.

Sometimes people mourn too long, it breaks their heart. Sometimes a medicine man can make medicine to stop the mourning, to not cause sickness. Sometimes he checks on the Spirit. When you die the Spirit departs from the body, it goes ahead of time, the Spirit knows you will die, so it leaves and goes to somebody else, like a newborn baby, it is a cycle.

All the medicine people know this and they can explain what happens to each Spirit. Like they would say this Spirit went to this person, so you do not have to mourn too much, a new baby is born, his Spirit lives on. The people feel related to that baby. Sometimes the Spirit stays close to that person, especially a strong medicine man.

People would be buried under stones, heavy stones, to prevent animals from getting at them. A lot of people stop at the graves of strong medicine men to talk to their Spirits. They ask the Spirit for help, for children to live longer. A medicine person can trace the Spirits to certain people, the cycle that they go through. My dad was a medicine man who could do that. Some of them remember how they lived in the last life. He remembered that his Spirit was in a woman in the last life. Some remember things from their past life. He was a very strong medicine man because he led a good life. Spirits were reincarnated, being born again, into the body of another person. *Yamoria* made laws that medicine power was not be abused, not to show off. This is the reason why medicine people follow the Spirit, so they will know what happened to them in past lives.

Stages of Life

Because of extinguishment of Native culture and beliefs, because of modern schooling and times, we cannot follow that anymore. But long time ago when Indians were left alone and followed their own way, the Elders would talk about the stages, from a baby to older. There was a special ceremony when girls first got their periods, it was a special celebration for that. They wish luck to the girl to produce children. They had a ceremony for boys too, they have it when the boy's voice changes. Sometimes the medicine man would help to identify when the boy becomes a man, they have a special celebration for that so that he will be a good citizen.

They had other stages like marriage, the Elders always provided guidance to people. They encouraged people to think seriously of marriage. Stages of life after you have children were also talked about. You get to a stage when you cannot do what you could do when you are young. That is why you cannot be lazy when you are young, you should work twice as hard because you are strong and quick. Elders tell youth that they should realize that they will not be able to do this when they are old. They have lots of stories of how people die, past medicine power, old age, going towards death. They use people as examples for other people so they can live a good life. Elders teach and guide people through the stages of life. Medicine power know when you are going to die, it takes off, it leaves the real old people. You know you will die when that medicine power leaves you. It goes somewhere else to help other people.

Time

They moved around the seasons. They go by animals, eggs of ducks, in the fall the caribou and moose are fat, it is a good time to get food. The Elders and hunters go hunting when the animals are fat, they save the fat, dried meat. Moose and caribou start to mate, they do not eat anymore, they lose all their fat in a matter of five to six days. The animals' mating season is important to people, they have to know when it happens. Fish also go upstream in early spring, so people have to know, the fish spawn way upriver, they all come down to winter in the big lakes. That is what Indians know, so they trap the fish. Seasons and animals are a big part of traditional life. They also trap for rabbit, marten, mink, to get clothes for children and babies. When warm weather comes after the cold winter, people are happy. They yell out, you could hear them all over, it is a happy time.

Language and Culture

We are going through a very powerful change, imposed on us. Today, children grow up differently, living on food from the store. People's lives are changing. Government has power to affect our lives. We are living in confusion. We used to listen to our Elders, that way we held on to our culture. But it is not like that anymore. Maybe it is not our fault. We, the Elders, feel helpless. Children are power and they are growing, but they do not want Indian culture, they want pizza, they want to go to Yellowknife. The school system teaches them too, that White people is the right way. The schools should do their best to find a new system in which education will save the culture. The culture is useful, it should be combined with modern times.

There are some people who have done this. I know this person who went to high school and university. He works in Norman Wells, he is well-off, but he never lost his culture, he talks Indian, first-class Indian language. He sets nets and rabbit snares, hunts beaver, his wife dries fish. They did not lose that. I am proud of him, everybody should be like that. Now it seems like people want to be like White people, it does not work, you lose everything. We pray to save our language and culture. We have to figure out how that will happen in schools and cultural institutions.

Indian Names

They had their own names, no John or George. They used animal names, they were named by their grandparents. Newborns would sleep with grandparents and they would name that baby, related to animals, Mother Earth, space, all related to creation. There was an old man named Sunstream, the sun ray, a ray sometimes comes through a hole in the tent. He was a medicine man, he grabbed it and swung on it and put it in his pocket. He was like a trickster. Those kinds of stories people like publishers do not believe.

Places were named in Indian. The government came here and surveyed, made maps and gave English names to places. They would name them after explorers, like Fort Franklin, it was named after an explorer. He came there and died, so it was named after him. Mackenzie was named after the first explorer who travelled that river. Now Indians are fighting for their rights to be recognized. The federal government gave money so that Indian names could be used. There is trouble because White people do not know them, some of the names are difficult to pronounce. White people are complaining. Fort Franklin is Deline [deline-ah], it is not our fault that that explorer died there. Deline has been there for thousands and thousands of years. For Great Bear Lake, there is an Indian name. There is a name for every point, every bay, all Indian names.

Economics

The main food was animal meat, they used fat too. Caribou was the main one. They used everything on the animals. They save the blood, they cook it and make soup. They do not boil it but keep it hot. They sometimes put caribou fat in it, boy, the Elders like that. They use the bones, they use the grease out of the joints. They pound the bones with a rock. They cook that too for hours. All the grease comes out of the bone, they cool it off and take all the grease out and they drink the broth. They save the grease in a caribou stomach used for a container. They pound the meat, dry meat. They also dry fish, they get lots of dried fish. They take a lot of this food to sacred places.

Transportation

They walked, pulled toboggans, used birch-bark canoes in summer. They also had moose and caribou hides for boats. Modern transportation came and life changed. It is good, but the bad thing about it is the loss of exercise. They used to paddle, women paddled, and children paddled. They were strong. The dog team came from the Chipewyan and they used dog teams. Some people had medicine power with dogs, some were stronger and faster. Traders came and brought dogs. Dog pulling came to this area. It was good and everybody had dog teams.

Dreams

Everything was based on medicine power and it controlled dreams. People recognize some people as true dream people. Sometimes it was a woman, sometimes it was a man. A short story: There was a woman who was very capable and independent and was a true dreamer. She had a dream that a man would be drowned under the ice. She was recognized as a dreamer. Her husband told her that she should tell the man that he should not go hunting alone. She went to see the man and told the person about her dream and told him to be very careful and always take somebody with him. She went home. The man never went alone for two years. He needed to go hunting beaver for food and clothing and that season was very good for beaver, so he went out alone. Two years had passed and nothing had happened. He got two beaver. It was in the fall, he put the beaver in a pack sack and it was heavy. He came to a stream, not very wide, but it was deep, he threw a stick across the stream, but the pack sack was real heavy. He stepped on this bridge that he made, it broke and he fell in the water. The pack strap went around his neck, he went underwater, and he drowned. He was found in the stream, because he did not listen to a true dreamer, true medicine power.

Medicines

Everything is based on medicine power. Some have bear medicine, very strong. At one time there were no people on earth, only animals. Animals had medicine power and the bear especially had strongest power. People today still recognize the bear as the strongest animal and they call him the boss. Strong medicine men usually communicate with the bear. At one time the bear taught medicine to a medicine man. All animals have medicine, the bear taught people what medicines or plants to use for sickness, to clean out stomach, headache, to heal a wound, rheumatism, all kinds. The bear has lots of knowledge. It comes from the bear. The medicine is very good, but now we are confused. Now we have doctors and nurses, with nice hospitals, and nobody want to go in the bush looking for plants, mosquitoes eating you up, even though it is good medicine. The best medicine is in the bush. The bear's bladder is one of the strongest. The bear is close to God, the bear knows what you are thinking, when you are in trouble you can talk to the bear and he will help you.

A man told me once that they had to travel far away to where there were no caribou. They used a small canoe, they got to the barren land. They saw white caribou and he shot one. He began to skin it. He shot the caribou in the ribs and he accidentally got cut by the broken ribs when skinning it. He got home that night and he got sick, his hand was blood-poisoned, it was swollen. They left by canoe, some people walked along the shore. They saw a bear and they had to kill it to get the bladder. It was heated, it becomes reddish. As you do this, you talk to it, you talk to the bear Spirit. They filled a cup with the bladder, and talked to the bear, 'Long time ago you could help anybody and you are still like that, we need your help. This man has lots of children and a wife.' He prayed to the bear Spirit. He drank the cup of bladder, it was really bitter. It was rubbed on his body and he was put to sleep. He woke up, he looked at his arm, he felt better, his hand was okay. Everything was okay. People took this story and talked about it to the Elders. The bear medicine is very good. When you are sick with a headache or sore leg, eat something of the bear and talk to it, you will get better. Bear Spirit is important. Plants were also used for medicine.

Healers

It starts with medicine power. Medicine power heals a lot of people. These medicine people have healed people. One guy was accidentally shot in the head while caribou hunting, he fell down and his gun shot off. They say that from the shot they could see the brain moving. He was pulled to camp. Everybody expected him to die. A bunch of medicine people came to see him, they started to make medicine. One medicine man asked for the gun that shot him and he began to sing. He put his hand on the barrel, smoke came out. He kept singing. He said later this person will not die, he will die of something else. The man got better and he lived to be 96 years old, he died of old age. It is sad but this healing is now lost.

Justice

Everything is based on medicine power. Long ago when medicine power was used, it was invisible power, they had a different way to deal with this. A short story: There was a wicked medicine man, somehow he got into conflict with a strong medicine man who died. He had three brothers, they heard about it and they wanted to look into why he died. They travelled a long distance to go to his grave, all three are medicine men who are Spirit men, one said he would try to talk to his brother, they sang. All of a sudden the dead person talked to them, he told them that he had been killed by another medicine man and that he had to go back to the Spirit world. The brothers made a strong medicine but they could not override the medicine man, they had to find something he did not know. One finally found medicine for shrinking, something that the medicine man did not know. They call for a caribou, it came in, they used medicine to call animals. They killed the caribou to get the medicine. The medicine man got sick as these brothers were burning the head and leg. Everything shrank, the medicine man got sick. The three brothers travelled to the village to see the medicine man. He was sick and they told him, 'There is a time when what you have done in the past catches up to you, you have killed lots of people.' Generally this is how bad medicine people were dealt with.

Indian people, here as an example, are not educated, they do not know how the law works, they do not understand what is going on. They have no money to pay fines. We are now trying to get our rights recognized, the government realizes now that too much has been imposed on Indian people, but it will take time to change the law. Elders are being involved in some places. It is starting now that people are talking about self-government and eventually maybe we could run our own courts. But it will take some time, because people are not educated.

Crimes that are alcohol related are things that could be dealt with by working for the community or going to outpost camps. By going to jail, it does not help or correct the person. The jail is not the Dene culture, it belongs to the outside world. Some say that the boys who go to jail live better there than at home, lots of food, TV. Some even have money when they get out because they get paid for work in there. They are not learning from it, they do not correct their lives. It would be good to have a big outpost camp and involve the Elders. They could start listening and they will benefit.

Non-Native People

We had been on our own. When the White people came here they mistreated us. They did not like the Indians but they liked the land. That was a big mistake, they should have worked with the Natives, agreed on things, helped each other. Everybody would be working together today. They came out with treaty business and put us on reserves. Now in the past few years, the government is trying to work with Indians. It is hard because we have been separate for a long time. The government is trying to correct treaty, provide education and housing, self-government. All these years the government ran those things for Indian people like welfare, school, nursing stations, all done by the government. Now Indians are starting to run some of these things, not always having things done for them. It is a communist system when they decide for us, and this has to stop. We have been living this way for so long, that it is hard to change. Everyone has to agree, business people too, they think Indians will interfere with business. Self-government would allow Indians to run their own affairs, take over everything. They need to find a way to work side by side with White people, but run their own affairs.

Pacific Coast Cultures

MARY ANNE MASON   (Shayshas)

Klemtu, British Columbia

'That's why I figure, well, this is a chance for me to tell. It was a tough life.'

Mary Anne Mason was born in 1921 in a fishing camp near her present home of Klemtu, British Columbia. Her traditional name is *Misquak*, which means Raven Woman. Mary Anne has six children, eighteen grand-children, and nineteen great-grandchildren. She was interviewed by Emily Faries in the late summer of 1994. When Emily arrived there was a big community feast. As a guest in the community Emily was the first one to eat, for which she felt very honoured.

Emily stayed at a lodge for guests in the community. She found that everyone was exceptionally nice and treated her like an honoured visitor. Mary Anne's home was very comfortable, and very busy. People of all ages came in and out throughout the interview to visit and say hi. Emily spent four days speaking with Mary Anne. Their conversation focused on the traditional lifestyle of coastal British Columbia, including the Potlatch, naming practices, and other ceremonies. Mary Anne also shared intimate details of her life history and her teachings, which focused on helping youth, and the importance of education.

Life History

I was born in a fish camp away from here. It is about five miles by boat. It's a fish camp where we dried fish. My grandmother was midwife, brought me into the world, but, you know, we lived here, but we camped there. So I was born in a camp, but I have lived and camped my entire life.

We had a little one-room classroom, up to grade six I guess. After grade six I went away to residential school, away from here. The residential school was in Chilliwack. It was run by the United Church. It was pretty good. From the stories I hear from other residential schools, it was a real nice one.

I think as far back as I can remember, when you are four years old you gradually start to really hear things, but you don't remember it. I started in with my grandparents. They sort of took over me, both sets of grandparents on both sides. They sit me down day after day. 'Don't do this, don't do that. This is what you are supposed to do, this is how you are supposed to do it. This is nothing that is expected of you.' This sort of thing, you sit there day after day learning all of these things because as a child you know they thought they'd start drilling it into me, but the thing is I didn't realize until later on why. There was a reason why they started at that early age. We don't find that today anywhere, but I went though all of that.

One of the things that stands out the most for me that I can remember later on in life was, help your people. My tribe, that's the Raven Tribe, is different from other tribes along the coast. If you are of that people that are of the Chiefs, the line, they said that's why you are taught at an early age, because far back then they knew that somehow I was going to have children, and who knows, one of them may have been the next Chief. And this is why they drilled all of this into me.

The different things of life, and that's why I figure, well, this is a chance for me to tell. It was a tough life. Not having to enjoy yourself. If somebody says something you don't answer back you just turn away and walk away. To a young girl that's hard, you want to pull your hair or something. You had to restrain yourself because of all the teaching that you had. 'Don't say this, don't do that, don't ever, you know, talk back to your

Elder.' If somebody talks to you, look them in the face and take in what they say. And do what you can. One of the things that stands out there in one of the rituals I had to go through was the teaching that they had, some day your people will have to look to you for a good example. To ask you something that not everybody can answer. And that means you have to learn all that you can, from the Elders. I think that I was lucky that I had the two sets of grandparents. All in all, when you grow up in that type of situation you learn how to take it. You learn how to take what's given to you, and what's expected of you.

I had a chance to be Chief but I turned it down. That was before women's lib came around. I was taught whatever the man says it goes. He goes first, not you, so somebody else can be Chief, and it went from my father to my son. In our tradition it goes from uncle and nephew. That's the way it's really supposed to go, but if the nephew really doesn't take to it or is not good leadership quality, then the Elders of your tribe gather together and choose.

My tribe is the Raven Tribe. It's called the Shayshas. We comprise four different tribes. The main one is Kitasoo, then Shayshas, then the Eagle Tribe, and the Wolf Tribe. So we comprise four. Sometimes there is conflicts, but we got all young Chiefs. You have to put up a big Potlatch, you invite so many different tribes, different communities to witness. What we did here because we made one young woman in Bella Bella Chief. We had to because my brother lived there, and he was one of the Chiefs. I had to go and put the Potlatch on, and invited Alert Bay, Bella Coola, Kitimat.

Potlatch is a time to get together to recognize a Chief being made or being put in his place because the other Chief had died. But he has to earn the right to that seat, and when the time comes, the family does this. Because it was my son, I had to put on that, and my family and children all got together and we had been gathering up clothing and money and food for a few years. With these invited guests from other places you had to give monetary and clothing, you know. We had to do two days of feasting, and with Chiefs from all different kinds of places.

Right now we have an elected Chief, and my son works in the band office, he is hereditary Chief. And there is another hereditary Chief that is in the band council, so they just work together. The elected Chief recognizes them. I guess if they didn't then they wouldn't get along. There are others that are bringing themselves up as Chiefs, but they are kind of like store-bought Chiefs. You know they spend the money on clothing and food and they bring themselves up. The saying that the White man says, 'There's too many Chiefs and not enough Indians,' it's almost coming into being. And I don't think that's right.

I think that we should stick to our traditions. It's hereditary Chiefs, that's why I mentioned that you had to be taught from an early age. Right now my son is Chief, we knew already as a family that my nephew is next in line, and he knows it already. He knows it already, that he is next in line. He must be about twenty-three. But every chance I get I tell him what is expected of him. It's not as hard as what I went through. The different things that he had to go through. But the main thing is that we hold ourselves as servants of the people. Even if you are Chief, you are there to help your people. If your people are hungry you go there and you feed them, and things like that. That was the tradition that we had been taught years before, that you had to go and gather. We had to put away, even these things that I am making every day. I am putting away for something that might happen within a family. It may not be immediate. Someone in a family needs help, then we all get up and go help, and that's the way it works in this area.

A Potlatch happens once in a great while. Sometimes it's long in between, but there are some people there that think I ought to get a name for myself, because names are the main things. If you are given a big high-class name you can't just take it and that's it. You have to do something. The hereditary Chief and his family have one year to get the Potlatch ready, you can't just get the name and that's it. In a year he has to invite so many communities to witness when they put the name on, when they dress him in his robe, and things like that.

The Potlatch is a ceremony. One of the first things they do is they call out so many people. I had four. The top one and then they all go down, and one young woman. She got a man's name. She is not just a woman today, she is a man because she spent quite a bit of money to get that name. To get that name she was the one that got the coffin and the clothing for my brother who was Chief that died. So in order for me to give a little justice to her, she is from a different tribe, we had to give her my brother's name.

The ceremony starts with them. They go out in just ordinary clothes and one by one it's the tunic first, a shirt, then the robe, and an apron and then they have this. I should call my son one of these days for you to see, like a headdress. He's got the whole outfit. One by one, different Chiefs are putting this on. But only one person from different places can see the name. It is just like baptizing them with the name.

Creation Stories

We have a story from the mainland called a Hershayshay story, and it's called. If I can open the first part of the Bible for you, but these stories were passed from generation to generation before that. Before the minister's preachers came. They had these stories about the first man that came to earth, in fact her daughter, the only daughter, she's got the name. But first of all the man was sent down to earth. They didn't say heaven, or God or Jesus or the Lord or anything like that, but somebody that made them sent them down. After a while they said he was too alone so they sent a woman down.

In the Bible it said it took a rib out of man and made a woman out of it. In our story it said they sent down a woman and she came down to earth like a down feather, just floated down to earth, and that's her name, it means just floating down, down feather. Just gently down to the earth where she joined the man. And that was his sister. This is something when we talk to the young people, and they say, 'You mean he married his own sister?' To that story it is yes, and they married their own, and along the coast very few tribes would allow that, to marry your first cousin. But in ours you can marry your own because of that story. And gradually they increased from there. It's a big long story, but I am just making it as short as I can.

Traditions

I find that the thing that is the most important for me that I don't find today and that should be stressed more often to the younger generation to learn all they can about their traditions, about who they are, because if you know who you are, you know who your relatives are, you know who you can get help from, and who you can help. In all walks of life there is different ways of looking at these things, but I find this is one of the most important things is that. To learn your traditions. To learn all that you can about your background, your identity especially, because a lot of the young people today, you know you ask if you are Native, you say I don't think so, you are talking like they are White. They don't think so because they are not all that brown, or I'm not an Indian, or I don't dance, or I don't talk Indian. Because that's one thing we are losing here is our language. We try hard, they are trying to teach them. They have teachers up at the school, so many years just trying the basics. We have two languages, Heiltsuk, and Tsimshian.

When I got sent away to residential school that's the only thing that I practically almost lost. I had to fight hard and work hard to get it back, to learn that again, because we weren't allowed to talk, you know. We had half a dozen other kids from this community. If we were caught talking we were punished. That's about the only thing that I know I almost lost. If you are away and come home for just a little while and come back again, you try so hard so you can understand your parents, but you are answering them in English. If you were like me when I was young, my parents cannot talk English. I would have to try and stick to our language, but they couldn't really hear me as I was gradually losing our language. So it was pretty hard.

Well, to me one of the things that, if you look at our little community today, something is lost here, and that's work. If you don't work and make use of your strength and your talents, what you know, you gradually lose it. We had a cannery, a fish cannery. For years we were able annually to go and work. And our fathers and mothers and uncles and brothers, after summers we would go dry fish for the winter, and from there go trapping. You know working all year round, making ends meet. When they start giving the Native people social assistance, that made lazy people out of them. People sit back and wait for that instead of making use of yourself because when you do that kind of work that you are capable of doing for yourself and your family you have that high esteem of yourself and others and I think that is something that the Native people all along the coast lost since they lost the canneries. The canneries closed down, it's not their fault.

There aren't that many, but gradually young people nowadays are getting that back through education. Education is one of those things. What I wish for every young men and women, boy and girl anywhere, Native and otherwise, is to get the best education they can get because for the rest of your life, whatever it is you go out to do, your aim, your goal is there, you work towards it. And these young people. I think three of my daughters are working in the school as teachers, and one is working in the band office, one is working in a band store. Making use of that education, and also making sure it is passed on to the younger generation. Because our parents weren't really educated so they didn't really know what it was about. The only thing my mother used to say, 'I want you to have something better than I had.' But she didn't know what it was. It was hard for them to send me away to residential school away from them, my grandparents. At the same time I think it helped them realize what they meant, something better than what I had.

We can't really fit into the White society because of maybe our traditions, they can't understand our culture, but if we work hard to try and get into their way of living, I think it's much easier for them to understand us, and I think, I know from working all of these years here and there. I have worked in the band store, I have worked in the clinic, and I have my own little business down here, and I've worked in canneries. I've got to know people, I've got to meet people, I've got to learn about people, I even met some people sometime. The church was new and they knocked on my door and they said, 'I hear you got the key to the new church. Can you come and open it? We want to see.' I said, 'Sure.' Before I went to the bottom of my steps one little old lady came, she was on one of those big yachts. She come really close to my face, so close I could see her breath. She said, 'Can you tell me where the Indians live?' So I went even closer to her face. 'You're talking to one' [laughs]. A lot of these people figure we are still living in caves, whatever. But when we get to meet people and let them understand that we are just as human as anyone else. If they accept us as we are then we can accept them more easily, and we can get together more easily.

Traditional Birthing

My grandmother and my mother were midwives from years back, it's been passed on. They tried to pass it on to me, but no thanks! You know I said no thanks! All the twenty-six years I worked in the clinic I only delivered one. I usually tell the ladies when I work with them, 'You got nine months to get to the hospital' [laughs]. But my grandmother delivered me, and my mother was a midwife too. So it's an age-old thing that Natives from way back have learned all this.

One of the things that my grandmother says, 'If we start teaching you how to deliver babies, there is one thing, one of the things that you have to do. As soon as you are ready I will do it with you and your mother will do it with you, we'll do it together.' And that's using a frog. I didn't want to touch a frog, let alone, so I said, 'No thank you.' The frog is to feel, they know when the frog is having and they could feel it, and you get the feel of the woman's stomach. I don't know how true that can be, but that's what they passed on from generation to generation.

There was only a couple of instances, when my grandparents told me so and so had a baby up in the woods. And I think she just squatted then and delivered her own child, in the bush. Because she just had the big long skirt on and she just delivered, pinned it on and it came down.

Didn't even lay down or anything, just got to work looking after her child.

There is usually two or three midwives at each one, but they don't all deliver. It depends on who you want for, you have the right to choose. Take for instance sometimes you hear about babies born with a cord around their neck. They have that untied before the baby is born, inside. How they do that I don't know because I never watched. And if the baby is feet first, they turn it around. Just like if you were with a doctor in the hospital they have instruments to do that, but they had midwives that knew all that.

The men had no responsibilities toward the child. In our tradition man was a man because he was a hunter, because he was a trapper, he was a man that got out and got food. He wasn't even allowed to carry the child in case it wet him, and the smell might stay on him and he wouldn't catch what he was hunting. In my time there was diapers, there was no disposables. Well, he wasn't even allowed to hang that up, even after it was washed, because of the smell. In our days people depended on the hunters to get the food. That was before these boats came that delivered your food, or places where you can get it.

I know one of the things that I was first taught to do, one of the many things I was taught, because I was a girl, by my aunt in a fish camp, how to fillet fish, so you can put them in a big smokehouse. How to put them up, because I was the oldest and I was a girl and my younger brothers were too small to do anything. I was also taught to go hunting with my father, to carry the game, whatever he got. Go up the river to get fish with him. My father was very unfortunate as a young man. He fell between logs and he got caught underneath a log jam and he lost his hearing and he couldn't hear nothing. That's why I had to go and do things with him because there was nobody else.

We learned how to cook as well. We learned how to cook bannock. How to cook the different kinds of meat that they had. The boys learned mostly hunting, up on the boat, and out in the woods. They knew the deer signs, the wolf signs, whatever they see on the tracks. They were growing up to be trackers.

Traditional Dwellings

Like I was talking about we used to have to go dry fish, and it's just a mud floor with gravel. Homemade beds with feather mattresses with boughs of trees underneath them. A fire in the middle and a hole. It's not like the houses today are so closed up. If you want fresh air you open your window. Ours was holes all around, get fresh air day and night. At least five families lived in there. Some called them longhouses, but we called them smokehouses because we smoked and dried the fish there. We stayed right in the place where they dried the fish. We smelled really fishy then [laughs].

Everybody took turns cooking. Everybody took turns cleaning up the house. The house was made out of cedar trees, with just holes for your windows. There was mosquitoes around, but they had their own repellent. It was grease, bear grease. It's mixed up with some kind of tree. I don't know what kind of tree it is that's beaten into pulp and mixed up there so the flies don't get at you.

Traditional Self-Government

That's why it's very important for people to be taught at a very young age that you are going to be one of the leaders in the community, a Chief, to be taught at that age that you have to be one of those that help your people. Chiefs and Elders are brought together and it could be both men and women, whoever is interested enough. If there is something going on in the community that somebody just came and they told us, 'Hey, we just saw so-and-so with somebody else's wife.' As an Elder I would go talk to another Elder or Chief. That's not right. Before something happens, before there is family trouble between the two of them or their children, we must step in. We call the man and we call the woman that he was with, and we call both husband and wife. Get them together, don't let it ever happen again. That puts a stop to that. If it's just plain ordinary stealing, they take them before the Chiefs and the Elders. I think the thing was they didn't have fines or different things like that. They had community work. You get wood for the Elder, or get wood for that old man there. Pile it up and put it away. That's part of your payment or punishment or whatever.

Elders

I've often been asked this, 'When do you become and Elder, who is an Elder?' The way my grandparents say, 'When you have your first grandchild you become a real Elder. Before that, as long as you are older than the person that seeks help, whatever it is, if you are able to help them you are their Elder. Whether it is a young man, young woman or somebody almost your own age. You know because I think they sort of train them to when they are still young to take part in anything that goes on, to know what's going on, know how to do things.

To me, and my part, being an Elder. I started being an Elder years and years ago, so it sort of, you just drift into it. It's almost automatic. You know what to do, you know how to help the people. The advice, sometimes I can sit here for a day or so with nobody coming. Then all at once I have somebody coming, whether it's alcohol or drugs or marriage problems or something like that. So you sort of almost have to be a role model. You have to do the right things, say the right things to help these people because you never know who is coming to your door, and you can't turn them down and say, 'I don't know, I can't help you.' Sometimes if we get to that part that it needs medical or those professional people then we can say what we want to say to them as Natives. I've had people from both, from all walks of life, seeking help or advice. To me colour doesn't make any difference. No matter who it is. Because at first when I worked in the clinic we were only supposed to look after Natives, but who is to say who gets hurt or somebody loses a finger, or has a bad cut on a boat. I can't say what colour are you? I just usually leave a blank space there. And then the public health nurse says, 'What's this?' I say, 'Oh, I didn't look up!' She just takes it at that.

I think in our line of duty as Elders and I call it a duty because it's something that the younger generation really needs to know some of the things, and I think today it's much more. It should be taught much more because of the situation that young people are in today. They come into this White society with a different view of the things of life. Where we the Elders see things different. Not because we are Natives, not because we are Indians, not because we are First Nations, but because of the things that were passed down for ages. We didn't have no books. We have no writings of any kind of our teachings. It's been passed down from generation to generation. It's up to each one of us to keep that going and that's why it's harder for this newer generation because they are much more into this White society, you know. A lot of it is good, but sometimes they drift into something that is very hard for them to see.

I make it a point to say I am here every chance I get when there is gatherings and everyone knows where Mary Anne lives. I am the only Mary Anne in the village. People that I meet, because I travelled quite a bit when I was able to, and if you are ever coming by and have time to drop in and have a cup of coffee, or if you feel like having something to eat just let me know and I will see what I can do. More or less you have to let, because more than ever these young people have to know where to go. I think it's important that the Elders make themselves known because sometimes it's just a matter of talking, getting it out of their system. They feel a little bit better because they unloaded it on somebody, but you all should try and help them in your own way, because the White people have all kinds of psychologists and psychiatrists and everything else that goes with it. I think that Native people have that built in to each one of us. We don't have to go to these psychiatrists. We don't have to go to school for that because we had that, our Elders a long time ago make you see what's happening over there, take a good look at it, study it and see how you can solve it. And they don't tell you right away, but after a while they tell you that this is how it should be. How to settle down into their own way of living, a good way of living.

I think there is too much of this thing today in every community, and that we let the young people have their own way. And yet we say it's the wrong thing to do, or something that they shouldn't do, without us saying anything. And then we say, 'I knew that was going to happen. I knew he was going to get into trouble.' And yet we don't do anything about it when we get the chance. Even as I have these little ones coming in, and sometimes I will just sit down and tell them a short little story. Because most of the stories that were taught, that was passed down from years back. It's not written, stories to teach a lesson, the do's and the don'ts. Don't make fun of this, don't say this and these other things that, you know. I think in every walk of life, an Elder has a very important role in a young person's life, or should be. We should make it known that we are there when you need us.

Heroes and Role Models

There are so many that I can say. I think the very first one for me that sort of took me were a couple on a mission boat. As a young girl we didn't have no books or nothing in the house, because my mother and father could not read or write. So the mission boat used to come and tie up on the float. I'd go down there because they had books. Not because I wanted to read, I couldn't read. But because of the pictures. I'd go through books with pictures there, and just make up my own stories there. I guess this missionary, and it happened to be Native, Haida people, Haida couple, named Dr Kelly, Peter Kelly, and his wife. They sort of took me aside, his wife at first, you know, tells me these stories. I couldn't really understand it. Yet she points out in her own way, then I can kind of grasp it. They took me outside one time and they said, 'Do you want to go to school?' That's how I ended up in residential school. Because residential schools in those days were for orphans or for hard-to-handle kids, but it just so happened that these two, this couple had an interest in me. That they knew I wanted to learn. That was my first people that I sort of looked up to.

And my mother especially, because she was the one woman that was almost always on call. That was before there was doctors and nurses here. She was a midwife, and also sort of almost a faith healer I guess. She didn't have no magic potions or anything. She had our homemade medicines, and she took that and she tried that, and sort of got me into the idea when I went to school that I wanted to be a nurse. I had a chance but my grandmother did not want me to stay away for five to six years without coming home. I had a chance to study in Chilliwack, but I couldn't make it. My mother was close enough that later on I was asked to work in the clinic.

Recreation

They had the Indian dancing and if you were able to see some of our Indian dances some of them are called play dances. They made up their own certain way of dancing for the kids to enjoy themselves, to let it out. They call it play dancing and you sort of put in animals or insects so the young kids will know what it is if they come across. There's a dance of the spider, and you know the way the spiders kind of go with their web. They had, I know when I was a young girl because I stayed with my grandparents, they got the intestines of the sea lion and it's almost like plastic, and sometimes it is filled with water and that's your ball. I just watched a game yesterday, the Americans and Brazil, volleyball. That's very familiar to what we used to do. We had cedar bark strung across two poles. There is no net or anything, but there is four on each side, but I thought of that because that sort of brought it back. At the same time they had almost the same thing as football. They made their own, they had bat and balls.

They had stick games, they called it. In this part they called it *lahal*, I think it's a kind of gambling. You had to guess, so many sit on that side. I don't really understand how they played, it was mostly men that played it. There was drumming and a kind of singing because they had to keep in rhythm. By the time I grew up all of these things kind of went away. The government said, 'No more dances, no more Potlatches.' So that sort of stopped for a while. We still practise the Potlatch, to make it perfect the

way they did it long ago. When the Potlatch is given you are giving everything that you got. You might just sit there with nothing after, but you
have done your part. This is to sort of bring you up to where you are supposed to be, but that was banned, and now it has come back, and we are
still learning how to do it the right way.

When the preachers, the ministers or church came. They are the ones
that, here in this community, they wanted people to be Christians,
because of the dancing and everything that was carried on he figured we
were heathens. He worked on the Chief. When he told the Chief, 'Tell
your people, when anyone wants to go heaven,' and he described heaven
to them and what will happen if they don't go to heaven. Every one of
them is not going to go to heaven unless you burn all of your old things.

We just have one sort of a newer totem pole. They had door posts, posts
in the corner of homes of totem poles. What have you, like, anything that
tells you what tribe you are on. Your husband and wife has their crests.
But all of that had to be burned. They say they are going to build a fire in
the middle, and everyone had to bring their robes, their hats, their
masks, their rattles and everything that is Indian was burned. This is one
community that not even one person hid anything, not even a rattle. So
we were just completely wiped out. That was in the late 1800s.

Gender Roles

If you are of a certain family you have to, and I say have to because it was
expected from you and your family. Like when I was a young girl, when I
first became a woman. That was something. You are put to bed for four
days, your aunts had to be with you to talk to you. You are curtained off,
isolated, and not eating for four days. That's where your aunts are there
so that you abide by the things that they want you to do. You have to lay
down a certain way. You can't get up unless you go to the bathroom.
That's the only time you get up. You stay in bed for four days, and the
fourth day your aunts are told they have to bath you and dress you and
they call the Elders and the Chief ladies to witness that you are getting up.
That's the second one, the baby being born your parents have to give
away quite a few things, then you become a girl and they give things away.
Then when you get married that's another big one. They have to be
doing things on your side as a woman too. It's the man's family, but the
woman has to know what's given to you as a wedding present. Everything
has to be written down a year after you get married it has to be repaid.

In our tradition, in our culture girls are very important, when they are born into the family, because we are the ones that reproduce. We are the ones that make the families grow. That's why they make it one of the important things. If a girl is born you don't just have to be the oldest of the girls. They have their own ways of doing for the boys, but I know more about the girls. One thing that I know about little boys is they trap little birds. They have little things to feed them. If they trap one the aunts make such a big issue out of that. They bring blankets and towels and stuff and they say they are wrapping up the bird. If they grow a little older and are lucky enough to get a deer, the uncles and the aunts get together again and do that for the boy. That's clothing, and blankets, and money and things like that. The people have to know that these boys are coming up, becoming a man, even though they are still small yet.

When you are a young girl, you are taught that a young man is of a certain stature, a certain family, a certain holdings. Say he has a trapline, he has certain names within a family. He has assets, his family has. The family they tell, you. But they don't tell you to go with that one. It's up to the grandparents to choose who. My husband was chosen for me. Yet as a young girl I went with every Tom, Dick, and Harry around, you know. I played the field. It's something that the young people of today do not want to understand and would not understand it unless they went through it. I went through it, I know, but one thing, the difference that I as an Elder today would not wish that upon any one of my grandchildren. I would like them to do what they do today, meet the one that they love because it took seven to eight years to settle down. I had children already, I said finally, 'My goodness, he's a good provider, he's a good man, he can be trusted, he provides things. There is a roof over our head. I must love him.' It took a few years.

There is a big long story to it. How they did it and things like that. It was decided by the grandparents, the mother and father had nothing to do with it. They had no say.

The grandparents are the ones that brought us up. They are the ones that taught us the do's and don'ts of life. There was no schools yet, and that was your teachers. That was the people you learned from. The father, in my case, I was the eldest, and the youngest ones came later on, they couldn't help my dad. So instead of just learning in the house how to bake bread and wash clothes and fix your bed and that, I had to go help my dad build boats and build houses. And I had sort of a dual role. I learned how to hammer the nail in. How to stain the boards. How to paint. I am thankful for all the things I had to learn.

Our traditions have it that your aunts or your uncles have to teach you most of this. The family values were so strong and so important so that you know who's who. Your aunt, your uncle, your grandmother, your grandfather. In our tradition there is no such word for cousin. First cousin, second cousin, kissing cousin, whatever, no such word. They are your brothers and your sisters.

I was fifteen when I got married and I got married to a man twenty years older than me. You have to be of a certain family. You can't be on your own, you can't ever say I want to do this, I want to go there. I want to go to Bella Bella and live there. We weren't even allowed to marry outside of our community. You have to marry within.

Two-Spirited People

In my day, and that's the big argument I have with my six children. Sometimes we sit by the table and we discuss what we see out there. More and more this thing is coming out and, 'Certainly there must have been in your day,' they said. And I said, 'I never saw one. If there was one it was so hidden that we didn't know anything about it.' Even before that there was no talk of anybody, lesbians or homosexuals. I say, 'My, it's just like what we have today. You guys live on noodles or TV dinners or things that you just microwave. It's new so this must be new.' If it was, even as far as a young girl having a child without being married was almost unheard of.

These young people of today learn so much on TV. Things like sex is so open. They can go to towns now and see different things. They can go to the nightclubs. They can see all these different things that are going on after hours. Which was something that was not flaunted. It's sacred. It's something that happens between married couples. That's what I told you with these Elders and Chiefs. If they knew of anybody going around with somebody else's wife or somebody else's husband they get together and they correct that right away before it gets into something that they couldn't get out of. That's why today that's almost lost. Young people today they don't want to be told anyway. They don't listen.

Tricksters

They had those in the Potlatches or just kind of dances and it is just certain kinds of people that can do it. Not everybody can go around and do it. If you ever go to these Potlatches the first part is serious. The tombstones have to be covered up and they have some kind of sacred mourning songs. Singing, then they uncover it and the family is there and they cry. Later on, halfway through the different dances, then these people come out. It is to make the families forget, to ease the pain a bit and make them laugh because they have been crying all this time for their loved one. It's time that they noticed that other people can laugh and they themselves can laugh or smile.

They have different masks. There is one especially that I like. It is done in Bella Bella and Bella Coola. This guy comes out with a funny mask on his face, and he imitates the dancers a bit. He fools around and he falls on the floor and later on he goes to one corner and puts something under his robe and it could be a pop, or a pail or pitcher with water in it. And then every once in a while he splashes. Everybody is scared and everybody covers up while he's coming down, you never know who he is going to splash. Sometimes he doesn't put his hands in the water, it's dry, but everybody is laughing. That's one that I know that I like, because it makes everybody laugh. Even the children are running around.

Music

Any kind of Potlatch, or a Chief could be just giving a feast sometime to honour part of his family or something that happened in the family. In our tradition, you can't afford to, in the olden days you didn't have too many stools or chairs. Sometimes not chairs, benches. So sometimes you sit on the bench and it sort of tips over and you fall down, or you trip on the road and you fall and you pick someone up, you have to do something to that person that picked you up. They have some kind of song that fits in. We call it washing ourselves. Our family gets up, you don't just do it for that, and everybody that comes they get a gift because of the mishap that you went through. It could be a boat that one of the young kids tipped over and somebody saved them. In every community this place was lucky.

There was one man that was my great-great-great-grandfather, was a composer. He was called even as far as Washington, and Alaska, to compose songs that would fit into whatever happened, dancing songs, whatever.

Art

It depended on a family and from there if you start on a totem pole you always have to start on the bottom. It comprises your crests. Somewhere along the line you have a bear story. There's a bear there, there might be a fish there, a salmon there, and something that is within your family, the doings that are going on. It has to be put in there what it's about. Supposing someone just saved another person from drowning, and they could just put a little man on there, and it tells the story. This is a bear story, this is a salmon story, this is a halibut story, this is when my uncle or brother was saved by different people and they had a big Potlatch, and gift givings and things like that. Totem poles are anywhere around the community. more or less in the olden days if there was a totem pole outside, supposing I had one outside here with all the different crests. I kick the bucket, that goes with me to the grave. They either just leave that there or make another one that stands. Usually the graveyard is filled with different ones, there might be small ones and big ones.

Daily Routines

It's just the usual chores. In those days, even before my time they didn't have hot and cold water, they didn't have electricity, they didn't have stoves, they didn't have carpets on their floors so they didn't have to have vacuum. They had mud floors, but they gathered gravel at least once a week that gravel has to be taken out somewhere and changed, taken out somewhere where the rain can wash it and if the rain doesn't come for quite a while they just leave it there and get a fresh bunch. That's your new flooring.

The beds that they talked about, that my grandparents had, was my people ate a lot of birds, ducks, geese, swan, you know things like that and they take the feathers and make mattresses. Underneath the mattresses it has to be the cedar or the, I think it's jack pine. It sort of makes your bed nice and springy. It has to be changed at least once a week under there. So they had different chores that you had to do, they had their outhouses, which was just a little hole and that has to be moved and put away, and anything that you get to eat, you just take what you need. Never more than what you need. It's always there.

I think that's something that is kind of hard today because people come and harvest things and they take as much as they can and just practically wipe out everything. We have a lot of things that we can't get now. We have to have licences to get it. We can't go out and get Abalone. I don't know if you ever seen an Abalone. They come on the rocks, it's a shellfish. This is pink and it has the meat in there and we take it out and that's a delicacy here. You have to dive for it or wait for the lowest tide to get it. We can't even get that today. If you are caught with one you get a heavy fine, Native or not.

Before the ministers came, before the preachers came, we knew, we still know and they knew before us and before them, that we had a Maker. And every day you get fresh food, you thank him for that, you thank him for the day, you thank him for the air that you breathe, your very being, because he made us. I thought, there must have been a minister before us that sneaked in or something like that, they say no, we knew, we know that we have a higher being.

Burials

People that were before my grandparents' time, they had boxes and just sat them in it and put them on the trees. I don't really know what it was about, but that's the way they tied it up on the trees, never buried underground. They had their own traditional burial ground for certain families. That's why it's important for these logging people, or people that come and mine and do different things in our land today to find out. Because here we moved, we migrated out here to the islands from the mainland and from there, there is all kinds of burial grounds at the different kinds of places that people lived. They didn't all stay in one place, there was different families.

The settlement that we had was on the mainland before we moved out here. It's over a hundred years ago now that we moved. One of the things that they taught, for people taking their own life. That was rare, people taking their own life. If you take your own life you will never rest. That teaching that they have, I don't want you to get lost somewhere or feel out of place somewhere. You know, away from your own people. That's one of the teachings that they had, don't ever think of taking your own life because girls having babies without being married, taking one's own life, and homosexuals, that was rare because of the teachings. It's the only life, it's a life that you have to take care of. It's a life that you can't change no matter how you try and change it because it's a life that's given to you to take care of. I think that's a teaching that sort of went away from us. I think just lately when we had three suicides we sort of brought that out. It's not nice to take your own life. We are talking to the young people of today because it is sacred, your body is sacred, you take care of it the best way you know how, keep away from alcohol and drugs. These sort of stuff you try to put into today's living.

There's always somebody in the family taking your name and your place. I already had about eight Indian names and I only got two left. And those two names that I got today are men's names. I go to the grave with that. And whoever does something out of the way for me gets those names. They have to earn those names. So therefore whoever gets it, I don't know if it's spirit, has to carry on the best way that they know how, what you were trying to do for your people, for your family and friends.

They never had anything going unless they prayed first. There is always somebody that does the prayer. There's chosen people to do that, a man or a woman. When you grow up in a family that believes so much there is no way that you can say there is no God because that was the teaching that was brought from years and years back and it's very important, and like myself for the past few days, where the way I felt for a while, and with my son-in-law getting so sick. I don't say I will take time out to pray. Any chance I get, whether it's in the middle of the night, or you wake up in the night, or the early morning before you put your clothes on, or come here before you have your breakfast, or any time during the day. To me it's like keeping in touch with your Maker or just thanking him for another day. Or thanking him for the blessings that the people get for having for friends and family and things like that. It's something that I know that I heard my grandparents. Only one grandfather didn't pray, but my other grandmother did. He closes his eyes when my grandmother prayed. 'Mm, mm,' that's all you heard from him. To me that meant he agreed with the prayer.

We have four clans here, Eagle, Raven, Blackfish, and Wolf. The Raven Clan can intermarry, but the rest of the clans you can't. We believe in God, we believe in a Maker, and he sent someone to look after you, sort of helps you through your difficulties, or helps you through your mourning, or your sickness. You know that somebody is there, watching over you, day and night.

I think grandparents are the most important ones in any family and the thing is supposing somebody lost their grandparents. It's more important to let the rest of their family know you are there for them. Their main grandparents might be gone, but you are there for them. And this is one of the family values that we have today because we let each other know we are there to help them, if they need someone to talk to.

Seasons

The season, like we could start with now, in this area, it's time to put away fish. Time to can fish, time to freeze fish. Different kinds of fish, shellfish

Abalone, if we could get it, to put it away for the winter. Deer has to be caught. With today's fridges and deep freezers that's easy enough, but in the olden days that's salted, that's smoked, and that's dried, and that's kept underground in a cool cellar. They dug a hole and they had boxes and that's how they were able to preserve. Like we have something that we get from Kitimat, we call it grease. It's something like corn oil. You can put it in making your tea biscuits or frying something. Grease is something, that if I had something wrong with my stomach, I could take a spoon of that and it would help me. You put it in your food, you boil fish and you put it in there. Well, you gather in spring in Kitimat, they only can get it there. So we in our area like before summer, early part of spring we gather seaweed. We preserve that, we dry that, we put it away, but we also trade it for this grease. So we still barter today.

In the spring too we get herring eggs, then we get seaweed, then we get salmon, then we dry it, then we get the different kind of meats that we can get up and preserve. Berries have to be gathered. Today we freeze it or we jar it and we get jam. There is also wild berries, but we can also get raspberries or strawberries from the stores. But in the olden days they dried their berries because they had no other way. Mostly everything was dried, dried fish, dried bark from the tree that we eat. And that's fall, it comes in the fall we are in the gathering season whatever there is, clams, different kinds of seafood, dried and freeze it now and jar it. It comes winter time, that's the time we eat it. So we have the four seasons, three seasons to gather, and one to eat.

We got salmon berries, we got blueberries, we got greyberries, we got wild currants, bunchberries, huckleberries, salalberries, we got wild crab apples. The grease comes from fish. You have to preserve it for a while. I don't know. We can't get it here.

Predicting Weather

The old people had their ways, like which way is that cloud going? Is it going south? If it is coming from there, there is going to be good weather coming. If it's coming from there you never know what kind of weather it is. Because they travel by canoe to hunt, to get whatever, it's important that they know what the weather is like tomorrow, and what, even the tide, because they paddled, and to get where they were going they had to know which way the tide is going. It gets there faster, but when the tide is low they just tie up for a while and wait for the right tide.

First of all it has to be the wind first. We do not get too many waves here unless it is a big storm because of the shelter we have from these islands.

The wind plays most of the big part in telling men that the clouds are coming fast from the south so we are not going to go out tomorrow because it's going to blow. That's about the only way they knew, from the clouds and which way it is going.

Native Culture and Language

You can't keep your culture unless you know your language because language, even me right now trying to tell you some of the things, I can't relate to it in English. As much as I can if I had my way it would just come right out in my language. It is so much easier to say it, but then you are of a different culture, you would not understand what I am trying to say. It's easier for me to relate to my people that way in our culture.

Each tribe, each clan, has their own set of names that are passed on from generations back. It's not a thing that you just pick out of a hat. It's something that you had to earn. Take for instance that girl you were talking about. She was talking about 'I'm an Indian, but I don't got no Indian name.' You don't, I can't just give you one because the names that I had are just given out to my family. She's further along the line, so you just have to wait your turn. The name has meanings because it has stories behind it. You can't pick up, just like I was telling you the other day her daughter has this feather, this down that came down from heaven. It relates to that story, the first man that came down, the first woman that came down. This is of the Raven Tribe that I am talking about. I can't talk about the Kitasoo because they got their own set of names and so have the Wolf and the Eagle, they got their own set of names that are passed on.

The names of places, the name Klemptu, it's a Tsimshian name because it is Kitasoo land, but the Kitasoo had a name like, like a safe harbour, but the bay is like this and it never used to have anything. If there is a storm they can come and tie up here. It's a safe harbour. That is in Kitasoo. You have to know when you get to someone else's territory. You cannot intrude unless you are married into this, then you can go in. I went to this one place with my husband where we picked wild crab apples. And him and I went up the flats, and we were picking here and picking there. The very next day, an older couple from here came, and they saw us up there. 'What are you doing up there? That doesn't belong to you, that belongs to a certain family.' There was nobody guarding it and nobody planted it, so we just went ahead and picked, just like bad boys and girls [laughs]. But they weren't even there to pick it.

There's a big change with our young people because a lot of our food they don't take, they don't eat. They don't know what it is. But we had to go out at different seasons of the year and put it away and dry it and smoke it. Today it's a little easier to preserve it. But if you didn't do it, you had very little chance of surviving. In the tradition that we have here I can't sit by and see some other family hungry. If I know of somebody that hasn't got enough bread on their table for their children, meat or whatever, then I can call my children together and say let's make a basket, let's make a box. We have to share, we don't let everybody else know, we do it quietly. That is a tradition that is kind of dying away quietly. You don't get that much help from your family, I still try to do it with my children. Let them know.

The epidemic was before my time, but it was talked of so much because there were very little people left that lived through it, and they had lost so many of their children, their fathers, their mothers, their uncles, their aunts. It was around 1918, around that time. There is something almost rare in the community and I think if they didn't have, I think it was some kind of boat that went by. If they didn't stop we would probably be, because where we are on the island, we could have still had. The reason why this place was founded was because it was a bay and there's lots of wood in there, and these boats needed wood for steam on their boat. Side-wheelers they called them. They had to come to get that and that's when the sickness came. At first it is just in the villages that somebody is sick, really sick. And by late night time they die. Gradually there are two or three of them the next day. It passed through the community just like wildfire. My grandmother told me there were just two people left that didn't get sick. A minister and his wife. They were Native people, but they weren't here, they were from Port Simpson. There were three of them, almost to the last day, there were two men and a woman. They had to do the burials. As much as twelve to twenty a day. I guess they must have been a tired couple.

It's like my father. 'I was so sick,' he said, 'I didn't even know my wife died beside me. I didn't know when they took her away, or when they buried her. It was days later when I found out, she was already buried.' That's how sick they must have felt. What they called the influenza, the flu, the great flu. The sickness that completely wiped out the Natives all across the coast.

Education

It would be much easier for me if I had one or two of my grandchildren sitting here so that I could talk to them about it. To me the most important thing is education. We have to have education no matter who we are or where we are from. Not only because of the competition, but the daily thing that confronts them every day. That you need to know a little bit more than what you know today. You need to know tomorrow and the day after that. That means you have to continually learn as you grow older. I often say to my grandchildren, years ago in my time I didn't need a grade twelve education to fillet fish or to dry fish. I didn't need that to pluck a duck, and how to cut it and prepare it for eating. I didn't need education to go get seaweed. It's practically built into you as a Native to do these things. You watch your older people, your mothers, whoever is in charge of you, every day. But today, even to open a can you need education in order to use that can opener.

I've lived through the day when people said, 'Watch that TV, there are people going to the moon.' And you wait and wait and see what happens, but they made it. And these different things that come every day. If you have others with you to explain it you understand it a bit. And that means you are learning again. I didn't say, 'Why are they trying to get to the moon? Why do they waste that money instead of feeding the hungry, clothing the poor? Why waste all that money going there?' You have some people that are educated, they read about it and learn about it, and explain it, and you get to know the reason behind the different doings that you see all over the world. There is a reason, there is something that is coming. They are preparing something ahead for the younger generation. Maybe I won't see it in my time. Maybe I won't go for a ride to the moon, but one thing for sure we know that some day if man has gotten there people will be going there for trips. What you get out of it I don't know yet. These different things, you need the education. You need it bad. Especially I said, there's so much competition, so much things to do, that each First Nation people should make it a point to make a goal for themselves, and I am saying this to the younger people. Set a goal and work towards that. Because once you get there, you alone will know the benefits, you will feel good about yourself. You will feel good about getting there. But also you are helping humanity itself rotate to doing good and helping others and passing on that education.

A few years back, even when I went to residential school, I heard about young people finishing high school. In fact in residential school I made lunches for half a dozen young people from the coast that started going to high school. To me, my goodness, they are smart, I guess there are a few people around. I never considered myself able to do that. I never really worked towards that, I just envy the people that worked towards that. Even today I can see the names of these people. One of them made it to be an M.P. We have doctors, lawyers today, men and women I know in Kitimat who are relatives of mine. We have people that are working in universities. That was very unheard of in my day. I always used to think, few people can make it. I never thought that all of us can make it if we work towards that goal. That's a big job, and like I said I am talking to the young people. But these young people are parents, which are the very most important teachers in the young lives of the Native people today. They are the first teachers.

The mother is the first one to hold the child in her hand. She is the first one that can speak, even with the child not able to answer or hear. Once she says a word, it goes inside and it is there for the rest of his life. It's going to come back and float up someday. You will remember the good things that you learned from your parents. It is very important that parents play a big part in the teaching and raising of the children because the next step is the way of the older people. Today I think that is kind of harder to do it. The grandparents are the professors and the parents are the teachers. The grandparents are the professors. They go a little higher than the parents in the teaching of the different things of life, and we hope that we don't completely lose that. But I know in every community there are Elders and grandparents that are taking that role and helping to teach the young people of today. Because we are in the computer age. We are in the age that they use laser beams in hospitals. As an Elder I can't really begin to understand what's behind it, but I can see, and I don't see older people using it. It's younger people. Young people are taking over, and I am very proud today that I can say, I see, I know, I hear, that there are graduates in nursing and all sorts of professional jobs that can be had today.

Like me I retired a few years back. I never thought at that time that they retired me that a person should retire until they are ready to jump in that hole. But today I think different. There's time for us to do what we can. There is time for us to sit back and let the young people take over. I don't think there is too much else that I can say except I am sure that every Elder, every grandparent everywhere, when they see their grand-children, the young people graduate, go to university, go to college, get jobs, not within a community, but outside, because in little communities like this we don't have very much job openings. With the amount of young people that graduate you have to sit at home and twiddle your thumbs, or else go out. That's why they have to learn to mix in with different people in all walks of life. To fit in, to learn of this other person's culture, to understand this other person. They in turn will understand you, that's about all I can say.

VINCE STOGAN (Musqueam)

Musqueam First Nation, British Columbia

'When I came home my Elders taught us that all our people who have passed on are still around us.'

Vince Stogan was interviewed by Emily Faries in the fall of 1994. She originally scheduled the interview in the spring, but his elder brother passed away, and their meeting had to be postponed. Vince Stogan's traditional name is *Tsimalano*, which has been passed on through his family for five generations. Vince is from Musqueam First Nation in the city of Vancouver, B.C. He works with the University of British Columbia, and travels across North America sharing and learning traditional Native teachings.

Life History

I was born in 1918 right here in Musqueam reserve. My dad and my grandparents were all from here. All my family from way back are from Musqueam. My older brother was supposed to have been the hereditary

Chief, my family was the line of hereditary Chiefs. My Indian name is *Tsi-malano*, which is the name I carried from my ancestors. I am not sure why my Elders gave me that name. My late brother was older than I was. The reserve is just inside the city limits. As the city grew it reached the reserve. Most of Vancouver has really changed since I was a little boy. There has been big changes in the last fifty years.

I went to school at a place called Chilliwack. It is about a two-hour drive from here. I went to a residential school. I was about six years old when they brought me into the school, and I stayed there until I was eighteen years old. Most people left the school when they were sixteen, but I worked at the school for the last two years at sixty cents per hour, which was a lot back then. I went to school up to grade eight or nine, but back then we were not allowed to go to high school. We were not allowed to go to high school, this is something I am kind of sorry about, because we lost our education. Those who made it, there were about four or five of them that went to high school, they were all right up there, well, they are all gone now, but one was in parliament in Ottawa and his name is Frank Calder, he was from up north. If I would have had the chance to go to high school, I might have made it to something, but the government would not give us the chance to go to high school.

But now I am really glad that I am working with UBC [University of British Columbia]. It is about a ten-minute drive from here. I am on the board for the Longhouse for Learning that they have there. This year they have thirty-eight Native students there, girls and boys. If we would have had the chance in the 1920s and '30s, we would have gone somewhere, but it did not happen like that for us at that time.

When I got out of residential school I went back to the reserve. We are fishermen here, we do a lot of fishing. The river is right down along the edge of the reserve here, the Fraser River, we do a lot of fishing. Once I got married, I worked in a logging camp for a long time. We came home about twenty-six years ago. My wife and I raised seven children, six boys and one girl. And they are all here, all my family is here, even my daughter has a house here. Our family is all here on the reserve.

Important Aspects of Culture

One thing that we have is our longhouse, but we do not talk about it too much. We have longhouses where we have spiritual dancing through the winter. We will be starting soon, this year, my first invitation was this Friday. We are going to re-enter the ones that were initiated last year. They will be having a ceremony for them this Friday. They asked me if I would go, it is a ceremony of its own. We do not talk about it, it is something that we try to keep from public, it is sacred to us. They should not be written down.

We have mask dancers here. They are different from up North, we have mask dancing here, but that is something we do not bring out in public either. We do not talk about it too much. There is quite a history to it on how it was brought out. Masks were found, that is something that is sacred and it is not brought out in public. My wife belongs to the mask dancers, just certain families belong to that, but I do not. It is just like naming our children, we have to do that fairly quickly because they are getting away.

The name that I carry is a name that the Elders gave me, it was my dad's and my grandfather's, it is passed down the line. What we do here is, we find out from both families of the children, we find out about the family tree. We cannot just go out and take just any name, it has to come from the family tree.

One of the things that it going on here in B.C. is everybody is claiming the names that are coming out, and there is quite a ruckus about it. So we have to go back to the family history, find out the names and bring them back down by naming our children and grandchildren. That is a ceremony on its own, it takes almost all night to do that. We hold the ceremony in the longhouse or out in the field. That is where those mask dancers come in those kinds of ceremonies. We can use that ceremony to bring in our children and our children's children. We all have our names now. Those kinds of ceremonies take a long time. If it's just for one person or one child, it does not take as long. This way here you have to go back and let the people know where that name comes from, what side of the family it comes from, from way back, we bring that name out, so nobody else can use that name. So that is something we are really careful about, the naming ceremonies.

Mom – everybody calls my wife Mom – and I do a lot of travelling to different places. We go to Salt Lake, Utah, Oregon, Maine, New York, and other places. We travel with a medicine wheel. A man that does it was Sun Bear, he is gone now, we lost him about three years ago, but we have been trying to carry out his dream and wishes. We are still trying, we still travel around. We go through Canada, we do a lot of travelling with the medicine wheel. They try to get all the healers in one place.

We teach people not so much our culture, but for spirituality. We do a lot of praying, when we help people, when we heal someone, in our way, not the church way, in the Native way. In our way, in our prayers, we use three different things that we were taught long time ago. That is, we call the grandfather our Creator, White man calls him God, but we call him the Creator. In our prayers we say prayers to the Creator, to the Great Spirit, we believe our people, our Elders are still around us. When I went to school it was pumped into our heads that if we are good we will go to heaven and if we are bad we go down to hell. We as Native people do not believe that anymore, we believe that our Elders are still around us, so we do a lot of ceremonies to please them. Here we do a lot of burning of food for the people who have passed on. At feasts, we feed our ancestors. We do a lot of that. It is starting to be where community burning takes place, as well as family burning. In the community burning, the whole community comes in at once, the last time we did one was in Seashelt, not too far from here.

Mom and I did a big one, there were sixty-eight plates. In family ones, we usually have eighteen to twenty plates, it all depends on the size of the family. So we do a lot of that, we do a lot of travelling. Now in our travels like in New York, we do burnings for them, too, for those who used to live in that area. It really works because when we got there nothing was going right for them. A person from New York had been here and he saw us doing that, and he asked us to do it during the gathering, but I said we have to do it before the gathering, to please the people who used to live here long ago. We did that and it sure made a difference for them. Everything went well. The past people who lived there were pleased with what happened. We do a lot of that here, it is starting to involve communities now.

I strongly believe that practising our culture helps us today. Here in Musqueam we have our longhouse in the winter. In the fall we have a community burning when all the Elders that live here come, we had a big burning. We ask the spiritual Elders who have gone on to the other side to guide us through the winter. In the spring we have another one thanking our Elders for helping us through the winter, we have two burnings. They are offering of food for the spirits. We put some food on a plate and burn them, not just anybody can do that, we have been taught by my dad and grandfather, that is the kind of work we can do, it is passed on in the family, not just anybody can do it. What I am doing now is teaching a few who are strong-minded to do this work. I am seventy-six now, but still going strong.

Traditional Dwellings

This is where we had longhouses, our people on the coast lived in these houses. Two or three families would live in one longhouse, they would hand-split the cedar. I saw one here made out of hand-split cedar and it was quite warm. That is the way our people lived. Longhouses were big, some were smaller, they would hold Potlatches in them, they would invite one another, we put up a Potlatch in our longhouse and we can put up four hundred people there. When people lived in longhouses, they had open fires. One corner would be one family's and in another corner, another family. That is the way they used to live.

The way we live now is different. We do not have to pack water or pack wood anymore. We are modern now. Our people long time ago did not have that. I remember when I was young I had to pack water for my cousin, we lost our mother long time ago when I and my brothers were about four to six years old. I used to stay with my cousin a lot, she was a big woman, so I used to help her out by packing water. We used to have wells that went way down in the ground, there used to be two or three wells around here. We would pack water by bucket. We are really spoiled now, no more exercise. The whole city of Vancouver is Musqueam territory. People long time ago lived all over this whole area, like Stanley Park, where UBC is now, our people lived here long before, we make it known that the city of Vancouver is Musqueam territory.

We respect other territories of Native people where we travel, like when we go to Salt Lake, Utah, their way is a lot different from the way we do things here. We respect them and we expect them to do the same for us here, we do that. I do not bring anything from the coast to their territory and do it there, we just sit back and let them do things their way, we honour that. It would be like if I went your way to see how your people do things, I would honour that. I would not say that is wrong, I would not do that.

A lot of Easterners are here in the city of Vancouver. They are Natives but they have no place to go, no reservations to go to, so they are forming their own thing here. That is where I get involved as one of their respected Elders.

Traditional Government

When we lost our dad, my late brother did not want to take on hereditary Chief, so we gave that up. Now we have elected one like every four years and then another Chief is chosen. We have nominations and all that, we got our Chief and councillors here, they are the ones that make decisions for us now. Long time ago, it was similar to that, but they were not chosen, they were hereditary Chiefs of each tribe. Education was not around in those days. They gathered all the Elders and they would decide what the people would do, like for the winter, who will be going fishing, who will be trapping, and all that. They would keep up the tribe, because we did not have reserves in those days.

Hereditary Chief line was passed on through certain families. They were the go-getters, they would go fishing, other people would depend on them a lot, they would have these Potlatches and that is where they would feed everybody and they would give out things to those people who needed it. As far as I know, women were not chosen to be leaders, it is just lately that women are doing that. In old days, they were not allowed to speak, it was always men who did.

Here in Vancouver, there are Native people from all over, a lot of them are Crees. What they want to do is have their own group, a governing body. The big problem we are having is everybody is fighting one another, it really slows things down. If they all got together, they would get things done a lot faster. If people could think as one, we would have one big voice. The biggest part of it is the money part. They all want to get a hold of the money, to carry on the work. I hope one day we will all smarten up and work together. I like the talking circles, they have helped a lot of people. In my line of work, I was taught by my Elders that we help people. We do a lot of counselling for people who are having problems.

Role of Elders

As for us, remaining Elders in Musqueam, we are trying to get the young people to go our way again. Education can make you think like a White man, we are trying to get our people to think our way. I believe that it is working. Even a lot of White people are starting to look to us now, they want to see the way we work things, they see it work a lot better than the government. Elders should make sure people learn how to be Native, to think Native. We are starting to do that in school now, we are teaching the young people our language. Pre-school, kindergarten, grade one, two, and three are being taught one-to-one in our language, for a half an hour of school time.

Other Native people are doing that too, to get our languages back. We had a big conference a few years ago, each tribe said they would try to have their language back by the year 2000. It is a goal that Native people are setting all over. By the year 2000 we should have our language back. When I went to residential school, they did not allow us to speak our language, they wanted to take that away from us. Well, they succeeded in a lot of ways. I was one of the luckier ones. When I came home, when I was eighteen, a lot of my Elders were still here in Musqueam. They would tease me about not knowing my own language. I tried hard to learn, I listened, and I got it back again. For us, we blame ourselves, when our children cannot speak their language. When Mom and I speak they think we are talking about them.

Role Models

Role models are the good teachers. We had Sun Bear from the U.S., he has a medicine wheel going and he touched a lot of people with this teachings, even non-Native people. We lost him about two years ago, so we are all trying our best to keep the medicine wheel going. We do a lot of travel, like today we are going to Oregon.

Traditional Roles of Men and Women

We are trying to hang on to that, especially teaching in the longhouse. It is usually the men who do the speaking, but now it is changing and women are doing some speaking too. We have a lot of good young people coming. Education made a lot of difference. In my time we were in boarding school and we were not allowed to go to high school. Today education is better and has changed a lot of things. We really like that. It is good to have the university, all our children are beginning to go to university now. Last year we had a graduation, there was one doctor, three or four lawyers. I think the Canadian government may be getting a little afraid of us now; they do not like that one day we will have a voice.

Traditional Parenting

It was mostly Elders who directed what children would be taught. I remember an Elder would come around and get all the young people out of bed in the morning and get them to the river to swim. This went on for a long time, but then the river got polluted and we could not swim in the water anymore. They have to swim in the mountains now where there are fresh streams. We still strongly believe in exercise of the young people.

Skills that were taught were basketry, weaving blankets out of sheep and goat wool. There were a lot of people that did that here, we are still trying to keep that up. There are also lots of carvers, totem pole carvers. We even have two or three silversmiths making jewellery here in Musqueam. We are getting back our own designs. We try to learn from the Elders our old ways on how they made designs. It is good to see the young people interested in that. Boys learned to be hunters and fisher-men mostly. Girls learned how to cure, smoke, preserve the fish, most of the time they cut them up and smoked them. My wife teaches those tradi-tional skills.

Arranged Marriages

Arranged marriage is something traditional here and we do not talk about it in public. We have mask dancing in weddings, the couple walks holding hands. Long time ago it would be Elders who chose the partners for the young people. We still have mask dancing in marriage ceremo-nies, but we still have to have a justice of the peace come in, because they do not recognize our traditional weddings. They just get remarried by the J.P. to make it legal.

Tricksters

In the winter months when we have gatherings, we use the mask dances. There is always a clown, his mask is made different from all the others, he makes people laugh, he goes after those mask dancers, pokes them on the back or something. People watch that while the ceremony is on. When we travel, Mom and I try to keep everybody happy, that is some-thing we learned from our Elders. At times we make them cry, but we make them laugh again.

For example, we had two deaths. I lost my sister and about two weeks later I lost my older brother, it really hit us, it hit me really hard. One of my nephews is from White Rock, close to the border here. He gathered some people last night and came here to my home and that made a lot of difference. In our traditional way they keep everybody laughing, it changed the atmosphere of our home here, everybody is laughing, we got away from that hurt feeling.

Music

It is mostly drumming, the small drums. We do not have the big drums. We have small hand drums. A lot of the songs are prayer songs. For example, if I'm called to open a conference with a prayer, sometimes I take my drum to sing. This weekend here in Vancouver we are having a big Pow-wow, but we have to leave to help some people in Oregon, I just have to go. I never know where I have to go next.

Work

Work is important, to keep moving. I honestly believe that. This is what I am doing now, even though I am getting old. I am now seventy-six and Mom is seventy-four, but that is what keeps us going, travelling and help-ing people. I will do that as long as I can help people.

Daily Routines

Praying is an important part of our lives, in our own way of praying. We do not pray like they do in a church, we pray to the Creator, Spirit World, Mother Earth, those three things. We strongly believe that our people, our Elders who have passed on are still around. So we pray to them to keep us. Most of the time it works for us when we are helping, healing someone.

Traditional Clothing

Clothes were made of cedar bark, it was woven, like a basket, but it was made soft. Now young people are trying to find out how it was done. Ani-mal hides, deer were used. They also got mountain sheep and goats, most of the blankets were made out of sheep and goat, they made wool. Long time ago, blankets were like money is today, the more blankets you had the richer you were, but there was a spiritual part. In Potlatches, blankets were important.

What happened here, my grandfather was the last one to put up a Pot-latch in 1920. In 1921 and 1924, Department of Indian Affairs came and took everything away from us, all our masks, everything. That is why a lot of it is in the Smithsonian. We are now trying to get them back. We got some back.

The Smithsonian in Washington, D.C. We had a meeting here about a year ago with these people. They said they would give us back if we build our own museum here, so we are talking to the people about it now. There is a museum at UBC, and lots of our traditional items are in there. If we can build our own museum, then we can get our things back, masks, robes, drums, blankets. We have a blanket that was made in 1916, we had to have it on a board because it was starting to fall apart.

At a Potlatch you give away everything that you own, chickens, horses, whatever you got, you start over again. I believe that is why Indian Affairs put a stop to it. Like, my grandfather gave all his horses away, he used to have lots, he gave everything he owned. We still have a totem pole here, twelve feet high, blankets were piled that high to twelve feet. People from the island used to come in by canoe and they would take all their stuff home, even a horse sometimes.

Burials

We had huts, fence around it, they just put people in these huts, pile them up, one family in each hut. We have to destroy all those, bury the bones in the modern cemetery. Government said it should not be done like that. The huts were made out of red cedar. The spirits live on, they are always around. My grandfather was a healer, but we help people with problems. I do a lot of counselling. I help them to cure that. They come here to our house or else we go to a Chinese café down the street. These Chinese people understand what we do when I am counselling, they do not interfere. They say they do that in China too, burning of food, spiritual counselling.

Traditional Beliefs and Christianity

Today a lot of priests and ministers are coming our way. Long time ago we were robbed of our language, today the Christian ministers try to help us. They no longer say that is wrong. I usually ask them to have a prayer with me, like before a burning. We pray hard for families who are having problems. They say they believe in our way now. Long time ago we had to listen and do it their way and you have to hide your own way, your language. Now it is turning. They are coming our way. They do not call it heathen anymore.

Prophecies

A lot of these things were passed down to us by our Elders. When I was younger and growing up, all the Elders wanted me to take my great-grandfather's place. A lot of the stories he told us when we were kids, here in Musqueam territory. These stories go far back, even my grandfather could not remember when they started, they go way back. Musqueam people have lived here for a long time. The Musqueam people were once a big nation. They owned the whole territory where the city of Vancouver now is, this is Musqueam territory.

The story goes that a long time ago northern people used to come down on big canoes, war canoes. Northern people used to have war with our people here in Musqueam. Sometimes they would win and sometimes we would go up there to raid them. They would be captured for slaves, like for our people here. Also some people that were taken from here are up north, in northern part of B.C. These captured people would live with that tribe.

No matter where we dig around here in our territory, even around UBC, artefacts and bones are always found. I kind of believe that wherever they were killed is where they were buried. There are bones found around the city of Vancouver, it may have been a battleground. These things happened way before our time. But right now we are trying to keep up with the White race, Western race, we are trying to get all our children to go to school, to get an education. Right here in Musqueam we have one woman and one man who are lawyers now, they went through UBC. Last year there was one Native doctor who graduated and he is right here in Vancouver with all the other doctors. He is doing really good. I meet him once in a while.

A lot of the things that happened long time ago, they would travel by canoes and paddles. These stories are passed on by our Elders, grandparents. The reason why I do this kind of work now is because my Elders pushed Mom and I in doing what we are doing now, to take my grandfather's place. When we were about forty-five years old, we noticed that all our Elders were going very fast and so we said okay we will do what our Elders want us to do and took over. We started on healing and working around longhouses. That is why I'm on the road all the time. By going back to our traditions, it will help a lot of people for their future. It has helped a lot of people in our travels, we travel all over and that is what we teach, we have workshops. I'm doing one workshop tomorrow here in our community. There are a lot of things I would like people to learn. I feel free in talking to people and it also helps me too. I'm doing the best I can. Going back to our traditional ways will help us in the future.

Stages of Life

Last night all the Elders met, we have an Elders' centre here. We talk about things that are going on here in B.C. and other parts of Canada. There are a lot of people here in the city of Vancouver that are urban Native people, they have reserves but a lot of them do not. We talked about that. We as Elders will try our best to help everyone, it does not matter who they are or what they are. A lot of the Natives here in the city want to get in touch with Elders here in Musqueam. So it is our role in this stage as Elders to help Native people. We have gatherings at the Elders' Centre to help people. Today I spoke for a while when I had the opening prayer.

I think Western people are starting to see and realize what we are doing as Elders. A lot of the big wheels, the big shots are starting to look to us now. They are already starting to schedule meetings here on the reserve, so our Elders do not have to go to town. We are going to have a meeting with the big wheels, the premier. They are going to meet with us here at the Elders' Centre. It looks like things are starting to open up for us as Native people.

Time

We did not have calendars and things like that, now we have three or four different wristwatches. My grandfathers would go by the sun mainly in the summer. In the winter time, if it is snowing, it is pretty hard to tell what time it is, but they could always tell what time it was. In the spring we do a lot of ritual work like burning food for the people who are gone. We do burning for our ancestors who are gone. We do that in this area. In the summer time, it is fishing time for us, a lot of our people go fishing. We still do a lot of ritual work in the summer time. In the fall we get ready for the winter season, we do a lot of rituals again, like burning, getting ready for the winter. In the winter time, we have our longhouse season. Then we start over again. It is hard to explain, you have to see it yourself to witness some of our gatherings, we can take three to four hundred people in one longhouse. We have naming ceremonies and things like that as well, mainly in the winter. They are like cycles.

Language and Culture

Language is important to our culture. In my time we were sent to boarding schools and they took our language away from us, but I was more fortunate because a lot of my Elders were still around when I left the boarding school, so I got my language back again. But a lot of our children do not understand the language, they cannot speak it. What we are doing now is teaching the pre-school. They are picking it up well.

Native names are passed on from generation to generation. My name is Tsimalano and that name has been handed down from my great-great-great-grandfather, five generations back. Five generations back, the Chief of the lower mainland was my great-grandfather, five generations back. His name has been handed down, family after family, now I have it.

Names of places have Indian names too. What is happening now, we named all the rivers and creeks in our language. The Western race is trying to spell it or pronounce it the way it sounds and we get mixed up on that. They spell it the way they think it should be, and a lot of times we do not know where that is. The Elders here speak the language so they know where places are and we understand the names.

A lot of the young people go to gatherings, to hear our language, to hear the Elders speak the language. We kind of blame ourselves for not speaking the language to our children. It may have to do with the boarding schools because we sure lost a lot of our culture and language. When we got caught speaking our language we got a strapping, we were punished. They watched us really close to make sure we did not speak the language.

Traditional Foods

We ate berries and lots of salmon, smoked salmon. Down here most of our people are fishermen and we smoke a lot of our salmon. It is saved for the winter. The past summer we went out fishing and we canned cases of salmon, not only for ourselves but for our family and whoever needs it. Lot of people get stuck and they came here, they try to buy salmon from us but we do not sell it, we just give it to them. One of my boys half-smokes and half-dries the fish. That is how we help people, for those who cannot do it, we give them the food. That is one reason why a lot of people got to know us. We are well respected.

Before the city of Vancouver was here a lot of our people were trappers. There was a lot of hunting. Right now we are on the outskirts of the city, long ago there was a lot of game. My grandfather used to say people would go to the area where UBC is now and bring home some deer. We did not have to travel far. Now we have to travel hours to get to the hunting grounds. We got deer, moose, elk, and sometimes mountain goats. But they have to travel a long distance, way up north. Around here the city is getting too big and too populated, all the game is gone from here. Now we need trucks to get into the mountains.

Relations with First Nations

There used to be some battles between some tribes, but not anymore. Long time ago, Native people would trade also. For example, we do not get any clams here on the mainland, so the island people would come and trade clams for blankets and other things. That was the way they traded. Even now people from the island come here, my wife is from the island. Her family comes here and brings clams and we give them salmon.

Dreams

I know that dreams were important in one's life and still today we believe that dreams are very important. My wife is the one who knows about dreams. A lot of times here dreams become reality. When you believe in dreams, they are connected to spirituality. We come to understand what they are, what they represent. Dreams can also tell about the future.

Traditional Healers

There used to be a lot of traditional healers here. Right now there are not too many left. A lot of them tried but could not make it, it is a lot of work. What I and my wife do has been handed down through our Elders. My wife's grandfather was a great healer, my grandfather was a healer too, so that made it easier to carry on their work. It was passed down in the family.

Life on the Land

It is very important to be close to the land. In our travels and in our prayers, we always have Mother Earth. There are three things we use in our prayers, we do not use the church way, this is a different way of pray- ing. We use the Creator and we strongly believe that. Next it is the Great Spirit. When we went to school it was pumped into our heads that if we were good Christians we would go to heaven and if we were not, we were going to hell. But when I came home my Elders taught us that all our peo- ple who have passed on are still around us. We can still keep our beliefs even though we are now in a modern world. Once we go the Western way we are lost. We encourage the young people to carry on. If anything happens to Mom and I, they can carry on what they have learned from us and other Elders.

Maps

There were no boundaries like no one really owned it. We live in this area here and going up north we come to a river and there is another band who live there, although we speak the same language. Everybody knows where another tribe's land is. Today we have reserves but long time ago there was no such thing. People lived all over.

Education

Residential schools affected our people through loss of language and culture. What we are trying to do is to forget the past and go into the future. That is what I mean by education. If we are going to live in this modern world we must have education. Otherwise they will keep pushing us down. Now we have one of our girls here who is a lawyer and she is doing very good on land claiming, she is working very hard on that. I encourage the young people to go to school and get all the education they can. For me, I stopped at grade eight. I believe that is why they put us in boarding school. They would not allow me to go to high school, which I could have. That is how far I got.

What I am doing now is trying to get these young people to get as much education as possible. We are going to have to live in this modern world. I strongly believe now that the government is getting a little bit afraid of us now. If we would have had the chance we would have been strong people now, one of the reasons why they kept us down is because they did not want us to learn. Native people learn fast, we have our own way of thinking. I encourage young people now to go to university. The Department of Indian Affairs is getting afraid of us now because our young people are learning fast. They still know two ways, their own and modern way. Those people who had negative experiences in school should return to their own culture.

I was eighteen when I left school. Since then I have listened to my Elders. I returned to our culture. When the Elders knew we really wanted to learn our ways, they started teaching us again. That is where we got most of our knowledge, from our Elders.

When I was initiated in the longhouse I used to have to stand for hours, listening to the Elders speaking. One would finish and another would get up. I would have to stand there and listen. I used to feel angry sometimes, wondering why they were doing that to me. But I found out later on why, because it is really helping us now. We can go through a lot of things through spirituality because we listened. So that is what I am grateful to my Elders for.

Justice

Justice of today has gone haywire. In the newspaper it shows that it is nothing to kill another person, you only get two years. On the other hand, there was a man who killed a neighbour's dog and he got fifteen years for that. The system is horrible.

Long time ago when young people did something wrong, they knew that they did something wrong. I think there are other ways to deal with crime rather than jails. Sometimes they could get them to work for the reservation, like cleaning up and doing their time. This way they are helping other people. Sending them out on the land would help them. Also someone who had knowledge should talk to these people, counselling. It is better than going to jail. They should also realize that counselling is better than being behind bars. I hear that there are other reserves that are doing that. When people go to jails, they just come out more angry.

One young man had a choice of serving two years of jail or doing community work. But after his time was up, he went back to the same place where he was. We got all the Elders together and we talked to him, we told him that if he did not behave, he would have to go to serve his two years it really smartened him up, he is now one of the best boys, he is helping everyone. So it worked for him.